CULTIVATION
AND
CULTURE

LABOR AND THE
SHAPING OF SLAVE LIFE
IN THE AMERICAS

CARTER G. WOODSON INSTITUTE
SERIES IN BLACK STUDIES

Armstead L. Robinson
General Editor

CULTIVATION AND CULTURE

LABOR AND THE SHAPING OF SLAVE LIFE IN THE AMERICAS

Edited by

Ira Berlin and Philip D. Morgan

UNIVERSITY PRESS OF VIRGINIA

CHARLOTTESVILLE AND LONDON

THE UNIVERSITY PRESS OF VIRGINIA
Copyright © 1993 by the Rector and Visitors
of the University of Virginia

"Coffee Planters and Coffee Slaves in the Antilles: The Impact of a
Secondary Crop" copyright © 1993 by Michel-Rolph Trouillot
"Provision Ground and Plantation Labor in Four Windward Islands:
Competition for Resources during Slavery" copyright © 1993 by
Woodville K. Marshall

First published 1993

Library of Congress Cataloging-in-Publication Data
Cultivation and culture : labor and the shaping of Black life in the
Americas / edited by Ira Berlin and Philip D. Morgan.
    p.   cm. — (Carter G. Woodson Institute series in Black
studies)
    Includes index.
    ISBN 0-8139-1421-3. — ISBN 0-8139-1424-8 (pbk.)
    1. Slavery—Economic aspects—Caribbean Area—History.
2. Slavery—Economic aspects—United States—History.
3. Agriculture—Economic aspects—Caribbean Area—History.
4. Agriculture—Economic aspects—United States—History.
5. Slavery—Caribbean Area—Conditions of slaves.   6. Slavery—
United States—Conditions of slaves.   7. Plantations—Economic
aspects—Caribbean Area—History.   8. Plantations—Economic aspects—
United States—History.   I. Berlin, Ira, 1941–   .   II. Morgan,
Philip D., 1949–   .   III. Series.
HT901.C85   1993
306.3'62'09729—dc20   92-31010
                                                                            CIP

Printed in the United States of America

CONTENTS

PART THREE:
THE SLAVES' ECONOMY

ACKNOWLEDGMENTS

ALTHOUGH HISTORIANS treasure the world of the independent artisan, historical scholarship remains a collective enterprise. The extent to which our understanding the past benefits by the joint efforts of many men and women becomes fully manifest in *Cultivation and Culture*. Although the anthropologists, sociologists, and historians who have contributed to this volume speak for themselves, we would like to express our appreciation to all those who helped make this work possible.

In the beginning was a conference. In the spring of 1989 a group of some forty scholars met at the University of Maryland as participants in a colloquium entitled "Cultivation and Culture: Labor and Shaping Slave Life in the Americas." It is safe to say that all came away with an enhanced understanding of the nature of slave societies. We especially wish to thank the Division of Arts and Humanities, the Department of History, the Department of Spanish and Portuguese, and the Afro-American Studies Program at the University of Maryland for their generous support in hosting this conference. Divisions and departments, however, do not by themselves extend hospitality or even pay the bills. For that we owe a debt of gratitude to Richard N. Price, Samuel L. Myers, Jr., and Saul Sosnowski, not only for sharing their scarce resources but also for their willingness to enter the general intellectual free-for-all that made the conference so rewarding. Terrie Hruzd oversaw the day-to-day operations of the conference and attended to dozens of other details involved in transforming the conference papers into a book, thereby easing the burden on contributors and editors alike.

Some of the papers presented at the Cultivation and Culture conference were published in a special issue of *Slavery and Abolition* entitled *The Slaves' Economy: Independent Production by Slaves in the Americas* in the spring of 1991. We thank the coeditor of that fine journal, Gad Heuman, for giving these essays and a shorter version of the editors' introduction an early hearing and its publisher, Frank Cass and Company, for permission to republish essays that first appeared in *Slavery and Abolition*.

Preparing this volume for print has been a long process. But the willingness of all contributors to share the editorial work has quickened the pace. While the editors read all the essays, the contributors reciprocated by a critical reading of the editors' introduction, a mutual exchange for which the final product is that much better. In addition, Sidney Chalhoub, Stanley Engerman, Sidney Mintz, and Stuart Schwartz also reviewed the introduction, improving it in numerous ways. Stanley Engerman's comments, coming at the end of the whole process, were particularly valuable and especially appreciated. All this work was made easier by the staff of the Center for Advanced Studies in the Behavior Sciences, where Ira Berlin spent a year in residence in 1990–91. Philip Morgan gratefully acknowledges the generous support of the National Endowment for the Humanities for a fellowship awarded in 1991–92 and the good advice he received from Peter Ripley at a critical stage in the proceedings. Cathie Brettschneider of the University Press of Virginia guided a complicated manuscript into print with competence and great good humor.

CULTIVATION AND CULTURE

LABOR AND THE
SHAPING OF SLAVE LIFE
IN THE AMERICAS

INTRODUCTION

LABOR AND THE SHAPING
OF SLAVE LIFE IN THE
AMERICAS

Ira Berlin and Philip D. Morgan

S LAVES WORKED. When, where, and especially how they worked determined, in large measure, the course of their lives. So central was labor in the slaves' experience that it has often been taken for granted. Recent studies have instead focused on the slaves' social organization, domestic arrangements, religious beliefs, and medical practices, that—along with music, cuisine, and linguistic and sartorial style—gave Afro-American culture its distinctive form during slavery. For the most part, these aspects of slave life have been understood as emanating from the quarter, household, and church, rather than field and workshop.[1] This emphasis has, however, obscured the activities that dominated slave life. After all, slavery was first and foremost an institution of coerced labor. Work necessarily engaged most slaves, most of the time.

For slaves, work was both Adam's curse—unrelenting toil from which they derived but few benefits—and a source of personal satisfaction and political self-assertion. The act of creation, which even onerous and exploitative work entailed, allowed slaves to affirm the humanity that chattel bondage denied. By making something where once there was nothing, slaves discredited the masters' shibboleth that they were simply property, countered the daily humiliations which undermined their self-esteem, and laid claim to the fruits of their labor for themselves and their posterity. The "fixed point of the negro's system of ethics," declared one knowledgeable observer of slave life in the American South just prior to emancipation, was "that the result of labour belongs of right to the labourer."[2]

Because work was both the source of the slaves' oppression and a

1

seed of liberation, it became the terrain upon which slaves and masters battled for the wealth that the enslaved produced. The masters' right to limit physical movement, fix terms of worship, and name children—however much this symbolized and even ratified the slaveholders' hegemony—was subsidiary to control over the slaves' labor. The struggle over the slaves' labor informed all other conflicts between master and slave, and understanding that contest opens the way to a full comprehension of slave society.

The conflict between master and slave took many forms, involving the organization of labor, the pace of work, the division of labor, and the composition of the labor force—all questions familiar to students of wage labor. The weapons workers employed—feigning ignorance, slowing the line, maiming animals, disappearing at critical moments, and, as a last resort, confronting their superiors directly and violently—suggest that, *in workplace struggles*, slaves and free workers had much in common. Although the social relations of slave and wage labor differed fundamentally, much can be learned about slave life by examining how the work process informed the conflict between wage workers and their employers. For like reasons, the processes of production were as much a source of working-class culture for slave workers as for free ones.[3]

Acknowledging the centrality of work offers a useful beginning in the study of slave life, but understanding the slaves' labor requires more. The exploitation entailed in the appropriation of the slaves' labor provides only the barest outline of the lives slaves lived. Most elementally, the work of slaves divides into that done for the master and that done for themselves. Slave societies thus involved two interrelated and overlapping economies: one organized by and for the master, although contested and constrained by the slaves; the other by and for the slaves, although contested and constrained by the master. Both entailed struggle over the slaves' labor, but they affected slave life in different ways.

The masters' economy predominated. The work extracted from slaves by their owners occupied most of the slaves' laboring time and thus inescapably circumscribed the lives of enslaved people. From the calories they expended to the music they played, no aspect of their lives was untouched by their work regimen—its physical and psychological demands, its organization, its seasonal rhythms, and its numerous divisions by skill, age, and sex. Indeed, labor was so inseparable from life that, for most slaves, the two appeared to be one and the same.

Appearances, however, never quite equaled reality, since slaves did not labor only for their owners. In addition to toiling in the masters' economy, slaves created their own, often at the behest of the master. The independent economic activities of slaves—variously called the "internal economy," the "peasant breach," or more simply the slaves' economy—had far-reaching consequences.[4] By producing food for themselves and for others, tending cash crops, raising livestock, manufacturing finished goods, marketing their own products, consuming and saving the proceeds, and bequeathing property to their descendants, slaves challenged their masters' authority and took control of a larger portion of their lives.

On the dual foundation of the masters' and slaves' economies, slave society and culture then took shape. The allocation of work by sex and age helped define gender and age conventions, influencing relationships between men and women, young and old. Although the occupational and social hierarchies of the slave community were never congruent, the distribution of work molded the slave community, propelling some men and women into positions of leadership and distinction, leaving others far to the rear. Likewise, work informed the culture slaves created, providing the ideological and material basis for their most precious institutions and beliefs. The character of the slaves' work, moreover, influenced the hopes and aspirations they carried into freedom, giving direction to the postemancipation struggle for equality. The legacy of slavery cannot be understood without a full appreciation of the way in which slaves worked.

I

Slave labor knew no bounds. Masters employed their slaves in every possible manner, from backbreaking drudgery to the most exacting crafts. Slaves worked in cities and in the countryside, in small shops and on great plantations. Exactly how slaves worked for their owners depended most vitally upon the requirements of particular crops and crafts, which shaped the nature of the work force, the organization of production, and the division of labor. These, in turn, rested upon the geography, the demographic balance of slave and free and black and white, the size of slaveholding units, the character of technology, and the management techniques prevalent at different times and in different places. Any systematic study of slave work must also consider the knowledge and skills of individual slave men and women, the slaves' origins, and those of their owners. The complex matrix of circumstances that determined the slaves' labor, moreover, changed over time and differed from place to place.

In every slave society, masters have tried to extract as much labor as possible from their slaves. Yet not all work required the same physical and psychological application and not all masters drove their slaves with the same ferocity. Work in the mines was typically more demanding than work in the fields, work in the fields more onerous than work in the manufactories and shops, and work in the shops more burdensome—at least physically—than work in the house. With respect to the cultivation of major staples, work with sugar was universally recognized as the most taxing. The work-year of sugar slaves was longer—more hours a day, more days a month—than that of slaves engaged in any other crop. Cane holing, manuring, and harvesting were three of the most exhausting operations known on New World plantations; morbidity and mortality rates were generally highest on sugar estates. Coffee and rice were considered more arduous to raise and process than cotton, and cotton more so than tobacco. Similar hierarchies existed in the cultivation of minor crops, ranging from pimento—considered quite exacting—to provisions requiring only light labor.[5]

In general, the intensity with which slave owners drove their slaves depended upon the character of a given slave economy, particularly the slaveowners' commitment to the production of staples for the international marketplace. Demands on slaves were different in periods of settlement when staple production was not yet an all-encompassing activity than in mature slave societies, when staple production informed every aspect of life. In pioneer societies or on the expanding margins of established societies, slaves worked hard to clear the land, to break the soil, to plant and harvest the first crops—but the unsettled nature of the society, the primitive division of labor, and the close interaction of master and slave allowed slaves a degree of latitude they rarely enjoyed in mature staple-producing regimes.[6] As the commitment to staple production deepened, the slaves' work routine became more rigidly defined. In some mature slave societies, complex managerial hierarchies separated master from slave, eliminating much of the personal interaction that had earlier mitigated slavery's more burdensome features. But while this growing division of labor condemned most slaves to the harsh reality of field labor, the elaboration of the plantation's occupational hierarchy allowed some slaves to secure privileged positions as domestic servants and artisans. On occasion, a few slaves even entered the managerial ranks as foremen and drivers.

The intensity with which slaveholders worked their slaves also depended upon the long-term evolution of staple production. Early on, staple producers earned bonanza profits as burgeoning metropolitan demand pushed prices upward. A golden age of staple production, however, generally spelled a dark age for the slave. When masters could make big profits, they expanded their operations at breakneck speed, importing Africans in huge numbers and working slaves to the threshold of human endurance, sometimes beyond. But as staple production rose, commodity prices fell. Slaveholders responded by cutting costs and increasing production, often expanding output despite falling prices. From the slaves' perspective, busts were no better than booms: slaveholders scrimped on the slaves' necessities, rented slaves away from their home plantations, disposed of unprofitable hands, and in general sought ways to drive their laborers harder than ever. Additional increases in demand created new cycles of staple expansion, particularly on new lands. Here, slaveholders could take advantage of the fertility of fresh soil and the most up-to-date implements and techniques, while older regions often had difficulty competing.

If, by contrast, metropolitan demand failed to grow, staple exports sagged. Where slaveholders found profits so small as to be unworthy of their efforts, individual slaves might gain their freedom and abolition become an open question. But such circumstances were rare, and to reach them slaveholders had to slip below the edge of marginality. Even in the face of a collapsing staple export, slavery proved remarkably adaptable. In the Minas Gerais region of Brazil, for example, slavery not only survived but grew vigorously after the mining boom faded. Links to the export sector were not severed, but *Mineiro* slaveholders successfully diversified, reoriented toward subsistence, and engaged in import substitution. Most slaves in nineteenth-century Minas grew cereals, raised livestock, or worked in craft and cottage industries. The pace at which slaves worked rested upon the owners' needs, aspirations, and abilities to adapt to changing circumstances.[7]

No matter what the source of their masters' demands, though, slaves resisted them. Determined not to be reduced to beasts of burden, slaves malingered, broke tools, turned truant, and sometimes simply refused to work. Agreeing among themselves—perhaps on the basis of their prior experiences, some of which derived from Africa—slaves established standards of their own with respect to the pace of labor, the length of the workday, the number of free days, and much else. When they could, slaves found practical applications for their expectations and endowed their practices with the force of custom and a sense of entitlement. Such customary practices defined, in part, the intensity of the slaves' labor, as well as the hours they worked, the division of labor, the rights of supervisors, and a host of other matters—all of which slaves fiercely defended. Although slaves remained subordinate until they broke slavery's grip, subordination was not impotence. Employing their numbers and their knowledge, slaves—no less than other workers—tried to shape their own world.

For their part, masters sought to deny the slaves' attempts at self-determination, arrogating to themselves control over all facets of the productive process. The ensuing conflict was intense and violent, often brutally so. In 1701, a group of Antigua slaves murdered their owner, Samuel Martin, when he forced them to work on their regular Christmas holiday.[8] Martin had badly underestimated the dangers that even the most powerful master faced in trespassing on what slaves believed to be their rights. Most slave owners had a deeper appreciation for the boundaries beyond which slaves would not be pushed and thus better understood the limits of their own power. Through continuous struggle and endless negotiation, both masters and slaves conceded what neither could alter, and, in time, both grudgingly agreed to what was acceptable, what might be tolerated, and what was utterly beyond endurance.

Such agreements gained force over time, but they remained inherently unstable. Slaves accepted them only as curtailing exploitation; for the slave, such agreements defined an outer limit, beyond which they would not be driven. In contrast, masters accepted them only as evidence of their dominance; for the master, such agreements defined the minimum they could expect from their slaves. In short, by insisting on what could not be denied, slaves limited the exploitation to which they might be subjected, while by accepting what could not be prevented, masters enhanced their claim to the slaves' labor. Masters let it be known that failure to produce to agreed levels would be met with the lash or the branding iron, with mutilation or even death. For their part, slaves let it be known that attempts to press them beyond agreed limits would be met with slowdowns, broken tools, truancy, and even insurrection. Both were true to their word, for—as Samuel Martin discovered—breaking the carefully negotiated "rules of the game" called the game itself into question.[9]

Well aware of the dangers involved and fearful that violations might disrupt much-prized social harmony, metropolitan authorities and local officials often sanctioned the customary relations established by the unspoken agreements between master and slave. Slave codes were not simply extensions of the masters' will but also a recognition of the concessions that slaves had wrung from their owners through constant struggle. Following Martin's death, the planter-dominated legislature of Antigua accordingly gave the slaves' traditional Christmas holiday the force of law.[10]

Yet the contest did not end with these uneasy bargains, which both sides regarded as temporary truces in a continuing battle, not as the basis of a permanent peace. At each turn, masters tried to intensify the level of exploitation, increasing the pace of labor and the length of the workday and decreasing the slaves' free time. Slaves resisted such encroachments, trying instead to reduce the demands encoded in customary practice. Whoever won or lost, the struggle itself taught slaves—as it taught masters—how they could turn even the most dismal circumstance to their own advantage. In the process, slaves developed ideas about the importance of labor, the role of property, and the relation of both to their own being; such ideas eventually stood at the center of the slaves' political cosmos.

Whereas the asymmetric struggle between master and slave was always the same, the terms of that struggle differed in different places at different times, for they not only rested upon the unequal resources and diverse experiences master and slave brought to the contest but also on the terrain of the struggle itself: the kind of work slaves did. The links between various forms of commodity production and the nature of slave life were numerous. Some had been forged even before the settlement of the New World.

As sugar production evolved in the Mediterranean between the thirteenth and sixteenth centuries, it became closely identified with the plantation—that is, with highly capitalized productive units in which large numbers of slaves, some of whom came from Africa, worked in gangs under the direction of European overlords. The huge profits sugar produced in the Americas reinforced the tie between sugar and the plantation, allowing the New World's great sugar magnates to construct vast estates boasting hundreds—occasionally thousands—of slaves. Of all the crops grown in the New World, sugar was the most demanding of labor: about two-thirds of all the Africans carried to the New World ended up on sugar plantations. It may be difficult to identify a typical sugar plantation, for, as David P. Geggus points out, in late eighteenth-century Saint Domingue the largest sugar plantation was seventeen times the size of the smallest. Still, sugar estates were consistently larger than all other types of rural holdings. Indeed, sugar planters created, as Robert Fogel has observed, the "largest privately owned enterprises of the age."[11]

Other commodities—coffee, rice, cotton, and tobacco—also forged links to the plantation, but the connection was not nearly as close. Most of these crops was at some time grown on farm-size units using free or servant labor, but some were grown only on small units. Tobacco planters, for example, could rarely afford large retinues of slaves, and even when they could, the dispersed settlement pattern dictated by the requirements of tobacco production compelled planters to divide their labor force into "quarters." In contrast, coffee was sometimes grown on estates that rivaled the largest sugar plantations but could just as easily be produced on a unit no larger than a tobacco quarter.[12] For other commodities—lumber, naval stores, cattle, and various small grains—the connection with plantation production was more distant still, although each of those commodities was produced on plantations or plantation-size units in some places, at some time.

Whether large or small, plantation or farm, the size of slaveholdings had important consequences for slave life. As a rule, slaves were sold more frequently and the division of labor more fluid on small than large estates. The rapid turnover of slaves and large number of divided households on small plantations generally made the slave family a less stable institution on small units than on large ones. Conversely, slaves on small plantations—at least in areas densely populated with slaves, such as parts of the antebellum South—tended to marry earlier than their counterparts on large plantations because they were less confined in their choice of mates. However, confinement to small units in regions of low population density, which was the experience of many coffee slaves in the Caribbean highlands, required travel over long distances to locate potential partners. Topography and demography left many coffee slaves socially isolated. Such isolation, Michel-Rolph Trouillot speculates, produced particularly intense interaction among the residents of small units. The closeness of living quarters typical of coffee estates "reinforced the frequency and intensity of cultural exchanges within the plantation."[13]

Relations between particular commodities and slave life, however, were governed by more than the size of the unit of production. Some commodities rooted slaves in a single spot; others promoted mobility. Sugar, rice, and coffee production required large capital investments on sprawling estates with numerous outbuildings, both industrial and agricultural, thereby tying slaves to a single place. To be sure, masters transferred slaves long distances within sugar, rice, and coffee regions. In fact, staple production often became like a relay race, in which one prime region held the baton before soil depletion led it to be passed to another, fresher region. The slaves who grew sugar, coffee, and rice followed the rather leisurely linear geographic movement of crops that they tended. In contrast, slaves growing tobacco were nearly always in motion, since tobacco exhausted soils quickly and required little capital investment in a single site. Tobacco slaves—like slave lumbermen and cowboys—experienced considerable mobility, which adversely affected their family life but promoted a knowledge of the world derived from dealing with a multitude of different peoples and circumstances. Whereas tobacco encouraged continuous short-distance migration, the expansion of cotton cultivation in the southern United States initiated a great migration that sent tens of thousands of slaves hundreds and even thousands of miles from their homes. Between 1790 and 1860 over eight hundred thousand blacks were forcibly transferred from seaboard to interior states. The demand for cotton, rich southwestern soils, and an efficient transportation system help account for this huge interregional trade, but in the final analysis all depended on cotton's ready adaptability to lands that stretched from South Carolina to Texas, from Florida to Tennessee.[14]

Different crops dictated not only where slaves worked but also when they worked. Various crops and commodities had different seasonal rhythms, each of which required slaves to labor intensively during some parts of the year and permitted them a measure of free time during others. Although planting and harvest were times of intensive labor for all agricultural workers, the seasonal cycles of some crops had a greater impact than those of others. Sugar production was marked by extreme seasonal variability: once harvested, sugar cane had to be processed quickly lest it degrade or spoil. Processing cane proceeded at a terrifying pace, slaves working day and night for a month or more. The seasonal breaks in tobacco were not nearly as sharp. Tobacco leaves ripened at different times. While they had to be picked at precisely the right moment to optimize their value, the time constraints were nothing like those of sugar production. In the Chesapeake, "the annual work cycle was almost wholly shaped by the seasonal demands of tobacco," Lorena S. Walsh notes, "which required constant attention throughout most of the year."[15] The absence of periods of intense activity did not necessarily lighten the slaves' work load, as planters often required their slaves to strip and stem the plant after dark. Nevertheless, tobacco cultivation moved with slow and measured tread through the year, while sugar raced at a furious pace for long stretches. The demands of tobacco were tedious and monotonous; those of sugar literally killing.

Like tobacco planters, most slaveholders tried to eliminate seasonal fluctuations by filling slack periods with an array of tasks. When crops were laid by, slaves turned to the business of repairing equipment, extending roads, and enlarging the estate by opening new fields and constructing additional outbuildings. Slaveholders also searched for secondary crops or crafts to complement the seasonality of the primary staple. In pre-Revolutionary South Carolina, rice planters integrated indigo into their agricultural repertoire, and in parts of the late colonial Chesapeake, tobacco planters added wheat to their cultivation cycle. Many Jamaican coffee planters and penkeepers hired out their slaves as jobbing gangs, combined coffee production with ranching, or supplemented either activity with the raising of pimento—all with a view to maximizing their income and keeping slaves constantly at work.

Secondary crops, sometimes grown together with the primary staple and sometimes distant from it, had a dynamic of their own. Michel-Rolph Trouillot suggests that secondary crops promoted diversity, whereas primary crops tended toward homogeneity. Even when grown in close proximity to the primary staple, secondary crops attracted different slaveholders and employed different slaves. By their marginal nature, secondary crops created an economic niche that allowed men and women whose color, late arrival, or lack of capital barred them from participation in primary staple production to enter the planter class. Coffee, a secondary crop par excellence in the Caribbean, was grown by free people of color in Saint Domingue, Grenada, and Dominica and by French migrants in Trinidad. Ironically, sugar may have served the same function in Louisiana as coffee did in Saint Domingue, as it was one of the few mainland crops in which free colored planters gained a toehold.

"Underdog" planters—socially as well as economically marginal— left their mark on slave society. Since they could hardly compete with the primary producers, they were forced to construct their labor force from the slaves primary producers had rejected. In Saint Domingue, coffee slaves were disproportionately African, generally drawn from those nations that sugar planters disparaged. Moreover, the success of these undercapitalized planters was frequently achieved at the expense of their slaves. Slaves who worked secondary crops were often rented in jobbing gangs and performed the hardest tasks.[16]

Even as masters filled the interstices of production with yet more production, the rhythms of work persisted. Seasonal demands peaked and with them tensions derived from working at breakneck speed. Slaveholders tried to defuse these tensions by sponsoring great celebrations upon the completion of the work. The few holidays slaves enjoyed—Christmas and Whitsuntide—followed harvest and planting, respectively. But the tensions remained, and such periods also marked peaks in the number of runaways and other such manifestations of discontent. Rumors of great Christmas risings existed in every New World slave society. The seasonal rhythms of work structured the contest between master and slave, as it did all else.[17]

The struggle between master and slave also proceeded differently depending on who the slaves were. Masters constructed their labor forces with care. Because of their enormous resources, sugar planters had the greatest choice of laborers. After a brief experiment with indentured Europeans, they opted for African slaves, making the sugar plantation—particularly during the height of the sugar boom—an outpost of Africa in the New World. Other planters followed when they could, searching for commodities as profitable as sugar and imitating the labor policies and practices of the great sugar magnates.

By their command of the labor market, the most successful planters could be even more selective, choosing as slaves those whom they deemed the best workers. Planters evolved a variety of criteria to judge the character and capacities of various African and Afro-American peoples, distinguishing among them by their strength, resistance to disease, willingness to work, and ability to reproduce. In greater part, such notions were shallow stereotypes with little basis in fact—as evident in the radically different opinions that planters in Brazil, Jamaica, and South Carolina held on the same African nation. But these ideas also drew on the planters' experiences in directing slave labor. The above-average height of people from certain African nations seems to explain why they were especially valued, although other alleged traits—a propensity for suicide or cannibalism, for instance—sometimes outweighed perceptions of strength or stamina. Such mixtures of rational calculation and baseless stereotyping guided the construction of the labor force in various slave regimes.[18]

To a considerable degree, the slaveholders' preferences determined the work slaves did. Slaveholders placed greater faith in creole or Afro-American slaves than in newly arrived Africans, perhaps because of the creoles' language skills and familiarity with the landscape and work regimen. Thus, while slaveholders frequently elevated cre-

oles to positions of authority and allowed them to work independently, they subjected "saltwater" slaves to close supervision and
often at the meanest drudgery. In late eighteenth-century Saint Domingue, David Geggus reveals, only one in ten African men—compared to one in four creole men—held positions outside the field.
Between creole and African women, the differential was even starker:
10 percent of creole women in the colony labored as managers, artisans, or domestics, while only 2 percent of the African women held
similar jobs. In general, the proportion of creoles increased with the
prestige of the occupation.

The influence of the masters' preferences was not confined to the
general distinction between creoles and Africans, for slaveholders
also distinguished among creoles by their knowledge, skills, and reputation—seeking out those slaves whose particular experiences fit
their particular needs. Moreover, since high-status creoles owed their
standing to connections with their owners and other plantation nota-
bles, many of them were of mixed racial origin. Like that of free
people, the slaves' social hierarchy was whiter at the top than at the
bottom.[19]

In addition, slaveholders guided the occupational opportunities of
Africans. For example, in Saint Domingue at the end of the eighteenth
century, slaves from the Congo constituted 43 percent of the African-
born slave men but 55 percent of the African-born artisans, 66 percent
of the fishermen, and 69 percent of the domestics. Less than a third of
the Congo slaves, however, worked in the colony's *sucreries*. Likewise,
the proportion of Hausa people employed in the boiler rooms was
more than twice that of Bambaras, Nupes, and Mandingues. Of the
Senegal people who did not work in the field, two-thirds were carters
and stockmen. Although much of this national and tribal division of
labor rested on crude stereotypes, it also reflected the slaveholders'
knowledge of the skills Africans carried across the Atlantic. In Saint
Domingue, as David Geggus suggests, knowledgeable slave owners
employed the Nupe's long equestrian tradition and the Fulbe's knowledge of cattle herding to their own benefit.

The decisions slaveholders made also affected the sexual balance
and age distribution of the slave labor force. Throughout the Americas, slaveholders preferred men, generally young ones—whom they
believed to be strong yet pliable workers.[20] Slaveholders with the
greatest resources had the best opportunity to act on their preferences.
As a result, disproportionately male populations emerged wherever
high profits allowed slave owners to draw directly on Africa for their

workers. The ratio of men to women imported in the sugar islands—particularly in the midst of the sugar revolution—was weighted heavily in favor of men. However, the sexual balance of the slave population of the sugar islands—as in most New World slave societies—did not long favor men, as slave women survived better than men in the New World. On one large Jamaican sugar estate, Richard S. Dunn calculates, nearly 20 percent of the incoming African men died during the first five years of residence, while only 13 percent of the women suffered a similar fate. Such an imbalanced mortality rate eventually swung the sexual ratio in favor of women, especially after the close of the transatlantic slave trade. But, once reversed, the balance did not always remain in favor of women. Movement to the frontier, Steven F. Miller demonstrates in his study of the American South, again weighted the labor force in favor of men, as slaveholding pioneers viewed women as "a dead expense."[21] From Alabama to Trinidad, frontier planters put a premium on slave men. Needless to say, the transfer of men to the frontier left the slave population of the older regions disproportionately female.

Try as they might, slaveholders could rarely design a labor force to meet their specifications. Even the most powerful slaveholders had but a tenuous hold on the local market for slaves and almost no control over the African market, which drew slaves from the interior of the continent to a multitude of coastal factories. Marked differences in the sex ratios of slaves taken from different regions of Africa—for example, the numbers of men and women were far more evenly balanced among slaves from the Bight of Biafra than among slaves from other parts of the coast—played havoc with the wishes of slaveholders on the western side of the Atlantic. If a New World colony received large numbers of slaves from the Bight, its planters would not be able to buy as many men as they would like. Moreover, marginal operators, unable to compete for slaves, were forced to take the scrapings of the international trade or to adopt other strategies, piecing together a labor force from family members, indentured servants, and wage workers or purchasing slave men and women in relatively equal numbers and encouraging them to reproduce.[22]

Once the labor force had been assembled, however, slaves began to construct alliances that turned their particular attributes to their own advantage. The slave masters' careful choices took on a different meaning when viewed from the quarter. Slaves who shared a common heritage, language, skill, or occupation quickly formed ties of friendship and kinship, and began weaving them into a cultural matrix of shared belief. Such shared beliefs were critical: only by joining together could slaves establish standards of their own to counter those of the owner. In numerous ways, common work experience reinforced shared values, and the culture that emerged provided the basis for opposition to the slaveholders' rule. By drawing together men and women of like background, slaveholders thus helped speed the process of community formation among slaves, and, ironically, bolstered opposition to their own rule.

Just as slaveholders chose their slaves, they also had the first say as to how their slaves worked. Masters organized their labor force by gang or task; they developed elaborate managerial hierarchies or worked shoulder-to-shoulder with their slaves; and they divided their labor force into simple or complex occupational groupings. Yet even the most powerful slave masters were constrained in their decisions by a variety of circumstances, none more significant than the requirements of crop and craft. By time-tested conventions, some commodities lent themselves to an organization by gangs and some to an organization by task; some to personal and others to impersonal command; some to a range of skills and others to no skills at all. Slaveholders honored such conventions, but only so far as they satisfied their desire for ever higher productivity and profits.

In the gang system, slaves labored in carefully defined groups—often segregated by age and sex—under the close supervision of white overseers or, on occasion, black drivers or foremen. Overseers and drivers pressed slave gangs with a degree of regimentation and discipline that called forth military or machine metaphors from all who witnessed them. Gang labor thus allowed planters to distribute workers according to age, sex, and skills, and provided them with a means of close supervision. The numbered gangs—first, second, third—of the great sugar estates suggests only the barest possibilities for those allocations. No matter what the assignment, gang labor left little room for the slaves' initiative, as slave gangs generally toiled from sunup to sundown.

Slaves enjoyed a good deal more latitude under the task system, which defined the slaves' labor by the work to be accomplished: so many rows to be sowed, so much wood to be chopped, so many acres to be harvested. Slaveholders surrendered the regimentation of gang labor, in some measure, because the task system allowed them to measure the slaves' work with precision, even in the absence of supervision. Advocates of tasking also observed that the system offered slaves an incentive to finish their work as quickly as possible. When their task was complete, the slaves' time became their own. Accordingly, slaves placed a high value on the self-regulated labor and the absence of direct supervision that tasking allowed.

Whereas gang labor was generally limited to plantation-size units, tasking went on everywhere—in plantations, farms, mines, and workshops. However, different crops and commodities became associated with different patterns of labor organization. For example, sugar was almost always linked with gang labor and, on mainland North America, rice with the task system. The regularity of these connections often made the tie seem determined, even foreordained, by the demands of the particular commodity and the circumstances under which it was produced. But there were no necessary linkages. Planters frequently debated the relative merits of task and gang labor, and, on occasion, switched from one to the other in an effort to maximize production. Some up-country Georgia planters, Joseph P. Reidy notes, established daily tasks for certain operations in an otherwise dominant gang system. Tasking grew in popularity particularly in the early nineteenth century and was even adopted by sugar planters as they sought to increase productivity, reduce costs of supervision, and lessen metropolitan criticism of the hard driving associated with the gang.[23]

Significant as gang versus task labor was, the contest between master and slave only rarely involved the choice. That decision resided in the master's purview, except perhaps when slaveholders switched from one system to another, in which case slaves could enter the debate.[24] Instead, masters and slaves struggled over the terms of labor under both gang and task. From the slaves' perspective, what distinguished gang and task labor was not the degree but the terms of exploitation. If tasking offered an alternative to the regimentation of the gang, slaves probably did not work less and certainly not at a slower pace under the task system. Slaveholders attempted to define the task so that it filled the slaves' entire work day. At day's end, only the strongest and most industrious slaves controlled their time. Often these men and women had to assist others—spouses, parents, children, and friends—in completing their work, keeping all in the fields late into the day and making a mockery of the independence tasking promised. Such manipulation made tasking—no less than the gang—an instrument of labor discipline and suggests why slaves sometimes demonstrated an ambivalence about task work, even actively opposing it on occasion.

The familiar contest between master and slave took different forms under the task and gang system. Just as some slaves contested the definition of the task, others pressed their owners over the length of the work day, the size and composition of the gang, and the pace at which it worked. A Mississippi planter complained that "all the whips in Christendom" could not drive slave gangs "to perform more than they think they ought to do, or have been in the long habit of doing." According to David Barry Gaspar, slaves who labored under the gang system in Antigua were sensitive to the composition of the labor force, becoming "extremely concerned" when their estates were short-handed and their gangs composed of youthful or aged workers.[25] Gang labor, unlike tasking, placed the struggle between slaves and their supervisors squarely on the ground whereas the crucial decisions over the definition of the task were generally made at some distance from the field.

The organization of work was only one of many factors of production that affected the way slaves labored, and hence the way they lived. Some slaveholders—a majority in some slave societies—worked directly with their slaves, following them down the same furrows or standing face-to-face across a bucksaw. Other slaveholders knew their slaves only through a long chain of command, which stretched from office-bound attorneys and bookkeepers to stewards, overseers, and drivers in the field. On the largest estates, such hierarchies allowed masters to absent themselves entirely, separating plantation ownership from plantation production. The wealthiest sugar planters took refuge in—or never left—their European metropoles, thereby removing themselves from direct contact with their slaves. On some Caribbean islands more than half the slaves belonged to absentees. Although few of the coffee, rice, or cotton barons retreated across the Atlantic, they periodically left their estates for a townhouse, relinquishing the day-to-day operations to plantation-based managers.

Labor within such hierarchies differed markedly from work on a farmstead with only the master, the mistress, their children, and their slaves in residence. Whereas farm slaves knew their owners—eating from the same pot, if rarely at the same table—plantation slaves labored under an ever-changing coterie of supervisors. Although working in close proximity to a master had its own pressures, working under an overseer tended to be more onerous. Throughout the Americas, overseers gained a reputation for abusiveness, occasionally sadistic brutality. Such reputations cast a long shadow over those overseers, who tried to balance their employers' demand for profits with the slaves' expectation of decent treatment. In the Chesapeake, as in many other places, planters tended to change overseers frequently, although long-established overseers produced the largest crops and had the least discontented slaves. But even under the best of conditions, slaves fared poorly when their supervisors had no direct material interest in their well-being.[26]

Still, slaves discovered advantages in the long chain of command, finding ways to play owner against steward, steward against overseer, and overseer against driver. While distance hardened the heart of many absentee owners, it sharpened the sympathies of others. Guilty over a failure to exercise their paternal responsibilities, absentee owners often sought out the opinions of their slaves—sometimes through personal visits, sometimes through special emissaries, and sometimes through memorials from their slaves. Overseers learned that a petition from the lowliest plantation hand might provoke the owners' wrath as quickly as falling output. The absence of the owner therefore encouraged slaves to express themselves, bond more strongly together, and select their own leaders.

The existence of deep managerial hierarchies also allowed a few slaves to enter the supervisory ranks, although almost always at the lowest level. Black drivers and foremen, operating under a white overseer or directly reporting to a master, accumulated power, prestige, and privilege. Although balancing the interests of their people with those of the master proved a difficult matter even for the most astute, drivers nonetheless enjoyed the benefits of rank—superior rations, clothing, and housing. Elevated from the ranks of field hands usually in their late twenties or early thirties, slave foremen worked longer and lived longer than their compatriots.[27]

Beneath slave foremen and drivers in the plantation's occupational hierarchy stood slave artisans. Many plantation crafts involved heavy manual labor and some artisans were "put to the hoe" for at least part of the year, but most skilled workers escaped the harsh regimen of the field. Although they often faced dangers, notably industrial accidents, that field hands did not, artisans—like drivers—enjoyed the benefits of rank. The artisans' clothes, food, and shelter were superior to those of field hands, and they also lived longer, healthier lives.[28] The control slave artisans enjoyed over their own time allowed them to travel off the plantation and to work independently, expanding their chances of buying their way out of bondage. Empowered by their special abilities and knowledge of the world beyond the plantation gate, skilled slaves frequently rose to positions of leadership within the slave community, often achieving superiority over drivers, who owed their elevated status to the owners' largess rather than to their own special skills.

Access to skill depended in some measure on the nature of the productive process. Before a slave could be elevated to a position of privilege within the slave hierarchy, there had to be a position to fill. Different crops and crafts demanded different repertoires of skilled and unskilled labor. Some commodities required a near army of skilled workers; others hardly any. Sugar belonged to the former category; cotton to the latter; other crops and crafts fell somewhere between the two. Although both sugar and cotton cultivation relied upon gang labor in the field, the different levels of skill entailed gave their respective labor forces distinctive configurations.

Sugar plantations, which combined agricultural and industrial functions within a single enterprise, boasted a complex division of labor, which began with the planting of ratoons or cane pieces and stretched through the harvesting, milling, and processing of cane juice into sugar crystals and molasses and its various by-products. Both the growth and processing of cane required large numbers of specialists, many of whom were highly skilled—coopers to make barrels, carpenters and masons to build and repair outbuildings, boilers and distillers to work in the sugar houses, and machinists to keep equipment in good repair. In addition, the daily operations of a sugar estate employed an array of specialists to tend the animals that drove the mill, to cook and clean for stewards and overseers, and to attend the children of the slaves. Nearly one-fifth of the slaves residing on sugar plantations had occupations other than that of field hand. Throughout the Caribbean, sugar estates had two or three times as many tradesmen as did coffee plantations.[29]

The division of labor on cotton plantations—even the largest ones—looked nothing like that of a sugar estate. Cotton required few skilled workers of any sort. Ginning cotton, unlike sugar processing, was a relatively simple operation that demanded no special abilities. Once ginned and packed into bales, cotton needed no further processing. Some cotton planters, particularly on the larger estates, engaged in cloth production, but this was an activity for old women and young girls, not prime hands. Since cotton could be stored outdoors under a tarpaulin, cotton plantations required few outbuildings, reducing the need for sawyers, carpenters, and joiners. And since cotton could be transported by flatboat, barge, or steamer, cotton plantations employed few teamsters, blacksmiths, saddlers, harness makers, and other workers to service wagons and the animals who pulled them.[30]

Much also depended upon the population beyond the plantation. Where slaves lived surrounded by substantial numbers of white non-slaveholders, skilled work was often given over to them, leaving the most skilled slaves without employment. Thus, when tobacco planters in the Chesapeake region of North America switched to small grain production, they initially turned to white yeomen to mill, market, and transport their grain. Only later did slaves gain control over these trades, and then only on the largest estates. White nonslaveholders, moreover, were not the slaves' only competitors for skilled status. In many places, free people of color dominated the artisanal trades, often to the exclusion of both black slaves and white freemen. The absence of competitors, white or black, allowed slaves in the Caribbean opportunities that hardly existed on the mainland. In Antigua, some slaves served as physicians to white and black alike.[31]

The proportion of laborers who were skilled—like the size of managerial hierarchies—was also a function of plantation size. There could be little specialization on small units, and most slaves—like their owners—were jacks-of-all-trades. If a small planter owned a slave who was not a field worker, that slave would almost certainly be a female domestic. Large units, by contrast, allowed for specialization. During the eighteenth century, Chesapeake slaves—even those belonging to the great planters—generally resided on "quarters" and did a variety of work, skilled and unskilled. On the home quarter, the seat of the planter's empire, the division of labor was much greater. George Mason remembered his ancestral estate as a self-contained village: "My father had among his slaves carpenters, coopers, sawyers, blacksmiths, tanners, curriers, shoemakers, spinners, weavers and knitters, and even a distiller."[32]

Almost universally, skilled labor was men's work. Unless the slave population was heavily male, the large number of men removed from the field meant that women composed the greater portion of those remaining. As New World slave populations consisted increasingly of creoles, their field forces became overwhelmingly female. By the early nineteenth century, Richard Dunn found that a young man's chances of remaining a prime field hand on the Mesopotamia plantation was one in two; for a young woman, it was five in six. In 1802 women accounted for thirty-three of the fifty-nine members of the great gang—which did the hardest field work—and thirty-six of the forty-five members of the second gang. Slave women rarely gained supervisory positions, and then generally only over children and other women.[33] The few exceptions to this rule appeared rooted in gender conventions transferred from Europe and Africa to the Americas, for the only women not working in the field were usually attached to the domestic sphere as housekeepers, nurses, seamstresses, or stockminders.[34] In short, woman's work in slave society, according to a perceptive observer of the Jamaican scene, was limited to "the house, with its . . . supposed indulgences, or the field with its exaggerated labours."[35] Although slave women were generally healthier and lived longer than their male counterparts, their exertions in the field took a heavy toll on their health, fertility, and longevity.

Conventions respecting age also determined the slaves' place in the occupational hierarchy. Richard Dunn traces the work history of one slave woman on Mesopotamia, Debby, from when she joined the labor force at age eight as a gleaner, through her placement in the grass gang at age nine, to her entry into the great gang as a first-class hand at fifteen, to her "retirement" as a shepherdess at age thirty-three. Debby died at thirty-seven. Such a neat meshing of the life cycle and the division of labor was only possible on the largest estates. Although all planters tried to integrate children into their work force at as early an age as possible and keep old people employed as long as possible, some forms of production lent themselves more to the employment of the young and old than others. Sugar production, with its complex division of labor, encouraged planters to incorporate children and old people into the gang system; other crops permitted steady employment for old and young only briefly during the year. On tobacco plantations, for example, children wormed the broad leaves, a disgusting job that planters believed was made for little hands. However, the remainder of the year, planters struggled to find tasks to keep them busy.

Like gender conventions, those of age were not rigidly fixed. On the frontier, the slave population was generally younger than in the settled regions. Upwardly striving planters—perhaps eager to avoid older hands familiar with customary work practices—found young people to be not only cheaper but more malleable workers. As Steven Miller has discovered, in 1840 slaves between age ten and thirty-six composed some 55 percent of the slave population on the cotton frontier of the American South compared to 47 percent of the population of the seaboard. Slaves were also employed differently on the frontier than in the older settled regions, with children entering the work force earlier and old people remaining longer.[36]

In large part, then, the labor demands of the masters dictated the composition of slave populations, and hence other aspects of slave life.

The slave family's very existence, for instance, rested upon the character of the work force. Until the number of men and women in the labor force approached sexual parity, adult slaves had difficulty establishing families. After slaves had formed families, the greatest threat to their stability came from their masters' response to labor demands—perhaps selling off some slaves in hard times, shifting part or all of the labor force to take advantage of new opportunities, or renting out some slaves to make additional money. The size of the labor force was also an important determinant of family stability and family structure. Slave families faced greater disruptions and households were more often composed of a single parent on small farms than on large plantations.

Work demands also shaped the demographic performance of slaves in vital ways. Work assignments and the intensity of work, for example, limited the fertility of slave women. A ninety-hour workweek, Richard Dunn observes, left Mesopotamia's slave men and women with "little appetite or energy for sexual intercourse." Work demands had an even more telling effect on mortality. On various Caribbean islands, death rates on sugar estates were twice, sometimes three times, as high as on coffee or cotton plantations. Work may also explain the greater longevity of slave women than men on sugar estates, for "although the grueling labor of the cane fields was performed mostly by women, men still did the heaviest and most dangerous tasks."[37] In addition, the labor demands of tobacco, cotton, and to a lesser extent, rice on the North American mainland help explain why its slave population grew naturally at a time when the slave populations of Caribbean and Latin American sugar societies were decreasing naturally. To be sure, work was not the sole determinant of demographic well-being, for disease, environment, diet, and ethnic background interacted with labor demands in complicated ways. But perhaps nothing more surely reveals the impact of work patterns on slave fertility and mortality than the seasonal pattern of infant birth and death on Mesopotamia.

At no time was the connection between slave work and slave life more evident than when the productive processes were altered. Changes in the terms of labor that accompanied the introduction of new crops, new technology, or even new supervisors upset the carefully contrived agreements that had been negotiated between master and slave. With the old rules in disrepair, everything was suddenly open to reconsideration. Both master and slave weighed the advantages of social stability against those of redefining customary practice. Seizing the moment, slaveholders added to the slaves' burdens, stretching the length of the day, increasing the size of the task, and

revoking established privileges. Understanding the dangers of concession, slaves resisted with new force. As both slaveowners and slaves
fortified their positions, tensions rose, and in the heat of the moment
slave society was recast. Whether such alterations were founded on
the advent of a new crop (wheat) or new technology (the plow) as in
the post-Revolutionary Chesapeake, or on the transit of slave society
from the seaboard to the interior as in the American South, or on the
introduction of a new variety of cotton as in up-country South Carolina, or on the reconstitution of the labor force as in various Caribbean
slave societies, such moments marked significant watersheds in the
development of slave societies.[38]

II

The introduction of new crops, technology, or labor organization not
only altered the masters' economy but also that of the slaves. For while
chattel bondage presumed the forcible extraction of the slaves' labor, it
required that slaveholders provide their slaves with subsistence and
protection. Slaveowners gladly accepted the benefit of the slaves' toil
but did not always meet their obligations. Often they commanded
slaves to provide their own subsistence, requiring them to feed, clothe,
and medicate themselves. Such bad faith burdened slave men and
women, who worked long hours to support themselves and their families after they had finished doing their owners' bidding. But, in a manner that characterized so much of the slave experience, slaves turned
the masters' additional demands to their own advantage, transforming
attempts to tighten the bonds of servitude into small grants of independence—"niches" or "breaches"—whereby they controlled a portion of their own lives. By appropriating their labor for themselves,
slaves articulated their own interests and the means of achieving them.
Nonetheless, relations between master and slave remained at once
"dependent and antagonistic," so that if the slaves' economy stood
apart from that of the masters—physically and ideologically—it never
formed, as Dale Tomich notes, "an independent 'peasant breach' with
a logic of its own."[39] Like the masters' economy, the slaves' economy
can be understood only within the context of the struggle between
master and slave.

In securing a measure of economic independence—as in other
areas of workplace struggle—slaves achieved their greatest success
where masters were most vulnerable. The masters' vulnerability

increased the slaves' bargaining power, enlarging the niches, or breaches, wherein the slaves' fragile economic independence rested. Such points of vulnerability differed under different productive regimes. Mahogany cutters in Belize derived a degree of economic independence from their ability to roam the forest, armed with axes and guns; cotton pickers in pioneer up-country South Carolina from the acute shortage of labor; tobacco hands in the Chesapeake from the small size of their productive units; sugar workers throughout the Americas from the necessity to harvest and grind the cane rapidly.[40] Thus, in every slave society, understanding the slaves' economy requires understanding the masters' economy: the nature of the labor force, the requirements of particular crops, the organization of production, and its seasonal rhythms.

The slaves' economy must also be studied in conjunction with the masters' need to ensure subsistence for their slaves. In the Americas, slaveholders employed three broad strategies to feed their slaves: they imported rations from outside the plantation, they supervised the production of food as part of estate labor, or they allowed or required slaves to feed themselves by ceding them a portion of their time and access to gardens (sometimes called houseplots or yards) and provision grounds (sometimes called *conucos, polinks,* or "negro grounds"). Such practices were not mutually exclusive, and they differed from place to place and changed over time. While some slave societies depended almost exclusively on rationing, others relied on slave provision grounds for most of their food requirements; most, however, developed a mix between imported and estate-grown rations and the independent production of food by slaves.

Slaveowners variously allowed, encouraged, or forced their slaves to provide their own subsistence when provisions were expensive or difficult to obtain. Such practices reached back to the beginning of plantation production on the island of São Tomé off the west coast of Africa in the sixteenth century. They were carried to the New World by the Portuguese and spread throughout the Caribbean by the Dutch.[41] Nonetheless, the practice of requiring slaves to feed themselves did not rest upon precedent; it developed only under particular circumstances. For example, in nonagricultural operations like mining, provisions were generally in short supply, whereas land was readily available and easily given over to slaves. Thus, mineowners in many parts of the Americas required their slaves to grow food, often giving them large blocks of time in lieu of rations. In the Colombian Choco, a five-day workweek was the general practice, so that slaves had two days to devote to raising their own provisions. On smaller *cuadrillas*, some slaves were given three days per week. But such practices were not universal. In the Minas Gerais region of Brazil, for instance, mine-owners often denied their slaves access to provision grounds and frequently ignored the law granting slaves Sundays and holy days to cultivate their own plots.[42]

The slaves' economy thus took shape at the confluence of the requirements of staple production and the demands of the established system of subsistence. Like the masters' economy, it was both an exemplar of the continuing struggle between master and slaves and part of the terrain on which that struggle was fought. Whereas masters saw the slaves' self-subsistence as a means to lower their expenses and raise their profits, slaves viewed their independent economic activity in a different light. Throughout the Americas, slaves believed they could enlarge and vary their diet from the produce of their own gardens and provision grounds. Moreover, by marketing their surplus and keeping the proceeds of those sales, slaves could also elevate their standard of living and gain the ability to move freely through the countryside, thus learning about the world beyond the plantation's borders. Finally, with their small accumulations of cash, slaves placed their domestic and communal life on a firmer base, offered "a start" to the next generation, and—on occasion—secured freedom for themselves and their loved ones.

Slaves pushed hard to establish and then expand the right to produce and market independently, demanding additional land and time to work it and pressing for greater freedom to sell the surplus. Frequently, they—not their owners—initiated independent economic production. After carving out their own grounds, slaves on one St. Vincent estate offered their owner a bargain: if he would allow them Saturday afternoon out of crop, they would feed themselves and expect him to supply only salt and basic provisions.[43] As always, slaves transformed the masters' grant of privileges, once in place, into entitlement. On the sugar plantations neighboring Vere, Jamaican slaves voted with their feet, refusing to be transferred to a parish where they would have to depend on rations for their food supply. In the Windward Islands, the continued presence of plantation yam grounds harked back to earlier days of provision production by estate labor. Referring to the slaves' custom of working for themselves on Sunday, a clergyman in the Leeward Islands declared that "Slaves have (or, which is the same, think they have) some Rights and Privileges, of which they are as tenacious as any Freeman upon Earth."[44]

Claiming a larger and larger share of the produce of their labor, slaves gained de facto—and occasionally de jure—proprietorship over a portion of what they had created. Like similar struggles with their owners over the pace of work, size of task, and the composition of work gangs, the slaves' contest over their right to produce independently sharpened their understanding of that struggle and their hopes for its eventual resolution.

The peculiar demands of staple production—be it sugar, coffee, rice, tobacco, or cotton—and the desire of slaveowners to provide subsistence for their slaves as cheaply as possible shaped the evolution of the slaves' independent enterprises. The availability of land, particularly land that could not be profitably employed in staple production, often induced masters to allow their slaves to feed themselves. Planters encouraged slaves to develop their own provision grounds in hilly or mountainous land—known as "gutsides" in the Leeward Islands—that bordered the great estates. The presence of vacant backlands allowed the slaves' economy to thrive in the Windward Islands of St. Vincent, Grenada, St. Lucia, most parishes or quarters in Jamaica, and the Leeward Islands of Montserrat, and, to a lesser extent, St. Kitts and Nevis.[45]

Conversely, where land was limited and fertile, staple cultivation soon took precedence and independent provisioning by the slaves assumed importance only under special circumstances. Once the commitment to sugar production had been made, a small, low-lying island like Antigua or Barbados essentially became an extensive plantation, where slaves were exclusively foreign fed, at least through the eighteenth century. Likewise, slaves in the Jamaican parish of Vere, which consisted of one large, exceptionally rich plain, devoted all their attention to sugar production and were fed by rations as long as slavery lasted.[46]

But a surfeit of land did not persuade masters to allow their slaves to produce provisions themselves if greater profits could be secured in employing slaves in staple production or if food could be obtained more cheaply elsewhere. The requirements of commodity production convinced some slaveowners to keep their slaves working the great staples rather than allow them to tend provision grounds. Planters in the extensive coastal plain of Demerara-Essequibo and Berbice refused to provide their slaves with provision grounds, even though nearby backlands were available, because the estates required labor for massive irrigation projects.[47] Similarly, when food could be imported cheaply or purchased easily from nonslaveholding Indians, whites, or even free blacks, planters did little to encourage the slaves' independent production, sometimes actively discouraging it. On mainland North America, for example, the presence of free whites—extending to a majority in most places—limited the development of the slaves' economy. Although there was land aplenty for slave provision grounds, North American slaveholders generally preferred to control the production of foodstuffs themselves or purchase provisions from the nonslaveholding population. Buying food and necessities from nonslaveholders offered important political rewards, since it tied the nonslaveholding population to the slaveholders' regime.[48]

Moreover, planters found advantages in provisioning. The cultivation cycle of some staples, most notably tobacco and cotton, easily accommodated estate production of foodstuffs. Planters dovetailed their provision and staple operations to keep their slaves employed full-time. Even sugar planters on mainland North America had land and time enough to have their slaves plant one or two crops of corn as well as vegetables. Eventually, certain regions specialized in provisioning. On nonstaple producing islands such as Anguilla, the Bahamas, and the Cayman Islands, slaves cultivated food crops as part of estate labor. In parts of the Chesapeake where tobacco could no longer be profitably grown, many slaves became farm laborers, not plantation hands. In addition, small-time, resident masters, who were firmly committed to their colonies, may have been far more wary of the independence that self-provisioning fostered among their slaves than were their grand, absentee counterparts.[49]

The availability of land and the dynamics of population thus only partially explain the emergence and growth of the slaves' economy. In the short term, masters continually altered the method by which they provisioned their slaves in order to assure dominance, meet the requirements of staple cultivation, and maximize profits. When export commodities commanded high prices, slaveowners tended to provide their slaves with rations; when exports mustered low prices, masters often obliged slaves to grow their own food. But, over the long run, the development of the slaves' economy—like that of the masters'—was tied directly to the evolution of a slave society and the slaveowners' changing commitment to staple production.

In the earliest years of settlement, when staple production was not yet all-encompassing, planters generally had spare land, which they put into provisions either through regular estate labor or by making it available to slaves to work for their own account. Even Barbados, which at the height of the sugar revolution exemplified a plantation regime that relied upon imported foodstuffs, contained slave provision grounds in the seventeenth and the first decades of the eighteenth century. In the early history of St. Kitts, sugar planters generally planted prime cane land in yams and provided fallow cane fields for their slaves to cultivate their own food crops. A similar pattern could be found on mainland North America. The slaves' economy took hold during the initial period of settlement in the Chesapeake, the Carolina low country, and the lower Mississippi valley.[50]

As the commitment to staple production deepened, planters usually began to provision their slaves directly—often on imported foodstuffs. Efforts to maximize staple production resulted in the withdrawal of land and labor from food crops. With an increase in the acreage devoted to staples, provision grounds for slaves contracted, unless there was sufficient marginal land—usually located in plantations' back lots—to which *polinks* or "negro grounds" could be relocated. Legislation regulating various aspects of the slaves' economy—trading, ownership of certain kinds of property, and travel—signaled new constraints on independent economic activities by slaves. The planters' desire to limit the slaves' economy was most evident on an island like Barbados, where by the mid-eighteenth century slaveholders had wrested provision grounds away from their slaves. Barbadian slaves thus came to depend almost exclusively on imported rations, growing little of their own food. But the pattern was familiar. During the height of the eighteenth-century sugar expansion in the Caribbean, even planters in home-fed colonies supplemented provision-ground supplies with imported food, sometimes under the pressure of metropolitan authorities. In Martinique, French officials required that planters furnish subsistence for their slaves and limited the growth of slave provision grounds.[51]

With the decline in the commitment to staple production, slaveholders again shifted responsibility for provisioning to their slaves, encouraging—sometimes requiring—slaves to feed themselves. The size of provision grounds and the time slaves had to tend them increased, again often under the pressure of metropolitan regulations intended to guarantee the slaves' subsistence. The slaveholders' new policies not only reflected a simple desire to cut costs but also changes in the structure of the labor force—which, in a mature slave society, included large numbers of young and old people. Such changes could be observed in the Caribbean, where by the early nineteenth century the provision-ground system had become the dominant mode of providing subsistence for slaves. At the time of emancipation, not only were some three-quarters of the slaves in the British West Indies feeding themselves but the surplus they produced supplied a large proportion of the free population. On some islands, slaves achieved a monopoly over the production of commodities like firewood and fodder.[52]

The evolution of staple production thus explains a good deal about the origins and growth of independent production by slaves. Still, the development of the slaves' economy no more followed a preordained pattern than did the development of the masters' economy. Within the same society, masters and slaves made different choices, depending— for example—upon the size and topography of their plantations, the character of the plantations' work force, the availability of transporta- tion, and of course the changing balance of power between master and slave. Moreover, natural and man-made crises—everything from hur- ricanes to revolution—set in motion sharp changes in commodity prices and the availability of provisions, thereby altering the dynamics of both the masters' and the slaves' economy. Indeed, that such crises often became the occasion for the appearance, growth, or demise of the slaves' economy suggests a reciprocal relation between the econo- mies of master and of slave. When planters found it difficult or expen- sive to buy the necessary foodstuffs, they gladly gave their slaves the land and the time to work it themselves; when provisions were cheap, they tried to limit the slaves' independent activity.

The war for American independence, which denied Caribbean slaves access to mainland foodstuffs and unleashed a wave of protest culminating in the Haitian Revolution, was the greatest of the traumas consequent on this pattern. In the Caribbean, where the ensuing disruptions caused massive starvation on some islands, planters re- verted to estate labor to grow provisions or turned the job over to their slaves, greatly enlarging the amount of land set aside for grow- ing provisions. Between 1750 and 1800 the average size of provision grounds in the British West Indies nearly doubled, increasing from four-tenths of an acre per slave to seven-tenths. By the beginning of the nineteenth century, slaves in many Caribbean societies had gained Saturdays—as well as Sundays—to work their grounds. The closing of the African slave trade, the disruptions of commerce that accom- panied the Napoleonic wars, and the metropolitan-sponsored cam- paigns to ameliorate the condition of the slave reinforced the shift toward independent provisioning in the Caribbean, generally by the slaves themselves.[53]

The revolutionary events of the late eighteenth century had a different effect in the North and South American mainland. Hard times in the Caribbean sent staple prices skyrocketing on the international market, and mainland planters rushed to increase production. Sugar boomed in northeastern Brazil and southern Louisiana, especially after the fall of slavery in Saint Domingue. As these mainland slaveholders transferred land and slaves into sugar and pressed their slaves to grow the great staple, the slaves struggled to maintain their own economies.[54]

The slaves' willingness to work independently derived first from the desire for a richer subsistence. The bounty of the slaves' gardens and provision grounds led many observers to conclude that the quantity and quality of food was better where slaves grew their own provisions than where they relied upon planters' rations. Throughout the Americas, slaves created a horticultural smorgasbord in their gardens and grounds, blending native American plants like cassava, European vegetables like *calavance* peas, African trees like *ackees*, and Oceanian fruits like mangoes. Able to cultivate their gardens with a minimum of interference, the Saramaka maroons of Surinam grew a staggering array of crops, and the diversity of vegetables, spices, nuts, fruits, and trees grown by Jamaican slaves, to take just one example, astonished all who saw it: *abbay* (African oil palm), Angola or pigeon or *gungo* peas, bananas, *bissy* (African kola nut tree), cabbage, calabashes, *calalu* (a name for various green vegetables), cashews, *chocho*, coconuts, custard apples, maize, *mammee* apples (*mammee* gum was used by slave doctors for chiggers and *mammee* bark against lice), naseberries, okra, oranges, palms, varieties of peppers, pimento, pineapples, pumpkins, shaddocks, and sweetsops, to name just a few. Root crops—especially the yellow and the white yam (of which there were many varieties, such as *afu*, *backra*, and *Negro*), together with eddoes and cocos—were the primary staples, with plantains and corn (both American and Guinean) as the leading secondary supplements. The centrality of the yam was evident: the term derives linguistically from the many African words meaning "to eat" or "food," rendered in Jamaican English as *nyam* and *ninyam*. To paraphrase John H. Parry, the history of the West Indies should be the story of yams, no less than that of sugar.[55]

In most parts of North America, slaves largely grew crops of European or New World origin—corn, turnips, cabbages, potatoes—but the most distinctive feature of their independent production was the cultivation of the dominant cash crop of their region. Many Chesapeake slaves produced at least some tobacco, the region's primary staple. In the South Carolina and Georgia low country slaves grew rice on their own grounds, while in the up country they turned to the production of "Mexican" short-staple cotton on a large scale, producing—in one up-country South Carolina district—about 7 percent of all the area's cotton in the mid-nineteenth century. Although the commercial orientation of slave production in the antebellum South may testify to the confidence of the mainland's planter class, slaves in the Caribbean also cultivated crops for export: ginger, arrowroot, gums, and oil nuts—although never sugar.[56]

As the prohibition of sugar cultivation suggests, slaveholders disliked and generally discouraged the direct competition of slaves, fearful that slaves would steal from their fields. Although the belief that slaves were naturally thieves was rooted more in their masters' ideology than the slaves' reality, thievery did play an important role in the slaves' economy. Many slaves held, as a matter of principle, that their masters' property was their own, or, in the slaves' idiom, "me no thief him; me take him from massa." Goods removed from the masters' field and house commonly found their way to market and added to the slaves' resources.[57]

Skills in animal husbandry also enriched the slaves' economy, not to mention their diet. Throughout the Americas, slaves raised a variety of barnyard fowl. In fact, in almost all New World slave societies slaves became the ubiquitous "Chicken Merchants," as one eighteenth-century Virginian put it. The slaves' poultry raising varied from place to place. Barbadian slaves reared Guinea fowls, ducks, and pigeons, as well as chickens; Louisiana slaves raised geese, ducks, and turkeys alongside their chickens. As Roderick A. McDonald explains, "raising poultry was ideally suited to the economy of the slave community since it demanded little investment of time or effort, required minimal capital outlay, and provided a steady income through marketing both eggs and the birds themselves." Perhaps, too, chickens were as important in ritual ceremonies elsewhere in the New World as they were for the Saramakas. The significance of this form of property ownership was well captured by a visitor to the Leeward Islands who observed that a slave's "poultry and little stock . . . are his wealth." A "negro without stock," he continued, was "miserable."[58]

In many parts of the Americas, slaves also gained access to cattle and other livestock during the initial periods of settlement. But the freedom of movement such stock allowed incurred the planters' wrath, and planter-controlled legislatures soon barred slaves from owning cattle and horses. Such laws curbed livestock ownership by slaves in many slave societies; in others, however, repeated passage of the same legislation indicates that slaves maintained control over their cattle and large stock. Indeed, in those societies where slaves participated in an extensive internal economy—like Jamaica—livestock ownership became quite widespread. By the nineteenth century, if not before, Jamaican slaves sold their cowhides, goatskins, and animal horns in foreign markets. Similar developments occurred elsewhere. At the end of the eighteenth century "small stock, goats, and hogs"— which were "for the most part the property of the Negroes"—supplied Antigua's shipping. Extensive woodlands and pastures facilitated stock raising by slaves on the North American mainland, particularly in low-country South Carolina and Georgia, where ownership of cattle by slaves approached or even exceeded Caribbean levels. Of the nearly ninety former slaves in Liberty County, Georgia, who lost property to federal troops during the Civil War (and who later applied for compensation), almost all—97 percent—testified that they had lost hogs and more than half horses, mules, and cows. After emancipation, a South Carolina planter who recollected that "a good many" slaves owned livestock seems not to have been exaggerating. The low-country slaves' "passion for ownership of horses or some other animal" became worthy of comment.[59]

But there was much more to the slaves' economy than the raising of animals, theft, or the cultivation of crops. Once given the time, slaves proved adept at exploiting the New World's natural resources. They hunted and fished, blending techniques they and their ancestors brought from Africa with those learned from Native Americans and Europeans. The creativity of Saramaka maroons—with bow and various arrows, fishtraps, and drugging techniques—was singular, but Afro-American slaves in general were inventive hunters and fishermen. Slaves also gathered nuts, berries, kept bees, and used wild plants to supplement their diet, decorate their households, supply their furnishings, and cure their ills. In Carolina, a visitor observed, "the Negroes are the only people who seem to pay any attention to the various uses that the wild vegetables may be put to." Of the 160 species of medicinal plants identified in Jamaica, over a third of them seemed to be of African origin. Throughout the New World slaves employed gourds and calabashes as containers, eating utensils, and musical instruments. Slaves also used local clays to make their own pottery, called *yabbas* in Jamaica and colonoware in the South Carolina and Georgia low country.[60]

In addition to making the land work for them, slaves manufactured many valuable items. Skills in woodworking, basketmaking, straw plaiting, and other crafts allowed slaves to fashion bedmats, bark ropes, wicker chairs, baskets, brooms, horse collars, canoes, and earthen jars. Slave shoemakers produced extra shoes on their own time; coopers produced extra barrels; carpenters carts and furniture; blacksmiths tools; and so on. Such products enriched slave life and provided slaves with essential commodities to trade.[61]

Given the opportunity to work for themselves, slaves marketed the product of their labor to their masters, fellow slaves, and neighboring nonslaveholders. Occasionally, they exported their produce. Slave-controlled markets—generally called Sunday markets no matter what day of the week they convened—became significant social and economic institutions in nearly every slave society. This was particularly true in the Caribbean, where the prevalence of urban locales and the sheer proportion of slaves engaged in independent economic production combined to make the Sunday market the essential mechanism of provisioning. From "day cut," as Jamaican slaves termed it, slaves began streaming toward the town center, carrying their produce on their heads, or, if relatively well-to-do, riding mules or leading asses. By the late eighteenth century, some ten thousand Jamaican slaves attended the market at Kingston and fifteen thousand Saint Domingue slaves gathered at the Clugny market at Cap Francois each Sunday morning. On smaller islands like Barbados and Antigua, where the commitment to staple production and the available land limited the slaves' economy, slave markets were neither as well attended nor as well supplied. But they were always significant institutions, for, in the words of physician George Pinckard, Barbadian markets in the early nineteenth century "depend almost entirely" on the slaves' enterprise, while the produce grown by Antiguan slaves, according to another estimate, prevented the island's whites from "starving."[62]

Marketing by slaves was generally more limited on mainland North America. The vastness of the land, the dearth of towns, and—most significant—the competition from white nonslaveholders constrained the slaves' ability to trade independently. Only in towns—such as the rice ports of the Carolina and Georgia low country or the small riverine villages of the Louisiana sugar country—did mainland North American slaves create Sunday markets approximating those further south.

But even where white nonslaveholders provided stiff competition, some slaves found opportunities to peddle produce and other wares. The growth of Chesapeake towns at the end of the eighteenth century found slaves and free blacks taking control of many of the marketing trades, so much so that one white farmer conceded that "a Black man (in this case a free negro) is much better for this business than a white."[63]

Where the absence of towns and cities limited the opportunities of slave hucksters, the plantation itself became the great entrepôt for slave-grown produce, with planters buying the slaves' produce for their own use, factoring the slaves' sales and purchases, and establishing stores at which slaves could buy and sell. Some planters gladly accepted these roles, even selling goods to their slaves at cost, with hopes that it would keep them at home. Beyond the boundaries of the plantation itinerant peddlers—often European immigrants—and storekeepers became the most important trading partners for mainland slaves, purchasing their produce and selling them liquor and other contraband goods.[64]

No matter what its form or extent, trading—through regularly scheduled markets or clandestine rendezvous with peddlers and shopkeepers—became an important element in the lives of New World slaves. By selling and bartering their produce and handicrafts, slaves acquired small amounts of cash to buy extra food, clothing, tobacco, alcohol, and an assortment of "luxuries." Perhaps because their lives were similarly impoverished, the slaves' shopping lists varied little from place to place. In the Leeward Islands, slaves purchased "tobacco and other little conveniences, and some finery too"; Jamaican slaves salted meat and fish; up-country Georgia slaves salt, blankets, coffee, and sugar; Louisiana slaves a wide range of foodstuffs and cloth, as well as pocketknives, combs, fiddles, umbrellas, and, in at least one case, a watch. Almost everywhere tobacco, alcohol, and cloth and clothing (usually of higher quality than the planters' allocations) were important items of consumption, as were bowls, pots, and other utensils. Jewelry and ornamental items were occasional purchases. Purchases of larger pieces of furniture, horses, cattle, and—in special circumstances—even other slaves required long-term savings and were accordingly rare events.[65]

Market day was also a social occasion of the first rank. Slaves dressed in their finest to attend market and their neat, even natty, attire turned heads. As Elsa Goveia observes, participation "in the Sunday market released" field hands "temporarily from the isolation and confinement of the plantations, and helped to make their hard life more tolerable." It was "the one occasion," Goveia continues, on which the field hand "was permitted to share in the greater freedom of the town slaves; and it enabled him to modify, in some degree, his heavy dependence on the master, by acquiring a little money of his own to use as he wished." Once the haggling had ended, market day became a time of great merriment, and slaves turned to more joyful pursuits, from religious observances to drinking, dancing, and gaming. Slaveholders and local officials emphasized the latter, denouncing the immorality that accompanied both markets and clandestine meetings with peddlers. But the planters' persistent efforts to regulate independent trading by slaves revealed deeper fears. Market day became the occasion for slaves—sometimes joined by free blacks and white nonslaveholders—to review their own standing and plan ways to improve their lot, generally to the disadvantage of the planter class. The process of redefining their own interests, which began in their gardens and provision grounds, crystallized in market-day banter. Even when slaves left the market with no more in their pockets than when they arrived, they carried away ideas of incalculable worth.[66]

Material benefits—however paltry from the planters' perspective—added considerably to the slaves' estate. Slaves supplemented these with payments for overwork and "wages" earned from hiring out their own time, both of which were also important elements in the slaves' economy. As with the uneasy bargains that underlay the masters' economy, slaveholders violated the slaves' independent productive activities at great risk to themselves. Slaves could be forced to work on their own time only under duress. When extra work had to be done— during planting and harvest, for example—slaveowners generally compensated their slaves, paying them for overwork on Sunday, in the evening, or on special holidays with equivalent amounts of time or with cash. Overwork payments became standard when it came to the ceaseless grinding and processing of cane, as with the onerous labor of digging and clearing canals. Slaves in up-country South Carolina also received incentive payments for picking cotton above a targeted quota. In almost every slave society some slaves won the right to hire themselves out on "free" days and in the evening, time otherwise given over to working their gardens or provision grounds. In Louisiana, for example, slaves accumulated considerable sums cutting wood and gathering moss, and smaller amounts by—among other tasks—ditching, sugar potting, collecting fodder, and serving as watchmen on their own time.[67]

If most of the proceeds of the slaves' independent economic activity went to meet immediate needs for food and clothing, some slaves managed to accumulate substantial estates, at times equivalent to those of moderately successful free artisans or farmers. At death, according to Edward Long, Jamaican slaves often had property valued between £50 and £200; "few among them," he added, "that are at all industrious and frugal lay up less than £20 or £30." In the Windward Islands, slaves saved similar sums, and some mainland slaves did equally well. During the nineteenth century slaves growing their own cotton in up-country South Carolina put away about a sixth of their earnings. Their savings became the basis of a complex system of credit arrangements within the slave community, whereby slaves financed one another's purchases and, in the process, knit their community more closely together.[68]

Such striking circumstances—slaves as bankers—made it easy to exaggerate the size of the internal economy and the wealth of the participants. By the best accounts, most slaves earned only pocket change. Nonetheless, both abolitionists and slaveholders found reasons—albeit different ones—to emphasize the slaves' prosperity. Edward Long estimated that a fifth of the money circulating in Jamaica was in the hands of slaves; Alexander Campbell, a Grenadian sugar magnate, reckoned that "one half of the current specie" in the Windward Islands was the property of Negroes; and a South Carolina planter thought that "in a small way a good deal of money circulated among the negroes, both in the country and in the towns."[69] Although the success of the minority could overshadow the desperate poverty of the majority and the tenacity of the slaves' economy could obscure its fragility, the few dollars that slaves earned played a large role in Afro-American life.

Much of the independence Afro-Americans secured during slavery—which manifested itself in the slaves' domestic, religious, and community life—derived from the slaves' economy. The extent that slaves wrested control of a portion of their lives from their masters owed directly to their own independent production. That independence began with the slaves' choice of how they would organize their gardens and provision grounds. In contrast to their work in their masters' fields, slaves generally decided what they would plant in their gardens and grounds, when they would plant it, where they would market it, and how they would employ the profits that accrued. Working beyond the watchful eyes of the master, mistress, and their minions, slaves labored with great intensity, demonstrating initiative and ingenuity in squeezing profits out of marginal land. Few observers failed to compare the difference between the desultory manner with which slaves worked their owners' fields and the energy and care they applied to their own crops.

Slaves worked in a variety of ways, but almost always the slaves' economy was a family economy, with the sexual division of labor established in the masters' fields shaping the roles played by slave men and women in their own gardens and provision grounds. In Jamaica scouting out the mountain land—not too different from the Saramaka maroons' practice of "examining the site" for their prospective gardens—devolved on family heads, generally men. Women, however, did much of the marketing, and children and old people worked in the garden. Although the slaves' economy provided a basis for a sexual division of labor within the slave household, independent production remained the concern of the entire family. House plots involved all members of the household, as best evidenced in the memorials they contained to dead relatives. Jamaican slaves, according to one account, formed themselves into "distinct parties" as they began work in their grounds, moving "with all their family, into the place of cultivation." Likewise, an ex-slave from the Georgia low country recollected how his family of nine had "all worked together" on their corn crop. Since slave families pooled their resources and worked in concert, they also made collective decisions on how they would consume their profits. Although funds earned by families on Louisiana sugar estates accumulated in the account of the head of the household—almost always a man ("married" women rarely had accounts in their own names)—all family members drew on them, although not equally. The symbolic basis of family life also had roots in the material one. In Jamaica the connection between independent economic activity and family life was symbolized by the *cotta*—derived from the Twi *kata*, "to cover"—a circular head pad traditionally made of plantain leaf or a twisted cloth, which was used to protect the head when carrying goods to market. What better way for slaves to signify a divorce then to cut the *cotta* into two, allowing each party to take half.[70]

Wealth amassed from independent production reached beyond individual households, supporting communal as well as domestic institutions. Slave-grown produce and slave-crafted goods allowed for small exchanges within the Afro-American community, thus providing a basis for a sociability that encouraged cooperation and mutuality between households. With their earnings, slaves purchased small gifts for one another, placed a few coins in the collection plate on Sunday, and assured a respected elder a proper burial. Slaves also pooled their scant resources for the benefit of the entire community. Labor exchanges were doubtless more numerous and significant than monetary ones and reinforced the cooperative ethos within the slave community. The wealth that slaves earned helped build churches and pay ministers and teachers. The arrival of the Union army in the American South unleashed a variety of complicated disputes over the ownership of antebellum African churches. Although white trustees held the legal deeds to these buildings and their contents, slaves claimed that the churches had been built and maintained by their own contributions. When the disputes reached the offices of the Freedmen's Bureau and local courts, slaves generally proved their case.[71]

Funds accumulated by the slaves' independent economic production also secured the future of their children, providing a "start" for the next generation. Slaves developed complex systems of inheritance. In Jamaica, when a family head was nearing death, he nominated a trustee or executor from among his kin to distribute his personal property to his legatees. Jamaican masters even permitted their slaves, Bryan Edwards claimed, to will their gardens or grounds; if a master decided to convert the slaves' grounds to estate use, he compensated the slaves for them. In the early nineteenth century slaves on the Codrington plantations began to bequeath their cottages, gardens, and personal belongings to other slaves, and in the Windward Islands slaves bequeathed rights of occupancy along with movable property. "They pass them on from father to son, from mother to daughter, and, if they do not have any children, they bequeath them to their nearest kin or even their friends," wrote one observer of the inheritance practices of Martinique slaves. Low-country South Carolina and Georgia slaves employed guardians to facilitate the transfer of property across plantation lines as well as generational lines.[72]

The slaves' economy reached deep into all of Afro-American culture. Gardens and provision grounds, Barry Higman suggests, permitted the elaboration of African-influenced conceptions of spatial order. Here boundaries could be fluid and irregular, as against the geometric and rigid European notions of order. Moreover, slaves infused their gardens and grounds with magical beliefs, many carried from Africa. Saramaka maroons closely examined potential garden sites in order to avoid forest spirits and snake gods and to placate the god who presided over their chosen location. In low-country South Carolina and Georgia slaves planted sesame or *benne* at the end of rows

in their private fields because it was thought to help ward off in-
truders. When one visiting absentee owner first saw sesame in Jamaica, "it was growing in a negro's plantation." Known as *wangla*, it
was used in *obeah* practices. Jamaican slaves also planted the cut eye or
overlook bean at the borders of their provision grounds as protection
from the evil eye. Thus, when the Intendant of Saint Domingue described the slaves' provision grounds as *"une petite Guinée,"* he was
more perceptive than he knew.[73]

Although slaves garnered numerous benefits from independent
economic production, they understood that their participation benefited the planter class. From the owners' perspective, the slaves' participation signaled acceptance of the legitimacy of the master-slave
relationship. For some slaves, this was too high a price to pay. They
refused to participate, not merely because of the extra work independent production entailed or because masters reduced rations to the
extent that slaves could feed themselves, but because participation
tacitly acknowledged the owners' authority.

Slaves may have also sensed the divisive effect that independent
economic production could have on their own community. The scramble for modest wealth could be no less mean and demeaning than the
scramble for great wealth. It unleashed a variety of conflicts—great
and petty—among slaves, as some tried to gain advantages at the
expense of others. These conflicts sometimes grew out of the opposing
roles of farmer and merchant, buyer and seller, even "employer" and
"employee." When plantation slaves took their goods to market, they
often found their produce engrossed by savvy urban hucksters—generally slave and free blacks—who controlled the trade, took the lion's
share of the profit, and left country folks with but small returns
on their labor. Where the slave trade remained open and provision
grounds constituted the dominant mode of subsistence, slaveholders
often assigned newly arrived Africans to creole families, for whom
they labored in return for subsistence until they could establish
grounds of their own.

While some creoles took seriously their mentoring responsibilities—often forming life-long friendships with the newly arrived—
others shamelessly exploited the initiates. Creoles forced newly arrived Africans to work long hours in their gardens and provision
grounds, even while the newcomers had also to labor in the owners'
fields. The newly arrived thus faced a double servitude. Such exploitation characterized other areas of the slaves' economy as well.

Privileged slaves—overseers, drivers, and artisans, for example—employed their elevated status to raise themselves at the expense of field hands. Those who controlled more extensive grounds hired the less fortunate to assist them, paying them just a small portion of what their labor was worth. Family members—especially children and old people—were not immune from such abuse, as household heads pressed them hard to assure group survival.[74]

Much of this exploitation was the self-exploitation of desperate people, pressed to the wall to survive. The self-exploitation that drove petty producers the world over was also the lot of New World slaves. But no matter its source, it gravely harmed the slave community, turning slave against slave. The padlocks slaves purchased to protect their possessions and the guards stationed at provision grounds testified to the extent of these tensions. So too did the denunciations by their more industrious compatriots of those slaves who refused to participate in the slaves' economy. According to a public prosecutor in Martinique, such attacks left nonparticipants so "ashamed" that they refused to accept rations. Independent economic production could divide as well as unite.[75]

It was not so much sloth but the lack of results that led many slaves to eschew independent economic production. No matter how hard they labored, their participation in the slaves' economy did not guarantee them a better life. Given time and the right circumstances, an industrious slave might gain a more varied and nutritious diet from gardens and grounds, but time was always short and agricultural conditions less than ideal. Provision grounds, by their very nature, were located on waste land, far from the slave quarter. The slaves' crops—no less than the masters'—were subject to the ravages of drought, storm, and vermin. If Saramaka maroons quite often faced famine because their gardens failed, it is hardly surprising that plantation slaves—exhausted by estate labor—experienced shortfalls from their plots. The hard reality was that hunger and malnutrition stalked societies that depended upon provision grounds for subsistence, whereas estate-supplied rations, particularly the corn and pork diet of North American slaves, were sufficient to maintain general health.[76]

Participation in the slaves' economy thus did not necessarily make slaves healthier, longer-lived, or more fecund. Much evidence suggests just the opposite. The natural increase of a slave population cannot be linked directly to the slaves' participation in a system of independent economic production. Barbados, where rationing was always central to subsistence, was the one British Caribbean sugar colony to have a slave population that maintained a positive natural increase, a position it achieved by about 1810; the one Jamaican sugar parish to have a naturally increasing slave population before emancipation was Vere, and it too had few provision grounds. In fact, an experienced observer maintained that Vere slaves were "the most comfortable" in Jamaica and claimed to be able to "tell a Vere Negro almost in a Hundred others from his fat, sleek Appearance." On the mainland, Virginia's slave population achieved a natural increase much earlier than that of South Carolina, although the slaves' economy was more active in low-country Carolina than in Virginia. The height slaves grew to also seems to correspond inversely with self-subsistence. Thus creole-born slaves in the Caribbean were significantly shorter than those of the United States, and, within the Caribbean, creole slaves living on islands devoted to intense sugar cultivation were shorter than nonsugar island slaves.[77]

Slaveowners appreciated that the slaves' desire for economic independence could be turned to their own advantage. By shifting part or all of the burden of subsistence onto the slaves themselves, owners reduced the time, effort, and cost of maintaining their slaves. Although slaves theoretically received compensation in time for producing their own food, the most reliable calculations indicate that slaves worked longer where they were responsible for their own subsistence than where they received rations.[78] Many masters also believed that slaves would labor more efficiently if they were given time to themselves after they had finished their daily tasks. Allowing slaves time for independent economic enterprise not only operated against malingering but also armed slaveowners with another means of disciplining their slaves: keeping them busy.

The slaves' economy could be made to support the masters' economy in less tangible ways as well. "The negro who has acquired by his own labor a property in his master's land," asserted Bryan Edwards, "has much to lose, and is therefore less inclined to desert his work." Other slaveholders concurred with Edwards's judgment. A Grenadian proprietor argued that "the more money the Negroes got for themselves, the more attached they were to the property," while a South Carolina planter proclaimed that no low-country "Negro with a well-stocked poultry house, a small crop advancing, a canoe partly finished or a few tubs unsold, all of which he calculates soon to enjoy, will ever run away." And even when slaves did run away, masters frequently echoed another lowland Carolina slaveholder who was "convinced runaways would not go far, being connected at home, and having too much property to leave." By extending or withholding the slaves' "rights"—to enlarge their gardens, attend markets, or trade with neighbors—slaveholders found another means to bend slaves to their will. By cloaking the raw, coercive nature of chattel bondage behind a seemingly consensual-exchange—the opportunity to subsist in return for labor in staple production—slaveholders masked the violent, exploitive character of their regime. Thus, if the slaves' economy fell short of producing the "obedient, property-respecting, and hardworking" slaves that masters so coveted but never quite possessed, slaveholders still had good reason to encourage slaves to provide provisions for themselves, to pay them for overwork, to allow them to attend slave-operated markets, to factor their slaves' purchases, and to respect their slaves' property rights.[79]

But no matter the benefits, slaveowners remained deeply suspicious of the slaves' independent economic activities. They feared that the slaves' preoccupation with their own enterprises and their dealings with free blacks and white nonslaveholders would dissipate their energy and undermine their dependence—material and psychological—on the owning class, wreaking havoc on the masters' economy. For if the slaves' economy made slaves complicit in their own oppression, it also imposed limits on the masters' rights. Slaveowners viewed the slaves' economy as antithetical to their own economic ambitions. Transforming the master-slave relation to one approximating that of buyer and seller or employer and employee—negotiation and consent replacing fiat and coercion—menaced the slave regime. At base, slaveholders understood that no matter what short-term advantages they reaped, allowing slaves to articulate their own interests through independent economic activities sowed the seeds of subversion and ultimately threatened their rule.

Slaveholders thus not only worked hard to curb the benefits that accrued to slaves as a result of their independent activity but to integrate the slaves' economy into their own. At every opportunity they tried to maximize the time slaves spent growing the great staples and to limit the time slaves worked their gardens and grounds. They determined which goods slaves could buy and sell freely, constrained the slaves' right to hire their own time and collect overwork, and—if given the opportunity—denied slaves the property they had earned on their own, thus enforcing their claim to a slave's entire being and its product. To the extent slaves succeeded in feeding themselves and earning a surplus, masters reduced rations and added to the slaves' responsibilities for supplying shelter, clothing, and medication. In short, slaveowners recognized the slaves' rights only to the extent that those rights affirmed their own domination.

Such actions contradict Bryan Edwards's claim that the slaves' economy manifested a happy "coalition of interests" between master and slave and strengthen Sidney Mintz's contention that the slaves' independent economic production represented only a "temporary resolution" of the "social contradiction arising from exploitation . . . that served the interests of both parties, oppressor and oppressed."[80] Like similar agreements regarding labor in the masters' economy, the slaves' economy rested upon bargains that were inherently unstable. As soon as slaves found a way to eke out a little more independence, masters sought new methods to drive them into greater dependence. As masters tightened bonds of servitude, slaves sought new avenues to enlarge their independence. If its outer limits remained fixed, the day-to-day dynamics of the master-slave relationship was constantly being negotiated and renegotiated. The contest had no end.

The tension between the masters' and the slaves' economies defined the struggle, a change in one initiating a change in the other. The introduction of so-called Mexican cotton into up-country South Carolina transformed the way slaves labored not only for their owners but also for themselves. Mexican cotton, which allowed for an easy separation of fiber and pod, reduced the slaveholders' need to employ additional hands in the evening and on Sunday, sharply curbing the opportunities for slaves to earn extra wages on their own time. The demise of wage work forced the slaves to shift their independent economic activities to gardens and provision grounds, where they grew cotton of their own. With the change, up-country slaves lost the right to travel and bargain for their own wages. The requirement that slaveowners market the produce grown by their slaves limited the slaves' mobility and restricted their access to the market. Slaveowners also became increasingly involved in how their slaves spent their money. Such changes redefined the rights of master and slave. Masters increased their sovereignty over the plantation and its residents, denying slaves the right to come and go as they pleased. Slaves lost contact with the larger world beyond the plantation, becoming more insular and dependent even as their independent income increased. As changes in the masters' economy took their toll on the slaves' economy, struggle between master and slave moved onto new ground.[81]

The contest over the labor that slaves performed on their own behalf assumed various forms, as did the contest over the slaves' labor on their owners' behalf. In some places, at some times, the internal marketing system stood at the center, with masters and slaves disputing the terms of participation. In a place like the Jamaican parish of Vere, where rations were the dominant means of feeding the slaves, the struggle for subsistence revolved not around time but around allowances. Elsewhere masters and slaves fought over the appropriation of free time; the size, quality, and placement of gardens and provision grounds; the organization of labor; or the very composition of the labor force. Each of these was in itself a matter of great complexity. On the question of time, for example, masters and slaves contested Sundays and Saturdays, night work, and holidays. Raising questions about the organization of labor brought into dispute the various advantages and disadvantages of gang and task work, as well as the composition of the gang and the definition of the task. Such matters, moreover, soon became enmeshed in other issues. When slaves in Martinique appropriated more time to themselves, masters tried to reorganize the system of production from the gang to the task system, so that when slaves failed to complete their assignments, slaveholders could reclaim their free Saturdays.[82] The slaves' initiative, in short, provoked a response from the owners, which shifted the terrain on which the struggle was fought, if not the nature of the struggle itself.

The contest between master and slave was never quite the same. During the early years of settlement in up-country South Carolina, shortages of labor and capital restricted the slaves' ability to cultivate their own land but allowed them to work for wages—a most unusual form of independent economy activity. Rather than just trading their own products on Sunday, as did slaves elsewhere in the Americas, up-country Carolina slaves also participated in a Sunday labor market. In time, however, the growing complexity of up-country society and especially the introduction of a high-yield strain of cotton transformed the slaves' economy. Deprived of the opportunity to work for wages, up-country slaves turned to growing their own cotton. Independent cotton production eventually allowed slaves greater material benefits, but they also lost much of their freedom to travel and bargain for themselves. As Woodville K. Marshall shrewdly observes of the struggles in the Windward Islands, much of what is termed resistance "may have been subsumed under a competition and scramble for land and labor resources."[83]

Others joined the contest between master and slave. Metropolitan authorities, local officials, white nonslaveholders, and free people of color—all of whom saw the struggle between master and slaves as impinging on their own liberty—added their voices to the continuing conflict. Clergymen were alternately horrified that masters forced their slaves to work on Sunday and that slaves used the Lord's day for their own labor. Regulation of Sunday markets also involved the great merchants (always white) and small shopkeepers (white and colored), as well as local authorities and metropolitan overlords. The number of participants and the complexity of the contest can be measured in the struggle over the Barbados market, in which some white hucksters profited by trading with or even robbing slaves while others saw their interests threatened by slave competition. Bridgetown merchants, meanwhile, feared competition from both black and white peddlers, whereas urban masters could not seem to decide where to stand: they profited from their slaves' ability to market yet worried about the losses suffered from slave theft. Small planters fretted over the slaves' production of crops like cotton and ginger, in which smallholders specialized; the grandees desired to prohibit the slaves' trade in sugar-cane, even as they encouraged the slaves' market in firewood and grass. Both plantation and town hucksters established mutually advantageous relations with the slaves, each providing markets for the other's goods; yet urban slave hucksters also grew rich at the expense of their rural counterparts.[84] These cross-cutting interests suggest how the slaves' economy became everyone's business, how the resolution of any contest between master and slave required the concurrence— whether silent or active—of all members of slave society, high and low.

In the constant struggle over the appropriation of space in gardens and grounds and the time to work them, the slaves' world took shape. Their most cherished beliefs about the centrality of labor to their own worth and the significance of property to their own independence grew out of their experience as workers—and particularly out of their independent labor. Such beliefs were given full voice in 1789 by a group of Brazilian rebels, who, after killing their overseer and fleeing to the forest, stipulated that they would return to the plantation if their former master gave them "Friday and Saturday to work for ourselves" and supplied them with boats and nets to fish on their own and land "to plant our rice wherever we wish, and in any marsh, without asking permission." They also demanded a large boat with which to market their goods. Once their economy was assured, these former slaves felt certain that their freedom would be secure and that they would then "be able to play, relax and sing any time we wish without your hindrance."[85]

Such notions of freedom, forged in the crucible of slavery, informed the aspirations of black people once slavery ended. The time slaves secured to work their own land became a kind of "rehearsal for reconstruction," during which slaves established their priorities, ordered their lives, and developed their own conceptions of freedom. With emancipation, freed people throughout the Americas made it clear that they wanted, above all, access to land and other material resources that they could work in family and communal groups. They wanted no part in gang labor or in any system that limited their control over what they could grow, what they could rear, and what they could sell. They understood these rights—the rights to work on their own and to control their own resources—as coincident with their independence. In short, they desired most to build upon the independent economic activity in which they had engaged as slaves.

PART ONE

The Labor Force

1

SUGAR PRODUCTION AND SLAVE WOMEN IN JAMAICA

Richard S. Dunn

IN 1823 an English artist named William Clark illustrated the various stages of Caribbean sugar production in a set of strikingly handsome color plates, the most detailed and graphic depiction we have of slave laborers at work in the British West Indies.[1] Clark shows gangs of slaves holing and planting the cane pieces, then harvesting and milling the ripe cane, then boiling the cane juice into crystallized sugar and distilling the by-product, molasses, into rum, and finally carting the cured sugar in huge hogsheads to the seashore for shipment abroad. This artist clearly romanticizes his work scenes: the slaves are grouped in picturesque tableaux, decorously decked out in jackets, trousers, and skirts, whereas other observers report that they toiled seminaked under the broiling sun. Yet Clark makes it abundantly clear that the slaves do all the work. In most of his pictures, a single top-hatted white man stands idly watching as scores of blacks labor strenuously. And slave women are performing much of the heaviest manual toil. While some work sites—the boiling house, the distillery, the quayside—are reserved exclusively for men, in all of the agricultural scenes large numbers of women appear. They drudge in the holing, planting, and harvesting gangs; they haul bundles of cane to the mill; and they labor in the trash yard stoking the boiling house furnaces.

Indeed, at the time Clark published his set of plates, the majority of the sugar workers in the British Caribbean were probably women. A good deal is known about the composition of the slave labor force in the early nineteenth century because the British government took an elaborate census every few years between 1817 and 1834. In 1823 about

49

717,000 slaves were registered in the twenty British Caribbean colonies, 435,000 of whom were attached to sugar estates. Sugar was a major crop in fifteen of these colonies, and virtually the only export crop in twelve of them. And among the fifteen sugar colonies in 1823, only Trinidad, Demarara, and Berbice had more male than female slaves. In Antigua, where Clark sketched his sugar laborers, there were 30,000 slaves in 1823; 78 percent of them lived on sugar estates and 53 percent were females. In Jamaica, the center of British sugar production, there were 336,000 slaves of whom 52 percent lived on sugar estates, while the others worked mainly on coffee estates or livestock pens. Overall, the Jamaican sex ratio was almost evenly balanced at this date, but the proportion on the large sugar estates was very much as in Antigua—about 53 percent female.[2]

Little has yet been published on the role of slave women in Caribbean sugar production, but the subject is surely of interest, since cane-field labor during the slave era was notoriously strenuous and exhausting. What follows is a case study of some five hundred women and girls who lived on a fairly typical Jamaican sugar plantation: Mesopotamia estate, in western Jamaica. Heretofore, no one has found a way to document the actual work histories of a cross-section of slave women, but the Mesopotamia records permit this sort of analysis. By reconstructing the individual careers of all the women on this estate between 1762 and 1831, I can establish that virtually every one of them labored in the cane fields, that most of them did this work for many years, and that collectively they performed much of the hardest sugar labor. Furthermore, the Mesopotamia evidence strongly indicates that sugar labor injured their health, impaired their fertility, and shortened their life expectancy.[3]

The fact that women outnumbered men at Mesopotamia and most other Jamaican sugar estates in the 1820s was profoundly ironic, because for 150 years the Jamaican sugar planters had been deliberately stocking their labor gangs with more men than women. They wanted laborers with strong physiques for heavy manual work, and they were only secondarily interested in providing wives for their slave men or in propagating slave children for future service. As sugar production in Jamaica rose from 1,000 tons in 1675 to 100,000 tons in 1800, and the slave population rose from 10,000 in 1675 to 330,000 in 1800, the planters found it more functional and economical to buy new prime-aged workers from the Atlantic slave traders rather than to rely upon their slave women to rear replacement workers from birth. They imported almost twice as many males as females from Africa. Three large samples of African slaves shipped to the island show a strikingly uniform sex ratio. During the years between 1674 and 1725, of 31,360 slaves shipped to Jamaica by the Royal African Company 61.9 percent were males.[4] Between 1764 and 1784, of 41,625 slaves shipped to Jamaica on 121 vessels, 62.2 percent were males.[5] Between 1791 and 1798, of 49,884 slaves shipped to Jamaica on 149 vessels, 61.7 percent were males.[6] These three samples, which constitute about 16 percent of the 750,000 slaves delivered to the island between 1655 and 1807, suggest that the planters acquired overall approximately 465,000 male as against 285,000 female African slaves—a sex ratio of 163.[7]

The preponderance of males on the slave ships was, however, quickly modified in Jamaica. Half the children born on the island were girls, and among the adult slaves the women lived longer than the men. A sample of the inventoried slave gangs on twenty-one sugar estates during the years between 1674 and 1701—the very time when the Royal African Company was importing 162 males for every 100 females—shows that the sexes were almost evenly balanced on these estates, with 105 working males for every 100 working females.[8] Unfortunately, no one as yet has reported on the demographic characteristics of the many hundred Jamaican slave gangs inventoried during the course of the eighteenth century.[9] But a census of the 18,980 slaves in the sugar-growing parish of St. James, taken in 1788 at the peak of the African trade, shows a surprisingly closely balanced sex ratio of 107.[10] Barry Higman, who has studied this subject more fully than anyone else, calculates that at the close of the Atlantic trade in 1807— when almost half of the Jamaican slaves were African-born and some 60,000 more males than females had arrived via the Middle Passage during the preceding twenty-five years—the island sex ratio was about where it had been in the late seventeenth century: 104.[11]

Though slave women survived better than men in Jamaica, their fertility was low. The population grew steadily in size up to 1807, but only because of the huge influx of new slaves from Africa. Throughout the slave trade era deaths always outnumbered births on the island, and after Parliament abolished the African trade in 1807 this trend continued. The Jamaican slave registration returns, compiled every three years between 1817 and 1832, disclose a crude birthrate of 23 per thousand as against a crude deathrate of 26 per thousand. Natural decrease was particularly evident on the sugar estates, where there were three recorded deaths for every two births.[12] By 1834 the slave population had declined by about 43,000, or 12 percent.[13] Furthermore, the deathrate for males (29 per thousand) continued to be higher than for females (24 per thousand), with the result that the slave sex ratio dropped from 104 in 1807 to 95 in 1832. Interestingly, on the island's 670 sugar estates the ratio fell still lower, to 92 in 1832.[14] And the imbalance was particularly noticeable on the largest sugar estates. Analysis of the slave returns for Westmoreland parish in western Jamaica shows that on the twenty-three sugar estates with two hundred or more slaves, the sex ratio fell from 88 in 1817 to 82 in 1834.[15]

Thus by the end of the slave era the big Jamaican sugar planters had created a far different labor force than they had intended, with significantly more women than men. Of course, the emergence of a female majority does not by itself demonstrate that women did much or most of the sugar work. But examination of the labor pattern at Mesopotamia estate, which was one of the twenty-three sugar plantations in Westmoreland parish with two hundred or more slaves, reveals a good deal about women's participation in sugar production. The records for this estate permit analysis of annual changes in the work force during the years between 1762 and 1831, and they establish that the women at Mesopotamia did indeed perform a great deal of the heaviest field labor.

Situated on the Cabarita River in the Westmoreland plain, five miles inland from the port town of Savanna la Mar, Mesopotamia was laid out around 1700 and was operated for more than a century by four generations of the Barham family: Dr. Henry Barham (who ran the estate from 1728 to 1746), his stepson Joseph Foster Barham (1746–1789), Joseph Foster Barham II (1789–1832), and John Barham (1832–1834). Though the Barhams became absentee proprietors in 1736 when Henry moved to England, the two Josephs each visited Mesopotamia for a year or two as young men and took uncommon interest in the spiritual and physical well-being of their slaves. They maintained a Moravian mission on the estate from the 1760s onward and required their bookkeepers to compile annual inventories of the slaves (taken on December 31 or January 1) so as to keep track of changes in the population. Eighty-six of these inventories survive, taken over a span of ninety-five years from 1736 to 1831, making the Mesopotamia slaves the best-documented Jamaican work force yet discovered.[16] At first, the Mesopotamia listings merely identified each slave by name and occasionally by occupation or value; from 1751 onward they provided annual death registers, with the date and cause of each slave death; from 1762 onward they added annual birth registers and also regularly supplied the age, occupation, and physical condition of each man, woman, and child; from 1774 onward they identified the mothers of all slaves born on the estate. By correlating these inventories, I have been able to trace 1,388 individual slaves—650 females and 738 males—who lived at Mesopotamia between 1736 and 1831. More important, I have been able to reconstruct the year-by-year careers of the 504 females and the 599 males who lived and worked there between 1762 and 1831, the period for which the prosopographical information is most detailed.

At Mesopotamia the slave population fluctuated greatly between 1736 and 1831, ranging from lows of 236 in 1744 and 238 in 1769 to peaks of 380 in 1793 and 421 in 1820. During this span nearly twice as many deaths (1,025) as births (541) were recorded, with male deaths (564) considerably outnumbering female deaths (461).[17] The Barhams replaced these lost laborers by purchasing some 599 new slaves, either from the African slave ships (142 males, 88 females) or from neighboring estates that were closing down or retrenching (192 males, 177 females). Thus, at any given time some of the slaves living at Mesopotamia were born and raised on the estate, some were born in Africa, and some (including many Africans) had developed family ties elsewhere in Jamaica before they were transferred to the Barhams' estate. The African-born slaves (except for children who were captured before their puberty initiation rites) would have been instantly identifiable to any observer because they bore the distinctive ritual scars or country marks of their ancestral tribes on their temples, cheeks, arms, breasts, bellies, or backs.[18]

Over time the Mesopotamia sex ratio changed significantly, as is illustrated in table 1.1. In the 1730s the sexes were evenly balanced; from the 1750s to the 1790s males were strongly dominant; and from the 1810s to the 1830s a female majority emerged. These developments strongly affected the composition of the work force on the estate. The earliest surviving inventory of 1736 shows a symmetrical slave population of 124 males and 124 females. No invalids were listed, which suggests that the workers were relatively young and healthy, and the proportion of nonworking children was greater than on any subsequent Mesopotamia slave list, which suggests that Dr. Henry Barham was encouraging family life and procreation. But after the Barhams departed for England, all this changed. In the 1740s and 1750s, fewer girl babies than boy babies survived infancy, fewer females than males were purchased, and more women than men died. By 1761 the sex ratio was 129. A year later, when age and health status were listed for the first time, more people were in their forties than in their twenties.[19]

TABLE 1.1. Slave employment by sex at Mesopotamia, 1736–1831

Year	1736	1751	1761	1771	1781	1791	1801	1811	1821	1831
Total slave population	248	285	270	250	254	361	352	306	417	328
Males	124	149	152	145	146	201	180	148	203	157
Females	124	136	118	105	108	160	172	158	214	171
Total workers	192	215	176	197	218	278	275	246	316	257
Males	98	111	107	129	128	163	146	123	161	129
Females	94	104	69	68	90	115	129	123	155	128
Total prime workers	—	—	159	125	173	192	199	146	203	178
Males	—	—	98	78	101	113	101	69	99	92
Females	—	—	61	47	72	79	98	77	104	86
Total prime field workers	—	—	87	78	109	139	92	91	153	104
Males	—	—	40	38	60	68	31	26	60	51
Females	—	—	47	40	49	71	61	65	93	53

Only 27 percent of the women were categorized as "able" as against 53 percent of the men, and 37 percent of the women were nonworking invalids. If the numerous invalids on the estate would only die, the Mesopotamia overseer wrote to Joseph Foster Barham, "a Happy Release it will be, for they are so Enfeebled by age, as to be scarce able to help themselves."[20]

It is difficult to explain why the women at Mesopotamia sickened and died faster than the men in the 1740s and 1750s. The discrepancy between the number of baby girls (54) and baby boys (77) who entered the records between 1736 and 1761 is especially striking. I suspect that the Barhams' attorneys and overseers were treating the women with particular brutality and had stopped trying to encourage procreation or to sustain family life. But this is impossible to prove, since the attorneys said little about the Mesopotamia slaves when they corresponded with the Barhams—except to complain that too many of them were old and sick and to pester for permission to buy new prime-aged workers from the African slavers. What can be said is that the pattern at Mesopotamia seems to have been common elsewhere in mid-eighteenth-century Jamaica. To support this contention, table 1.2 presents 102 slave inventories from fifty-six Jamaican sugar estates (not counting Mesopotamia) in chronological sequence.[21] Inspection of this table suggests two interesting points: first, that the sex ratio at Mesopotamia was reasonably in accord with that of other Jamaican sugar estates (except in 1736), and second, that the labor gangs on the

TABLE 1.2. THE SEX RATIO AT MESOPOTAMIA
COMPARED WITH OTHER JAMAICAN SUGAR ESTATES

Date	Estate	Inventories	Male slaves	Female slaves	Male sex ratio
1674–1701	21 estates	21	609	579	105/100
1676–1709	Bybrook	8	417	394	106
1703	Angels, Palmers Hut, Prospect	3	114	163	70
1730	Worthy Park	1	132	104	127
1736	Mesopotamia	1	124	124	100
1740s	Burtons, Decoy, Rose Hall, Wallins	4	791	356	222
1757	Island	1	95	75	127
1758–66	Duckingfield Hall	4	827	674	123
1760–69	Mesopotamia	10	1492	1107	135
1762–84	Spring	2	95	111	86
1780–89	Mesopotamia	10	1580	1144	138
1775–83	Dundee	3	312	233	134
1784–96	Worthy Park	11	2240	1978	113
1800–09	Mesopotamia	10	1711	1642	104
1817	22 largest Westmoreland estates	22	3207	3657	88
1817	Mesopotamia	1	152	169	90
1834	22 largest Westmoreland estates	22	3070	3725	82
1834	Mesopotamia	1	148	168	88

Sources: The 1674–1701 inventories are in the Jamaica Archives; Bybrook is in Helyar MSS, Somerset Record Office; for Angels, etc., see Sheridan, *Sugar and Slavery*, p. 216; for Worthy Park, see Craton, *Searching for the Invisible Man*, pp. 54, 81; for Burtons, etc., see Michael Craton and James Walvin, *A Jamaican Plantation*, p. 151; Island is in Barham Papers, Bodleian; Duckingfield Hall is in the Greater London Record Office; Dundee is in the Scottish Record Office; Spring is on a University of Pennsylvania microfilm; the Westmoreland estates [Mesopotamia is here excluded] are in T 71/178, 723, PRO.

island were most highly skewed between the 1730s and the 1780s. This was probably the time period in Jamaican slavery when the sugar planters came closest to creating a work force where men performed most of the heavy labor. In the case of Mesopotamia at least, the decision to rely on the slave trade for new young male workers had long-range consequences. By 1761 there were few women of child-bearing age living on this estate—unlike the situation in 1736—and few girls who could become future mothers.

From the 1760s to the 1780s Joseph Foster Barham I instructed his attorneys and overseers to encourage maternity, but the number and proportion of women and of women workers remained low. During these years, the attorneys purchased few women or girls from the African slave ships. In 1789 Joseph Foster Barham II succeeded his father and changed this policy. Repelled by the Atlantic slave trade, he stopped dealing with the African slavers in 1793. Hoping to make his estate self-sustaining, he urged that his young women be shown special indulgence, and he bought 228 slaves from three local Jamaican estates—in family groups, with a balanced sex ratio. Barham greatly enlarged his slave force between 1781 and 1821, doubling the number of his female slaves (see table 1.1). From 1809 onward the females on this estate outnumbered the males, reflecting the islandwide trend. By 1811 the sex ratio among the prime workers at Mesopotamia had dropped to 90 and among the prime field workers it was down to 40. However, from Barham's viewpoint his pronatalist policy was a failure. There were still five recorded deaths for every three recorded births at Mesopotamia. The proportion of young children remained smaller than in 1736. Barham bought no additional slaves during the 1820s, and the population of his estate quickly declined from 417 to 328 during his final decade of ownership.

From 1762 to 1831 the reported crude birthrate at Mesopotamia never exceeded the crude deathrate, except briefly in the 1780s among the female slaves. And the deathrate among females was always lower than among males (see table 1.3). The Mesopotamia deathrate was particularly high during the last two decades because Joseph Foster Barham II had acquired a good many elderly people when he bought families of slaves from other Jamaican estates. But Barham was always far more concerned about the low birthrate. By the 1820s he was blaming the women on the estate for their failure to reproduce more effectively. He charged them with destroying their health through promiscuity, and he threatened to put any women who had abortions or miscarriages into a special jobbing gang which would be hired out to perform especially taxing manual labor.[22] In 1825, when two women named Beany and Dido were delivered of stillborn children, they were sent to the workhouse in punishment; in 1826 they were back at their regular jobs as field workers, but Beany was henceforth characterized as "ill disposed" and Dido as "evil disposed."[23]

Beany and Dido were not the only women at Mesopotamia to register discontent. The records identify twenty-nine women who ran away from the estate at least once between 1762 and 1831; nineteen of them ran away repeatedly; two managed to escape permanently. The youngest of these fugitives were in their mid-teens and the oldest in their mid-fifties, but most commonly they absconded when in their twenties. More of these runaway women were born in Africa rather than at Mesopotamia, indicating a pattern of flight by African newcomers that has also been found in the North American slave-based

TABLE 1.3. BIRTHRATES AND DEATHRATES
AT MESOPOTAMIA, 1762–1831

Decade	Female birthrate	Female deathrate	Male birthrate	Male deathrate
1762–1771	16.7	35.2	8.8	37.8
1772–1781	13.8	24.0	13.5	34.0
1782–1791	22.2	19.8	17.6	29.1
1792–1801	24.3	28.3	21.0	35.9
1802–1811	18.0	26.7	16.4	35.9
1812–1821	19.8	35.6	19.9	37.4
1822–1831	20.1	39.8	21.0	44.9
Total	19.7	30.6	17.2	36.5

colonies.[24] To be sure, the women at Mesopotamia resorted to flight less frequently than the men. Between 1762 and 1831 the records identify eighty-three men and boys who took off at least once—which is 14 percent of all the males. But a principal reason why the women escaped less often than the men is that many of them had young children to take care of, children they loved. Of the twenty-nine female absconders from Mesopotamia, twenty-one were childless and another seven had been brought to the estate late in life from other Jamaican plantations after their children (if they had any) were grown. The only exception to this pattern was Dido, who became "evil disposed" after she was sent to the workhouse in 1825 and ran away in 1831, abandoning her eight-year-old daughter, Georgianna. This suggests that the Mesopotamia women's maternal feelings were much more powerful than Joseph Foster Barham II appreciated.

Biographical portraits of three women suggest what it was like to be a female slave at Mesopotamia. A woman named Deborah or Debby (like most of the other slaves, she had no listed surname) is representative of the largest group, those born on the estate. Just about half of the 650 female slaves recorded as living at Mesopotamia between 1736 and 1831 fell into this category.[25] For these slaves childhood was a harsh rite of passage; 19 percent of the Mesopotamia-born girls died before age two, and another 8 percent before age sixteen. Debby was one of the survivors. She was born in November 1792. Her mother, Katey, was a thirty-year-old Jamaica-born field worker who had come to Mesopotamia six years previously from a neighboring estate without a husband but in a large family group—her parents, four siblings, and a nephew.[26] Debby's father is unknown. She had a younger brother, born when she was four, and so grew up surrounded by close kin. Debby was excused from labor through age seven, started work as a gleaner at age eight, cut grass in the third field gang from nine to fourteen, and then progressed to harder field work in the second gang from fifteen to sixteen. At age seventeen, she was incapacitated for a year with a serious infectious disease, the yaws, but was categorized as "able" at eighteen and returned to the second gang. When she was twenty-one, she was advanced to the first field gang or great gang—where the work was physically most demanding—and stayed there until she was thirty-three. Debby had three daughters—Princess, Sarah, and Deborah—born when she was twenty, twenty-three, and twenty-six; the father or fathers of these girls are unknown. At age twenty-five, she was one of twelve women who received a reward of £1 "for raising her children" (all three of her girls were teenage field workers on the estate when the last Mesopotamia inventory was taken in 1831). When she was twenty-nine, Debby's health status was downgraded from "able" to "weak," but she remained in the first gang. At age thirty-four, she lost her left arm (probably to the yaws) and held no job for a year, but then worked for another three years as a shepherdess. She died of "debility" in March 1830 at age thirty-seven and was memorialized in the plantation records with the following commentary: "lost her arm, subject to fits, and ill disposed."

A second group of slave women was brought to Mesopotamia from neighboring Jamaican estates between 1736 and 1831. The career of a woman named Sophia illustrates the experiences of the 177 females in this category. Generally arriving in families, these people ranged in age from very young to very old; 22 percent of the females were under the age of sixteen and 36 percent were over the age of forty, so that only a minority were of prime working age when they came to Mesopotamia.[27] Sophia arrived as a young girl. Born around 1779, she came to Mesopotamia in June 1786 at the age of seven, acquired for the modest price of £30. She was the youngest child in a family of nine slaves purchased from Three Mile River, a nearby Westmoreland sugar estate. Her father, Qua, was a driver, and her mother, Betty (past hard labor when she came to Mesopotamia), was a nurse. Although Sophia's father died when she was eleven, her mother and six siblings all survived for more than twenty-five years at Mesopotamia, so that Sophia always had plenty of close kin. She was excused from labor through age eleven, an unusually long time, which suggests that she was in poor health as a child. She started to work in the grass gang at age twelve, moving to the second gang at age fifteen. She was incapacitated with the yaws at exactly the same age as Debby, seventeen, but recovered sufficiently to be put back in the field at eighteen. By age twenty-three, she was in the great gang, where she remained until she was thirty. She had three children—Elizabeth, George, and Nancy—all mulattoes and so presumably fathered by one or several of the white managerial staff.[28] Her daughter Elizabeth, born when Sophia was twenty, died in infancy, but George and Nancy (born when she was twenty-two and twenty-six) reached adulthood and were employed on the estate as a carpenter and a domestic respectively in 1831. By age thirty-one, Sophia was described as "obstructed" and weak; she was transferred back to the second gang. Here she put in fifteen more years of field labor, but between age forty and forty-two she attended the Moravian missionaries.[29] At age forty-eight she was back in the first gang. She became pregnant again at age forty-six, but either she miscarried or her baby died immediately, because she had no listing in the following year's birth register. When the final Mesopotamia inventory was taken in 1831, Sophia was still working (at age fifty-three), although clearly beyond her productive prime. She was shifted from the second gang to the easier job of gardener at fifty-one, was downgraded again to the job of nurse at fifty-two, and was described as suffering from dropsy.

A third group of slaves was imported to Mesopotamia directly from Africa between 1736 and 1831, including eighty-eight females. Although fewer in number than the slaves born on the estate or the slaves acquired from other Jamaican plantations, Africans purchased directly from the slave ships were especially prized by the Barhams' managers because they were almost all in their teens or twenties and could be put directly to work. At Mesopotamia incoming African females endured the initial shock of enslavement and gang labor noticeably better than the males. Some 7 percent of them died within two years and 13 percent within five years, whereas 20 percent of the new African males died within five years.[30]

A woman named Juliet is typical of this group. Like a number of other African women, Juliet survived for many years. Born about 1781 on the Guinea coast, she was transported to Jamaica on a ship that reached Montego Bay in March 1792. Joseph Foster Barham II's agent reported: "I went there and picked for you 11 very fine young boys and 9 girls which I hope will turn out well."[31] Like most of the other eight girls in this group, Juliet was listed as eleven years old. Unlike Debby and Sophia, Juliet thus had no immediate kin at Mesopotamia, but she did at least arrive with a band of companions her own age. She was put to work in the grass gang at age eleven and soon advanced to the second gang. At age twenty-three, she joined the first gang, where she worked until she was thirty-five. When Juliet reached thirty-four, however, her health began to fail, hovering between "able" and "weak," and from age thirty-seven onward she was always "weak." She was shifted back to the second gang when she was thirty-six, developed a lame foot by age forty-two, worked four years as a grass cutter, and became incapacitated at age forty-seven. In 1831 Juliet was still alive, although an invalid, at age fifty. She bore no children. Five of the other eight Guinea girls who arrived at Mesopotamia with her in 1792 were also childless. The remaining three, however, produced twenty children among them; Matura (the most fecund African female on the estate) had eleven children, Clarinda had eight, and Clarissa had one. In 1831 four of these Guinea women were still alive, having spent forty years at Mesopotamia; only two of the eleven males who arrived with them survived that long.

The experiences of Debby, Sophia, and Juliet suggest certain features common to female life on a Jamaican sugar estate. To be sure, Debby had a shorter career than the other two, dying younger, and Debby and Sophia were mothers, whereas Juliet was childless. But all three women were field hands forced into a cyclical labor pattern. Starting off with relatively easy work as children, they worked desperately hard as young adults; as their health broke down they sank gradually back into the equivalent of child labor status, when they survived past age thirty-five or forty. For Debby, Sophia, and Juliet—as for most other women on the estate—labor in the first field gang was the primary job assignment; the work they did as young girls and as older women was much less productive—and much less taxing. Examination of the careers of all of the females at Mesopotamia reveals that some never graduated beyond the second field gang, while a few others escaped field labor altogether. But the vast majority of the Mesopotamia women—nearly 90 percent—labored in one or both of the principal field gangs during their prime working years.

The overall pattern of primary employment for female slaves at Mesopotamia differed notably from the pattern for male slaves. The contrast becomes plain when we focus on the 216 women and 322 men whose adult careers on the estate can be traced in full—that is, the slaves who were recorded as reaching the age of sixteen in or after the year 1751 (when systematic annual inventory keeping began) and who died before December 1831 (when the last inventory was taken). At about age sixteen members of both sexes were assigned to the lines of work they would hold throughout their prime working years—the only exception to this rule being the drivers, who were elevated to their responsible supervisory positions considerably later, when they were already middle-aged. There was a clear order of rank among the prime slave occupations: drivers and craft workers were reckoned to be the most valuable and skilled slaves, stock and field workers came next, followed by domestics. At the bottom of the scale came the marginal workers—such as jobbers, gardeners, fishermen, and rat catchers—who had low valuations because they were incapable of more demanding adult employment. Among the 538 men and women whose complete careers at Mesopotamia can be reconstructed, only twenty-four never held a job. These people, who mostly came from other Jamaican estates, were too old or sick on arrival for even marginal employment.

The Barhams and their agents systematically excluded the female workers at Mesopotamia from all of the most highly skilled and highly valued jobs (see table 1.4). A few women were drivers, but only of the children's grass gang, which was really marginal employment. No women were craft workers such as carpenters, coopers, boilers, and distillers. No women tended the cattle or worked in transport jobs, where they could have enjoyed some measure of independence, as well as lighter physical labor. More women than men served as domestics, but since the proprietors of Mesopotamia were absentees after 1736 there was little need for domestic labor on this estate. The few women employed as domestics by the white supervisory staff had much easier work than the female field workers, but because they were not contributing to plantation productivity, they had lower valuations than field hands of the same age. Most of the marginal occupations at Mesopotamia were also reserved for the men, and the women who were too frail for field work could only become domestics, doctors (just one female doctor was employed on the estate at any one time), nurses, midwives, field cooks, washerwomen, fowl keepers, grass cutters, or water carriers. The water carriers at Mesopotamia were always crippled women who had lost an arm or a hand, usually in a sugar mill accident; presumably they carried water containers on their heads.

On Jamaican sugar estates, field work was of course ubiquitous, but women had much less chance than men of escaping from the holing, planting, and harvesting gangs. For the 322 Mesopotamia men whose careers can be fully examined, the likelihood of becoming a prime field hand was one in two, whereas for the 216 women the odds were five in

TABLE 1.4. PRIMARY OCCUPATIONS OF 528 ADULT MESOPOTAMIA SLAVES
BY SEX, 1751–1831

Occupation	Females	% F	Males	% M	Total	% of slave workers
Drivers	3	1.4	13	4.0	16	3.0
Craft workers	0	0.0	42	13.1	42	7.8
Craft and stock workers	0	0.0	11	3.4	11	2.0
Stock keepers	0	0.0	16	5.0	16	3.0
Stock and field workers	0	0.0	22	6.8	22	4.1
Field workers	182	84.3	177	55.0	359	66.7
Domestics	6	2.8	3	0.9	9	1.7
Marginal workers	13	6.0	26	8.1	39	7.2
Nonworkers	12	5.5	12	3.7	24	4.5
Total	216	100.0	322	100.0	538	100.0

six (see table 1.4). Furthermore, large numbers of women were assigned to the first or great gang, which performed the most strenuous
field work. In June 1802 the Mesopotamia overseer reported that he
employed thirty-three women and twenty-six men on the great gang;
since two of these women were pregnant, he allowed them to work on
the second gang, along with thirty-six other women and nine men,
doing lighter work such as cleaning canes.[32] This was the standard
pattern during the last three decades of slave work at Mesopotamia.
Between 1801 and 1831, 83 percent of the women field hands worked
in the great gang for at least one year and 44 percent worked there for
at least ten years. In these years the great gang was always primarily
populated by women. And while it was customary in Jamaica to pair
the weaker workers in the great gang with the stronger ones, many of
the women must have been paired together, laboring in regimented
lockstep and keeping a collective pace with the other members of the
gang, as they dug the deep square holes in which to plant new cane
shoots, as they weeded and manured the young cane, as they cut and
bundled the ripe cane stalks at harvest time.[33]

A central feature of life at Mesopotamia was that a great majority of
the women were subjected to an exhausting routine of manual labor
throughout their prime child bearing years. To demonstrate this point,
table 1.5 compares the labor assignments of all the young women and
men on the estate—from age twenty to age thirty-four—between the
years 1801 and 1831. The 130 women age twenty to twenty-nine spent
88 percent of their working time in the two field gangs, primarily in the
great gang, and were given practically no extended released time to

TABLE 1.5. Occupational assignments of young adults at Mesopotamia by sex, 1801–1831

	20–29 year age cohort		25–34 year age cohort	
	130 Women	123 Men	127 Women	120 Men
Number of work years assigned to:				
First gang	618	432	542	434
Second gang	228	125	133	50
Other employment	85	395	122	352
Nonworking invalids	30	22	38	16
Attending young children	2	0	23	0
Total work years	963	974	858	852
Percentage of labor assigned to:				
First gang	64.2	44.4	63.2	50.9
Second gang	23.7	12.8	15.5	5.9
Other employment	8.8	40.6	14.2	41.3
Invalids	3.1	2.2	4.4	1.9
Attending young children	0.2	0.0	2.7	0.0
Total labor	100.0	100.0	100.0	100.0
Percentage of labor by total cohort:				
First gang	31.9	22.3	31.6	25.4
Second gang	11.8	6.5	7.8	5.9
Other employment	4.4	20.4	7.1	20.6
Invalids	1.5	1.1	2.2	0.9
Attending young children	0.1	0.0	1.4	0.0
Total labor by sex	49.7	50.3	50.2	49.8

care for their young children. The 127 women age twenty-five to thirty-four present a slightly different pattern. They still labored primarily in the great gang and put more time into field work than the men of their age cohort. But a rising percentage were in broken health and had to be shifted into secondary occupations, or became invalids.[34] Another small but significant development was that several healthy female field workers age twenty-five to thirty-four were exempted from field labor altogether, because they had numerous small children who needed care. Matura was removed from the first gang at age twenty-nine when she produced her sixth living child; Cooba at thirty-one with her fifth; Sally at thirty-two with her sixth. But there were limits to the Barhams' pronatal policy: women with only two or three living children were never excused from field work on this account.

The gang labor performed at Mesopotamia had a quantifiable impact upon the health and life expectancy of the field workers. Both the male and female field workers at Mesopotamia had shorter working careers, poorer health records, and earlier deaths than the slaves who held more privileged jobs.[35] The 177 men examined in table 1.4 who were assigned to the first and second gangs worked for 13.2 years on average—7.5 years less than the average stock keeper—and then had to be shifted to easier work. They put in an average of 20.4 years of adult labor altogether and died at age 42.2, whereas the ninety-four more privileged male drivers, craft workers, stock workers, and domestics labored 24.1 years on average and died at age 44.8. Because there were so few privileged female workers, it is difficult to construct a meaningful comparison among the women. Nevertheless, the contrast between field workers and drivers and domestics is striking. The 182 women field workers examined in table 1.4 worked for 15.6 years in the first and second gang on average—13.7 years less than the average domestic. They put in 20.9 years of adult labor altogether and died at age 45.3, whereas the seven privileged women drivers and domestics worked 32.4 years and died at age 55.6.[36]

The Mesopotamia statistics further indicate that the women were generally in poorer health than the men. The 216 women whose working careers can be fully traced were categorized as "able" only 41 percent of the time. They were described as "sick" or "weak" or "diseased" 43 percent of the time, though they continued to work, for the most part in the field gangs. And they were designated as "invalids," incapable of any kind of labor, 16 percent of the time. The 322 men were slightly better off, being described as "able" 48 percent of the time, "sickly" 45 percent of the time, and "invalids" 7 percent of the time. Nevertheless, the women demonstrated greater powers of endurance than the men. The average female field worker stood up to gang labor for 2.4 years longer than her male counterpart, and she lived 3.1 years longer. Among the twenty slaves who toiled for thirty years or more in the cane fields, fifteen were women. Three of them— Bathsheba, Eve, and Priscilla—worked in the fields for forty years, a record matched by none of the men. Nearly a quarter of these women passed the age of sixty, as against 15 percent of the men; five of them lived past eighty, whereas only one man did so. It is striking to see how many among these 216 Mesopotamia women reached retirement status: thirty-one were excused from labor for ten or more years and eight for twenty or more years before they died. Phillis was the champion in this respect. A field worker aged about fifteen in 1736, she was given a high valuation of £70 in 1756 but was removed from gang labor at

TABLE 1.6. SLAVE MOTHERHOOD AT MESOPOTAMIA

	Total women (136)	Jamaican women (97)	African women (39)	Field workers (126)	Nonfield workers (21)
Number of children					
0	64	44	20	58	6
1	27	17	10	26	5
2	8	5	3	9	3
3	10	9	1	11	1
4	8	6	2	8	3
5	2	2	0	3	0
6	6	5	1	6	1
7	5	5	0	4	0
8	1	0	1	1	1
9	1	1	0	0	0
10	1	1	0	0	0
11	1	0	1	0	0
12	1	1	0	0	0
13	0	0	0	0	0
14	1	1	0	0	1
Total children	250	198	52	195	55
Age cohort of mother					
15–19	17	15	2	12	5
20–24	68	51	17	64	4
25–29	66	49	17	59	7
30–34	47	37	10	33	14
35–39	31	27	4	18	13
40–44	18	16	2	7	11
45–49	3	3	0	2	1
Total children	250	198	52	195	55

age forty-three in 1764 because she had contracted venereal disease. Thereafter, she occasionally worked as a midwife or nurse but was mainly an invalid—for thirty of her last thirty-seven years. Phillis died in 1801 at approximately eighty.

Against this background, let us reconsider the question of low fertility among the Mesopotamia women. There were 136 females on the estate during the years between 1774 and 1831 whose complete birth histories can be charted.[37] Table 1.6 considers their collective maternal record. Of these women, seventy-two bore 250 children, while the other sixty-four had no recorded live births. It must be emphasized that these statistics exclude all abortions, most miscarriages and stillbirths, and many neonates. The bookkeepers occasionally noted that women were pregnant at the time of the annual inventory; twenty-eight such pregnancies were observed, but only thirteen of these were reported as births or stillbirths the following year, the other fifteen being unaccounted for. This suggests that something like half of the pregnancies at Mesopotamia terminated in miscarriages, stillbirths, or infant deaths within a few days of birth. There seems to have been much more of a problem on this estate with births than with conceptions. For the 136 women whose birth histories are complete, the records list fourteen pregnancies (of which only five came to reported term), one miscarriage, and two stillbirths. Three of the seventy-two mothers died in childbed. Fifteen of their 250 reported children died within two weeks of birth, and twenty-one others within one year of birth—or 14 percent of the total. But the most striking fact is that nearly half of these Mesopotamia women never bore *any* children who survived long enough to enter the estate records.

The African women at Mesopotamia—as elsewhere in the Caribbean—had especially low birthrates.[38] Among the thirty-nine African women with complete birth histories, only nineteen had recorded live births, as against fifty-three of the ninety-seven Jamaican women. The African mothers averaged 2.7 children each, as against 3.7 for the Jamaican mothers. It has been argued that the African women produced fewer children than the Jamaican women because they nursed their young for upwards of three years, with the result that spacing between conceptions was wider.[39] But the Mesopotamia evidence does not support this contention. For one thing, on this estate ten of the nineteen African mothers bore only a single child, so spacing between births was not an issue. The African mothers who did have more than one child, however, spaced their babies just as the Jamaican women did, becoming pregnant optimally about every two years.[40] Three of them had large families. Between the ages of nineteen and thirty-seven Matura bore ten children evenly spaced at two-year intervals, and she produced her final baby at age forty-two; seven of her children lived to maturity. Clarinda bore eight children at two-year intervals between ages nineteen and thirty-three, four of whom reached maturity.

If nursing practices do not account for the low African birthrate, alternate explanations are also problematical. Some African women had short birth spans because they were already twenty-five or thirty years old when they arrived in the Caribbean. But the thirty-nine African women with complete birth histories at Mesopotamia had all been brought to the estate before or during puberty. African women may have had special difficulty finding marriage partners. On the sugar estates in Trinidad, where the slave registration records contain extraordinarily detailed information about tribal origins in Africa and family formation in America, it is evident that the African men chose wives whenever possible from their own nations or from linguistically similar communities.[41] The Mesopotamia records supply regrettably little information about national origins or family structure, but they do indicate that over a third of the African women who were purchased by the Barhams from neighboring estates were married (almost always to African men) when they came to Mesopotamia. By contrast, three-quarters of the locally born women purchased from neighboring estates came to Mesopotamia single, or had children but no husbands.[42] The African women at Mesopotamia were generally in poorer physical shape than the Jamaican women; they were more frequently described as "sick" or "weak." And assuming that their sexual partners were primarily African-born men, at Mesopotamia the young African men were almost exclusively employed as field laborers and could have been so exhausted by their twelve-hour workdays and their ninety-plus–hour workweeks during crop time that they had little appetite or energy for sexual intercourse.

However one explains the peculiarly low birthrate among African women, the fact remains that the Jamaican-born women at Mesopotamia also produced strikingly few children.[43] One probable reason for this was the nutritional inadequacy of their diet. Caribbean slave rations were seriously deficient in protein and low on fat content, which may well have delayed the women's age of menarche, disrupted their menstrual function, and speeded menopause.[44] Among the Mesopotamia mothers there was indeed a general pattern of delayed first births, long and irregular birth intervals, and early final births. Though the bookkeepers on this estate never recorded slave stature, the teenaged slave girls in Trinidad and St. Lucia, according to the registration returns, experienced their adolescent growth spurt as late as age fifteen—which indicates that their sexual maturity was quite delayed.[45] However, the nutritional argument fails to explain why a housekeeper and seamstress named Minny was able to produce fourteen offspring in thirty years, or why a field worker named Cooba bore twelve children in twenty-five years. Similarly, the pervasiveness of disease on this estate must also have been a contributing factor, yet a clear correlation between ill health and infertility is hard to establish. On the one hand, Harriet and Olive were described as "dreadfully diseased" and Jenny as "dreadfully ulcerated," and all three were childless.[46] On the other hand, Luna gave birth to five children (four of whom died young) after she was unable to work any longer because she was incapacitated by bad sores; Ophelia gave birth to three children after she was unable to work because she was infected with venereal disease (all five of Ophelia's children lived to maturity); and Sabina gave birth to three children after she started to experience epileptic seizures (two of whom died young—although Sabina herself lived to age sixty-three).

The white managers at Mesopotamia suspected that the slave women practiced abortion and infanticide. The records state that several of the Mesopotamia newborns who died during infancy were "overlaid" by their mothers or carelessly dropped; but were such events intentional or accidental? In my opinion, the numerous miscarriages and infant deaths at Mesopotamia are better explained by the heavy work load imposed upon pregnant women and young mothers. Barry Higman calculates that a field worker on a Jamaican sugar estate labored 4,000 hours annually—as compared with 2,900 hours for a British factory worker in 1830, or 1,500 hours for a factory worker today.[47] Among the 136 women at Mesopotamia with complete birth histories, 126 were field hands, and the great majority of them were assigned to field labor in the first gang during their child bearing years. Very few teenaged girls bore children on this estate. Women aged twenty to twenty-nine years produced more than half the babies at Mesopotamia, and 92 percent of the mothers in this age group were field workers (see table 1.6). Rather belatedly, the estate managers recognized the deleterious effect of cane planting and cutting on the "breeding" women (as they called them), and starting in 1808 they began to excuse from gang labor mothers who had produced about six children.[48] Five of the 126 women field workers whose birth histories can be traced bore large families of eight to twelve children, and four of these women were retired early from the first or second gang so that they could take care of their young offspring. Only Clarinda continued to toil in the first gang through the birth of her last two daughters, twins, at age thirty-three, doubtless because three of her previous six children had died in infancy. As table 1.6 indicates, most of the women who gave birth in their forties, at the tag end of their reproductive span, had been removed from field work. And the most fecund mother at Mesopotamia, Minny, never did *any* work in the cane fields. One of only four black women assigned permanently to domestic work, between the ages of fifteen and forty-five Minny produced fourteen children.

TABLE 1.7. THE SEASONAL PATTERN OF BIRTHS
AND INFANT DEATHS AT MESOPOTAMIA

	Births	Norm (100)	Infant deaths	Norm (100)
January	31	91	12	162
February	28	83	6	81
March	37	109	6	81
April	40	118	10	135
May	24	71	7	94
June	34	100	8	108
July	23	68	6	81
August	32	94	8	108
September	32	94	7	94
October	42	124	7	94
November	37	109	5	68
December	47	139	7	94
Totals	407		89	

There was a seasonal pattern of live births and infant deaths at
Mesopotamia, from which the impact of the sugar labor system upon
mothers and their babies can be inferred. On this estate slave births
were most frequent in the three-month period from October to December and least frequent in the three-month period from May to July; and
young children were most likely to die in January or April (see table
1.7).[49] Crop time or sugar harvest, which began in January and continued with interruptions into June, was the period of most intense
labor at Mesopotamia. When the sugar mill was in operation, members of the first gang worked at least ninety hours (including three
nights) per week. The other period of especially heavy duty came in
September and October, when the field gangs dug cane holes and
planted the new cane. If we calculate nine months backwards to
conception, it appears that a woman who conceived in March, in the
middle of crop time, and who came to term in December, just before
the next harvest season, stood the best chance of giving birth to a live
child. A woman who conceived in October, during the planting season, and came to term in July, shortly after crop time, stood the poorest
chance. During the first two years of its life her child was at greatest
risk in January, when the weather was cool and the mother was
absorbed in crop labor.[50]

One final element in this scenario needs to be considered: the
vicious behavior of the white overseers and attorneys toward the slave
women. The Mesopotamia records are silent about the number of

floggings and other punishments administered to the slaves, but discipline was undoubtedly severe. The Jamaican estate manager Thomas Thistlewood, who supervised a small slave gang at Egypt sugar estate a few miles from Mesopotamia, recorded in his richly detailed diary that during the year 1765 he ordered thirty-one slaves flogged a total of forty-nine times, mostly for stealing food or running away. Thistlewood was somewhat less brutal with the women than with the men, since he generally gave them only fifty lashes apiece as against one hundred or more for the men. But fifty lashes could certainly endanger a pregnancy or traumatize a nursing mother. In this one year he flogged thirteen women twenty-one times, put four of them in shackles for a week or two at a time, and forced one rebellious woman to wear an iron collar and chain. Thistlewood was also violent in another way. He was a sexual athlete, who kept a slave mistress and fornicated every few days with other women he encountered—mostly in the fields or pastures, sometimes in the corn loft or curing house, more rarely in his own private quarters. During 1765 he recorded having intercourse with his mistress one hundred times and with twenty-three other slave women on fifty-five occasions. Several of the women he flogged he also raped during the course of this typical year. One afternoon when he had sex in a field with a slave named Maria, Thistlewood observed: "Just before, saw her and Mr. Smith, the overseer of Orange Grove Estate, in the Morass. He gave her money, how much I can't say."[51] Thistlewood generally paid his own slaves one bit and neighbors' slaves two bits.

Thistlewood had his counterparts among the white attorneys, overseers, craft supervisors, and bookkeepers who operated the Barhams' estate. Miscegenation was frequent at Mesopotamia. In 1736 only three mulattoes were listed among 248 slaves, but by 1791 there were ten mulattoes among 361 slaves, and by 1831 there were nineteen mulattoes and quadroons among 328 slaves. Altogether, the Mesopotamia women bore forty-three children fathered by white men between 1762 and 1831—over 10 percent of the total births. This was a high ratio considering that on average about 110 sexually active black men lived at Mesopotamia and only eight white men (which included the Moravian missionary). Twenty-three mothers of mulattoes and quadroons can be identified. Eight of the thirteen house servants who worked on the estate between 1774 and 1831 bore at least one mulatto child. The mothers of colored children tended to be young, as might be expected. Mulatto Nelly, who worked in the Great House at Mesopotamia, was only fourteen when her quadroon son John was conceived by an unknown white man, and half of the other colored children were conceived when their mothers were between the ages of fifteen and twenty-one. Nelly was one of four mulatto women on the estate to produce quadroon children, none of whom were manumitted by their fathers. Evidently the whites at Mesopotamia were not attracted to African women. Only two Africans—Coumba and Matura—bore any mulatto children, and they had one each.

The case of a woman named Batty suggests what it was like to be the mistress of a white man at Mesopotamia. She was born at Mesopotamia in August 1773, although neither her mother nor her father can be identified. Batty was excused from labor through age nine, started work in the grass gang at ten, was advanced to the second gang at thirteen, and probably to the first gang in her early twenties. She was a healthy young woman who seemed destined for a standard career as a field hand. At age twenty, she bore her first daughter, Martha, who died of intestinal gripes three weeks after birth. About three years later Patrick Knight, the white carpenter at Mesopotamia, made Batty his mistress. At age twenty-four, she bore Knight a daughter, mulatto Annie, followed at age twenty-seven by a second daughter, mulatto Peggy. The year after Peggy's birth, Batty was taken out of field work and installed as a domestic in the bookkeeper's house. In 1802, when Batty was twenty-nine, Patrick Knight hired her from the estate, employing her as a domestic in his own house. He also asked Joseph Foster Barham II's permission to purchase the freedom of his daughters, Annie and Peggy. Two years later, after Barham gave his grudging consent, the girls were manumitted, while their mother remained a slave. For fourteen years Batty served in Knight's house and in his bed; at age thirty-four she bore him a son, mulatto Edward, and four years later another daughter, mulatto Mary.

But Knight was evidently losing interest in Batty and her progeny. He made no attempt to manumit Edward or Mary. And perhaps Batty was seeking free choice for herself. When she gave birth to her last child at age forty-one, it was a Negro girl named Hannah (father unknown). By this time Batty was described as "weak" and was beginning to develop the coco bays, a loathsome disease akin to leprosy. In 1816, when Batty was forty-three, Knight dismissed her, and she became a washerwoman on the estate. She was an invalid for a year at forty-four, worked as a grass cutter for three years, and was an invalid again from ages forty-eight to fifty. At this point her mulatto daughter Mary, who had been working in the overseer's house, died of fever at age twelve. Batty resumed work as a children's nurse and then as a nurse in the plantation yaws hospital. When she was fifty-two, her eighteen-year-old mulatto son Edward was manumitted; he had been working as a waiting boy in the Great House when anonymous "friends" wrote to Barham, offering to pay £140 for his liberation. No one offered to pay anything for Batty's freedom. Still working at the yaws hospital until her final illness, she died of dropsy in September 1830, aged fifty-seven.[52]

The story of Batty's rise and fall illustrates several of the distinguishing features of slave life for women on Caribbean sugar estates. Had Batty been born in West Africa rather than Jamaica, she might also have been enslaved, for huge numbers of women were captured in tribal wars and forced into slavery in eighteenth- and nineteenth-century Africa; they were reckoned to be more useful than adult male slaves as agricultural laborers and domestic servants. Like their Jamaican counterparts, the African slave women were often brutally treated. They seem to have produced very few children. But their work was far less strenuous than Caribbean gang labor, and if they were sexually and psychologically victimized, racism was not at issue; their oppressors were fellow blacks rather than white masters like Patrick Knight.[53] Had Batty been born into slavery in Virginia rather than Jamaica, she would probably have worked either as a field hand or as a domestic, but again this labor was much less taxing than the field work she performed as a young woman at Mesopotamia. She might have been sexually abused by her white master, but miscegenation was less overt and probably less frequent in Virginia than in Jamaica.[54] The Virginia slaves were flogged less often; they were better fed and in better health. And the women in Virginia bore large numbers of children, so that the black population continually expanded at about the same rate as the white population. This is perhaps the most fundamental contrast between slavery in the antebellum South and the Caribbean. For the slave women at Mesopotamia—and on other Caribbean sugar estates—the distinguishing features of life included exhausting manual labor, a lethal disease environment, savage physical punishment, inadequate food, sexual abuse, broken health, and infertility. These were the grim realities behind the picturesque scenes in William Clark's handsome portfolio of color plates from 1823, the harsh facts underlying his romantic tableaux of slave laborers at work in the cane fields and in the sugar factory.

2

SUGAR AND COFFEE CULTIVATION IN SAINT DOMINGUE AND THE SHAPING OF THE SLAVE LABOR FORCE

David P. Geggus

D URING THE SECOND half of the eighteenth century Saint Domingue became the world's leading producer of both sugar and coffee. The two crops occupied different ecological spaces in the colony and had different histories. Most sugar estates in the humid coastal plains had been in existence several decades when the main expansion of coffee cultivation occurred in the highlands during the thirty years after 1763. A comparison of the work forces on sugar and coffee plantations therefore reflects the influence of several factors besides the exigencies of different work regimes. It compares long-established and pioneer settlements, as well as large-scale and small-scale enterprises. It contrasts life in the tropical lowlands with life in the mountains (at usually two- to four-thousand feet), thus implicating differences of climate and disease environment. These geographic, temporal, and economic factors made for significant differences in the composition of the slave labor force on the two types of plantations, which also helped shape the contrasting life-styles in *plaine* and *morne*.[1]

The plantation was the primary social unit in most New World slave societies; within its confines slaves spent most of their lives. The size of the work force was therefore critical to slave life. Saint Domingue plantations were large by eighteenth-century standards, although never as large as the planters, their descendants, and historians of the colony have claimed. A common proclivity to generalize from the most striking examples has been reinforced by the mythic stature of "The Pearl of the Antilles." On the Bréda estate at Haut du Cap, Toussaint Louverture's birthplace, for example, there lived about

TABLE 2.1. WORK-FORCE SIZE:
SUGAR PLANTATIONS

	Mean size	N	Range
1745–92	177	100	34–584
1745–69	171	12	42–464
1770–79	181	29	56–584
1780–89	188	66	34–566
1790–92	202	21	50–404
North	182	65	42–584
West	177	29	34–566
South	113	6	75–176

Note: The total number of cases exceeds 100
because slave lists from different decades were
available for some plantations. Of these, either
the most complete or the latest was chosen for
inclusion in the overall and provincial samples.

150 slaves, not the more than 1,000 claimed for it by Ralph Korngold. The Pébarte coffee plantation, endowed with 1,000 slaves by Thomas Ott, in fact possessed only 60. Contemporaries similarly estimated the labor force of the famous Galliffet estates at 1,200 or 1,500 slaves, when it never numbered more than 900 on the three sugar estates and about 130 on the two coffee plantations. Even those who thought the average sugar plantation had 200 or 250 slaves exaggerated.[2]

Sugar-estate work forces or *ateliers* seem to have been largest in the North Province of Saint Domingue, which produced most of the colony's semirefined sugar. They were slightly smaller in the West Province, which mainly made muscovado, and smallest in the South, the slowest of the three provinces to develop (see table 2.1). On the one hundred sugar estates for which statistics are available, one-eighth of the colony's total, the mean slaveholding was 177 persons and the median only 156. Work-force size continued to increase through the second half of the eighteenth century, but during the decade prior to the Haitian Revolution the average sugar plantation still contained fewer than two hundred slaves. Yet at that time these were among the largest slave gangs in the Americas, comparable to those of Jamaican sugar estates and much larger than those in Brazil or the rest of the Caribbean. Nonetheless, a few could not even muster the forty-five workers that contemporaries considered a minimum for a sugar estate,[3] and, given that the largest unit was seventeen times the size

TABLE 2.2. FREQUENCY DISTRIBUTION
OF SUGAR PLANTATIONS
BY WORK-FORCE SIZE

N Slaves	N Estates	% Estates	% Slaves
0–99	26	26	10
100–199	38	38	33
200–299	25	25	32
300–399	7	7	13
400–499	2	2	5
500–599	2	2	7
Total	100	100	100

of the smallest, it is difficult to identify a typical plantation. Those with under one hundred slaves made up one-quarter of the total, and small estates persisted down to 1791. Even so, one-quarter of sugar-plantation slaves lived on the big estates that were home to three hundred or more slaves, and two-thirds of Saint Domingue's slaves lived in units of more than 170 slaves (see table 2.2).[4]

Sugar estates varied even more in their physical dimensions than in the size of their work force. In a sample of fifty plantations, acreage ranged from 47 to 1,084 hectares (see table 2.3). As usual, the mean measure was skewed by the largest cases, the median size being only 191 hectares. Some of the variation was incidental to the production of sugar, denoting the presence of waste land such as salt marshes, forests, or livestock ranches, but total area still correlated highly with work-force size.[5] Estates became gradually smaller over time, but the mean area in cane grew steadily each decade and was about a hundred hectares on the eve of the Revolution.

In the North, estates were one-third smaller than elsewhere in the

TABLE 2.3. MEAN PHYSICAL DIMENSIONS (IN HECTARES):
SUGAR ESTATES

Area	(N)	Cane	(N)	Plant cane	(N)	Ratio of slaves : cane	(N)
272	(52)	92	(61)	33	(24)	2.07	(58)

Note: The carreau, the colonial unit of measurement, was converted at 1 = 1.13 hectares, though some prefer 1.26 hectares. Where their area was unknown, cane pieces were assumed to measure 4 carreaux.

TABLE 2.4. WORK-FORCE SIZE:
COFFEE PLANTATIONS

	Mean size	N	Range
1767–92	48	107	7–304
1770–79	34	6	26–48
1780–89	45	87	7–304
1790–92	82	13	17–225
North	43	71	7–304
West	76	18	10–225
South	38	18	8–146

colony but had a greater area than others in cane. The ratio of ratoons to plant canes was roughly two to one, although limited evidence suggests that the West and South relied less on ratoons and planted more frequently.[6] This perhaps reflected their less abundant rainfall, though the use of irrigation in the West made for an exceptionally high output per hectare in most of its parishes. More frequent replanting and the greater agricultural yields doubtless explain why, outside the North, planters tended to employ more slaves per hectare of cane.[7] Despite these differences, the average output per estate probably did not differ much between the two main provinces, the North and the West. Robert Stein's idea that medium-sized plantations typified the northern plain is certainly misleading.[8]

Coffee plantations were considerably more diverse than sugar estates (see tables 2.4 and 2.5). Since they demanded far less capital investment, they were generally smaller. A quarter of them had fewer than eighteen slaves. However, the largest coffee plantation had a work force nearly ten times the median size of thirty-three slaves. The average *atelier* was about one-quarter the size of the average slaveholding in sugar cultivation. On the one hand, one-third of the slaves on mountain coffee plantations lived in units of more than one hundred slaves, comparable to most sugar estates; on the other hand, another third lived in groups of fewer than forty-five. Work forces appear to have been larger in the West than in the North and South provinces, and they increased sharply in size during the closing years of the Old Regime.

Coffee plantations ranged in size from a mere 15 hectares to 1,328 hectares, with a median size of 104 hectares (see table 2.6). Many were in the pioneer stage of development, and the average area cultivated

TABLE 2.5. FREQUENCY DISTRIBUTION
OF COFFEE PLANTATIONS
BY WORK-FORCE SIZE

N Slaves	N Estates	% Estates	% Slaves
0–19	29	27	7
20–39	36	34	20
30–59	14	13	13
60–79	10	9	13
80–99	6	6	11
100–199	9	8	22
200–299	2	2	9
300–399	1	1	6
Total	107	100	101

in coffee was only some 27 hectares. Plantations were much smaller in the North than in the other provinces, but the number of coffee trees per holding apparently was greater. As in the case of sugar cultivation, the North's earlier development and more intensive cultivation accounted for the difference. Over the years, blocks of land must have been sold from the original extensive concessions to finance development. The overall ratio of one slave to 1,100 trees was somewhat lower than that recommended by contemporaries, but it varied enormously from one plantation to another, presumably according to soil fertility and the age of plantings.[9]

On both coffee and sugar plantations, the agricultural work load per capita apparently was lighter where the plantation work force was larger.[10] However, this probably reflected a tendency of the larger estates to employ more slaves as domestics and artisans, rather than a lower intensity of agricultural labor. In any event, opportunities for social mobility—as for family formation and for the preservation of African culture—must have depended in good measure on the size of the work force. Its importance was modified, however, by the prox-

TABLE 2.6. MEAN PHYSICAL DIMENSIONS (IN HECTARES):
COFFEE PLANTATIONS

Area	(N)	Coffee	(N)	Coffee trees Nos.	(N)	Ratio of slaves : trees	(N)
145	(76)	27	(20)	79	(62)	0.9	(61)

imity of plantations and their density of population. On the coast-alplains of Saint Domingue, where there were two slaves to every three hectares, it was easier for slaves of different estates to mingle than in the mountains, which had half the population density and where travel was difficult. In the North, however, the situation in the intensively cultivated mountains was close to that of the plains. On the pioneer settlements of the western and southern highlands slaves lived much more isolated lives.

In the late eighteenth century, most of Saint Domingue's coffee plantations were of fairly recent foundation worked by recently imported slaves. During the 1780s half their work forces had no slave over 60 years old, and, on one in seven, all slaves were under 40. This was true even in the North, where coffee had been cultivated longest. Only 3 percent of the coffee slaves were thought to have reached 60 years of age, as opposed to 8 percent of the slaves on the sugar estates. In the highland coffee plantations, 57 percent were young adults between 15 and 39, as compared to 50 percent in the plain.[11] Coffee plantations naturally had more African and fewer creole slaves than did the sugar estates (see table 2.7). Even so (and although males formed a two-to-one majority in the slave trade), men seem to have outnumbered women by only a slightly greater margin in the mountains than in the plains.[12] The proportion of children was almost identical on sugar and coffee estates. These features were common to both types of plantations in the period before the Haitian Revolution and to those regions of the West and South where the slave regime was preserved through much of the 1790s, even though the latter regions were affected by losses, chiefly of men and Africans.

Apart from during the revolutionary period, the sugar estates displayed relatively little temporal and regional variation, though the North Province was clearly the most creolized region and had the smallest proportion of adult men. The proportion of children proved remarkably similar for different provinces and in different decades, except that it was high for the pre-1770 period, reaching 31 percent in one sample of 1,973 slaves. The proportion of children fell on the sugar estates around 1770, and creoles soon came to form a majority of the slave population. This conjuncture appears anomalous, since creole women generally seem to have had more children than Africans. Moreover, this was the period when planters began to promote child rearing. Probably the rapidly growing numbers of imported (mainly adult) slaves and perhaps the greater longevity of creoles diminished the proportion of children in the slave population. Regional variation

TABLE 2.7. COMPOSITION OF SUGAR AND COFFEE PLANTATION WORK FORCES

| | Men | Women | Children | Slaves | Sex | Mean % per estate | | | Estates |
		(percentages)		(N)	ratio	CR	CR/Adults	Col.	(N)
Sugar, 1760–92	42	36	22	14,455	115	56	47	2.7	59
Coffee, 1767–92	45	34	21	3,719	120	36	22	1.6	66
						% of total slaves			
						CR	CR/Adults	Col.	
Sugar, 1796–97	33	40	28	9,254	91	67	38	2.6	76
Coffee, 1796–97	36	36	28	6,242	103	47	18	1.6	121

Note: CR = creole; Col. = mixed racial descent; Children = 0–14 years.

was more important among coffee plantations. The North proved both considerably more creolized and had more children (25 percent as opposed to 16 percent) than the other provinces, while the sex ratio was notably higher in the South (138 males per 100 females).

The slave population appears, however, to have been more evenly balanced between males and females than the colonial censuses suggest. These show the sex ratio of the slave population falling from around 150 at mid-century to about 130 in the 1770s and close to 120 in the 1780s.[13] It is likely that the censuses overstated the sex ratio because of the underregistration of the oldest slaves, who were disproportionately female. Saint Domingue clearly never experienced the severe sexual imbalance of many Brazilian and Cuban plantations. It may even have had a slightly more balanced population than that of contemporary Jamaica.[14] As Saint Domingue planters consistently imported more slave men than did its neighbor and as it is usually assumed to have had a less creolized population, this is surprising.[15] Saint Domingue creoles had a sex ratio of about 95. Different regional samples of African slaves reveal sex ratios between 133 and 160, substantially below those of newly imported Africans, which averaged 180 in the eighteenth century, rising to 201 in the 1780s.[16] This reflects the higher mortality rates suffered by males and by Africans and also suggests that slave deathrates may have been higher in Saint Domingue than in Jamaica.

Saint Domingue's African-born slaves made up a fascinating ethnic mosaic that varied through time and across different regions, as well as between different types of plantation (see table 2.8).[17] French planters employed an elaborate lexicon to identify the origins of their slaves, one which deserves to be taken seriously. Although not that of modern ethnography, it was the product of both African and European observation, and planters based their business decisions upon it. Even though most of the main *nations* identified by colonists could be found on all types of plantations, to a significant degree sugar and coffee planters tended to buy Africans from different ethnic groups.

Overlaying this contrast between sugar and coffee planters, however, was another contrast between the composition of slaves imported into the colony's three provinces. To some degree, these provincial variations reflected the incursions of British and Dutch contraband traders in regions neglected by the French slave trade—particularly the south coast. More important, though, French slavers themselves delivered a different ethnic mix to each of the colony's three provinces, apparently in response to the differing mix of crops. The resultant regional labor supply naturally limited choices, so that the purchases of all local planters reflected those of the majority. Regional variation was thus a function of crop-related planter preferences.[18]

Coffee planters bought a proportionately greater number of slaves of those ethnic groups that Saint Domingue slaveholders as a whole disdained—Bibi, Mondongue, Igbo, and Congo (see table 2.8). Conversely, the most highly regarded *nations* (those shipped from the Bight of Benin) could be found more frequently on sugar estates. Less well-established in the market, buying in smaller quantities but with greater urgency so as to bring their lands under cultivation,[19] coffee planters were less selective when purchasing slaves than were sugar planters. They also had less need to be, as coffee cultivation made fewer demands on its work force than the planting, harvesting, and processing of sugar cane. Planters based their African ethnic stereotypes on a variety of factors, including physical strength, health, dietary preferences, and agricultural experience, as well as ascribed attributes of a more fanciful nature. The slaves' average height was of especial importance to planters (see table 2.9).

Within a given region, Central African Bantu were 50 percent more prevalent in the mountains than on the plains, whereas African peoples shipped from the Bight of Benin were more common on sugar than coffee plantations. The latter were more highly valued in Saint Domingue because they were considered physically strong and both men and women were good agriculturalists, accustomed to wielding a hoe and able to take charge of their own provision grounds.[20] At least one contemporary commentator favorably mentioned their above-average height.[21] Congo slaves were notably shorter, and in

TABLE 2.8. ETHNIC COMPOSITION OF THE AFRICAN-BORN SLAVE POPULATION BY PROVINCE AND PERIOD

	North 1778–91		West 1785–91		West 1796–97		South 1796–97
	Sugar	Coffee	Sugar	Coffee	Sugar	Coffee	Coffee
Bantu							
Congo[a]	40.8	63.9	31.3	47.3	21.0	35.3	36.0
Mondongue	2.5	4.2	0.8	2.6	1.5	2.4	4.1
Mozambique[b]	0.6	0.1	0.8	2.6	1.0	2.9	2.0
Bight of Benin							
Arada (Ewe-Fon)	10.5	8.9	14.9	5.7	16.1	9.1	5.1
Fon, Dahomet[c]	1.3	0.4	0.1	0.0	0.1	0.0	0.0
Foëda (Hweda)	1.9	0.0	0.8	0.0	0.2	0.1	0.0
Adia (Ewe-Fon)	2.0	0.7	0.1	0.0	0.7	1.1	0.3
Nago (Yoruba)	8.9	5.5	16.1	9.2	18.6	12.2	9.3
Barba (Bariba)	0.8	0.1	0.8	0.0	1.6	0.4	0.3
Cotocoly (Tem)	0.3	0.0	1.8	1.1	3.2	2.3	0.6
Taqua, Tapa (Nupe)	0.8	0.5	1.3	0.7	3.0	1.4	0.6
Tiamba/Kiamba (Gurma)[d]	2.5	1.1	2.5	1.5	2.7	2.1	2.0
Aoussa/Gambary (Hausa)	0.7	0.4	4.9	1.8	4.3	2.7	2.4
Other[e]	0.2	0.1	0.1	0.0	0.2	0.0	0.0
Bight of Biafra							
Igbo, Ara, Arol	2.5	2.3	5.6	10.5	7.2	8.8	13.0
Bibi (Ibibio)	0.0	0.0	0.0	1.8	0.4	1.5	2.3
Moco (Anang)	0.0	0.0	0.1	0.0	0.1	0.3	1.3
Gold Coast							
Côte d'Or[f]	0.9	0.7	0.1	0.0	0.1	0.1	0.3
Bandia, Banguia	0.0	0.0	1.5	0.0	1.1	0.8	0.0
Caramenty (Akan-Ga)	0.0	0.0	0.7	0.7	2.4	0.4	0.0
Mina (Akan)	3.4	1.0	3.0	0.4	0.2	1.2	2.7
Senegambia							
Sénégal	1.4	0.7	1.5	2.0	1.7	2.2	2.5
Bambara	4.0	2.0	3.0	5.9	3.5	6.2	5.9
Poulard (Fulbe)	0.7	0.4	0.8	0.2	0.5	0.6	0.9
Mandingue	3.0	2.9	0.5	0.0	1.0	0.3	1.6
Windward/Ivory Coasts							
Kissi	0.4	0.2	0.0	0.0	0.1	0.0	0.2
Sosso, Tini (Susu)	1.2	0.3	0.2	0.2	1.6	1.0	1.4
Mesurade/Canga[g]	2.5	0.9	0.7	0.2	0.2	0.6	2.2
Cap Lao	0.0	0.0	0.9	2.8	1.6	0.8	0.0
Other[h]	2.2	1.0	1.4	0.4	0.3	0.1	0.1
Other	4.1	1.5	4.0	2.4	4.2	3.2	2.5
N slaves	2,143	973	1,059	457	2,641	1,578	1,576

[a]Includes some Mayombe, Moussondi, Solongo, Mayaque, etc.
[b]Includes a few Maconde and Macua.
[c]Includes 1 Damballam.
[d]Includes 1 Gurma.
[e]Samba, Judah, Mahi, Couëda.
[f]In French, the term included Cap Lahou and sometimes also the Bight of Benin. Some Dongoua/Dangouana (Dankwa?) included.
[g]Includes some Miserable.
[h]Aquia, Thémené, Bobo, Timbou, Bula, Coranco.

their homeland agricultural tasks were to an unusual degree left to women.[22] They also proved unhealthier (though only in the plains). Sugar planters expressed a strong aversion to them, although they often commented with approval on what they perceived to be their cheerful disposition.

Slaves from the Bight of Biafra, who were also short, were generally concentrated on mountain plantations. Said to be sickly, the Ibibio were small in stature and had a correspondingly low reputation. The Igbo, however, were the subject of conflicting opinions, as well as somewhat taller, and their position was, fittingly, more equivocal.[23] Slaves called "Mandingues" also attracted a mixed assessment, though—in keeping with their exceptional height—sugar planters appear to have favored them. In this case, the diversity of colonial opinion may reflect the diversity of Mande-speaking peoples to whom this label was attached.[24] The height of the Susu, Kissi, and other peoples from the Windward Coast may also explain their selection by sugar planters.[25]

Height, however, did not override all other criteria in the eyes of most planters. Slaves from southeast Africa, usually called Mozambiques, were taller than average but were said to have weak chests, still characteristic of the modern Makonde.[26] They were also considered unhealthy, perhaps because they were among the few Africans in Saint Domingue not to have been raised in a yellow fever hyperendemic zone and thus lacked immunity to that disease. This suggests another reason why the Mozambiques were most often found in the mosquito-free highlands. The Mondongues approached average height but were avoided by sugar planters, doubtless because of their widespread reputation as cannibals who were difficult to feed.[27] Colonists expressed contrasting opinions concerning the tall Bambara,[28] and they and their "Sénégal" neighbors (presumably Wolof, Serer, and Tukolor) appear to have been regarded differently in different provinces.

The premium placed on physical strength by sugar planters probably explains why the favored ethnic groups tended to exhibit lower sex ratios in the mountains than in the plain. Sugar planters tended to preempt the slave men, forcing the coffee planters to buy relatively more of the less desirable women. The sugar planters' priority also explains why the sex ratios of sugar and coffee work forces were not more divergent, notwithstanding their difference in age. In the case of the ubiquitous Congos, however, the general preference for slave men was counterbalanced by the greater agricultural experience of the

TABLE 2.9. HEIGHT OF SELECTED ETHNIC
GROUPS (MEN AGED 20–59)

	Mean (cms)	Median (cms)	N
Bantu			
Congo	164.2	162.4	335
Mondongue	165.3	165.1	110
Other C. Bantu	165.1	165.1	34
Mozambique	167.6	167.8	131
Bight of Biafra			
Igbo	165.6	167.8	73
Bibi	164.6	167.8	21
Bight of Benin			
Arada	167.3	167.8	50
Nago	166.7	167.8	120
Barba	165.1	165.1	11
Taqua	168.5	165.1	33
Aoussa	170.0	170.5	120
Thiamba/Kiamba	166.5	167.8	37
Adia, Cotocoli	165.6	162.4	13
Gold Coast			
Mina	166.6	165.1	41
Windward Coast			
Sosso	169.0	167.1	12
Kissi	166.2	167.8	10
Cap Lao	165.8	167.8	11
Mesurade/Canga	166.7	165.1	51
Senegambia			
Bambara	169.3	167.8	85
Sénégal	169.5	167.8	53
Poulard	171.9	172.5	30
Mandingue	170.3	170.5	92
Unidentified Africans	166.5	167.8	340
Black creoles	167.3	167.8	314

Source: Lists of fugitive slaves in *Affiches
Américaines*, 1788, 1789, and 1790. No Congo
were counted for 1789 or for the second half of
1788.
Note: The *pouce* was converted at 2.707 cms.

slave women, proportionally more of whom went to sugar than coffee plantations.

The sugar estate commonly functioned as farm, factory, ranch, country house, and hospital, as well as a place of sugar cultivation. It provided a range of employment that, within the confines of American slavery, was extremely diverse. All in all about one-fifth of the slaves had an occupation other than that of field hand. The proportion might be larger or smaller, depending on whether gatekeepers, child minders, and hedge cutters (minor posts generally given to the aged or disabled) and those in the hog pen and chicken coop (usually children and young adolescents) are included. About one in four adult slaves held a post that conferred some prestige and represented a degree of social advancement (see table 2.10). Only one in eleven of these principal specialists were women, even including the midwives, who tended to be retired field slaves. Men were eight times as likely as women to escape from the drudgery of field labor to a position of some independence and responsibility.[29]

Since coffee cultivation was a less complicated undertaking than sugar cultivation, the division of labor on mountain plantations was correspondingly simpler. Occupational diversity and social mobility were much more limited, especially for men. Only one in eleven adult slaves held a responsible position: about 13 percent of the men and 4 percent of the women.[30] There was of course no factory house to provide an alternative to field labor. Roofers were a good deal more common than in the plains, but overall artisan posts were rarer, held by about 2 percent of the adult population, as opposed to 4 percent on the sugar estates. Work with livestock was also less common. Carters, muleteers, and herdsmen accounted for less than 2 percent of the adult slaves on the highland plantations, but more than 3 percent of those on the *sucreries,* which in addition also employed millers and ploughmen. Domestic servants were, however, more numerous on the *caféières,* where they constituted about 4 percent of the slaves, as opposed to the sugar estates' 2 percent. This doubtless reflects the greater proportion of resident owners in the coffee plantation sector. Creole extravagance in this area seems to have been exaggerated.

Africans made up more than one-third of sugar estate specialists on the eve of the revolution and a large majority of those on coffee plantations. Nevertheless, on both sugar and coffee plantations there was a clear-cut preference for creole slaves, particularly for jobs performed by women and for posts attached to the plantation house or allowing travel off the plantation (coachmen, muleteers, and carters).

TABLE 2.10. Percentage of slaves on 34 sugar estates
with major occupational specialization
(by origin and sex)

	Adults	Men	Women	Sample
		(percentage)		size
All slaves	24	41	5	4,956
All creoles	28	52	7	2,169
Foreign creole	47	42	67	15
Colored creole	34	45	24	134
Black creole	27	52	5	2,020
All Africans	18	29	2	1,985
Timbou (Jalonka)	5	18		38
Mina (Akan)	10	17		69
Sénégal	10	20		30
Côte d'Or	12	13		17
Mesurade	12	25		33
Arada (Ewe-Fon)	13	23		209
Foëda (Hweda)	13	56		39
Adia (Ewe-Fon)	14	24		42
Tiamba/Kiamba (Gurma)	15	19		47
Sosso (Susu)	16	25		25
Nago (Yoruba)	16	31		181
Mondongue	17	30		48
Fon	17	57		23
Congo	18	28		803
Mandingue	22	33		59
Igbo	22	42		46
Bambara	29	37		77
Poulard (Fulbe)	31	33		13
Taqua/Tapa (Nupe)	31	38		16
Barba (Bariba)	44	54		16
Aoussa/Gambary (Hausa)	53	53		15
Unknown origin	26	45		802

Source: Inventories of 34 sugar estates, 1778–90.

In the 1780s specialist posts were held in the highlands by 23 percent of creole men and 10 percent of African men, 10 percent of creole women and 2 percent of African women. All these features recur in earlier and later periods, with the predominance of creoles merely varying with their prominence in the general population.[31]

The predominance of creoles was a good guide to the status of a given occupation. This was particularly clear in the contrast between master carters, carters, and their assistants, or between masons—whose tasks were varied and demanded mobility—and coopers—whose work was repetitive and localized (see table 2.11). Most sugar boilers continued to be Africans down to the Revolution, probably because creoles preferred to avoid the stifling heat of the factory building. Africans might be chosen over creoles for the position of slave driver, but the few African *commandeurs* found in the plain were generally second or third drivers on the least creolized estates.

Of the Africans, Congos were by virtue of their numerical predominance more commonly found in specialist positions than any other group. However, some *nations* had greater success in avoiding field work than others (see table 2.10). This was especially true of the tall peoples from the savanna regions. With the exception of the Fulbe, they were disproportionately selected as sugar boilers, which was by far the commonest post available outside of field labor. They appear to have had an aptitude for standing long hours over steaming cauldrons.[32] The following proportions of the men were employed as *sucriers:* Hausa, 57 percent; Bambara, 25 percent; Nupe, 23 percent; Mandingues, 22 percent; Africans in general, 16 percent. However, 25 percent of both Igbo and Yoruba worked as sugar boilers, although they were only of average height. While the prominence of Yoruba as *sucriers* is hard to explain,[33] the large percentage of Igbo specialists on both coffee and sugar plantations may have been due to their poor reputation as field workers. Such reasoning may also have been applied to the "slow-moving" Bambaras. The planters' avoidance of those deemed the ablest agriculturalists, the Aradas, also points to this conclusion.

Of the ethnic groups generally praised by planters for other talents—Congos as domestics, craftsmen, and fishermen; Sénégals as domestics and stockmen; and Bambaras as craftsmen[34]—only the last were disproportionately placed in responsible positions. However, this was because few of the Congos and Sénégals became sugar boilers, the most numerous specialists. The distribution of "privileged" slaves within each ethnic group demonstrates that colonists clearly took into account the traits they ascribed to different African peoples. One-fifth of Congo specialists were artisans, a higher proportion than in any other ethnic group. Bambara were almost as prominent as artisans, and in fact slightly more likely to be selected. Among the few Africans to work in proximity to whites, as servants and cooks, Congos were everywhere especially visible, perhaps—as it was said—because of their temperament and linguistic aptitude. Similarly, two-

TABLE 2.11. DEGREE OF CREOLIZATION OF MAIN OCCUPATIONS
ON 34 SUGAR ESTATES

Occupations[a]	Creole[b] (percentage)	"Colored"[c] (percentage)	No. of known origin
Male			
Agricultural			
Slave driver	87		60
Ploughman	83		6
Master carter	90		20
Carter	74	1	104
Carter's mate	41		39
Miller	92	10	53
Master boiler	43		37
Sugar boiler	44	1	288
Stockman[d]	56		39
Fisherman/canoeman	25		4
Artisans			
Wheelwright, smith[e]	88		8
Mason	81	19	31
Carpenter/joiner	68	10	50
Cooper	55	8	64
Roofer	50		6
All artisans[f]	66	10	161
Domestic			
Coachman	100	19	16
Servant/maitre d'	100	17	6
Valet/hairdresser	83	17	6
Cook	71	5	21
Cook's help	80		5
Female occupations			
Slave driver	100		2
Housekeeper	100		3
Servant	90	38	21
Laundrywoman	89	11	19
Nurse	74	10	31
Midwife	91	27	11
All domestics	87	17	95

Source: See source note for table 10.
[a]In cases of multiple employment, only the first occupation listed was
counted.
[b]Includes foreign creoles.
[c]These are included within the creole figures.
[d]Includes those in charge of cattle, mules and horses, but not those who
watched over the smaller livestock.
[e]Includes *machoquiers*, who repaired tools.
[f]Includes 1 saddler, 1 brickmaker.

thirds of the Sénégal (and Fulbe) specialists worked with animals, as carters and stockmen, though in domestic service Sénégals seem to have been extremely rare.[35] Put another way, Congos, who constituted 43 percent of the African male sample, made up 55 percent of the African artisans, 66 percent of the African fishermen and canoemen,[36] 69 percent of the African domestics, but only 32 percent of the African *sucriers*. Even so, Congos also constituted 47 percent of those working with livestock, although few could have had relevant experience in Africa and they were not credited with any special aptitude for this activity in Saint Domingue. Numerically few in Saint Domingue, peoples with experience of handling livestock provided only a tiny proportion of the stockmen. Prominent among them, nonetheless, were Nupe, who had a long equestrian tradition, and the Fulbe, West African cattle herders par excellence, who enjoyed the greatest chance of any slaves of working with livestock.[37]

In sum, slaveholders acted on their ethnic stereotypes when choosing slaves for particular positions. Often they accentuated the negative, paying more attention to undesirable attributes (lack of aptitude for field work or insufficient height and strength) as to skills learned in Africa. This did not greatly modify the distribution of ethnic groups, to the extent that Congos predominated among the Africans in all occupations. But among different *nations*, the probability of performing different types of work varied considerably.

If the slave elite was dominated by men and creoles, women and Africans made up the bulk of those at the bottom of the plantation hierarchy, the field hands. Those aged 15 to 49 who were in good health—those whom the colonists called *nègres travaillants*—formed just under half of the adults or 37 percent of all sugar plantation slaves in the 1780s. Rarely did they make up more than one-half of a workforce. On fewer than one in seven estates did men predominate among these key workers, and then only by small margins; 62 percent were women in the 1770s, 64 percent in the 1780s. Roughly speaking, in a typical gang of seventy field slaves, one-half were Africans, equally divided between males and females, about ten were creole men, and more than one-third young creole women.

The productivity of a plantation depended on the health of its slaves. While the proportion of the slaves in any particular *atelier* lodged in the plantation hospital fluctuated considerably from month to month, generally 8 to 10 percent of a sugar estate's work force was permanently incapacitated to some degree.[38] An average proportion for coffee plantations is less easy to ascertain, as the slave lists of many small plantations record no sick at all—which might denote a clean bill of health or merely minimal record keeping. In any event, it is certain that on both sugar and coffee plantations women were healthier than men and creoles healthier than Africans. It is also likely that sugar and coffee plantations did not differ greatly as to the proportion of their work forces who suffered from chronic ailments.[39] The incidence of day-to-day illness may well have been different, as contemporaries in both the French and British Caribbean commented that life in the mountains was healthier for slaves and masters alike. Coffee slaves were less exposed to insect-borne diseases because of the altitude of the plantations on which they worked, and to accidental injuries because of their work regime. Why then did highland plantations not have fewer slaves who were permanently sick?

A solution to this puzzle seems to lie not with the work or disease environments but with the physical condition of the African slaves purchased. It appears that creoles living on coffee plantations were much healthier than creoles on sugar estates, although Africans were less healthy in the mountains than in the plains.[40] Since coffee planters were less selective in the slave market than sugar planters, they accepted more slaves with deformities, diseases, and other disabilities. Plantation mortality and morbidity reflected the process by which the labor force was constructed.

In pre-Revolutionary Saint Domingue, epilepsy, insanity, blindness, and pulmonary disorders proved more common among creoles than Africans. As a process of selection, the slave trade screened out many people with congenital disorders. However, the Africans' "advantage" was counterbalanced by their immigration into an unfamiliar disease environment and their concentration in low-status occupations. The fact that Africans were generally shorter than creoles suggests that Africans also had experienced poorer nutrition in childhood.[41] This problem was perhaps aggravated in the Caribbean by changes of diet and, for some men, lack of familiarity with farming, since slaves grew most of their own food. Among both Africans and creoles, the higher levels of male morbidity were entirely accounted for by cases of hernia. Although the grueling labor of the cane fields was performed mostly by women, men still did the heaviest and most dangerous tasks. Hernia was the most frequently identified disability on coffee as well as sugar plantations, but it was strikingly more widespread on the latter, where it affected nearly 3 percent of adult males. Cases of maiming and loss of an eye were also more prevalent on sugar estates, where quite clearly accidents were more common.

The largest African ethnic groups had levels of morbidity close to the African mean, allowance being made for their different sex ratios. On the sugar estates, the Arada, Nago, and Igbo were nonetheless healthier than the Congos. This accords well with their respective reputations among slave owners. The unhealthiest, with two to three times the average level of morbidity, were the Timbou (Jalonka), Thiamba, Kiamba, and Sénégal, followed by the Mandingues (of whom 16 percent were incapacitated). The resulting pattern may be connected with differences in traditional diet. Mandingues—and perhaps other people from rice and millet-growing regions of Africa—adapted with difficulty to the cassava, plantains, and maize of Saint Domingue. They may also have had less resistance to disease than Africans from the Bight of Benin, whose subsistence was based on maize, a more nutritious staple.[42]

Disconcertingly, this pattern was largely reversed on the mountain plantations. The Mandingues and Sénégals once again had above-average levels of morbidity, but Congos were healthier than the average African; the Ibo, Arada, and Nago were notably less healthy. One physician observed that, although Congos were the most affected by stomach disorders (*mal de ventre*), they did well in the mountains, where they were known as hearty eaters.[43] It appears that their familiarity with life at higher altitudes and the availability of plantains, their preferred foodstuff, gave them definite advantages over people from the lower-lying hinterland of the Guinea coast. These men and women, in turn, were better suited to life in the plains, being likely to possess immunities to insect-borne diseases. Such resistance to disease would also explain why the Timbou of the Futa Jallon highlands suffered such exceptionally ill health on the sugar plantations.

Little is presently known about mortality or birthrates of slaves in Saint Domingue. As in other slave societies, the tendency not to record the birth or death of infants makes the investigation of either quite hazardous. It is therefore difficult to distinguish the impact of high infant mortality from that of low fertility.[44] The problem is magnified when the best available measure of fertility is the ratio of children below age five to women aged between 15 and 44. To an unknown degree, therefore, the following discussion of fertility also concerns infant mortality as well.

At the end of the colonial period measured fertility levels of slaves on Saint Domingue plantations were exceedingly low, even by the standards of Caribbean slave societies (see table 2.12). In the sugar sector, average fertility indexes fell slightly but continuously each

TABLE 2.12. Plantation fertility
indexes (children aged 0–4
per thousand females aged 15–44)

	Mean	Median	N
Sugar			
1755–96	326	290	84
1755–91	328	281	59
1796	323	326	25
Coffee			
1767–98	437	373	118
1767–92	356	333	56
1796–98	509	441	62

decade from the 1760s to the 1790s, and they were lowest in the North Province, where at the plantation level the median fertility index was only 277. Fertility tended to be lower on sugar than coffee plantations.[45] This might reflect the latter's healthier location, but it seems chiefly attributable to the lighter work regime. Indigo plantations, which shared the same unhealthy lowland location as sugar estates, seem to have enjoyed rather higher levels of fertility.

Efforts to correlate fertility with a range of relevant factors has met with little success, perhaps owing to the small size of the samples, the crudeness of some of the measures employed, or the complexity of the subject itself. The factors examined were work force size and sex ratio, per capita work load,[46] the proportion of disabled and sick women, and the percentage of fertile women who were creoles or aged 25 to 34 (the late twenties being the age of peak fertility). For sugar estates the only correlation approaching significance was work load, and that only in the North Province.[47] As slave-cane ratios were lower in the North than elsewhere, this suggests there might be a critical threshold beyond which the punishing labor of sugar cultivation began to impinge on slave women's fertility (or the life expectancy of their infants). On the coffee plantations the most significant factor was workforce size,[48] which indicates that the difficulty of finding a suitable partner was more important in the mountains.

The weak correlation between creolization and fertility is difficult to explain, since on most plantations where mothers could be identified creoles appeared to be more fertile than Africans in all age groups—with the exception of coffee plantation females over age 30, for whom

TABLE 2.13. Mean percentage of slave women identified as mothers, by age, ethnicity, and crop type

	15–19		20–29		30–39		40–49	
	African	Creole	African	Creole	African	Creole	African	Creole
Sugar plantations	0	8	19	49	42	39	24	34
Coffee plantations	14	19	46	72	47	100	35	17

Note: The data concern only mothers with living children, of whom the true proportion is understated, since usually only the mothers of children aged under 15 are identified. Ambiguously identified mothers were deleted from the sample. The figures represent the means of percentages derived from thirteen sugar estates and seventeen coffee plantations. The figures referring to coffee plantation creoles in their thirties and forties derive from very small samples.

the samples were very small (see table 2.13). Fewer were childless, and the mothers had on average more children. However, the fertility of African women is understated because an unknown number had spent only a short time in Saint Domingue.[49] Still, this factor is unlikely to have accounted for even half of the very considerable gap between African and creole childlessness in women under 30. African women must have rarely borne children during their first five or ten years in the colony. On the sugar estates the African and creole rates of childlessness were broadly comparable for women in their thirties; the African-creole differential reappeared for women in their forties, although in less extreme form. This suggests that the African women experienced a shorter child-bearing span than creoles, ceasing to have children earlier as well as beginning later.[50] One-tenth of the births to creole women were to mothers aged 40 or over but only one-twelfth of those to African women, despite the fact that almost no Africans gave birth before age 20 (see table 2.14). The median and modal age at birth of the creole mothers was 26; among the Africans the median was 28.5 and the mode 27.

Tentative though they are, as they derive from small samples, the findings regarding mother's age at childbirth on sugar and coffee plantations make an intriguing comparison. To a striking degree slave women on the coffee plantations gave birth at much younger ages than in the plain. Among Africans the median age at childbirth was 26, and among creoles 20. This was not due merely to the greater youthfulness of the mountain work forces, for greater proportions of both Africans and creoles are listed as mothers in almost every age group, and most particularly among those under 20 (see tables 2.13 and 2.14). In other words, the adverse impact of sugar cultivation on fertility

TABLE 2.14. DISTRIBUTION OF BIRTHS TO SLAVE WOMEN, BY AGE, ETHNICITY, AND CROP TYPE

	Percentages of total births							No. of births
	10–14	*15–19*	*20–24*	*25–29*	*30–34*	*35–39*	*40+*	
Sugar plantations								
Africans	0.0	1.3	25.0	28.9	19.7	17.1	7.9	76 (100%)
Creoles	0.6	14.9	26.0	27.6	11.6	9.9	9.9	181 (100%)
Coffee plantations								
Africans	6.2	13.4	24.7	24.7	13.4	11.3	6.2	97 (100%)
Creoles	14.6	29.3	36.6	9.8	2.4	4.9	2.4	41 (100%)

Note: The coffee plantation creole sample's comparability with the others is limited by its lower average age.

was not uniform, affecting young women, especially young African women, with particular severity.

Evidence drawn solely from the sugar plantations suggests that low fertility might have been in large measure due to late attainment of puberty, especially by African women. Africans were indeed said to achieve menarche later than creoles,[51] and the small stature of African women affirms that low fertility can plausibly be attributed to childhood nutritional deprivation. However, data from coffee plantations considerably complicate the picture. In the sugar estates sampled, only one African—aged 19—gave birth before age 20, and the youngest mothers were two creoles of 14 and 16. On the mountain plantations, even African women apparently as young as 11, 12, and 13 gave birth. In both *plaine* and *morne* early pregnancy was linked with miscegenation, but it cannot be explained by it. White or mulatto men fathered only one-fifth of the children born to slave women under 20 in the highlands and one-quarter in the plains, where a staff of European bachelors ran most estates. To judge from the childbirth evidence, sexual relations between white men and African women appear to have been uncommon.[52]

Most coffee plantations, then, achieved fertility indexes markedly higher than that of the typical sugar estate, despite the disadvantages of small size and a predominantly African population. They were able to do this presumably because of their lighter work regime and perhaps also their less restricted food supply. It is less certain, however, why sugar cultivation should have affected in particular the fertility of the youngest women and the Africans. The interaction of work load and nutritional factors may well have been especially detrimental to the fecundity of adolescents. And because of the proximity of the seaports, the incidence of prostitution—accompanied by abortion, contraceptive practices, and venereal disease—was no doubt higher in the plain than the mountains, as numerous contemporaries noticed.[53] These factors, however, were more relevant to creoles than Africans, whose diverse fertility patterns need further investigation.

Though much remains to be learned about slave society in Saint Domingue, late eighteenth-century sugar and coffee plantations obviously constituted different social worlds. In the densely populated plains, the estates that imposed rectilinear order on the tropical landscape were peopled by relatively large, diverse communities several generations old. The majority of their inhabitants were locally born slaves, and work forces formed an occupational hierarchy based on birth and sex. Coffee plantations, recently cut out of the mountain forests and far removed from the bustle of the towns, had more of a frontier atmosphere. Their work forces were younger and smaller and had little internal differentiation. The slaves had fewer avenues for advancing themselves within the plantation hierarchy, and they lived more isolated lives, albeit in a healthier environment and under a less demanding work regime.

The African presence was much stronger in the highlands than in the plain and also more homogeneous. Between half and two-thirds of the Africans on coffee plantations derived from the Congo basin, itself an unusually homogeneous cultural area. It is unclear, however, that African cultural traits were more easily preserved in the mountains. The survival of linguistic communities and the finding of a spouse of common ethnic background was probably better facilitated by the greater size of sugar estates. The coffee plantations' more intimate scale and the greater likelihood of their having a European family in residence also promoted creolization through day-to-day contact between whites and slaves.[54]

The contrast between *plaine* and *morne* was not clear-cut. Each sector exhibited considerable diversity, particularly in plantation size and demographic composition. Regional differences were important, usually reflecting the age of settlement. However, the provincial variations in the ethnic composition of the African population were themselves crop-related in origin. They derived from ethnic stereotypes based on the agricultural practices of different African peoples, their dietary habits and general health, but above all physique, especially height. Within the colony as a whole, and within a given plantation, these characteristics had a demonstrable influence on the type of work an individual slave could perform and on the composition of the slave community. It remains to be discovered how far a similar regionalism marked the culture of Saint Domingue's slaves and of their descendants in independent Haiti.[55]

Sources (1745–1792 Sample)

Abbreviations: AD = Archives Départementales; *Affiches* = *Les Affiches Américaines;* AN = Archives Nationales, Paris; "Afrique" = Gabriel Debien, "De l'Afrique à Saint-Domingue," *Revue de la Société Haïtienne d'Histoire et de Géographie* 135 (1982); BIFAN = Gabriel Debien et al., "Les origines des esclaves des Antilles," *Bulletin de l'Institut d'Afrique Noire,* ser. B (1961–67); Not = Notariat de Saint-Domingue, Archives Nationales, Section d'Outre-mer, Aix en Provence; "Papiers privés" = Marcel Châtillon, Xavier de Boisrouvray, "Papiers privés sur l'histoire des Antilles," *Revue française d'histoire d'Outre-Mer* 216 (1972); RSHHG = *Revue de la Société Haïtienne d'Histoire et de Géographie;* Siguret = Rosaline Siguret, "Esclaves d'indigoteries et de caféières," *Revue française d'histoire d'Outre-Mer* 199 (1968).

Sugar Plantations
Astier: Not reg. 293, 29 août 1788; Auvray (Trou, Terrier Rouge, Grand Bassin): MS. g. 105, Bibliothèque Municipale, Rouen; Barré Saint Venant: Françoise Thésée, Gabriel Debien, *Un colon niortais* (Niort, 1975); Baudard Saint James: C9B/37, AN; Baudin: 5F/256, AD de la Sarthe, Le Mans; Beauharnais: 251 AP 3/5, AN; Beaunay (Quartier Morin, Trou): 1Mi/16/R4, AD de la Sarthe, Le Mans; Belle Hôtesse: T 210/1, jan./août 1784, AN; Bertrand du Platon heirs: Not reg. 1388, 23 avril 1784; Bobin: *Affiches,* 1781; Bongars: T 520, AN; Borthon de l'Etang: BIFAN 23 (1961); Boyer: "Afrique"; Bréda (Plaine du Nord, Haut du Cap): 18 AP 3, AN; Breteuil, 1779: E 1748, AD des Yvelines, Versailles; Breteuil, 1787: Fischer Collection, Howard University Library, Washington, D.C.; Bretton Deschapelles: Françoise Thésée, *Négociants bordelais et colons de Saint-Domingue* (Paris, 1972); Brossard/Laguehay: 3E 780/15 bis, AD de la Lot-et-Garonne, Agen; Budan: Not reg. 1391, 25 mai 1787; Butler: Gabriel Debien, *Etudes Antillaises* (Paris, 1956); Caignet: AN, T 210/4; Canejolles: "Afrique"; Chabanon heirs: T 210/1, AN; Chavannes; T 210/1, AN; Clérisse/Hirigoyen: Papiers Clérisse, château d'Hastingues, courtesy of J. Cauna; Conflans (Varreux, des Sources): T 1113, AN; Corregeolles: "Papiers privés"; Cottineau: Gabriel Debien, *Plantations et Esclaves* (Dakar, 1962); Couré: *Affiches,* 1788; D'Aux: Papiers d'Aux, marquis Baudry d'Asson, courtesy of G. Debien; De La Mare: *Affiches,* 1788; Delaunay-Mahé: "Afrique"; Desforges: Château de Cussac, courtesy of Général Bermondet de Cromières; D'Orlic and D'Orlic/

Bomale: Rodrigue Papers, box 1, Overbrook Seminary, Philadelphia; Dupocy: Not reg. 292, 13 mai 1787; Durand de Beauval: Gabriel Debien, Pierre Pluchon, "Trois sucreries," *Bulletin du Centre des Espaces Atlantiques* 2 (1985); Dutour/ Sauvage: Not reg. 294, 14 mai 1789; Ferret: *Affiches*, 1781; Fleuriau: Jacques Cauna, "Une habitation de Saint-Domingue," thèse de doctorat, Université de Poitiers, 1983; Foäche: Debien, *Plantations et Esclaves;* Fontenelle/Lefebvre: Not reg. 419, 23 juin 1779; Foucauld: "Afrique"; Fournier De La Chapelle: Not reg. 1388, 13 jan. 1784; Galbaud du Fort: Olivier Frémond de la Merveillière, "L'habitation sucrière d'une famille nantaise," *Bulletin de la société archéologique de Nantes* (1935); Galliffet (Grande Place, La Gossette, Desplantes): 107 AP, 127/4, AN; Gascard Dumesnil: Not reg. 1388, 1 dec. 1784; Gaschet/Hardy: Not reg. 295, 8 avril 1791; Gourgues: Rodrigue Papers, box 1, Overbrook Seminary, Philadelphia; Gravé: Not reg. 1387, 16 juin 1783; Gruel: Moreau de Saint-Méry, *Description . . . de Saint-Domingue* (Paris, 1958), 2:610; Hay: Not reg. 294, 12 juillet 1789; Hué de Montaigu: T 356, 25 mai 1785, AN; Jolly: Not reg. 418, 24 août 1778; La Barre: Gabriel Debien, *Comptes, profits . . . de deux sucreries* (n.p., 1945); La Ferronaye: T 210/2, AN; La Forgue Desmangles: Not reg. 1393, 26 fev. 1779; Lebray: Not reg. 418, 7 juillet 1777; Lemmens: Bernard Foubert, "L'habitation Lemmens," *RSHHG* 154 (1987); Leroux des Isles: Not reg. 1389, 29 avril 1785; Longpré/La Rochalard: *BIFAN* 24 (1963); Loyseau de Montauger: Gustave Vallée, "La sucrerie Loyseau," *La Porte Océane* (1955); Lugé: M. Reible, *La sucrerie Lugé* (n.p., 1976); Macnemara: MS. 65/60, AD de la Vienne, Poitiers; Mauger: Gabriel Debien, "Les esclaves des plantations Mauger," *Bulletin de la Société d'Histoire de la Guadeloupe* 43 (1980); Maulde: 10J/33, AD du Pas de Calais, Arras; Merle: Not reg. 418, 23 fev. 1778; Mondion (Limbé): Not reg. 294, dec. 1789; Montholon: Not reg. 1390, 10 jan. 1786; Moreau de Riancourt: Château de Cussac, courtesy of Général Bermondet de Cromières; Motmans: Debien, Pluchon, "Trois sucreries,"; Pailleterie: 10J/33, AD Pas du Calais, Arras; Paterson heirs: Not reg. 294, 29 mai 1789; Philibert de l'Hermitage: Not reg. 294; Pihéry de Civray: A. Latrou, "L'administration d'une habitation," *Revue Historique des Antilles* 6 (1930); Pimelle: Bernard Foubert, *Une habitation à Saint-Domingue* (n.p., n.d.); Pons: Not reg. 419, 14 mars 1780; Raby, Pierre Léon, *Marchands et spéculateurs dauphinois* (Paris, 1962); Rivaud: *BIFAN* 23 (1961); Robin: "Papiers privés"; Robiniaud/Leroux: Not reg. 418, 4 oct. 1777; Rouaudières: Gabriel Debien, *Lettres de colons* (Laval, 1965); Rouvray: Not reg. 294, 7 mars 1789; Saint-Mesmin: Debien, Pluchon, "Trois sucreries"; Saint-Michel, 1783 (Quartier Morin, Pte. d'Icaque): B 6042, AD de la Charente-Maritime, La Rochelle; Saint-Michel, 1790 (Quartier Morin, Pte. d'Icaque): C9C/7, AN; Santo Domingo: *BIFAN* 27 (1964); Tréhazar: *BIFAN* 27 (1965); Théobald Troumigny: "Afrique"; Turpin/Flaville: Not reg. 418, 26 mai 1778; Unknown (Ouanaminthe): *Affiches*, 1788; Vaudreuil (Plaine du Nord, 1745): "Papiers privés"; Vaudreuil (Cul de Sac, 1789, jan. 1791, and Plaine du Nord, 1788): T 561, AN; Vaussanges: *Affiches*, 1781; Venault de Charmilly: E 1246, AD de la Loire-Atlantique, Nantes.

Coffee Plantations

Andrault: Gabriel Debien, *La fortune et la famille d'un colon* (Niort, 1978); Ardisson: Not reg. 1387, 31 oct. 1783; Baon: 107 AP 127, AN; Bergeron/Duluc: Siguret; Berquier: *Affiches*, 1788; Bersaudy La Roussellière: Not reg. 294, 8 sept. 1789; Bertet: Not reg. 1389, 24 nov. 1785; Bertrand: Not reg. 294, 1 mars 1789; Biguérier: Mossmeier Collection, Louisiana State Museum, New Orleans; Bongars, North, 1785: Not reg. 1389, 23 fev. 1785; Bongars, West, 1790: Gabriel Debien, "Histoire de deux plantations," *Revue de la Province du Maine* (1968); Bongars, West 1780: T 520, AN; Brisson: Dxxv,/111/884-6, AN; Brossard: 3E 780/15 bis, AD de la Lot-et-Garonne, Agen; Brosse: Siguret; Brun: Siguret; Cael/Pébarte: MS. 11/66, South Carolina Historical Society, Charleston; Candie/Dupuch: Not reg. 1388, 18 mai 1784; Carrère: *BIFAN* 25 (1963); Carteau: Not reg. 859, 22 juillet 1787; Castella: 107 AP 127, AN; Charrier: *Affiches*, 1788; Charron: Siguret; Chartier: *Affiches*, 1788; Chatard: doc. 20, Chatard Papers, Baltimore, courtesy of F. Chatard; Châteauneuf: Not reg. 1391, 10 sept. 1787; Clément: Jérémie Papers, L3-30, University of Florida, Gainesville; Clérisse: Clérisse Papers, Château d'Hastingues, courtesy of J. Cauna; Darbat: Siguret; Dartis: *BIFAN* 24 (1963); Dauzat frères: Not reg. 1387, 13 juillet 1783; De Boismartin: Dubois Martin Papers, Maryland Historical Society, Baltimore; De Chesse frères: Not reg. 419, 10 avril 1790; De La Tour: Thésée, *Négociants bordelais*; Delaunay, Grande Rivière: *Affiches*, 1788; Delaunay: *Affiches*, 1788; Delosset: Not reg. 1625; De Thèze: Roger Massio, "Inventaire de deux habitations," *RSHHG* 90 (1953); Douault: "Papiers privés"; Dugas: Not reg. 1387, 8 juillet 1783; Dumas/Mignet: Not reg. 1394, 12 mars 1786; Du Mont: Roger Massio, "Plantations de Bigourdans," *RSHHG* (1953); Dumourier: T 210/4, fev. 1786, AN; Duplessis: Not reg. 1625, 2 août 1787; Dupuy de Grandpré (Plaisance): Not reg. 1098, 29 mai 1788; Dupuy de Grandpré (Marmelade): Not reg. 780, 14 avril 1786; Duval: *Affiches*, 1788; Faux: Not reg. 1388, 17 mai 1784; Gagnard: Not reg. 293, 27 mars 1788; Géraud: Not reg. 1098, 22 mai 1788; Gillet: Not reg. 1390, 14 dec. 1786; Girard de Grandfils: "Afrique"; Guihard/ Lesec: Not reg. 1389, 10 fev. 1785; Guilhou: "Afrique"; Harriet: Not reg. 295, 23 août 1791; Jolly/Dubuisson fils: Not reg. 1393; Joubert de la Baume: Jérémie Papers, L3-1, University of Florida, Gainesville; Lahogue: Not reg. 780, 26 juin 1786; La Rivière: Minutes, Bourges de La Flèche, 4E/vi/968, AD de la Sarthe, Le Mans; La Robinière: Not reg. 1393, 4 nov. 1782; Lasniel: *Affiches*, 1788; Ledieu/Linotte: Not reg. 1390, 2 juin 1786; Ledoux: "Afrique"; Lehinas: Siguret; Lemaire: Not reg. 1390, 31 mai 1786; Lemaître: *Affiches*, 1788; Leroy: Not reg. 1393, 14 avril 1782; Lesec: Not reg. 294, 8 juin 1787; Maphaud: *BIFAN* 25 (1963); Margaillau: Not reg. 1156, 13 oct. 1787; Maulèvrier: Gabriel Debien, *Etudes Antillaises* (Paris, 1956); Michelet: Not reg. 422, 30 sept. 1784; Milscent de Musset: Not reg. 781, 15 juin 1787; Mondion: Not reg. 294, dec. 1787; Montléart: *Affiches*, 1788; Navailles, Saint Louis: Jacques Cauna, "Les propriétés Navailles," *RSHHG* 158 (1988); Norroy: Not reg. 1394, 5 juin 1787; Panson: *Affiches*, 1788; Pébarte: MS. 11/66, South Carolina Historical Society, Charleston; Peyrigné-Lalanne: Massio, "Plantations de Bigourdans"; Pincemaille: Not reg. 1388, 16 sept. 1784; Poudensan: *Affiches*, 1788; Poulle: "Afrique"; Pouvillon: Not reg. 1389, 10 avril 1785; Preele: *Affiches*, 1788; Puilboreau: *Affiches*, 1788; Raby du Moreau: Léon, *Marchands et spéculateurs;* Renard/Jalès: Siguret; Rigalle: Not reg. 1387, 25 juin 1783; Rogier: *Affiches*, 1788; Rossignol: Not reg. 422, 30 sept. 1784; Royé: Not reg. 1388, 2 avril 1784; Rozès: *Affiches*, 1788; Sigoigne: Not reg. 1099, 7 août 1788; Tardivy: Not reg. 422, 15 jan. 1784; Testu: Gabriel Debien, *La fortune et la famille d'un colon* (Niort, 1978); Theuvet: Siguret; Tournié: Not reg. 202; Unnamed (Grande Rivière, Nouvelle Bretagne, Jérémie, Léogane, Côtelettes): *Affiches*, 1788; Vignave: *Affiches*, 1788; Vigoureux: Not reg. 1389, 2 mai 1785; Villatte: Not reg. 295, 23 mars 1791; Vincendon-Dutour: Dugas Vallon Papers, South Caroliniana Library, Columbia, S.C.

Note: Where discrepancies existed in manuscript or printed sources between data and summaries of data, the former were usually preferred. Missing data were occasionally inferred from context where it seemed safe to do so.

PART TWO

The Economy

3

SUGAR CULTIVATION AND SLAVE LIFE
IN ANTIGUA BEFORE 1800

David Barry Gaspar

WORK WAS THE dominant force in the lives of slaves. In 1716 Clement Tudway, the absentee owner of the Parham Hill plantation on Antigua's north coast, put the matter succinctly and expertly when he said that "from the Negroes' Labor all produce must Come." This accurate summation of the role of slaves in making the sugar plantation profitable, and of the central function of work in binding slaves and masters together, was the nucleus around which Tudway constructed a set of careful instructions to his new "Agent, Manager and Overseer." Tudway's main message was that his slaves should not be allowed to neglect their duties; they should be well treated, but at the same time the plantation manager should choose "a Diligent driver" to make them work.[1] Similar ideas about slaves as the sinews of the plantation shaped the perceptions and expectations of Antigua plantation owners during the seventeenth and eighteenth centuries. This essay explores the relation between plantation work and the development of slave life and culture in Antigua during this period, focusing on three interrelated themes: work specifically performed for the master during regular hours of labor (master's time); work performed for the benefit of the slaves themselves, on their own time (the slave's free time); and the leisure and recreational pursuits of slaves during their free time.

English settlers first colonized tiny Antigua (280 square kilometers) in 1632. After abandoning tobacco, the colony began to produce sugar on a large scale for export by the last quarter of the seventeenth century. The emerging sugar revolution transformed the environment, institutions, and values of the island. The earlier white-settler

101

society with a few indentured servants was replaced by a racially
stratified slave society of white masters and servants and African
slaves. All blacks were subordinated to all whites, regardless of social
rank. Deforestation accompanied the expansion of sugar cultivation,
as slave labor carved plantations out of the woodland. Planters with
sufficient means acquired most of the cultivable land and established
the largest plantations; as men of both property and standing in this
aggressive island community, they also exercised political power in
the legislature. As in other sugar colonies, economies of scale, plantation milling capacity, land transportation, and the supply of cultivable
land together determined the optimum size of an Antigua sugar plantation, which John Yeamans, the island's agent in London in 1734, put
at close to three hundred acres. Yeamans estimated, however, that
there were few plantations of "above, or even so much as 300 acres of
land fit for sugar." Without that amount of land, he added, "No
Planter can be enabled to bear the great Expence of the Buildings &
Utensils Necessary for making Sugar." At this time, a few large and
many middling and small planters cultivated the "improvable land,"
which seems to have been the general pattern for much of the eighteenth century. The proper ratio of slaves to acres of land under cane
was 1:1 or 2:1. Accordingly, planters were always striving, conditions
permitting, to strike an economic balance between slave force and
acreage. The Reverend Robert Robertson, who owned slaves in Nevis
(Antigua's island neighbor) during the early eighteenth century, observed that once planters secured the land, labor was the next most
important "Requisite to Sugar-making," but fewer than 150 slaves
could not advantageously work a 200-acre plantation.[2]

By the second decade of the eighteenth century, Antigua was the
leading sugar colony among the British Leewards, and the island's
black majority—which dated from the seventeenth century—towered
above the white population. In 1708 blacks totaled more than 80 percent of the population (12,943 blacks, 2,892 whites); by 1756 the black
population had increased to a little over 90 percent (31,428 blacks,
3,435 whites). Nearly twenty years later, in 1774, on the eve of the
American Revolution, blacks still constituted more than 90 percent
of the overall population (37,808 blacks, 2,590 whites). The steady
growth of a black majority was achieved through continuous importation of Africans, which concealed the impact of persistent heavy mortality and low birthrate caused by the heavy burdens of life and labor
under slavery.[3]

In 1734 Governor William Mathew explained to the Board of Trade that among the reasons for Antigua's poor economic performance was "the want of negroes" to work either land already under cultivation or newly prepared land. Planters tried to maintain an optimal number of working slaves, but they faced a daunting task if mortality, sickness, or infirmity among their slaves coincided with scarce supplies of fresh cargoes from Africa or with difficulties hiring local slaves. They complained frequently that they needed more slaves, and some even considered sending their own ships to West Africa.[4] Many sugar plantations appear to have been regularly short of workers. If conditions of labor on plantations with adequate numbers of working slaves were normally hard, they were many times worse on understaffed estates, especially during peak work periods in the annual cycle of production. In general, the work routines of Antigua slaves were shaped by the size and topography of the plantation, the quality of its soil, weather variations, the number of working slaves, the character and disposition of the plantation owner and other management personnel (including slave drivers), the plantation's operations during the annual cycle, the plantation's milling and manufacturing capacity, the number of livestock that might ease the burden of some kinds of work, and the performance of the sugar market. These factors, together with the special characteristics of a particular plantation environment, greatly affected the nature of the work of the slaves.

If the seventeenth century was preindustrial, as Sidney W. Mintz has observed, then the sugar-cane plantation, which was "an unusual combination of agricultural and industrial forms," was also "probably the closest thing to industry that was typical" of that century. Sugar plantations were factories in the field: sugar cane was cultivated in the fields, while sugar and rum were also processed on the premises.[5] In Antigua, as elsewhere in the Caribbean, slaves performed most of the work in field and factory. It is therefore appropriate to explore the nature of the work that such slaves performed on the "master's time" to uncover some of the processes that shaped the contours of slave life.

Richard B. Sheridan notes that because of "the manifold tasks to be performed, the seasonal nature of labor, the combination of field labor with the manufacture of raw sugar and rum, and the large number of slaves on a typical sugar plantation, elaborate specialization and division of labor developed."[6] In Antigua, however, specialization was c.ıly an ideal to which the largest planters aspired, and then only if their plantations were adequately staffed. Many middling and small planters who had fewer slaves would have found this model of specialization elusive. It is perhaps for this reason that in 1737 the evaluators of the two badly understaffed plantations of the deceased owner Main Swete (one of 337 acres, the other of 90 acres), while methodically listing the value of each of the eighty-eight slaves, bothered to identify the occupations only of Jackey, the driver, and of Nanny, the "doctress."[7] Whatever the size of the plantation and its work force, however, the demands of sugar production created a distinct seasonal cycle of labor.

There was much manual work throughout the year for the field hands, who constituted the majority of the slaves on the plantations. During the wet season, from May or June to December, they prepared the ground, manured it, planted canes and provisions, and weeded; during the harvest months of the dry season, from January to June or July, they reaped the ripened cane.[8] Ranked at the bottom of the slave occupational hierarchy, field hands undoubtedly performed the hardest physical labor. Because of the heavy demands of field labor, Antigua planters ideally allowed recently arrived Africans, or "New Negroes," a seasoning period to get accustomed to the plantation environment before they joined the field gangs. Writing to absentee owner Charles Tudway in 1758, Francis Farley advised that if Tudway rented out his plantation, then he should bind the renter to replace any slave who died with another young slave of the same sex within six months. Otherwise, when the lease expired, he would find himself in need of "Seasoned Negroes" acclimated to life and work on a sugar plantation. Farley declared that "a plantation Cannot be Carried on without Negroes Accustomed to that Business & these are very seldom to be bought." If seasoned creole or island-born slaves were scarce or more expensive than newly arrived Africans, Antigua planters did their best with slaves who came off the ships from Africa.[9]

The most laborious work required of field hands was holing the ground with a simple hoe or preparing holes for planting cane cuttings from which new plants would sprout. Hoe culture, with its reliance on heavy manual labor, persisted in the sugar islands even after eighteenth-century farmers in Britain adopted new labor-saving tools like plows. Among the supplies ordered for the Tudway plantations in 1770 were one dozen "Negro Cutlaches," twelve dozen "Mens Hoes," fourteen dozen hoes for the women, and five dozen hoes for the children. On a visit to Antigua in 1787, John Luffman recorded that holing stiff ground was the "heaviest labor" performed by field hands.[10] In addition to the great physical strain that it forced slaves to endure, hoe culture banished the incentive to use cattle for applying manure to the fields. Thomas Norbury Kerby, an Antigua planter, explained in 1789 that animal-drawn carts conveyed manure to the field, from which the field hands filled small baskets that they carried on their heads to the cane holes. Some slaves prepared manure using various ingredients, such as dung, cane trash, marl, clay, loam, lime, salt, ashes, shells, sea moss, sand, rags, and soot.[11] Several decades of sugar cultivation caused Antigua soils to require manuring, certainly by the mid-eighteenth century. Farley's advice in 1758 was that "one Acre of Land well manured & properly planted Will make more Sugar than two Acres planted in the Usual way."[12]

Because of the strenuous work that holing and manuring entailed, Antigua plantation managers often hired slaves from other plantations when they were needed—and they hired out their field hands for holing operations when they could be spared. By the middle of the eighteenth century, such work, usually contracted for by the task, was "so exhausting that planters sometimes saved their own Negroes by hiring others . . . at a rate of £8 or £10 per acre." The manager of the Tudway plantations considered money that went into hiring slaves for holing to be well spent. Writing in 1783, he explained that "The Negroes in the Plantations are not always sufficient to hole all the Land that is to be planted, especially if they are Sickly, or if they are weak and low in Flesh, from dry Weather and a want of Ground Provisions, and perhaps good Water; in either of which Cases they must be eased in their Work, or some of them will be lost, and the loss of one good Negroe would amount to much more than the Money paid for holing many Acres of Land, besides the inhumanity of severely working the Slaves when they are in Distress." Earlier, the Swete plantation paid £43.17s.6d. to Colonel Burton for a little over ten acres holed by his slaves at £4 an acre. In one day's work a gang of forty to sixty slaves could hole an acre, each slave finishing from sixty to one hundred holes. Colonel Samuel Martin, who owned a large plantation in the parish of St. Mary, advised planters in *An Essay Upon Plantership* that "Hoe-ploughing, or holing stiff land is an heavy labour, that ought to be relaxed often by easier work." Dr. James Adair went further. He recommended that planters feed field hands more nutritious provisions to combat the bad effects of hard labor and sickness that were so prevalent during the wet planting season.[13]

During the planting cycle field hands also tended to the fields of ratoons, in which the stumps of canes were left to sprout new plants. Some proportion of the plantation's fields were either newly planted or in ratoons, which matured earlier but did not yield as much sugar. In 1737, of the thirteen fields under cane and occupying a little over 150 acres on the Tudway family's Parham Hill Plantation, there were seven fields with ratoons and six with new plants.[14]

Working from sunrise to sunset, with breaks for meals in the morning and at noon, field hands were ordinarily organized into gangs. Through this form of labor organization field work could be completed by all of the able-bodied slaves, while less able slaves could also be employed advantageously. One gang of the most capable hands worked at the heaviest tasks. Younger slaves were placed in another gang to help with manuring the fields, weeding, and collecting fodder for livestock. Samuel Martin advised that the field gangs be organized according to "age, sex, and strength."[15] In 1798 the Leeward Islands slavery amelioration act regulated the hours of labor: slaves should neither be called out to work before five o'clock in the morning, nor should they be kept at their chores later than seven in the evening, except during the harvest or for some other compelling reason; half an hour should be allowed for breakfast and two hours at noon or "Dinner Time."[16]

Slave gangs worked "in unison, under direct and close supervision" of the white overseers and black drivers, whom planters placed at the top of the occupational hierarchy. Most drivers were men chosen for their maturity, physical strength, intelligence, and knowledge of staple culture. Even more important, perhaps, in the planters' choice of a driver was the ability of that slave (even if physically disabled to some degree) to command the respect and cooperation of the other hands. Drivers were usually acculturated Africans or creoles, ranging in age from early twenties to mid-thirties. They were often elevated from within the ranks of the field hands, where they had acquired experience to handle the duties of leadership and supervision.[17] In 1737 there were three drivers on Parham Hill plantation: old Tony (aged seventy-two), Attaw (aged thirty-three), and Cuffi (aged thirty-two). These men were listed in the plantation inventory after the tradesmen but at the top of the list of all of the other slaves. By 1750 Attaw, now forty-six, was still a driver and valued at £110. He was first on the inventory of 222 slaves, followed by two new drivers who had been ordinary field hands in 1737: Baby's Cudjo, aged thirty-four, valued at £110, and Kate's Quamina, aged thirty-one, valued at £90. Old Tony from the 1737 inventory was not listed, while Cuffi had been banished for his role in the islandwide slave plot of 1736.[18]

The true character of sugar production as agro-industry appeared starkest during the busy period of crop time. As early maps indicate, windmills displaced animal-powered mills in Antigua by the early eighteenth century.[19] Most planters tried to get their mills grinding as early as possible after Christmas, depending upon the maturity of the canes and the number of fields that had to be cut during the dry season. The instructions to John Jeffers, manager of the Codrington family's Cotton Plantation in 1715, stated that he should start "with all the 3 mills a new years day without fail except it falls on a Sunday." In 1737 the harvest for Parham Hill plantation began on February 21, probably because drought had "scorched" the fields in several places. Similar conditions in 1774 delayed the start of harvest on the Tudway plantations until late February or early March, but a long wet season also played a role. Where good harvests were concerned, Antigua planters were obviously at the mercy of nature: the juice of the canes could be damaged by weather that was either too dry or too hot. If they were anxious about when to start grinding, planters were equally concerned about when to stop so as to avoid the hurricane season, which usually started in July or August.[20]

The wheels of the mighty plantation machine turned in harmony during harvest. Cutting the canes, transporting them to the mill for grinding, boiling the cane juice, and the other processes for making sugar and rum all went on simultaneously. Most of the able field hands chopped down the tall canes. According to one description of the process, "The Negroes, provided with cutting bills . . . arranged themselves as when hoeing, each taking his or her respective row. The upper part of the Cane, comprising plant and top, is first cut off, the plant is separated, and the Cane is then divided into junks of about three feet in length, cutting close to the earth. The green top is used to bind the junks with bundles of twenty or thirty each. The cutters strip the trash from the Cane as they proceed, and move it from one to another, till it is collected in swaths about twenty feet apart; this is done that the junks of Cane may be unencumbered in the intervals, while being bound by the inferior gang." Slaves later collected the cane trash, which was used as fuel for the boiling house, and the green tops of the canes, which were fed to the cattle.[21]

How did the harvesting work of field hands compare with holing and planting? In 1790 Kerby told a committee of the House of Commons that harvesting was laborious work, "but I do not think one of the most laborious, and is performed with such alacrity and good spirits that it seems trifling." The hardest work occurred "during the time of holing and dunging the land, although during the croptime the Negroes are employed many more hours in the course of the day." Adair described labor during harvest as "very light." Indeed, the slaves acquired "flesh and strength" at this time. Apart from the nature of the work itself, the slaves generally fared better because the dry harvest season was not as conducive to sickness as the wet planting season and because during the harvest they consumed much cane juice and sugar.[22]

During harvest other plantation slaves besides field hands were hard at work. Several slaves were engaged in transporting the canes to the mill in animal-drawn carts guided by mule men, who generally took care of the livestock and transported sugar to the warehouses or wharfs. On plantations where there were not enough animals to pull the carts, slaves were substituted, carrying the bundles of cane to the mills on their heads.[23] In the mill the canes were crushed to extract the juice. Several slaves were employed in unloading the carts, piling the cane bundles, feeding the cane into the mill, and extracting and piling the crushed cane stalks, which were also used as fuel in the boiling house. Mill operations "in a good breeze" demanded "the greatest exertion of everyone on the estate."[24] The raw cane juice flowed along conduits to the adjoining boiling house, where it went through several stages of preparation until it was ready to crystallize or "strike." There were different ways to know when this stage had been reached. Nevis planter John Pinney believed that it was best "to dip the forefinger and thumb into the boiling liquor and see whether it would make a thread between them." Others relied on "eye art," a visual evaluation which required "a critical Exactness" because there were a number of ways to "deceive the most attentive and experienced eye." When the sugar was ready to crystallize, the boiled-down mass was cooled and placed in hogsheads, then stored in the curing house, where molasses drained into other containers, leaving behind the raw muscovado sugar. Slaves who worked in the still house used the molasses and skimmings from the boiling house to make rum. During bad weather and "when they are working hard," slaves often received allowances of grog or rum.[25]

Slave boilermen were among the most skilled and trusted on the sugar plantation. Assisted by other slaves, the head boiler was "of equal importance to that of any other slave official." He was supposed to know "how the cane had been raised and treated, the kind of soil in which it grew, whether the soil had been richly or slightly manured, the age of the cane, its species, whether it had been topped short or long in cutting, and whether it had been arrowed, bored or rat-eaten."[26] Given this information, the head boiler modified the boiling process for best results. Naturally, planters chose boilermen carefully.

In 1753 Scottish absentee Walter Tullideph instructed his manager to "choose ye most Sensible of my people to be boylers and firemen" and to motivate them "with proper encouragements as feed and their ground of a spare day or ye like." Yet Tullideph, who understood that such privileged slaves might abuse their status, added that even they should be punished "when they deserve it."[27] In 1784 the manager of the Tudway plantations gave "a smart Correction" to one of the boilers for carelessness. He believed that the boilermen often made poor quality sugar through lack of attention to their work, but more often the weather and quality of the soil were responsible. The manager explained that "it is not at all times we can do as we please with the Cane Juice, and . . . it is sometimes impossible for the most skillful boiler to make good Sugar of it."[28]

The vital work of the boilermen and other slaves assigned to the manufacturing processes could be quite dangerous. Accidents on the job were common. Even the most prudent slaves found it unhealthy to work for extended periods in the steamy boiling house and the still house. In the 1740s, the plantation attorney, Benjamin King, reported that the boiling house of Betty's Hope plantation needed to be extended twenty-five feet and five boiling coppers must be added, because these improvements "would greatly quicken our work, and our crops would be sooner taken off every year, as well as preserve ye Slaves from Night Work which is very injurious, it being at present common to boil all night, notwithstanding the mills are burn'd out of wind by seven a Clock every Evening, and Besides the Distruction of Negroes." King also opposed night work because the sugar was of poorer quality "from ye Impossibility of Skimming the liquor so clean and ye Sleeping of ye Negroes."[29]

Gradually, black tradesmen displaced white during the early decades of Antigua's development, a trend that some observers believed contributed to the dwindling size of the white population.[30] The work of these slave artisans was important to the proper operation and maintenance of the plantation. On the Tudway plantations in the 1780s masons were always busy "in keeping the Buildings . . . in repair, in repairing the Negroe Houses, and the Stone Walls round the Cane Pieces." As a result, masons were not always hired out when requested. Carpenters also could "seldom or never be spared," because wood deteriorated much faster than stone. They too were kept busy attending to "Roofs, Negroe Houses, Worm-Tubs and Parts," in addition to many other jobs that frequently arose.[31]

Slave doctors and doctresses practiced folk medicine mostly

among blacks, but some whites also used their services.[32] Among other slaves not connected with field work were domestics, mostly women and young girls. Attached to the planter's household or that of other white plantation personnel, such as the manager, if the plantation owner was an absentee, domestics included housekeepers, cleaners, cooks, butlers, seamstresses, waterwomen, waitingmen or footmen, coachmen, waiting maids and nurses (wet and dry), each with her or his own expertise. Although their work may have been less laborious than that of the typical prime field hand, domestics faced special stresses as a result of living close to whites. Where field hands need not have daily contact with whites on most large plantations, domestics were almost constantly under orders, within sight and earshot of those in authority and at the mercy of their whims and idiosyncrasies.[33]

On Antigua plantations, age, sex, racial ancestry, color, individual skills, and capacity for work determined occupational standing. If the working strength of the plantation was concentrated in the tradesmen and male and female field hands, many old or otherwise incapacitated slaves were also assigned lighter work. The 1740 inventory for Betty's Hope plantation listed the following categories among 312 slaves: tradesmen (27 in number); "Able Working, field Men" (44); "Old and Infirm Men" (23); "Old and infirm Women" (37); "Able Working Field Women" (70); "Large Boys Work with hoe" (35); "Smaller Boys & infants" (30); "Large Girls work with hoe" (16); smaller girls and infants (30). The old and infirm men were described as "belonging to the field but not constant able Workers," while the old and infirm women were not fit for field work and were employed at whatever they were able to do. Inventories describing the physical condition of slaves might note a variety of disabilities and illnesses, such as "Ruptured," "Black Scurvy," "Joint Evil," "Eliphantiecess," or "Asmah," that sometimes disqualified slaves from regular field work.[34] The hard labor and life of the sugar plantation was directly responsible for many a sad case of disability.

Fewer slave women than men in Antigua commonly worked at occupations requiring special skills. As a result of this division of labor, which was determined not simply by biological difference but also by social conventions about women's work and place, planters routinely assigned a greater proportion of women than men to field gangs. Writing in the 1780s, Jamaica planter-historian William Beckford commented that "a negro man is purchased either for a trade, or the cultivation and different processes of the cane," while "the occupa-

tions of the women are only two, the house, with its several departments, and the supposed indulgences, or the field with its exaggerated labours."[35] Among the seventy-six slave men on Parham Hill
plantation in 1737 were twelve tradesmen (more than 15 percent of the
plantation work force) and one doctor. The tradesmen consisted of
three masons, five carpenters, and four coopers. Excluding the three
drivers, most of the other slave men were probably ordinary field
workers. Of the seventy slave women listed, seven (10 percent) specialized in "domestic" labor: two "House" women, three cooks, one
nurse, and one "Sempstress" for the white servants. Most of the
remaining sixty-three able-bodied women worked in the field, because
other specialized occupations were not open to them. Evidently slave
men were not employed as domestics.[36] On larger plantations where
the number of slave men and women were nearly equal, the number
of tradesmen would have increased proportionately because of the
great amount of work to be done year-round, without necessarily
requiring a similar increase in the size of the female domestic staff. It is
likely that most slave women on Antigua plantations labored beside
slave men in the fields at some point in their lives.

On plantations with a sufficient number of slave men and women,
the division of labor by sex was easier to apply than on plantations that
had few slaves or too few slave men. In the latter case, the slaves may
have been driven to work harder, or women may have been forced to
do some of the heavy manual work usually assigned to men. In
discussing slave resistance, especially on plantations, due consideration should therefore be given to the stresses of labor and whether
the plantation was short of able workers.

Although Caribbean planters, visitors, and others often referred to
the difficulties of managing shorthanded plantations, historians have
not paid much attention to this dimension of plantation life. The field
operations of Caribbean sugar plantations were obviously labor intensive, and one Antigua planter observed in 1790 that, in general, "those
estates which are best handed, or have most Negroes, make in proportion the largest crops." He added that slaves were also aware that their
number affected their workload, and if the slave trade were to end,
they would be "extremely concerned" for obvious reasons. Thus it was
not unusual for Antigua slaves to express "much satisfaction whenever they heard of the arrival of a ship with Slaves, and frequently
apply to their masters to purchase a few more helpmates."[37] The
manager of the Tudway plantations explained in 1774 that all of the old
settled sugar plantations in Antigua tended to be short of hands:

"There are a great many superannuated and Infant Slaves, who cannot do anything, which, with the Sick, Stock keepers, Watches, Tradesmen, attendants at the Sick House, and upon the white people in the Estates, and now and then some run away, reduce the numbers of Negroes working in the Field very considerably." He noted that few of these old plantations could regularly call out more than a third of their field slaves. In 1784 the appropriately named New Work plantation under his charge was so badly in need of workers that he was "obliged to do the chief part of the Work there with the Slaves of the Old Work [plantation], tho' that Estate is but barely slaved."[38] Shifting workers from one plantation to another was only a temporary solution, and planters ultimately had to decide whether to buy or hire additional hands, draw children into the work force earlier, or employ their less able workers.

On shorthanded plantations, slave women who were required to take on the heavy labor of men, particularly outside the field, exposed themselves to serious injury. In the 1740s Betty's Hope plantation was "in absolute need of 50 Negroes." The manager advised against buying them "full grown, as such slaves are allways Obstinate, and Stubborn, & seldom Comes on kindly to Labour. Negroes from 12 to 15 Years of Age will prove best. . . . We are at present so weak in Negroes that the Women are Obliged to do the Labour of men, such as making fire, Carring Potts of Sugar of 100 Weight wch often Occasions Violent Disorders & Miscarriages, and tends greatly to the Detriment of the General Interest." Another of the Codrington plantations, the Garden, faced a similar predicament, not having men enough to "Shift the spells in Crop time and frequently Obliged to make fire under ye Coppers and Stills with Women." A shortage of hands could also lengthen harvesting time. On one of the Codrington plantations in 1780, for example, had there been a "heavy Crop, there would have been almost unsurmountable difficulties in taking it off, at a proper & seasonable time." The hard life of labor to which Antigua slaves were normally exposed was clearly worse on shorthanded plantations. In 1754 Samuel Redhead noted that nine more slaves had died than were born since 1751 on the Codrington plantations, which, "considering the circumstances being obliged to work them pretty Smartly, is a small difference. When we come to be fully handed I hope the even ballance will be on the Other Side as then the labour will not be so hard. I judge an addition of one hundred & fifty workers more will be a pretty compleat Strength and enable us to do great things."[39]

That Antigua planters, at the best of times, could count on only a portion of their slaves to tend the fields can be demonstrated through an examination of Betty's Hope plantation in 1751, where details of the occupational distribution of the slaves according to such criteria as age, sex, and strength can also be analyzed. Of the 277 slaves belonging to the plantation, there were 140 males and 137 females. Only 143 slaves (56 males and 87 females), not quite 52 percent, were fit enough to be assigned to field work. The first gang of "able working" slaves numbered 98, a little over 35 percent, of all the slaves on the plantation. While three-quarters of the slave women worked in the field, less than half of the men were similarly employed; one-third of all men were tradesmen. Clearly, a larger proportion of slave women than men worked in the field. The occupational distribution was also more distinctly varied for men. On Betty's Hope plantation, the weaker and younger slaves were also assigned to tasks more compatible to their condition, so that they, too, were productive to some degree. The small gang of grown boys and girls, probably twelve years or older, did good service in the field.

Runaways and sickness among the Betty's Hope slaves often reduced the number of field hands that could be employed: "We seldom exceed 60 Negroes able to make Cane holes unless it is at particular times when the Tradesmen have been taken in the Field to assist." The plantation was, in fact, woefully shorthanded: "As Betty's Hope Land in general is poor it never having been manured, there requires at least 60 or 70 able workers to be added to the present gang." In this situation, the work of young boys and girls made a difference; the small gang of around thirty young workers did "much more work in proportion than the Great Gang." Had it not been for them, "the Estate would be greatly distressed." The practice of shifting tradesmen from their regular occupations to help in the field indicates in another way the extent of the demand that might be made upon the slaves of plantations that were not "well slav'd." Even the supposedly specialist tradesmen were affected, to say nothing of the other ordinary slaves who had any health or strength left or the children who were old enough to work. In 1715, on another of the Codringtons' plantations, the manager was instructed "to keep all the Masons in the field."[40]

Perhaps the most striking feature of gang labor on plantations was its high degree of regimentation. But because sugar plantations were enterprises "with an industrial labour regime and a pronounced market orientation," all workers were subjected to the regularities and disciplines of field labor. Samuel Martin compared a sugar plantation to "a well-constructed machine, compounded of various wheels, turn-

ing different ways, and yet all contributing to the great end proposed."
The motion of these wheels had to be well coordinated for optimal
efficiency. Using a different metaphor, James Ramsay wrote that the
"discipline of a sugar plantation is as exact as that of a regiment."[41]
While the enforced discipline of plantation labor under racial slavery
created tensions and conflicts between masters and slaves, it also
shaped the worlds of the slaves through the amount of work demanded of them, the kind of work they did, and the few hours that
they called their own.

The Reverend Robertson observed cogently that sugar culture allowed "as little Respite from Labor as perhaps any sort of Business
whatsoever any where else." Compared to the many hours they spent
working for the master, Antigua slaves were allowed little time to rest,
to create a life of their own, or to interact with one another outside the
workplace or the context of work for the master. However, even in the
long shadow of the master's will, they successfully created space for
themselves in the interstices of the slave system. In response to the
stresses of slavery, Antigua slaves developed important forms of resistance, from malingering and flight to outright rebellion. Much of
their resistance was carried out in the context of work. It would be fair
to say that the culture of work and the culture of resistance were two of
the primary shapers of slave life. Robertson summarized this well
when he acknowledged that runaways took off when "their Labour, or
Attendance is most wanted."[42]

The plantation slaves of Antigua made full use of their "free time"
to improve the quality of their lives beyond that of mere beasts of
burden and toil.[43] Most of this time was concentrated at the end of the
workweek, between Saturday noon and Monday morning. The heavy
demands of harvest sometimes cut short this respite, but most plantation slaves looked forward to being "off" for a day-and-a-half, and they
devoted much of this time to activities for which no other time was
available. The most common of these was attending to provision
grounds on the plantations. However, because of Antigua's small size,
few planters set aside ample acres of land, and the provision-ground
system which characterized the domestic economy of Jamaica, a much
larger territory, was not as common in Antigua. Food for slaves was
made available through a less uniform system. Some plantations allocated "Negro ground" on which individual slaves cultivated their own
small sections, or else slaves worked under supervision on the plantation's common provision ground. On the Codrington plantations in
1755 "one or two Canes pieces" were "every year in Provisions for the

Negroes." Between 1739 and 1759 on Winthorpe's plantation, slave gangs raised potatoes, yams, and guinea corn under supervised labor on a central plot of land, and they also received weekly rations from the plantation store. Antigua slaves raised mostly yams, but also eddoes, potatoes, plantains, guinea corn and, by the 1790s, American corn.[44]

At the end of the eighteenth century, Jamaica planter-historian Bryan Edwards observed, in regard to feeding the slaves, that the provision-ground system represented "a happy coalition of interests between the master and the slave." This comment is more relevant to the character of the fully developed system than to its origins, which remain obscure. For the British Leeward Islands, at least, provision grounds may have been allocated to combat the prevalence of theft by hungry slaves, starting in the seventeenth century. Because "the many Thefts and robberys Committed in this Island by Negroes have been for the greatest part occasioned through their Masters not planting or allowing them any provision or Soe exceeding Little that they are not able to Subsist upon it," the Nevis legislature ruled in 1682 that "Every Master of a family owner or Renter of any plantation shall for Every working Slave hee hath, man or woman, plant one thousand plants Ground in provision upon penalty of one thousand pounds of Sugar to bee immediately paid, five hundred to the publick Receiver and five hundred to the Informer, and all persons are hereby required to Give an account of any that Neglect to perform this Act." While such legislation does not appear in the Antigua records, similar problems associated with slave theft may have persuaded the planters to follow their neighbors in Nevis.[45] Custom and opinion, which were the foundation of local colonial laws, often did not crystallize into actual laws during Antigua's formative years as a sugar colony, but they nevertheless shaped relations between master and slave significantly.

In any case, most sugar planters in Antigua relied wholly or partly on the rationing of imported supplies to feed their slaves. Antigua, unlike Jamaica, was largely foreign fed. Reliance on outside sources tempted planters to keep their food bill as low as possible and to provide slaves with only the barest minimum of imported rations. Walter Tullideph found another solution. In 1757 he sent his slave Charles to Maryland merchant Henry Lowes to be sold, "the only reason" being that Charles had "a voracious appetite which will better suit you than us." Short supplies, brought about by a variety of causes, often resulted in subsistence crises and increased hardship for slaves. The worst subsistence crisis of the eighteenth century occurred during the American Revolution, when food supplies from the mainland colonies were severely curtailed. Every year during the hurricane season, which could stretch from July to September, supply ships also avoided the Caribbean. This interruption of trade exacerbated the hardships associated with food scarcity, which started during the dry months of harvest when yields of locally grown provisions were low. Therefore, according to Robert Dirks, field slaves "endured prolonged periods of backbreaking labor while subsisting on stingy rations, storable grains and starchy tubers," during planting time in the wet season. This was the "hard-time" or "hungry-time" described in Barbados.[46]

Drought, a constant visitor to Antigua, often made matters worse. Elderly slaves who had grown up on the island retained memories of recurrent drought and perceived these visitations as part of their lives. If it was not easy for island-born slaves to cope with the difficulties of drought, life must have been unbearable for traumatized Africans who had recently stepped off the slave ships. Compared with hurricanes and accidental fires, wrote Robertson, drought was "the surest and severest" of all the disasters common to the sugar islands, particularly the Leeward Islands. In his words, "the Drought is generally followed by an Army of Worms, Flies, and other Insects, which eat up what little green things are left on the Earth; then comes a scarcity of Indian Provisions, and a proportionable Dearth of those from England, Ireland, and the North Continent; then a most dreadful Mortality among the Negroes and Live-Stock, Crops next to nothing, and Ships returning with dead Freight." As there were no rivers in Antigua, planters stored water in tanks, and slaves dug ponds on the plantations to collect water. There were four ponds on one Codrington plantation, The Cotton, in 1755.[47]

Apart from working on their provision grounds on Saturdays and Sundays, Antigua slaves used their concentrated stretch of "free time" to take care of household chores, tend to the small kitchen gardens near their quarters, repair their houses, make handicraft goods, collect wood for sale, visit and care for the sick, interact as families, participate in group entertainments, often accompanied by music and dancing—and to rest. Sunday was the preferred day for these activities, but some slaves also attended worship at the Moravian and Methodist chapels and at the Anglican church by the later eighteenth century. Robertson admitted in 1729 that "I scarce know one Master who pretends to hinder, but rather encourages his Field-Slaves to work for themselves on the Lord's Day; nay he is esteem'd, and always proves, the best Slave who chuses rather to work on that Day than to make it

wholly a Day of Rest, or of pleasure." Masters paid their field slaves for
Sunday work as porters.

On Sundays, too, slaves held or were allowed to hold their own
markets. The main market was situated at the southern end of the
main town of Saint John's, at the junction of three roads that ran in
different directions through the country region beyond.[48] Robertson
explained that the development of markets and other features of the
autonomy that slaves enjoyed on Sundays originated during the early
days of the slave society's emergence in the seventeenth century,
when planters "overlook'd and abandon'd" them for a day after the
week's hard labor. The result was that "such of them as were naturally
industrious, or ambitious of making a finer Figure than their Fellows,
or had several Wives to please and gratify, employ'd the Day in labouring for themselves." Other slaves "made it a Day of Rest, and for
greater part a Day of Sport, till the Thing was found, when it came to
be look'd into by the Publick, to have grown to such a Head as not to
be soon or easily crush'd." By the early eighteenth century, slaves
claimed Sunday "as peculiarly their own." Robertson admitted that
"without doubt many of the Masters were not fond of disputing the
Point with them, as believing that this unbounded Liberty of doing
what they listed on the Lord's Day made their Slavery fit the easier all
the rest of the Week." In this context, Antigua slaves transformed
privilege into a right that masters or legislators dared not tamper with,
except to regulate the conduct of slaves on Sundays.

While Robertson, writing in the 1720s, believed that steps might be
taken to convert Antigua slaves and those in the rest of the Leeward
Islands to Christianity, he thought that these efforts should neither
interfere with the Sunday markets nor with the slaves' custom of
working for themselves. Whatever regulations governed or even restricted the Sunday activities of Caribbean slaves, Robertson noted
that "no Attempts that I know of were ever made in any of our Sugar-
Colonies to hinder the Field-Slaves from Labouring on their own
Account on the Lord's Day, and were any such to be made as the Case
stands now, they would, in my Opinion, prove wholly fruitless, if not
worse." Should a planter be "so mad as to command his Slaves to work
in the Field" on Sunday, "they would disobey him, and run away with
one consent." Robertson's central point was that "Slaves have (or,
which is the same, think they have) some Rights and Privileges, of
which they are as tenacious as any Freeman upon Earth can be of
theirs, and which no Master of common Sense will once attempt to
violate."[49] According to a report of 1789, with the exception of the

Christmas holidays, which had the force of law, other privileges were supported simply by custom or "Humanity and good Policy."[50] The Antigua legislature never passed a single act to recognize and support the Sunday markets during the entire slave period. In 1831, however, the legislature announced its intention to abolish the markets as part of a program to ameliorate slavery. Faced with such a threat, the slaves responded. To defend and extend their right to the markets they demanded legal guarantees of a new common market day. When the legislature refused, intense slave unrest followed.[51]

With Sunday markets firmly established as a central dimension of commercial and social life among Antigua slaves, slaveholders set about regulating what they could not prevent. The comprehensive 1697 "Act for the better Government of Slaves" contained at least three clauses that were in some way related to Sunday markets. The first prohibited slaves from leaving their plantations on Sundays without tickets or passes from their masters giving them permission, or unless a white servant accompanied them. Passes were required to show the names and the number of slaves, who were granted leave to proceed from a stated place to a specific destination. The only slaves exempted from these regulations were "Such as usually wait On Their [Masters'] person or go in Liveries." A second clause prohibited all slaves, who were lawfully absent from their plantations, from selling goods after ten o'clock on Sunday morning, by which time they were supposed to return home. Slaves who violated this law could be arrested and whipped, and owners could redeem them in the manner prescribed for fugitives. Clearly stated, the intent of the law was so that "no Staying to drink rum, or other mischievous devices may be encouraged by over long Staying, or numerous Assemblying together." A third clause ruled that no person should sell "any Rum at all" to slaves on Sundays, "or any Sort of dry goods, (by barter or otherwaies)." Each offense carried a fine of £3. In 1702 a new act declared that slaves should find their way home by ten o'clock on Sunday morning "to the Intent that all Opportunities of Idleness and Robbery may be taken away," but this rewording obviously did not alter the meaning of the earlier formulation. These resolutions were not enforced, however. In 1788 Luffman observed that slaves began to assemble by daybreak at the St. John's market, and by ten o'clock it was crowded: "This is the proper time to purchase, for the week, such articles as are not perishable."[52]

Antiguan laws intended to control the conduct of slaves on Sunday had no lasting effect. In 1714 Antigua legislators passed a new act "for the better regulating Negroes and the suppressing their Conspiracies and Profanation of the Lords' Day." The full text of the act has not survived, but its title suggests that slaves persisted in regarding Sunday "as peculiarly their own." In 1715 the legislature drew attention to the failure of the 1702 act.[53] Seven years later they repealed the 1714 act because it proved to be "highly inconvenient and, instead of answering the good Ends proposed," it had "put the Public to great and unnecessary Changes, begot Riots and Disorders between White Men and Negro slaves, and in a great Measure rendered . . . Slaves a prey to idle and ill-disposed persons." These "Riots and Disorders" evidently occurred when slaves defended themselves against whites pretending to prevent "Negroes carrying on a Trade in Stolen Goods between the Town and Country." Governor John Hart explained that whites were authorized "to Seize the Goods, Provisions or whatever they found with a Negro not haveing a Ticket from his Master which, the next Justice was obliged to condemn to the use of the Person making the Seizure." Many whites conspired to turn the law to their advantage. One of them "would demand a Negroes Ticket; if he had none the Seizure was made; if he had one it was taken and torn and then the Negro unavoidably fell into the Hands of the others, who way laid him at some distance and plundered him for want of it." That kind of robbery became so prevalent that "no Negro could pass with Security with any Goods of his Masters or his own."[54] In this way, slaves who were on their way to market on Sunday with their goods, stolen or not, often lost everything.

At the markets, barter was the predominant mode of exchange among the slaves who undoubtedly brought stolen goods, but they also offered for sale a variety of merchandise that they had acquired lawfully, including portions of their weekly rations. Among the most common items for trade were poultry, fruits, vegetables, roots, handicraft goods, and livestock.[55] Some food crops were cultivated more easily on some parts of the island. The markets therefore provided a way for slaves to vary their diet somewhat. According to one Antigua planter at the end of the eighteenth century, yams—which thrived in light soil—were raised in the east, northeast, and northwest districts of the island. Eddoes grew well in clay soil; corn did well in either. Plantains did best in rich, moist ground, or near rivulets.[56] Market sellers of these various goods were most probably women.[57]

Not all slaves who attended the markets came to trade. Markets were also social occasions, many slaves often traveling miles as porters or vendors to attend the lively central market in St. John's town. Slaves

from the easternmost parish of St. Philip had to cover between thirteen and fifteen miles to reach town. Daniel McKinnen remarked,
following a visit to Antigua in 1802, that on Sunday "the whole negro
population of the island seems in motion. The clothes in which they
appear, and the property they display on these occasions, would
induce one to believe that the rigors of slavery, on many estates, are
not a little softened by the liberality and benevolence of the masters."[58]
McKinnen should have given more credit to the initiative of the slaves
themselves, many of whom used every available opportunity to improve their lives.

While the markets were in progress white constables and the militia were on duty to maintain order. Fights often broke out. The 1723
slave act observed that Antigua slaves "do frequently on Saturdays in
the afternoon, and Sundays, gather and assemble in great Numbers in
and about the Town of St. Johns, and commit Riots, and sometimes kill
one another, to the great Terror and actual endangering of the Inhabitants." The act ruled that slaves caught fighting were to be whipped
publicly by order of a justice if "any Slave draws a Knife, either in
assaulting another, or in his own Defence." After the market ended
many slaves hung about town to gamble or otherwise divert themselves in "Otto's Pasture, and Long's, or Morgan's Pasture" nearby;
others made their way to the grogshops, several of which, according
to a report of 1740, were located, not surprisingly, next to "Otto's
Pasture and the Negro Market" in one of the most disreputable sections of town. Other slaves left town for the plantations, where they
organized afternoon dances.[59] On the one full day that they could
claim their own, Antigua slaves used their time as they saw fit to color
and enrich their lives in ways that were unconnected with work on the
master's time. These activities often strained or broke the boundaries
of behavior permitted by law.

A fraction of the free time of Antigua's plantation slaves came at
Easter and Christmas. Robertson explained that the catharsis these
holidays provided was as important to the texture of slave life and
ideal relations between master and slaves as the Sunday markets and
the slaves' customary right to work for themselves. Antigua slaves
were granted holidays at Easter and Christmas "to be employ'd in
such Labour or Diversions" as did not subvert law and order. Especially at Christmas, slaves used the relative freedom of mobility
and expression that the holiday made possible to invert the master-
slave relation through various festivities. During such seasons of "unbounded freedom" in the sugar colonies, when the slaves were "un-

usually idle and dissipated," whites guarded the towns and patrolled the highways at night "for fear of Mischief from the Combinations of their Slaves."[60] Merriment, excitement, and the possibility of revolt clearly went hand-in-hand. Robert Dirks has shown that among the seventy documented cases of slave revolts and conspiracies in the British sugar colonies between 1649 and 1833, more than a third occurred or were planned to take place in December. Whether these affairs were planned or spontaneous, the December "riotors and insurgents," according to Dirks, "responded to conditions they themselves did not entirely appreciate." The "pronounced seasonality in the slaves' regimen," however, probably played a significant role in the complex process that made Christmastime potentially explosive.[61]

Antigua slaves were deeply attached to the holiday season, and they defended their right to it—sometimes successfully. In December 1701 fifteen Coromantee slaves from the Gold Coast killed their master, Major Samuel Martin, allegedly because he had forced them to work during the Christmas holidays. In response to a report about the incident from Governor Christopher Codrington, the Board of Trade in England noted that since the cause of Martin's violent end "seems probably to have been some extraordinary Severity towards his Negroes we are the more Sensible of the expediency of a Law for restraining inhumane Severity not only toward Christian Servants but Slaves." Francis Le Jau, a missionary of the Society for the Propagation of the Gospel in Foreign Parts and resident of the Leeward Islands during the late seventeenth century, added his own condemnation of planters for treating their slaves "worse than beasts." Up to the time that Martin was killed, holidays for slaves at Easter and Christmas were not guaranteed by law, the validation of the slaves' rights to this time residing instead in custom and opinion. However, in 1723 the Antigua legislature recognized the slaves' right to Christmas holidays by passing a special law. Slave resistance, in fact, caused these slave-owning legislators to reconsider how their material interests would be better served. The 1723 act acknowledged that "great Disorders have happened, and Murders have been committed by Slaves, because their Masters have not allowed them the same Number of Days for their Recreation at Christmas, as several of their Neighbours have done." The law therefore ruled that masters were to give all slaves, "except those necessary about their Houses," Christmas day and the two following days "as Play-Days for their Recreation, and no more, or other Days." Slaveowners who violated the law faced a fine of £20.[62]

The law regarding Christmas holidays was, however, repealed in

1778. The new act explained that the "Alterations of Times and Circumstances" had made it and another law about militia duty at Christmas "improper." Furthermore, these laws had long been "so slightly or irregularly" enforced that their original intent regarding militia duty had been nullified. Thus, new laws were "absolutely necessary and proper." The act stipulated that Antigua slaves should have for their Christmas holidays "the whole Time from Sun-set on Christmas Eve to Sun-rise of the twenty-eighth Day of December, in each Year, and no more, nor any other Days in the twelve Christmas Days Holidays." The force of this law differed little from that of the 1723 act, although the wording was more precise to avoid misunderstanding about the duration of the holidays and to avoid abuses. Slaves who would not necessarily have a claim to the holidays were carefully identified as those about their masters' "Houses or Person." With the consent of their owners, though, such slaves could join the others in enjoying the holiday season.[63]

During the last decade of the eighteenth century, when the slave trade came under heavy attack in Britain, planters of Antigua and the other Leeward Islands tried to deflect the abolitionists' criticism by initiating legislation to reform the worst abuses of slavery. Most of this legislation was included in the Leeward Islands Amelioration Act of 1798, which addressed a number of issues that would later affect the quality of slave life.[64] Only a handful of regulations dealt directly with the question of conditions of slave labor. Parts of the act set new standards regarding time for rest, meals, and work but only indirectly addressed the issue of the actual amount of work that could be expected from a slave. At the same time, some women were to receive special consideration in regard to work. In the face of the approaching abolition of the slave trade, the sugar planters paid particular attention to conditions that affected the health and reproductive capacities of slave women. Thus, the act decreed that all slave women with six living children who were born while the mother and father lived together as wife and husband were entitled to be assigned only light work. Similarly, another clause stated that women who were at least five months pregnant were to be employed only in taking care of children on the plantation or in other light work. That the planters of Antigua and the other Leeward Islands intended these rather minimal regulations to improve the conditions under which plantation slaves lived and worked gives some indication of the harsh conditions that existed before.[65]

It is impossible to separate work and slave life in the Americas, so tightly and intricately were they intertwined. To examine the one is to uncover, at the same time, dimensions of the other. Of all the approaches the historian might choose to adopt toward slave life, an analysis of work is arguably among the best. Slaveowners intended work to define the existence and status of the slave. On the sugar plantations of Antigua in the seventeenth and eighteenth centuries, slaves represented the chief investment of proprietors, who organized their work routines with profit foremost in mind. So long as it was possible to obtain replacements for slaves who were no longer productive, Antigua planters paid little attention to preserving the health and lives of their work force—up until the very end of the eighteenth century, when they realized that access to slaves from Africa would be terminated. Under the harsh regimen of plantation slavery during the seventeenth and eighteenth centuries, however, Antigua slaves coped, but survival was a constant struggle. The use slaves made of their free time was an important part of the struggle. It gave them opportunities for release from the pressures of life and labor connected with the master's time. Thus, the duration of both kinds of time and the meaning that slaves attached to each category were significant shapers of slave life and primary products of the work environment. However, that environment was only partly determined by the requirements of sugar production. In whatever ways the specific character of work on Antigua plantations influenced the development of slave life and culture, other facets of the plantation and colonial environment must be taken into account, including the attitude of African and Creole slaves to forced labor; various other elements of their culture; the physical environment in which they lived; and the attitudes of slaveowners toward labor, especially the labor of people who were regarded as inferior. The process of sorting out the relative influence on slave life of the many dimensions of the environment of slavery in Antigua begins to explain the extent to which the slaves were able to modify the work process.

4

COFFEE PLANTERS AND COFFEE SLAVES IN THE ANTILLES: THE IMPACT OF A SECONDARY CROP

Michel-Rolph Trouillot

C OFFEE ENTERED THE Americas in the second decade of the eighteenth century, at a time when the export-oriented production of other agricultural commodities—notably sugar, cotton, and indigo—already informed both the organization of labor and the social life of most of the Antilles. In part because of this, the introduction of coffee into the New World did not lead immediately to large-scale, export-oriented cultivation. Furthermore, since the European coffee plantations in the Indian Ocean region were proving quite profitable to Dutch and French entrepreneurs, monopolies soon shielded Old World production from Caribbean competition. Coffee from Martinique, Guadeloupe, and Saint Domingue found its way to Europe, but only in small quantities. Of the Caribbean coffee producers, only Suriname had any importance on the world market. In most of the Antilles large-scale cultivation thus lagged until the 1730s, when some of the restrictions against the importation of Caribbean coffee into Europe, notably France and England, were lifted.

From the mid-1730s, however, coffee became a secondary crop of major importance in the Caribbean. Between 1734 and 1873 coffee cultivation increased so rapidly that few contemporaries failed to notice its social and economic impact. In many cases, profits from coffee exports were second only to those from sugar, and although a distant second, they were substantial. Immediately prior to the Revolution, the value of coffee exports in Saint Domingue matched the value of white sugar exports and equaled more than two-thirds of the value from the export of raw sugar. Between 1805 and 1814 the annual average value of coffee exports in Jamaica was nearly half that of

124

sugar.[1] Coffee was also significant in the Spanish territories. In Puerto Rico and Cuba coffee occupied a substantial amount of land, in part because of the large numbers of small properties on which it was produced. In Puerto Rico the acreage in coffee often surpassed that of sugar cane during the first four decades of the nineteenth century. In Cuba, where coffee exports were significant from the 1790s to the late 1840s, the 1827 census counted 2,067 coffee haciendas, twice the number of sugar mills.[2]

As the units of production multiplied, the number of slaves cultivating coffee also increased. Monocultural coffee cultivation in Jamaica occupied 15 to 17 percent of the slave labor force between 1810 and 1832. Estates where coffee was produced in combination with other crops employed another 2 percent of Jamaica's slaves. This left coffee far behind sugar (70 percent) but still the uncontested leader among the secondary crops. In post-1780 Martinique coffee production often employed almost as many slaves as all the other secondary crops combined. A similar situation existed in Guadeloupe, where a sample of 213 *habitations* shows 23 percent of the slaves living on *caféières*. In Dominica coffee slaves were even more numerous than slaves engaged in sugar production.[3] In short, from the second quarter of the eighteenth century to the third quarter of the nineteenth century, hundreds of planters in various islands saw their fate tied to this crop, and they exacted the labor of thousands of slaves to make its cultivation profitable.

That these planters shared similar goals of profit and faced roughly the same material requirements does not imply, however, that the overall consequences of coffee cultivation were always the same. Time and space matter, because of the changes in the world economy and because of the varied responses of specific territories. The impact of coffee on a particular slave colony was shaped by—among other things—the availability of African slaves, fluctuations in the European market, and competition from other producers in the Caribbean region and elsewhere. On the basis of these global changes, the evolution of slave-based coffee production in the Antilles can be divided into four periods.[4]

The mid-1730s to the early 1760s, the first period, was a time of rapid growth. Building upon the changes of those years, the second period—1763 to 1791, from the Peace of Paris to the slave uprising in Saint Domingue—was the golden age of coffee production in the Antilles. The aftermath of the Haitian Revolution, characterized by abrupt changes in the international market—specifically, an initial rise in prices, followed by overproduction and the crisis of the 1830s and 1840s, when Brazilian competition became intense—crippled most Caribbean planters. These years can be considered the third period. Thereafter, Caribbean slave-based coffee production declined sharply.

Within each of these periods, responses to booms and busts varied in accordance with the local availability of land and capital, affecting the sociospatial organization of particular territories differently. On many mountainous islands coffee planters could develop interior enclaves. Elsewhere, coffee competed for space with sugar—usually without success. Three different outcomes can be identified. First, certain societies were wholly dominated by coffee; Dominica from the 1730s to the 1830s is a prime example. Second, in some territories a significant amount of coffee production occurred in the crevices of a sugar-dominated plantation economy. Most of the British sugar islands—certainly Jamaica before 1790, Saint Domingue between 1734 and 1763, Martinique during the same period and later, and Cuba in the second half of the nineteenth century—fall into this category. Finally, there were territories with coffee-dominated enclaves, that is, colonies where the presence of an internal frontier, in combination with the demographic and social significance of free people who were not sugar planters, resulted in the settlement or consolidation of coffee-dominated parishes or municipalities. Among these stand Guadeloupe and Saint Domingue after the Peace of Paris, Jamaica after the coffee boom of the 1790s, and possibly Puerto Rico in the first half of the nineteenth century.[5]

The development of coffee cultivation and the social organization of space it produced occurred in different contexts. In most of the French colonies and in Jamaica coffee became the most important secondary crop, but only after these colonies had already entered a mature plantation phase dominated by sugar. In Dominica, by contrast, coffee production paralleled the development of the plantation system, and its importance preceded that of sugarcane, which became the dominant crop only after the coffee crisis of the 1830s and 1840s. In Cuba and Puerto Rico coffee experienced a long period of incubation, which paralleled the revitalization of sugarcane cultivation.[6]

These different sequences suggest that the overall impact of coffee on slave life and culture varied according to the intersection of two processes: economic exploitation and creolization. Coffee was almost everywhere a secondary crop, and secondary crops gained in importance only to the extent that they could fit within—or modify—local and international arrangements created to accommodate the dominant crop. With success often hinging upon local adaptation, secondary crops tended to promote diversity, whereas sugarcane—the primary crop par excellence—favored homogenization. Coffee attracted investors who were economically and socially differentiated. The production of secondary crops like coffee thus enhanced the opportunities of various groups within the free population—white, black, and "colored." It also limited and hampered the chances of others.

In post-1763 Saint Domingue, for instance, the presence of an internal frontier allowed free people marginal to the sugar economy to gain significant control of production within growing coffee enclaves. *Gens de couleur*, free blacks, and recent immigrants—including members of the petty nobility unable to penetrate the world of sugar after the Peace of Paris—were largely responsible for opening new coffee parishes in the interior. They took their chances with coffee and, for a time at least, high returns rewarded many, enabling them to improve not only their economic position but also their social status—no small achievement for nonwhite planters.[7] Free coloreds seem to have found an economic niche with coffee, among other crops, in Grenada as well. In Dominica free coloreds—especially those who traced their descent from the days of French control—constituted a significant share of the owners of coffee plantations. In the first decade of the nineteenth century "French" owners also dominated coffee production in Trinidad.[8]

Indeed, in many Caribbean colonies coffee seems to have been the preferred crop of the underdog in the free segment of the population—free blacks, European settlers of modest means, and ethnic or religious minorities. Their chances varied from one colony to the next, but the attraction of coffee can be easily explained: a combination of limited capital requirements and relatively high returns, which stemmed in turn from the physical properties and requirements of the crop, its cultivation and mode of preparation for the market, and the rapid expansion of European demand after 1763. Of course, conditions of establishment varied from place to place, and so did actual costs. Even within the same colony the mode and time of development resulted in significant differences among enclaves, as the cases of Jamaica and Saint Domingue suggest. Both colonies boasted coffee enterprises whose operating capital or labor force rivaled that of some sugar plantations. But most coffee plantations were relatively modest enterprises. More important, as far as coffee was concerned plantation size was neither a simple measure nor a condition of success. In Saint Domingue it may have been possible to operate a *caféière* with as little as one-sixth of the capital required for a sugar plantation. In 1835 the average coffee plantation in Guadeloupe was worth 42,318 francs, compared to 323,984 francs for a sugar plantation.[9] Coffee *could* be a small investor's choice, an underdog's stepping stone, and many in the Antilles tied their fortunes to its promise.

Not that an owner's underdog position among the free was any help to their slaves. At times, quite the opposite was true. Owners and managers of small plantations often sidestepped seasonal variations in the use of the labor force by putting their slaves to other tasks. In mid-eighteenth-century Guadeloupe small coffee and cotton growers with twelve to fifteen slaves rented their slaves to the sugar plantations. In nineteenth-century Jamaica the few coffee planters with large holdings did the same. Such practices, also common in other territories, may have jeopardized the slaves' welfare even more than the regular routine of sugar production. One suspects that the sugar planter who rented slaves from coffee plantations exploited these coffee gangs to the fullest. Thus, the mortality rate on coffee-labor plantations was slightly higher in Jamaica between 1829 and 1832 than on monocultural coffee units. Birthrates on coffee-labor units were among the lowest, even lower than on jobbing units, and higher only than on units engaged in wharfage during the same period.[10] To put it bluntly, the underdog among the free achieved success and survival at the slave's expense. Indeed, placing increased pressure on the slave was often the most expedient means for the owner to shed his underdog status.

Both the social and ethnic origins of the owners mattered, since they affected language, religious practices, daily behavior, and attitudes—often in ways that still remain to be deciphered. The concentration of colored coffee owners of French descent in northern St. Andrew, in Dominica, contributed to the cultural distinction of that enclave. Even in the late twentieth century northern St. Andrew remains more attuned to French-derived ways than many areas of Dominica—and certainly much more than the southern part of the same parish, where the influence of English-speaking Protestant sugarcane attorneys was much greater during the slavery period.[11] Northerners within the parish still speak a French-based Antillean Creole, while Southerners speak English or the English-based Kòkòy. Northerners remain primarily Catholic; Protestant denominations have much larger congregations in the southern part of the parish.[12] Clearly, throughout the Americas the origins of masters and the crops that slaves produced combined to influence cultural patterns in distinctive enclaves in ways that remained relevant long after emancipation. For instance, the cultural role of residual "French" coffee owners in Windward Islands other than Dominica and in nineteenth-century Trinidad needs to be ascertained, as does that of lower-class Frenchmen and *gens de couleur* in Saint Domingue. Meredith John, who has found that African men of French and Spanish owners were more likely to survive than slaves who lived on British estates in Trinidad, hints that this may have been due to the low rate of absentee ownership among Catholics.[13]

The form and timing of the integration of coffee as a secondary crop also affected the ethnic composition of the slave labor force on the various units of production. That coffee plantations followed the initial expansion of sugar in many Caribbean islands explains in part their smaller proportion of creole slaves. After the Peace of Paris plantation owners in the emerging coffee enclaves of Saint Domingue turned to the cheapest and most abundant source of labor. Their adversaries claimed, no doubt exaggerating, that their new enterprises employed as many as three-fifths of the slaves introduced in the colony between 1767 and 1777. But the coffee revolution certainly contributed to the great number of "Congos" in the highlands of Saint Domingue, not only because Congos figured heavily among the imports at the time of the coffee boom but also because coffee planters of modest means had difficulty competing for slaves from the preferred ethnic groups.[14] A similar concentration of Africans obtained in the Jamaican coffee enclaves of Manchester and Port Royal after the 1790s.[15]

The correlation between coffee and a relatively high African presence was not universal, partly because different histories of settlement afforded coffee planters different alternatives. Notably in Puerto Rico, because of the prior development of the free population creole slaves worked alongside of free wage laborers on coffee plantations in the first half of the nineteenth century. In late eighteenth-century Guadeloupe Africans made up about 19 percent of the labor force on the *caféières*, compared to 23 percent on sugar plantations. In 1813 the proportion of creoles on Trinidad coffee plantations was higher than on sugar units (or on cacao plantations for that matter), in part because coffee was then declining and sugarcane expanding.[16]

When and where the correlation between African slaves and coffee was strong, it influenced the sexual balance of the slave population. Males often predominated among the Africans on coffee plantations, which may have been due to the purchasing patterns of coffee planters, as well as the disproportionate employment of female slaves in the sugarcane fields.[17] In addition, coffee planters preferred to use males during the initial period of settlement, when clearing forest land was of utmost importance.[18] Thus, inventories of "young" coffee plantations may show a smaller proportion of women than those of long-established units.

The influence of any crop on the labor force was neither restricted to the period of expansion nor even to the period of cultivation. Slaves who survived the demise of their plantation, who witnessed sudden shifts in cultivation patterns, or who gained their freedom were not suddenly transformed into new individuals. They carried with them a cultural baggage weighted down by their immediate past. Because of the insecurity inherent in their owners' underdog status, coffee slaves were quite susceptible to abrupt occupational changes. As a secondary crop, coffee was often perceived as having an uncertain future in societies fixated on sugar, and coffee planters tended to sell or diversify in situations where sugar planters chose to maintain the old order. Hurricanes, plant blight, erosion, epidemics, and especially slumps in export prices led to the transfer of slaves from coffee to sugarcane plantations.

Examples are numerous. In Jamaica, as many as four thousand slaves from about seventy plantations were moved from coffee to sugarcane production between 1805 and 1815. In Cuba as many as thirty thousand slaves may have been transferred from coffee to sugar during the crisis of the 1830s and its aftermath. Undetermined numbers of slaves were also transferred when total coffee acreage decreased at the beginning of the nineteenth century in the colony of Guadeloupe. On Marie-Galante, one of the islands in the colony, coffee acreage decreased from 17 percent of the total in 1790 to one percent in 1835. Similar transitions occurred in British Guiana and in Martinique in the 1830s.[19] In Dominica the change occurred *after* the end of slavery. In the late 1830s, in the midst of the coffee crisis, a blight affecting the trees severely eroded the fragile confidence of the coffee growers. Many uprooted their trees, and those who could converted to sugarcane.[20] Thus, many former coffee *slaves* became sugar plantation *laborers*. And in Haiti, the impact of behavior and attitudes learned on the coffee plantations carried over after the Revolution.

The significance of these many histories within history—the conditions of settlement, expansion, or demise—can, however, easily be exaggerated.[21] If the larger context of production mattered, it did so because it influenced daily life on the plantations themselves. The overall impact of coffee cultivation was felt by the slaves, first and foremost, right on the plantations on which they labored. Three characteristics of those plantations had a particularly significant impact on slave life: their relative small size, their highland location, and their comparatively simple and undemanding organization of labor.[22]

Relative smallness of both the labor force and the material property itself was the norm among coffee plantations throughout the Antilles. Compared to sugar plantations—some of which had their own internal road system and their "negro village"—coffee estates were ventures of quite modest dimensions, in terms of both living space and cultivated space. More important, coffee plantations had many fewer slaves than sugar estates. Even in Jamaica, where both the initial investment and overhead costs of coffee planters were substantially higher than on other islands, there were 128 slaves per coffee holding as opposed to 223 per sugar plantation in 1832.[23] By and large the slave populations of coffee plantations were much lower, even in late eighteenth-century Saint Domingue—no exemplar of small sugar ventures. Prior to the Revolution most *caféières* there had forty or fewer slaves.[24] By 1835 the average *caféière* in Guadeloupe occupied 31.5 hectares and employed eighteen slaves, compared to the 143 hectares and seventy-nine slaves of a sugar plantation. In Dominica there were thirty slaves per coffee plantation in 1827, compared to 112 for sugar. In Martinique between 1822 and 1847 the average labor force on sugar plantations fluctuated between sixty-three and eighty-eight slaves, whereas the average number of slaves on coffee plantations was always below ten during the same period.[25] By 1813 there were seven slaves per coffee unit in Trinidad, compared to fifty-five per sugar plantation, most slaves living on units with a labor force of under twenty.[26] In St. Lucia, only a little over a third of coffee slaves worked on units with more than forty slaves. In mid-nineteenth-century Puerto Rico, coffee haciendas averaged as few as sixteen slaves, whose work was supplemented by a smaller number of wage earners—about six per unit.[27]

The highland location of coffee enterprises also influenced slave life and culture. Coffee slaves faced greater rainfall and cooler temperatures than slaves working in the plains, although observers disagree on the impact of these environmental factors on health and longevity. More important perhaps, highland location often meant isolation, and that, together with the small size of the labor force, produced distinctive relations between masters and slaves, as well as among the slaves themselves. Qualitative evidence, such as the descriptions provided by J. P. Laborie—a planter from Saint Domingue who wrote a much-used text on coffee cultivation—suggests an exceptionally close personal relationship between masters and slaves. In addition, a greater sense of community, or at least greater individual interaction, may have existed among coffee than among sugar slaves. In that sense, even though coffee estates may have operated as plantations (with a plantation labor process focused on an export economy), their social relations may have been closer to those prevalent on haciendas.[28]

At the same time, coffee slaves had less choice than their lowland counterparts in their personal decisions, and not just because they were more often under the close supervision of their masters. Size and isolation limited the slaves' movement beyond plantation boundaries (though not necessarily marronage), reinforcing the sense of seclusion. Laborie, who found the isolation personally advantageous, was reluctant to let his slaves go to the market and tried to confine them to a noncash economy. "The negroes in my district never went abroad," he observed. "I brought from the Cape all the articles which my negroes desired. These they received at the first cost, so that all the profits from the retail were saved to them. The payment was made in fowls, eggs, or other production at stated or market prices."[29]

This passage, as many others in Laborie's textbook, indicates that coffee planters exerted great control over their slaves. One wonders who set the "stated or market price" for the slaves' products. Yet Laborie's words also suggest a dependence on slaves unmatched in the lowlands. Many coffee planters were resident owners, for whom isolation meant both greater interaction with the slaves and greater self-sufficiency of the unit. Moreover, since coffee land was relatively cheap, planters were perhaps more willing to devote a substantial portion of their estate to the welfare of their slaves, especially since the labor force represented by far the highest share of their investment. Thus, for a number of reasons, coffee plantations—especially the caféière-résidences—tended to have substantial provision grounds, cultivated by the work force as a whole or allocated to individual slaves. A few combined both systems, relying primarily on large provision grounds for grains such as rice and maize, but with smaller gardens allocated to individual slaves. The Villars and Raby du Moreau plantations in the northern part of Saint Domingue set aside an amazing 33 percent of their cultivated area for provisions. Coffee units also tended to raise relatively more animals for internal consumption in relation to the size of their labor force, as well as a high proportion of slaves employed as domestics.[30]

Size and isolation generally increased cultural exchange, both between masters and slaves and within the slave population, thereby influencing the socialization of children, the institutionalization of religion, and the development of languages. Under most circumstances, greater interaction and self-sufficiency meant in turn a higher intensity of cultural exchange within the same unit. Although Afro-American cultures basically emerged from the crucible of the plantation *system,* their greatest growth took place somewhat on the margins of the *units,* in the space and time not devoted to the cultivation of export crops. This means that, in relatively densely populated areas, contacts across plantations were as important as contacts within the same unit. Social relationships and cultural encounters occurring on holidays or at market were far more vital than their infrequency might suggest.[31]

Size and isolation often affected relations within and across coffee plantations. First, given the relatively small size of the labor force, the social and cultural resources available in situ were restricted. For instance, once the labor force fell below a certain size, slaves of the same unit found their choice of marriage partners severely limited. Second, given the highland location of most units and the frontier character of many coffee parishes, spouses—and, for that matter, priests, friends, economic partners, teachers, and playmates—were also hard to find across plantation boundaries. Thus, coffee slaves had fewer ready-made choices in the creolization process.

This also meant, however, that other kinds of choices were more readily available. For if coffee slaves had fewer materials to draw from, they also had more freedom of combination.[32] For instance, whereas a slave had a limited choice in picking a local "specialist" (a priest, a drummer, or a healer), it is likely that both the local specialist and the majority accommodated more rapidly to each other's ways. Negotiations over cultural differences may have been carried out more openly and, perhaps, behavioral patterns became more profoundly entrenched.[33] The density of living quarters played a major role in this scenario, as the relatively crowded conditions in coffee slave houses reinforced the frequency and intensity of cultural exchanges within the plantation.[34] Further, in the absence of strongly established cultural conventions, coffee slaves probably had more room for improvisation, for adopting ways that would have seemed strange in the lowlands.

For instance, the post-1763 preponderance of newly arrived Congos on secluded *caféières* in the southern highlands of Saint Domingue affected Haitian culture to a degree that seems to qualify Mintz and Price's general rule that "fully formed Afro-American cultures developed within the earliest years of settlement."[35] The issue is the unit of analysis, the boundaries of the culture being formed. By the second half of the eighteenth century the north of Saint Domingue was more creolized than the south.[36] The fact that so many "Congos" ended up among themselves on highland coffee estates after 1763 may have modified the effect of prior creolization in the south. However, had an equal number of central African slaves been settled in the southern plains rather than the isolated units in the coffee parishes, the newly arrived Africans would have felt the impact of beliefs and behavior developed in the colony prior to their arrival much more strongly. Coffee slaves were no better or worse off culturally than others. Rather, the particular characteristics of the labor force within a given plantation—ethnicity, age, sex ratios, language, and religion of origins—mattered more on coffee units than on the larger sugar plantations or on the cotton and indigo plantations located in the lowlands.

Although the special features of slave life on a coffee plantation often evolved more in the time and space left free by the organization of labor, the slaves' culture on the coffee plantations of the Antilles was profoundly influenced by their work regimen. A number of contemporaries with axes to grind—sugar planters, attorneys, or high-level administrators often tied to the plantocracy—tried to establish coffee's reputation as a destroyer of slaves. They claimed that climatic and labor conditions in the highlands combined to decimate a large proportion of the labor force on coffee-producing units. The diatribe of Hilliard d'Auberteuil against this "deadly gift of Arabia," which he held responsible for the death of almost forty thousand slaves in Saint Domingue, was but one extreme case within this litany.[37] But mortality rates on coffee plantations were generally no higher than on sugar units.[38] Though the climate of the highlands must have been harsh on those slaves coming from African lowlands, tasks were less exhausting and labor organization less complicated on coffee than on sugar plantations, in part because the work process, from planting to delivery of the product to the exporters, was simpler.

Coffee production was a protracted but not particularly complicated process. The varieties of coffee then prevalent in the Antilles took four to seven years to mature, depending in part on the environment and in part on the spacing between the young trees. Coffee berries were picked when red and—ideally, at least—"washed" without delay in large basins of masonry where water softened the bark, thus preparing the beans for decortication. After a few days, the berries were put out to dry, usually on cement platforms or *glacis*. Dried berries were run through a rudimentary mill—activated most often by two mules, sometimes by water or by wind, or more rarely by two or more slaves—where the barks were broken open. After the milling, workers completed the decortication process by hand, discarded the spoiled berries and the barks. Acceptable beans were then bagged and ready for market.

The labor cycle on coffee units had two peaks, one occasional, the other seasonal. The occasional high point was the clearing of forested land intended for cultivation; the annual climax was the crop season. Coffee planters favored highland settlements on virgin soil, with cultivated sections on hillsides and living quarters on whatever passed for a flat surface. The initial clearing of forested land was by far the hardest of all tasks. Periods of intensive clearing recurred after installation, with planters pacing the rate of deforestation for a range of obvious reasons, such as conservation of tree cover, of labor, or of capital. Some planters hired gangs to perform clearing, as those who used their own slaves jeopardized the health of the most robust men, especially Africans forced to perform in wet weather.[39] Felling trees was throughout a hazardous operation.[40] The initial planting of coffee was also burdensome, especially the digging of thousands of holes each a foot in diameter and about sixteen inches deep to receive the young plants.[41]

Once a coffee plantation was settled, however, the work regimen was much less exhausting than that on a sugar estate, even in crop season when labor output reached its annual peak. Crop time varied widely, both in duration and in regard to the time of the year when it occurred, even though some patterns emerged in specific territories— spanning from nine weeks to three months and a half, most often after the end of the summer.[42] Nevertheless, crop time was arduous. Laborie, for instance, reduced his slaves' free time, often making them work part of Sunday, although with compensation.[43] But it was rather the intensity of the regimen than the difficulty of the tasks themselves that increased during crop time. The workday was extended and the mill often operated late into the evening, but it could be attended by as few as six men working in rotation. Further, even with the increased hours during crop time, the annual average hours that coffee slaves worked for their masters were generally lower than those of slaves working on sugar plantations.[44]

Apart from at crop time, work on a coffee plantation was rather monotonous, requiring few skills and little differentiation of the work force. Vanony-Frisch found only 3 percent of the slaves in Guadeloupe listed as skilled, compared to 13 percent on the island's sugar plantations. On Trinidad in 1813 coffee plantations had a higher percentage of field laborers (60 percent) than did estates devoted to any other crop. Large-scale plantations in Jamaica mimicked the three-gang system of the sugar estates, most likely for tighter control of labor output, but apparently with no long-term differentiation of tasks as such. When and where it occurred, the division of labor emphasized sex and age rather than skill, which in turn limited possibilities for promotion. For instance, drivers tended to be men, while women and children were generally employed in fertilizing the fields with manure. The very old and the very young sorted the beans after decortication.[45] The important tasks were mainly weeding, pruning, and picking the berries.

The workday was quite long by modern standards but rather uneventful. In Saint Domingue slaves went to the fields before sunrise, with a half-hour respite for breakfast at about nine o'clock. On some plantations a longer break occurred at midday, from about twelve to two, and work resumed until sunset. However, many Saint Domingue planters skipped the second pause altogether, deferred breakfast until later in the morning, and stopped the working day earlier, about an hour and a half before sunset.[46]

Supervision was generally limited, even in crop season. On Saint Domingue Laborie found it "neither necessary nor perhaps proper (particularly where the drivers are trusty and skillful) that the master or overseer remain constantly behind the negroes at work, and still less when they are weeding or gathering."[47] Picking berries was not the easiest of tasks, and slaves fell, hurt themselves, or damaged the trees by trying to reach for coffee berries while carrying increasingly heavy containers—baskets or bags sometimes tied to their arms or their necks. Still, overseers monitored slaves more to control the quality of their work and to prevent damage to both trees and berries than to regulate labor output. Indeed, as coffee cultivation expanded in the Antilles, many planters adopted the task system, assigning their slaves specific chores to be completed within a certain time period, sometimes a week, more often a workday. On some coffee plantations, chores were distributed according to such quotas. More generally, picking coffee berries was done by task throughout the Antilles: containers rather than drivers and overseer measured labor output.[48]

The prevalence of the task system meant that slaves could control some of their labor time and share in the decision-making process. However minimal that share, labor organization allowed for slave individuality and differences, and the slaves knew it. Laborie observed that women in particular, "who are more handy at delicate work than men, pick considerably more" than the assigned quota. Planters offered rewards for this additional work, and slaves voluntarily completed extra tasks to gain the corresponding gratuity. More significant, slaves routinely used the task system to shorten the length of the time spent in their masters' fields.[49]

Given this work regimen with its comparatively undemanding annual cycle and its relatively short workday, coffee slaves may have looked idle to white contemporaries, especially sugar planters. Thus coffee planters were accused of spoiling their slaves, often by the same people who accused them of mistreatment. After visiting a coffee area in Saint Domingue, one sugar planter complained that the owners there "did not know how to take advantage of their slaves who did whatever they wanted outside of harvest time."[50]

The nature of the work regimen allowed coffee slaves to enjoy a relatively favorable rate of natural increase throughout the Antilles, with minor exceptions (St. Lucia, for example) and with some wide variation. But equally important, the pattern of work permitted slaves great latitude for activities of their choice within the confines of the plantation. If isolation and size restricted some resources, labor organization—and the control over time that it afforded—in turn created opportunities to use advantageously the resources that were available. Laborie's observation that coffee slaves tended to prefer a single break may have reflected not just the planter's self-serving wishes but also the slaves' inclination to complete the masters' tasks as fast as possible in order to be free for activities of their choice.[51] Time not taken up with plantation work was time available to weed provision grounds, to raise fowls for barter or sale to neighbors and master alike, to care for family members, to carve a drum, to share a tale, or to plan for a holiday. The sugar planters' stereotypes of idleness notwithstanding, such time was to some extent "free," inasmuch as, within the confines of slavery, it was time in which to exercise one's capacities to one's own benefit.

Coffee plantations left some room for slaves to express individuality—and notably more than was true for slaves on sugarcane units. However, the aggregate impact of such individual choices on slave societies of the Caribbean cannot be inferred in any mechanical manner. The assessment can only be made for one territory at a time, and with a careful appraisal of the larger contexts sketched earlier in this essay.[52] The manner in which coffee's trajectory intersected with that of a particular colony's, the chronology of this encounter, the cultural accomplishments upon which it built, the social organization of space it generated—all, in turn, shaped the slaves' daily life.

5

OBLIGATION AND RIGHT: PATTERNS OF LABOR, SUBSISTENCE, AND EXCHANGE IN THE COTTON BELT OF GEORGIA, 1790–1860

Joseph P. Reidy

FROM THE 1790s through the 1850s cotton and slavery were nearly synonymous in the American South. If historians have dwelled upon the influence of cotton on regional and national affairs, attention has only begun to focus upon the organization of labor on plantations and farms, the foundation of slave-based production. Close study of the slaves' working lives reveals the interconnection between developments in the fields, life in the quarters, and the world beyond the plantation. Examining the way slaves worked also provides insight into the larger struggle between masters and slaves for control over the slaves' minds and bodies and over the products of their labor.

As one of the earliest centers of short-staple cotton production, up-country Georgia provides an excellent field for exploring the work process. Focusing upon the relationship between cotton and subsistence in turn illuminates the realms of production and exchange over which slaves exercised discretion. Whether slaves labored for themselves or their owners, the rules governing labor, subsistence, and exchange were continually revised in a process of constant—if unequal—struggle. Through subtle and overt means both master and slave communicated their interests and preferences, and an operational consensus grudgingly emerged. When new circumstances undermined these arrangements, a new round of negotiation began. In Georgia's short-staple cotton belt between 1790 and 1860, three distinct, though somewhat overlapping, phases of this process occurred: the first, dating from the 1780s to approximately 1820, laid the foundation of cotton agriculture; the second, from 1820 to the late 1830s,

138

marked the spread of cotton culture over much of the up country and the consolidation of the planters' political domain; the third, from roughly 1840 to the Civil War, initiated a series of economic crises that eventuated in slavery's demise.

The history of King Cotton coincided with the history of up-country Georgia, the area lying between the piney woods and wire-grass region along the coast and the foothills of the Appalachian mountains.[1] In the 1760s white settlers began moving into this region, especially along the Savannah River, which separates Georgia from South Carolina. After the Revolution state-sponsored land lotteries and land grants to Revolutionary veterans propelled the region's population upward. The newcomers divided into three major streams, the first originating in the more northerly sections of the piedmont plateau itself, the second in the tidewater region of the Chesapeake Bay, and the third in the coastal low country of Georgia and South Carolina. The largest group consisted of the small farmers from the piedmont, who subsisted by hunting and gathering from the wild and raising grains and various domesticated animals. These farmers grew some cotton and tobacco for home use, but only a fraction owned slaves and few engaged in commercial agriculture.[2]

In contrast, tidewater and the low-country planters—large and small—migrated to the backcountry expressly to grow commercial staples. Following the Revolution a settlement of Virginians had established tobacco plantations along Broad River northwest of Augusta.[3] Once Eli Whitney developed his gin, the advantages of cotton far outweighed its disadvantages. It neither spoiled as easily as tobacco nor required as much painstaking cultivation. By 1800 cotton had supplanted tobacco. Yet, like tobacco, cotton grew in small patches as well as large, thus accommodating growers regardless of the size of their landholdings and slaveholdings. Lacking experience with raising short-staple cotton commercially, masters and slaves applied their knowledge of other crops to the new circumstances.

Planters and farmers were far from unanimous regarding the finer points of both cotton culture and labor organization. The clearest distinction was that separating tidewater agriculturalists from low-country ones. From the Chesapeake planters brought knowledge of the system of mixed agriculture devised during the late colonial period as an alternative to tobacco monoculture. Mixed agriculture involved a combination of tobacco and various grains and grasses, with complementary, rather than competing, seasons of peak labor demand. To adjust the size of their work forces or to generate cash for agricultural improvements, masters sold, freed, and hired slaves. Manumission and hire reflected concessions to the political ideology of the Revolution, which reinforced the slaves' traditional pursuit of freedom; sale represented a reaction against the slaves' heightened political awareness. Among the slaves who were retained, Upper South masters sought to suppress all traces of revolutionary enthusiasm by asserting maximum control. George Washington's prescription was work, "as much in the 24 hours as their strength without endangering the health, or constitution will allow of."[4]

Although long days promised high profits, they also entailed long hours of supervision. Even when planters employed overseers, the range of duties associated with mixed agriculture required the division of slaves into small, essentially unsupervised squads. In the circumstances, slaves developed considerable agricultural skill and expertise in the use of specialized tools. In the intervals between their other duties slaves cultivated garden patches and took game from the woods and waters of the Chesapeake Bay area.[5]

Low-country planters, second to none in their desire to profit from slave labor, differed substantially from their tidewater counterparts in the best means to that end. The task system of cultivation that prevailed on their rice plantations explicitly rejected Washington's notion of maximum exertion over the greatest span of time in favor of assigning each slave a particular task, following the satisfactory completion of which the slave was entitled to leave the field. Low-country planters also differed from their tidewater counterparts in their attachment to hoe agriculture. Although aversion to the plow owed much to soil conditions in the low country, it also reflected a supposition of technological backwardness among coastal slaves.[6]

Far from promoting leisure among low-country slaves, the task system obligated them to provide most of their own subsistence during the time left after completing their task. Planters made land available for provision grounds and authorized slaves to raise animals and to hunt and fish from the wild. What slaves did not consume, they disposed of in trade networks that incorporated fellow slaves, masters, and the community at large. Planters who championed this system contended that it provided not only the best motivation for slaves to work industriously but also the most humane method of accounting for "the ability of the hand."[7]

Whether they hailed from the tidewater or the low-country, planters and farmers generally migrated to up-country Georgia with kinfolk and neighbors, many of whom shared the same religion. These reconstituted communities preserved the social fabric of the seaboard South and provided a framework for meeting the challenges of the new environment. When time came to build dwellings or clear new lands, planters often swapped slaves as well as advice. They also compared notes on cotton. Common understandings and practices sometimes emerged out of these exchanges. But in the Georgia up country as a whole diversity outweighed consensus. Individual farmers retained numerous idiosyncrasies passed down from their forefathers; these customary practices often operated in the realm of superstition, beyond the reach of the most forceful argument.[8] In short, with no one entitled to claim expertise through first hand experience, pioneer cotton culture invited every man to fend for himself.

From the start, however, the largest planters appeared determined to minimize the effect of chance in mastering the new environment and the new crop. Seizing the opportunity to exploit the natural fertility of the soil and to breathe new life into slavery, slaveowners organized their laborers into closely supervised gangs and administered the whip in frequent doses. They worked slaves long hours, making the workday the length of the solar day, and sometimes longer. They provided rations of bacon and corn from plantation stores but generally obliged slaves to prepare meals on their own time. And they placed highest priority upon raising cotton, planting "only as much provision, as serves to fill up the intervals" in cotton cultivation and "regarding the culture of provisions as altogether a secondary object."[9] Such a method of organizing plantation labor, they hoped, would guarantee both high yields and proper subordination—a habit that many slaves had broken during the turmoil of the Revolution.

The new regime left slaves little time to provide their own subsistence, sometimes restricting such activities to Sunday only. On many plantations slaves did not even enjoy all of the Sabbath, in that they had to perform essential chores such as feeding stock on the Lord's day. Most slaves were also required to police their quarters and wash their clothes on Sunday, further reducing the time available for rest and supplementary subsistence activity. The work regimen in upcountry cotton plantations thus broke spirits as well as bodies.

In more subtle yet no less decisive ways, however, slaves helped design the new system of cotton growing. Their success depended to some extent upon whether they had accompanied their owners to the up country or arrived via the regional slave trade. The former had the advantage of familiarity with their owner's ways and an established understanding of "rights" and "privileges." Slaves and masters from the low country, for instance, adapted the task system to the cultivation of cotton. Slaves sold as individuals to the up country fared differently depending upon whether they were purchased by a large planter or a smallholder.[10]

Slaves sold to a planter with an established work force stood little chance of influencing work patterns, although they may have been able to preserve after-hours privileges such as gardening, hunting, and fishing. Large slaveholders put little premium upon the diversity of a slave's prior experience (unless it included knowledge of a craft). Similarly, they did not necessarily prize a slave's ability to work without direct supervision. Attachment to old ways on the part of such slaves might prompt punishment instead of reward, especially when accompanied by the desire to rejoin loved ones from whom they were now separated.

When sold to a master with a small slave force and a diverse farming operation, though, individual slaves may have been able to preserve some control over their labor as well as privileges to hunt and fish. In such settings slaves often labored alongside masters in a kind of "sawbuck equality," wherein the pace and duration of labor and the frequency and extent of breaks would have reflected mutual considerations. Slave men also hunted and fished, with and without their masters. Although slave women were not exempt from field labor, most of their duties were household chores shared with their mistresses. A common dwelling housed all. Such familiarity bred practices that flagrantly violated accepted canons of behavior in the older settled areas. Visitors to the up country never ceased to marvel at the sight of slaves taking meals with their masters and addressing them on a first-name basis.[11]

Few slaves adjusted easily to the new rigors of field labor on cotton plantations. They had to draw upon reserve energy simply to keep up with the physical demands without incurring punishment. Charles Ball, a Maryland slave sold south around 1805, graphically described what Chesapeake slaves endured in a newly settled cotton-producing region.[12] In comparison with work in tidewater tobacco fields, Ball found the labor in cotton fields more "excessive" and "incessant throughout the year." Slaves worked under "captains" who set the pace for others to follow. Laggards were whipped, often mercilessly, in a ritual devised to impress minds as well as bodies. Besides the manifest danger of clearing malarial lowlands, much of the routine work was also unhealthy. Slaves pulled fodder, for instance, in the early morning and late evening dews of August, producing "agues, fevers, and all the diseases which follow in their train." And the slaves' diet rarely sufficed for the demands of their labor. In short, cotton plantations concentrated "the utmost rigour of the [slave] system."[13]

Even work that did not require physical strength still presented challenges, as Ball's description of learning how to pick cotton makes clear. Taking great pride in his physical strength and capacity for hard work, Ball found picking cotton a tremendous challenge. Fearing that his initial lack of dexterity had diminished his "character" among fellow slaves, he applied himself with "great industry and diligence" and soon exceeded the daily quota, though he never merited the distinction of "first rate." Picking cotton, he believed, "may almost be reckoned among the arts" such that a "man who has arrived at the age of twenty-five, before he sees a cotton field, will never, in the language of the overseer, become a crack picker." Overseers cracked many a whip attempting to disprove that axiom.[14]

These rigors notwithstanding, even plantation slaves managed to find time for gathering plants, nuts, and berries, and for fishing and hunting. In many cases, such activities were more a matter of necessity than choice, given the parsimonious nature of planters-on-the-make. Because these masters also seemed to demand the most labor, their slaves had neither the time nor the energy to supplement their diets. Necessity required invention, and slaves with prior experience growing provisions or gathering from the wild devised ways to do so in stolen moments. In some cases, masters capitalized on these skills. Charles Ball, for instance, had learned to fish along Maryland's Patuxent River as a young man. After discovering this expertise, his owner placed him in charge of a fishery. Although he and his fellow slaves had to put in long hours to meet their quotas, they worked under minimal supervision and ate well.[15]

Ball hunted with equal prowess. Like other slave hunters, he tended an assortment of traps at night and used a dog, especially when pursuing opossums and raccoons. Ball even kept firearms. In fact, he considered himself a "proper" hunter only after obtaining a gun. At one point, he arranged with his master to work on a weekly task—fixed at the beginning of each week—so he could spend half of each Saturday hunting. He even constructed a deer blind. Slave hunters with skills such as his could enjoy meals of fresh game several times a week.[16]

Slaves on up-country Georgia cotton plantations also sought access to land for gardens. Not every planter granted such permission, and those who did often imposed restrictions. Patches might be located "in some remote and unprofitable part of the estate, generally in the woods." Gardeners might have to clear new land each year so that the previous year's patch could be incorporated into the plantation's fields. Despite such obstacles, though, slaves raised "corn, potatoes, pumpkins, melons, &c. for themselves."[17]

The new cotton regimen left only Sunday for such subsistence pursuits, and slaves pressed their traditional claims over Sunday in new directions. Slaves so inclined encountered little difficulty hiring their own time on that day. They worked for nonslaveholders as well as planters, in cotton crops as well as at assorted tasks and jobs, and often earned between fifty cents and a dollar and a half per day. During cotton-picking season, Ball recalled, the intensity of competition prompted masters to "offer their own slaves one half as much as the cotton is worth, for each pound they will pick on Sunday" to prevent "them from going to some other field, to work." Ball pondered over "the moral turpitude of violating the Sabbath, in this shameful manner," but his need for subsistence overrode his religious scruples.[18]

Slaves did not miss the irony. Describing himself as "a kind of freeman on Sunday," whose sole object "is to get employment . . . where he can make the best wages," Ball observed that "by the exercise of his liberty on this day" a slave was able "to provide himself and his family, with many of the necessaries of life that his master refuses to supply him with." Although this "liberty" remained severely circumscribed, the rules governing Sunday labor recognized the principle that slaves were entitled to compensation for labor performed on their own time. Ball noted the absence of whipping and "abusive language." None of his numerous employees either "insulted or maltreated" him. Nor did they superintend his labor closely. Yet, he remembered, "I worked faithfully, because I knew that if I did not, I could not expect payment; and those who hired me, knew that if I did not work well, they need not employ me." In exchange for lost rest, slaves who worked on Sunday regained the control over their labor they had lost during the other six days. They also forced the masters to acknowledge, however grudgingly and provisionally, what Frederick Law Olmsted later described as "the agrarian notion" that formed "a fixed point of the negro system of ethics: that the result of labour belongs of right to the labourer."[19]

Despite its adverse effects upon rest and recreation, Sunday labor enabled slaves to purchase such necessities as salt, cloth, and blankets, and such items of taste as coffee, sugar, and tobacco. Slaves sometimes traded a portion of the ration provided by their owners for other goods. They also bartered or sold animals they had raised or captured and a wide variety of handicrafts, including moccasins, baskets, brooms, bowls, mats, mattresses, and horse collars.[20] Not all slaves enjoyed equal access to these networks. As a rule, those living on yeoman homesteads did not have the same advantages as those on plantations or in towns. Slaves proximate to highways and waterways could trade with itinerant peddlers and ships' crews, laws to the contrary notwithstanding. Slave wagoners and crewmen played an especially important role in promoting such exchange, but they did not monopolize it.[21] Planters did not suppress this independent economic activity, in part because they benefited directly from its products, and they considered it a safety valve for discontent. Slaves depended upon it even more as a source of goods and an outlet for creative energy.

From the Revolution through the War of 1812 these developments were more important for the direction they indicated than the numbers of masters and slaves directly affected. After all, most of the white settlers in the up country were subsistence-oriented yeomen until well into the nineteenth century. Most slaves lived on smallholdings where the organization of labor more closely resembled the mixed-farming squads than cotton-plantation gangs. And not all planters endorsed the need for reorganization. Those from the low country, in particular, retained the traditional preference for hoe culture and the organization of labor according to tasks, as did their slaves.

The success of the first generation of settlers attracted new waves of migrants to the up country. During the 1820s Georgia officials ousted the Creeks and Cherokees from the westernmost and northernmost regions of the state. Tens of thousands of slaves were transported from the Upper South to work on cotton plantations established where once Indians held sway. As slaveholders increased in number slavery lost some of its prior identification with colonial aristocrats and was seen more as a democratic institution—at least from the white man's perspective. Tens of thousands of new acres were cleared and cultivated, with cotton profits financing purchases of still more land and slaves and fostering commercial expansion. But cotton mania also resulted in the rampant exploitation of natural resources. Growers paid little heed to replenishing soil nutrients or preventing erosion. By the early 1830s nearly the entire eastern half of the piedmont showed signs of severe use: not only had the topsoil washed away but rainwater had also cut deep gullies into the fields.

To combat agricultural decline, planters interested in improvement developed a program of "scientific management" encompassing seeds, soils, animals, implements, and techniques but whose "starting point" was the proper "management of . . . negroes."[22] The strategy focused upon field labor. Arguing for the superiority of closely supervised gangs, planters sought to eliminate all remnants of the task system and the lax practices characteristic of the pioneer days. Yet they had no illusions about the "Herculean task" of "reducing to a system and order the complicated operations of a plantation, where nothing like system or order ever prevailed."[23]

To the masters' Hercules, slaves offered more than the proverbial twelve labors, especially where they had preserved elements of the task system. James Henry Hammond, who operated several plantations on the east bank of the Savannah River and whose experience was representative of a broad trend, struggled for twenty years to disabuse his slaves of their low-country ways. But they parried his efforts, clinging tenaciously to their customary discretion over field labor and their prerogatives regarding gardens, hunting, and fishing. Hammond opposed task labor for its tendency to promote overexertion; he also frowned upon the relative independence slaves enjoyed after completing their tasks. In his view, steady, moderate labor "from sunrise to sundown" with appropriate intervals of rest accomplished several objectives: it guaranteed good health and greater output while it reduced the amount of time at the slaves' disposal. Undermining the slaves' subsistence activities made them more dependent upon his largess, a vital component of the social order that he and other paternalistic planters idealized.[24]

Other advocates of gang labor resorted to newly found principles of "justice." One typical critic faulted the "old system" of tasks as neither "reasonable . . . [nor] just" in requiring "the same quantity of work" from all hands. Whereas a "strong young man" could finish by mid-afternoon and then go "home to work in his own field, or enjoy himself in any manner he thinks proper," a "delicate female" only "with difficulty" finished "by sun-down." "The one who least requires it," the observer concluded, "has plenty of leisure and time to rest himself, whilst the other who needs this the most has the least."[25]

Opponents of the task system left no stone unturned. One partisan argued that by dividing the work force into "fast and slow hands" supervised by individual foremen, "more work is obtained, every one does in proportion to his ability, and all are insensible of the quantity they actually do beyond the usual task."[26] Another advocate of the change added refinements, proposing several gangs, ranging from full hands ("all the strong and active of both sexes") to quarter hands ("all of the young and the old negroes"), with the respective gangs assigned "work suitable to their abilities." "There is always on all plantations," he insisted, "work requiring different degrees of strength to accomplish, which would enable a planter to assign to each gang, its appropriate labour." Such a system would promote "the spirit of emulation . . . which is always highly desirable, and which makes them work with more cheerfulness, and . . . makes them execute the work better."[27]

Although these self-styled improving planters of the 1830s sought complete dominion, they rarely achieved it. Compromises resulted, the most common of which featured the preservation of individualized tasks for certain field operations, such as hoeing.[28] One Georgia planter reported having settled upon daily tasks of one hundred rows of cotton, each a hundred yards long. For the first two hoeings, he considered these "good, though not severe tasks." Subsequent hoeings "were light, and the workers were often out of the field by 12 o'clock."[29] In those circumstances it was possible for slaves to control both their pace of work and their disposition over the rest of the day.

Slaves who lost control over their labor in the field clung tenaciously to such after-hours prerogatives as hunting and fishing. Not even the growing body of antebellum legislation that addressed these matters abridged the slaves' rights to nature's bounty. Laws that pertained to fishing, for example, aimed to protect the public at large— slaves not excluded—against depredation by commercial fishermen. One such law that applied to the Ocmulgee River in central Georgia required "any person [or] persons, their agent or agent, slave or slaves" fishing with seines to wait at least one hour between hauls. It also banned the laying of "any seine, gil net, or other obstruction across the main channel, so as to prevent the free passage of fish."[30] Fishermen who jeopardized life, health, or property in other ways, for instance, by poisoning the water, merited special legislation. Whereas whites who violated such laws faced fines ranging from $50 to $200, slave or free black violators operating "without the coercion of his, her, or their owner, or overseer" suffered thirty-nine lashes on the bare back.[31] But neither slaves nor free persons fishing with hook and line or small nets violated the letter or spirit of these laws.[32]

Slaves likewise enjoyed unimpeded access to animals of the wild. Legal restrictions on hunting scarcely existed before the 1850s and even then aimed to conserve large animals such as deer in areas where they were scarce. Typical legislation applied to only one or two counties, banning hunting during the spring and summer, when the deer reproduced. Some laws banned camp-hunting (the ancient practice of using fire to flush animals from cover), a source of "great injury . . . arising from firing the woods," which stampeded stock as well as game, "often destroying whole herds."[33] These laws notwithstanding, no regulations applied to small game, which had been the preferred quarry of slave hunters from colonial times.

Individual masters often took a more restrictive view of slaves' hunting. To their minds, perambulatory slaves attracted trouble, and nighttime activity sapped daytime diligence. The slaves' dogs also raised the masters' hackles. "Kept nominally to catch raccoons," one skeptic complained, the dogs were "actually employed to catch hogs." Others cited the "half-starved" curs' penchant for sheep.[34] But because masters and slaveless yeomen also kept dogs for similar purposes and to similar ill effect, lawmakers were reluctant to pass dog laws. Slaves benefited accordingly, subject to the limitations imposed by their masters.

Although gardening privileges raised assorted ticklish issues in their own right, most slaves in up-country Georgia kept gardens with the consent of their owners. They tended the patches on Sundays and at night, at times by the light of torches held by sleepy children.[35] Alternatively, slaves bargained for Saturday afternoons off. Some convinced their owners that tasks such as plowing were better accomplished by appropriating time from the crop instead of doing the work piecemeal; of course, the use of plantation work stock and implements further expedited matters.[36] Slaves also negotiated with individual masters for discretion over chance intervals of time, such as that lost to inclement weather. Although not necessarily suitable for gardening, these intervals were ideal for other productive activities such as making handicrafts.[37]

Having agreed upon the principle of slave-kept gardens, slaves and masters wrangled over the crops to be grown. Although slaves desired to raise whatever they pleased, masters did not generally approve of cotton or corn, lest, in the words of one owner, the "temptation" be afforded to "an unscrupulous fellow to mix a little of his master's produce with his own."[38] Yet some slaves won such permission, often provided they planted nankeen cotton, the distinctive brown tint of which would prevent confusion about which cotton belonged to whom. Still others labored under no such color coding. Their masters simply marketed their cotton with the plantation crop, paying them what it fetched, confident that the practice would promote industry and loyalty rather than laziness and theft. Slaves on a single plantation might earn as much as $2,000 for one year's cotton crops.[39]

The privilege to keep animals followed the same pattern. Chickens did not generally pose problems, in that they scratched for their own food and stayed close to home. Pigs were a different matter. Except just before slaughter, when they were penned for fattening, they fed on mast forage from the woods. Commonly held rights to the open range did not exclude the animals of slaves. By some accounts, however, slave-owned pigs had a particular knack for finding holes in the fences surrounding cultivated fields and feasting on the forbidden fruit. But antebellum law obligated landowners to protect their crops and exempted animal owners from liability for damages when fences did not meet strict requirements.[40] Although aggrieved farmers could do little but fume, masters could, and did, take more decisive action. Probably a majority forbade slaves to keep pigs—more through fear of theft from smokehouses than of damage to crops. Masters who authorized the keeping of pigs generally insisted upon purchasing the fattened animals for plantation purposes, thus reserving jurisdiction over hogmeat entirely to themselves.[41]

It is not entirely clear how slaves divided self-subsistence activities among themselves, but they seemed to have mobilized their available time and energy within the framework of households. To the extent that plantations facilitated household formation, the process of plantation consolidation strengthened the slaves' ability to produce for their own ends. Husbands, wives, children, and unrelated coresidents each did a part. Some duties were divided between the sexes. Nocturnal hunting and fishing was strictly the province of men, just as spinning, weaving, washing, and mending was women's work. Performance of other tasks depended upon the circumstances of individual households. Men, women, and children tended gardens as need dictated. Watching over pigs—like similar tasks involving animals in the woods, whether domesticated or wild—seems to have been the responsibility of men and boys.[42]

In short, as planters increased their influence, opening new land and purchasing slaves from the Upper South, they adopted gang labor as the premier method of organizing production and safeguarding organic society from the "natural" vices of the laborers. Slaves suffered an acute loss of control over their working lives as a result. But—even as masters consolidated their power—slaves registered unforeseen benefits, as a single plantation-based slave quarter replaced the scattered living arrangements of smallholdings. Besides the various psychological and cultural benefits of community life in such settings, the households of the quarters provided a structure for both meeting the subsistence needs of the slaves and reinforcing their rightful claims to such self-subsistence activities as gardening, gathering, hunting, and fishing.

Between the bank panic of 1837 and the secession crisis of 1860–61 planters continued to amass wealth and power, and slaves continued to maneuver for greater control over their lives. The depression that followed the panic altered the options available to masters and slaves. For marginal cotton growers, especially those faced with deteriorating soils, the depression meant bankruptcy. Large numbers departed Georgia for fresh land in the west; others moved to the undesirable sand-hill regions of the black belt or to nearby towns. Solvent planters picked up the pieces. Aside from the opportunity to accumulate wealth—in many cases to build dynasties—the depression enabled such planters to impose greater discipline upon their slaves. Whereas prior to the depression planters had frequently faulted smallholders and their slaves for breaches in the etiquette of slavery, now many of the offending masters were gone. Slaves had little choice but to succumb to stricter discipline.

To overcome the combined calamities of exhausted soil and low prices, the most financially stable cotton planters hoisted the banner of agricultural improvement higher than ever. They invested in new implements, including an assortment of specialized plows, cultivators, and seeding drills. One planter wondered how the preference for hoes had survived so long "in this utilitarian and labor-saving age." To prevent erosion, reclaim worn fields, and increase soil productivity, they experimented with horizontal plowing, ditching, and manuring. They diversified into fruits and vegetables, grains and grasses, and cattle and sheep. To conserve time and timber, they adopted new fencing materials and designs. And to disseminate information, they formed agricultural societies and sponsored fairs.[43] These planters viewed the depression as a blessing in disguise, and they championed agricultural reform as though it were a political crusade.

Planters who, of necessity, adopted new tools and practices spent more time supervising field operations; they also promoted increased division of labor and specialization among their slaves. An early advocate of plow cultivation touted a method of weeding corn entirely "unassisted by the hoe." Success hinged upon the proper layout of furrows. He did that work himself because "even the most careful" of his slaves was subject to "make a wrong start, and consequently lay off the whole field catacornered . . . rendering it incapable of being worked to advantage, and causing mortification and vexation to the agriculturist." The planter entrusted only his "most intelligent and careful hands" with the delicate tasks of seeding and plowing close to the plants; his "more indifferent ploughmen" were responsible for the middles of furrows, where they could do the least damage. Planters who lacked the resources or the time to initiate such changes balked, as did those who considered slaves suited only to the simplest chores with the simplest tools. One opposed diversification on the grounds that it involved too much "dibbling and jobbing" such that his slaves had "little to show for their labour by May-day."[44]

Plows called for drastic changes in field routines. One planter bluntly challenged the view that "the quality of plows" had "no bearing upon the management of negroes." He asked rhetorically, "if a negro has to push his plow in, hold it steady, guide it and the horse, is [he] not a used up negro to all intents and purposes?" Good plows were the proper antidote. But the range of implements did not end with plows; it included "cultivators, sweeps, shovels, bull tongues, etc., etc." for breaking up soil between rows and for clearing it away from or throwing it toward the roots.[45] Acquiring the vocabulary particular to these implements, not to mention learning the finer points of their use, required practice, and inexperienced hands damaged many a machine before achieving facility. But given that the new techniques required skill more than brute strength, women might do the job as well as men. Slaves from the Upper South, where plows were in extensive use by the mid-eighteenth century, may well have adjusted to these demands more readily than those from the low country, where hoes predominated. But in either case, more plows meant more cotton, which translated into more, not less, work.[46]

These changes produced others. Greater numbers of slaves came into contact with temperamental animals, both man and beast suffering as a result. Slaves worked animals hard, not so much out of cruelty or spite as from the demands of the plantation regimen. Frightened or angered animals kicked and bit; unsure feet trampled crops. Slaves paid many a pound of flesh for their bungling, even as planters took it as new evidence of the slaves' stupidity. Although mules had been slowly gaining in popularity, planters undertook the systematic conversion from horses and oxen to the heartier mules during the 1840s. Charles Ball recalled "much trouble" in his early dealings with mule teams, "having never been accustomed to ploughing with these animals." At least he had had experience plowing with horses; low-country slaves—who lacked such experience—had to master animals, tools, and techniques at the same time.[47]

Planters intended the reorganization of production to serve broadly political as well as narrowly economic purposes. At the national level and beyond, they aimed to silence the critics of slavery. Higher crop yields would undermine abolitionist arguments about the inefficiency of slavery. The manifest prosperity and harmony of organic society would also highlight the duplicity of societies (such as the North) whose "free labor" principles produced a bitter harvest of poverty and social unrest.[48] Closer to home, individual planters hoped to increase the size of their slaveholdings and, in the process, to impose the kind of "system and order" that they found disturbingly absent on most smallholdings. This consolidation augmented the planters' political power within the black belt and, by extension, in the state and in the nation.

To slaves in Georgia's cotton belt, the personal ties between master and slave that undergird paternalism assumed uncomfortable new dimensions during the depression, and the discomfort persisted through the Civil War. Owners adopted a new level of scrutiny, imposing greater regimentation and limiting the slaves' discretion over their actions, both in the fields and in their quarters. Planters' fixation on increasing cotton crops often resulted in additional subsistence burdens upon the slaves, just as they had for Charles Ball half a century earlier. Yet to a large extent the change gave new legitimacy to the slaves' right to self-subsistence. Planters who prized mutual interdependence and personal loyalty viewed such privileges as a means of promoting fidelity and good behavior in the face of more intense labor and abolitionist agitation. In the final analysis, slave-grown provisions reduced plantation expenses. When slaves convinced the most respectable planters (the most "intelligent" in the contemporary phrasing) to authorize such privileges, slaves of those owners who took their cues from the elite often benefited as well.[49]

The mutual understanding between masters and slaves regarding the slaves' self-subsistence failed when the slaves pressed the collateral right to market their produce and other goods without restriction. The law took an equivocal stand on the matter. The Georgia code, for example, permitted them to "traffic on their own account" in "articles of their own manufacture, or agricultural products of their own raising, or poultry raised by their master's permission, or articles of the like character usually permitted to slaves," provided they had "written permission of the master specifying the particular articles to be sold."[50] But during the 1850s a larger political agenda intervened. Many masters viewed with alarm the proliferation of commercial activities that allowed slaves to dispose of their products. With outlets for trade multiplying masters feared an increase in pilferage from plantation fields, chicken coops, and smokehouses, and a comparable increase in their slaves' consumption of liquor and other proscribed items. Although such trade was not new, masters worried about its unprecedented scope and the boldness of its practitioners.[51] Slaveholders, ministers, and grand jurors railed continuously against the slaves' independent commercial activity, but words had little effect.

Independent trading by slaves also contradicted the paternalist image of the slaves' utter dependence. Masters opposed the "spirit of trafficing" that grew from slaves' unrestricted trade. "To carry this on," one opponent argued, "both means and time are necessary," neither of which slaves "of right possessed." Another maintained that "negroes are not capable of managing [their own affairs], and that if left to themselves they would not obtain a support." Still others insisted that they be the sole purchasing agents for their slaves' surplus goods. Such masters wished to interpose themselves between the slaves and the realm of market exchange, where, in their view, naive slaves were sure to be cheated. Many slaveholders simply forbade their slaves to produce any marketable items. Slaves did not generally welcome such interposition. Whether to obtain goods of their own choosing, to turn a small profit, or to assert greater control over their lives and the products of their labor, they traded on their own authority, despite express orders to the contrary.[52]

The slaves' defiance took on greater importance as tensions between North and South increased. Masters saw danger everywhere but, as earlier, could settle upon no unified course of action. Up-and-coming planters, who viewed cotton as their ticket to larger slaveholdings, greater wealth, and more power, argued against diversification and similar improvements. But established planters, who had championed such changes from the 1830s, saw unprecedented need for self-sufficiency as a hedge against possible economic strangulation by the North. Among other things, this division of opinion shattered the state's most prominent agricultural society.[53]

The struggle over the slaves' labor and subsistence during the 1850s further polarized slaves and their owners. To the owning class, it was not simply that slaves wished a greater range of privileges but that the slaves' demands echoed in somewhat different, but unmistakably clear, tones among growing numbers of Northerners. By the same token, owners increasingly viewed their slaves as an abolitionist fifth column in their midst. They had little desire to send signals of sub-missiveness to enemy agents, but many reasoned that granting slaves a material stake in the plantation order was the surest way to forestall disloyalty.

The history of cotton cultivation in the Georgia up country illustrates the dynamic evolution of the master-slave relationship. At the beginning of the nineteenth century the newness of the country, the crop, and the people guaranteed variety in production methods and work routines. In addition to discretion over their working lives, slaves also maintained considerable control over their own subsistence. But by the 1830s the planters—who had earlier attempted to impose new discipline over their slaves—began to gain the upper hand. Slaves rapidly lost control over field operations but registered some success in preserving—and in some respects extending—their independent economic activities.

By trading a portion of their own produce beyond the plantation, Georgia slaves crossed the boundary into the corrupting world of commerce that most masters wished to keep impermeable. Slaves who ventured in that direction satisfied a variety of material and psychological needs. Yet, like those slaves who bargained for privileges to keep gardens or to hunt and fish, slaves who traded what they had produced paid a physical as well as an emotional price. On the one hand, they understood that such privileges did not reflect humanitarian impulses so much as paternalistic ones designed to reinforce a sense of personal loyalty to the grantor. On the other hand, they knew that engaging in such activity without permission risked punishment, perhaps sale.

Still, even as masters gained leverage by granting such privileges, slaves gained a measure of control over their lives. In the context of the total domination that masters desired, this was a crucial achievement. But in the larger context of national politics, the ramifications were even greater. The slaves' persistent efforts to market the products of their toil became a source of social and political irritation that helped prod the masters to secession and the nation to abolition.

6

PLANTATION LABOR ORGANIZATION AND SLAVE LIFE ON THE COTTON FRONTIER: THE ALABAMA-MISSISSIPPI BLACK BELT, 1815–1840

Steven F. Miller

URING THE QUARTER century bounded by the close of the war of 1812 and the depression of the 1840s the expansion of short-staple cotton production reshaped slave life in the U.S. South. Slaveholders eager to establish themselves on fresh lands forced the relocation of hundreds of thousands of slaves to the piedmont of the Carolinas and Georgia, further westward to the Mississippi valley, and beyond. Owing to the closure of the legal African slave trade in 1808, the vast majority of these involuntary migrants were Afro-Americans taken from established plantation regions of the seaboard South—predominantly from the tobacco and grain districts of the Chesapeake and the long-staple cotton and rice areas of the South Carolina and Georgia low country. Drawing on different work experiences and cultural traditions, slaves and slaveholders fought their continuing battle for control over labor and subsistence, but on new physical and social terrain. In the process, they forged a new slave society, which, although it derived its people and institutions from the older settled regions, over time reshaped them both.[1]

Focusing on the formative period of plantation society in Alabama and Mississippi, between roughly 1815 and 1840, this essay will discuss some elements of that transition. The two new states began the period as territories inhabited largely by Indians but by its end had become an integral part of the upland cotton kingdom, thereafter ranking consistently among the largest producers of the staple. Fueling the explosive growth of cotton production was the labor of slaves brought into the states by migrating planters and farmers or sold there by traders. The slave population in the two states grew sixfold be-

155

tween 1820 and 1840, as the southwestern cotton regions became home to an ever-larger proportion of American slaves. Whereas in 1820 a mere 6 percent of Southern slaves lived in Alabama or Mississippi, nearly 20 percent did by 1840.[2]

Those slaves lived in both small and large units, on forty acre farms that produced little or no cotton and on one thousand acre plantations that produced little else. Virtually from the beginning, however, plantations—substantial estates with twenty or more slaves—gained ascendancy in regions of fertile land and convenient access to market. Settlement took place in circumstances conducive to the establishment of large estates, especially in the fertile valleys of the Mississippi, Tennessee, Tombigbee, and Alabama rivers. Strong world demand for cotton kept prices generally high, with peaks in the late 1810s and the first two-thirds of the 1830s.[3] Cotton prosperity generated credit to finance purchases of land and slaves and pay the expenses of establishing new agricultural enterprises. At the same time, the national government's policy of Indian removal and the disposition of the public land worked to the advantage of large purchasers. Rather than having to muscle out yeomen farmers and other smallholders, prospective planters with cash or access to credit could easily purchase vast acreages and build plantations from the ground up.[4] Matters reached a climax during the "flush times" of the 1830s, when the opening of new land coincided with a cresting cotton market to create conditions not unlike those of the tobacco and sugar booms of the seventeenth century.

By the time the panic of 1837 deflated the boom, most slaves in Alabama and Mississippi lived in holdings that, by the standards of the cotton South, constituted plantation-sized units. In 1830, for example, only about 20 percent of the slaves in Lowndes County, Mississippi, resided in units of twenty or more; ten years later, well over half did. Augmentation of smaller holdings by natural increase or purchase accounted for some of the shift. But, more significantly, a sizable number of newly arrived slaveholders began operations in Lowndes County with enough slaves to work a plantation. Between 1837 and 1845 one-fifth of the slaveholdings brought into the county by their owner or owner's agent numbered twenty or more slaves and 48 percent of the slaves brought by their owners arrived in such large units.[5]

Slaves relocated to the cotton frontier, whether by owners or by slavemongers, were disproportionately young, since planters preferred to "stock" new estates with people in their teens and twenties.

Not only were such men and women more immediately valuable as laborers but they were also better able to withstand the westward trek, to survive new diseases during the "seasoning" period, and to re-produce in the new country. With these considerations in mind, a planter in Alabama directed his brother in Virginia to forward no slaves over the age of forty-five, "excepting 2 or 3 healthy old women to cook and a trusty old man to attend to the hogs"; other old folk were to be "[exchanged] for children of any age." Numerous "old planters" in Mississippi similarly advised a newly arrived émigré from Maryland that in choosing slaves for a new plantation "it is better to buy *none in families*, but to *select only choice, first rate, young hands from 14 to 25 years of age*, (buying no children or aged negroes)."[6]

Many slave owners could not tailor their holdings according to such criteria, either because they lacked the means to purchase expen-sive young slaves or because their scruples prevented them from ridding themselves of old people. But enough of them acted on their preference for young hands to make the slave population in Alabama and Mississippi substantially more youthful than that of older slave states. As of 1840 slaves between the ages of ten and thirty-six com-posed about 55 percent of the slave population in Alabama and 57 percent in Mississippi, whereas only 47 percent of slaves in eastern Virginia and 48 percent of those in South Carolina fell into that age group. And while men and women aged thirty-six and older made up nearly 18 percent of the slave population in longer-settled slave states, they amounted to only 12 percent in Alabama and Mississippi.[7]

Whether slaves arrived in traders' coffles or with longtime owners, the forced migration disrupted their lives. The demand for young slaves on the cotton frontier meant that thousands of young adults and teenage children were separated from their parents, not to men-tion from other relatives and friends. Slaves sold or taken to the southwest as individuals or in small groups moved into an unfamiliar world amid unfamiliar faces. Even transfers in toto of large plantation holdings severed the ties of kinship and friendship among slaves that had extended beyond those holdings.[8]

The forced migration strained the always unstable entente be-tween masters and slaves. For slaves bound for frontier Alabama and Mississippi, separation from familiar people and places was only the beginning. The trip out, generally made overland and during the winter, exposed them to severe weather and often to equally severe discipline.[9] Moreover, because many slaveowners did not escort their slaves personally but sent them in the custody of a relative, neighbor, or hired agent, slaves often did not enjoy what small comforts might accrue from personal appeal to the master's humanity or self-interest. Learning that he and his family were to be transported to Mississippi by an agent of his owner rather than the owner himself, a Virginia slave "became dissatisfied & Complained of the disappointment & feared he was in bad hands for Care & protection."[10] Distraught at being torn from kinfolk and friends, some slaves ran away in desperation during the trek, often attempting to return whence they came. Those who finished the journey were bitter about their removal from their old homes and apprehensive about their new one.

The slaves belonging to the Virginian William B. Beverly provide a case in point. At least one of them perished en route from Virginia to Alabama in late 1830, and several others died soon after their arrival. Because Beverly rashly decided to move without first securing land in the new country, the slaves lived in temporary quarters while their owner sought unsuccessfully to rent land for them to work. Some of them were hired out in the meantime. Resentful of their compulsory relocation and smarting from the recent loss of their fellows, Beverly's slaves turned on their owner, becoming more and more "demoralized." Their refractory behavior led Beverly to deride them as the "meanest parcel of negroes for the number, that ever left virginia."[11] For Beverly and his slaves, as in many another instance, the move to the black belt intensified the fundamental antagonism between the owner and the owned.

Slaves on the cotton frontier came into a work regimen shaped in part by the nature of the staple crop but perhaps even more by the necessity of clearing land. Because only a minuscule amount of land in Alabama and Mississippi had been cleared prior to the arrival of planters, the work of preparing new ground for cultivation vied with that of growing crops during the settlement period.[12]

The carving out of a new plantation took place in two overlapping, but analytically distinct, phases. Cultivation of crops could not begin in earnest until at least a rough clearing was completed. The first phrase thus involved extensive preparation for field work: cutting trees, grubbing out and burning underbrush, constructing cabins, outbuildings, and fences.[13] Depending on the condition of the land and the size of the working force, that could take a good deal of time. An efficient slave man, able to clear at best about one-eighth of an acre per day, required some four months to clear twelve acres, enough land for himself or another full hand to cultivate. Working only in the out-of-crop months of the cotton planting cycle—roughly the two months between early January and early March—such a slave man could clear only about one-half the amount of acreage he could tend.[14]

Awaiting the clearing of new fields, large slaveholders who relocated to Alabama or Mississippi often had more laborers than they had land for them to work. After four years of opening a new estate in Alabama, the slaves of a former South Carolina planter had cleared about four hundred acres—an amount their owner deemed insufficient for a work force consisting of about twenty-five field hands.[15]

The demands of clearing differed substantially from those of the second phase, field labor. Clearing was work best suited to young men. Not only were women, children, and old folk of limited utility in the arduous tasks of cutting trees and building cabins, but the high cost of provisions in newly settled portions of Alabama and Mississippi discouraged slaveholders from sending any slaves who could not be of immediate service. Women and children, opined the transplanted Virginia planter William B. Beverly, were "a dead expense" in a milieu suited to "axemen." A kinsman who served as overseer on an Alabama estate purchased by Beverly's father came to the same conclusion. Between chopping trees, rolling logs, and grubbing out cane roots, he reported, establishing a plantation in the woods required "a good deal of hard work." The slaves under his charge—including a substantial number of women and children—were not up to the task. Complaining that "the [logg?]ing is too hard for those you have," the overseer requested that his employer purchase "about 7 or 6 young men boys 16 to 20 years old, for it is absolutely necessary to have more male strength on the place." Awaiting more men, he increased the burden on those slaves he had on hand.[16]

As plantations matured and fields opened, however, slave women and children became far more valuable. Field labor in cotton required no special physical strength. Although men generally predominated among plow hands and women among hoe hands, the presence of women behind the plow was by no means unusual, especially on smaller estates. In picking—work that above all involved manual dexterity and stamina—women ranked among the most productive workers and children as young as ten were useful hands.[17] Moreover, as cotton needed only rudimentary processing at the point of production (unlike sugar and tobacco), plantations that grew the staple required few workmen with artisanal or other special skills.[18] For all these reasons, the resident populations of cotton plantations in

Alabama and Mississippi came to include about as many women as men—much as in the older settled cotton regions of the South and the Caribbean.[19]

The shifting work patterns of frontier plantations put a premium on flexibility in allocating slave labor, encouraging temporary arrangements by which planters adapted their work force to the tasks at hand. Two strategies predominated. In the first, planters dispatched a party of young slave men, often supervised by a kinsman or an overseer, to "make an improvement," waiting to send out or purchase other hands until land became available for them to work. In typical fashion, a Virginia planter directed his son-in-law, who was preparing to settle on land recently ceded by the Choctaw Indians in Mississippi, to forward "a hand or two to build your Cabbins fence & clear Lands &c, & make ready for a larger force to enter for the purpose of makeing Crops." Among large slaveholders who could afford to work an estate back east while opening one out west, the sending out of advance parties was more the rule than the exception.[20] By such means numerous large slaveholdings were transferred in piecemeal fashion from the seaboard to the interior.

The experience of the slaves of James A. Tait and his father Charles Tait suggests something of the process.[21] In early 1818 James Tait and several slave men arrived in the public domain in Monroe County, Alabama Territory, "entirely alone, in a wilderness." Having laid in supplies of meat and meal, Tait and his slaves—technically squatters on government land—began "preparing a few acres for the cultivation of Indian Corn." While young Tait and his slaves readied the new homestead, Tait's father was working other slaves belonging to the two men on a cotton plantation in Elbert County, Georgia. After that year's harvest Charles Tait dispatched a cadre of Georgia slaves to the new country. They numbered about sixty, twenty owned by James Tait and forty by his father. All told, about twenty-five ranked as working hands. The black emigrants severed connections with friends and kin back in Elbert County, even as they renewed old ties with their fellows who had been among James Tait's advance party.

The slaves arrived in mid-January 1819, when James Tait vowed to "set them all to regular business in the morning." They had plenty to do. That year they cultivated 80 acres of corn and 175 of cotton. In addition, they had by early 1820 "cleared a big field on the upland . . . and some in the swamp." Owing to the increased acreage under cultivation, to the maturing of younger slaves into more seasoned workers, and to the "two or three more ten year olds" put into the fields, the Taits yielded some eighty bales of cotton, about double what they averaged in Georgia. By the end of 1820, nearly three years after the groundbreaking, the Taits' new place bore certain hallmarks of an established plantation: the presence of an overseer and the erection of a gin house. Thereafter, the Taits augmented their work force through purchase as their slaves readied more land for the plow.

As an alternative to the piecemeal reconstitution of a slave force, many slaveholders resorted to hiring. By hiring slaves, slaveholders could transfer hands among one another according to the needs of their estates. Some migrating planters left the seaboard states with most or all of their slaves, expecting to hire out those not immediately needed. In December 1833, for instance, several slaveholding families embarked on a land-hunting expedition from North Carolina to Alabama, taking with them "near 100 negroes." On their arrival, reported an acquaintance, they intended "to hire their Negroes to pick out Cotton, were advised they could get 75 Cents pr. Day for them." Similarly, when John Horry Dent of South Carolina resettled in Alabama a few years later, he kept in his custody only four or five of his forty-five slaves, "hiring out the remainder to the best advantage."[22]

Hiring followed regular patterns. Typically, slave women and working-age children whose owners' plantations had scant land open to cultivation were rented to perform field work on more mature estates, especially during the harvest, when demand for hired slaves peaked. Domestic servants, whose skills did not suit the rustic world of log cabins, were also prime candidates for being hired out to more established proprietors. Meanwhile, slave men were most often rented out to clear land or construct cabins for newly arrived planters. Men and women alike tended to be hired in small units, a practice that splintered many large slaveholdings. For example, after twenty-five slaves belonging to a North Carolina owner reached Sumter County, Alabama, in 1835, they were parceled out to twelve different hirers, most of them in units of one or two. They were employed in essentially the same manner, although sometimes changing masters, for at least seven years.[23] Although most hired slaves probably returned to work for their owners after a few years' absence, slave hiring, like the gradual reconstitution of slaveholdings, protracted the process of establishing settled slave communities on the cotton frontier.

Although the character of the labor force changed as crop production became incorporated into the routine of nascent plantations, the necessity of opening new ground determined the nature and pace of field work. A portion of the burden fell on each available hand—male and female, young and old. While felling trees remained almost exclusively the province of slave men, the women and older children cleared brush and burned debris. To a larger extent than their counterparts in the seaboard plantation regions, they also shared in the arduous chores of rolling logs, grubbing roots, and digging stumps. Louis Hughes, a Virginia slave sold as a teenager to a Mississippi planter around 1840, claimed that he had never seen "women put to the hard work of grubbing until I went to McGee's," and that "such work was not done by women slaves in Virginia." Hughes was incorrect in asserting that women were exempt from such tasks in Virginia; nevertheless, his observation speaks volumes about the unaccustomed burdens put on slaves during the settlement period.[24]

The emphasis on clearing also tended to compress the crop year, thereby intensifying labor in the field. Awaiting the opening of new ground, planters delayed planting until the last feasible moment. Preparatory work such as clearing and fence building, a Mississippi planter noted, ordinarily began in mid-February and lasted "two or three weeks, unless the farm is mostly new; in which case the clearing of the new ground continues four or five weeks." Given such a late start, planters and overseers had to push slaves all the harder to finish picking before winter wind and rain damaged the standing crop. Moreover, until a planter had enough open land to employ all his hands profitably, slaves were liable to be set to clearing at any slack moment during the crop cycle. Girdling or "belting" of trees, for example, occurred in the summer after field crops were laid by; grubbing, brush burning and log rolling went on intermittently throughout the year. Confined to the winter months and usually involving only a portion of the work force on mature plantations, such tasks went on year-round on frontier estates and affected everyone.[25]

Careful ground preparation was essential for proper cultivation of the staple. Roughly opened land would suffice for corn crops, which if need be could be planted with a sharp stick and required relatively little cultivation. But cotton did not yield well in crudely prepared fields. Obstructions such as stumps and roots made plowing difficult and necessitated labor-intensive hoe cultivation. For that reason, planters generally planted newly cleared land in corn for at least a year, waiting until slaves had improved its tilth before devoting it to cotton. If a planter "choose to purchase a place in the woods," wrote an authority on cotton growing as late as 1866, "it will be impracticable to plant cotton the first or second year. He must content himself with being a corn planter. . . . Cotton will not do well in new ground."[26]

The introduction of new varieties of the staple that were easier to pick gave planters additional reasons to hasten the clearing of cotton fields during the 1820s and 1830s. Because the new strains enabled field hands to pick about twice as many acres of cotton, improving planters attempted to expand the acreage per hand by supplementing hoes with mule-drawn implements such as harrows, cultivators, and scrapers in hilling and weeding operations. But such tools could not be employed successfully, as one Mississippian noted in 1833, "until the land is a little freer from stumps and roots" than was typically the case in newly opening areas.[27]

In attempting simultaneously to transform untamed forests and prairies into cultivable fields and to hasten along the business of cotton growing, planters in frontier Alabama and Mississippi made heavy demands on their slaves. They sought to lengthen the working day, to exact heavy labor during seasonal lulls in the planting cycle, and to extend their supervision, either personally or via overseers, over all phases of work. As they did, however, the planters confronted slaves who were no less determined to resist what they insisted were violations of customary practice and encroachments on their own time.

The contest, as always, was unequal. But the slaves were not without leverage, especially because the planters were themselves in a somewhat vulnerable position. Just beginning operations in the Southwest, and usually heavily indebted, newly arrived slaveholders could ill afford to alienate altogether the workers on whose labor their future depended. Moreover, as a class the frontier planters were a far cry from the self-assured aristocracy they would become by the late antebellum period, having not yet secured their political dominance in the new country and unsure of their ability both to mobilize non-slaveholders to maintain slave discipline and to fend off challenges to slavery itself. Frontier planters faced the problem of extracting prodigious amounts of labor from unwilling and unruly slaves while not completely demoralizing their hands or endangering their own precarious position atop the social order.

In endeavoring to cope with the problem, nearly all planters employed some variant of the gang system. The advantage of gang labor, from the master's perspective, lay precisely in the authority gained over work time and the degree of supervision this allowed. With the labor force of frontier plantations seldom exceeding twenty or so hands, work groups tended to be fairly small—as much squads as "gangs"—and seldom as homogeneous and carefully differentiated by function as those on sugar plantations, for example. Indeed, only during the planting and weeding periods of the cotton crop cycle did various gangs perform distinct sorts of work. Although nothing inherent in upland cotton cultivation prevented organization of labor by the task, even planters newly arrived from the low country and accustomed to working slaves by the task converted sooner or later to the gang system in opening upland cotton plantations. By the 1840s those few Alabama and Mississippi plantations that operated under the task system stood out by their idiosyncrasy.[28]

Even when slaveholders instituted task work, its continuance remained subject to their sanction. The slaves of James Tait worked by the task for some twenty years beginning in 1826, Tait having adopted it "in compliance with the persuasions of an old S. Carolina overseer," only to find the regimen abruptly changed when their owner concluded that "it will not do." "Tasking, done forever done," he declared. "The evils attending it too numerous to mention here." Although he refrained from enumerating the "evils," Tait's description of his revised labor arrangements made clear what he believed them to be. Under the "new rules," he explained, the slaves "rise at daybreak, eat and start to work 1/2 an hour by the sun; work all day without tasking." In asserting his own control over the length of the workday, Tait came belatedly to the same conclusion his neighbors had reached long before.[29]

Within the framework of the gang system, slaves and slaveowners struggled over field labor. Slaves, who arrived in the new black belt with diverse work experiences, suddenly found themselves thrown into new daily and seasonal work routines. The transition was especially jarring for those who hailed from the Chesapeake, since their relocation to the southwest generally marked their first encounter with cotton cultivation. Besides performing the heavy work endemic to the settlement period, they had to learn the skills and seasonal rhythm of cotton planting and often adapt to a more tightly disciplined and regimented way of working. Slaves brought up under a regimen of tobacco and mixed farming in the Chesapeake discovered that cotton imposed its own cadence on the agricultural year. For Charles Ball, a Maryland slave sold onto an up-country South Carolina plantation early in the nineteenth century, initiation into the land of cotton was like entering another world. Accustomed to performing a variety of farming tasks individually or in small groups with minimal direct supervision, Ball despised the tedium and regimentation of work in the cotton fields. He particularly hated the picking season, which kept workers in the field from as early as August to as late as February, whereas the outdoor work of harvesting in the Chesapeake tobacco belt was completed by November and subsequent processing of the staple was "comparatively a work of leisure and ease." During the cotton harvest, owners and overseers drove slaves hard, lengthening the workday at both ends and punishing slaves who failed to meet daily quotas.

As Ball and countless other "raw hands" discovered, meeting the quotas was no easy task. "It requires some time to enable a stranger, or new hand, to acquire the sleight of picking cotton," Ball explained. The knack was so difficult to acquire that a slave not brought up to pick cotton stood little chance of becoming "a crack picker."[30] A slave's familiarity with cotton work was a valuable attribute for southwestern purchasers in the domestic slave trade; sellers took pains to point out when slaves they wished to sell had been "well trained to cotton making, cotton picking, etc." It was as much their unfamiliarity with cotton culture as their lack of immunity to local diseases that made "Virginia negroes" generally less valuable to Mississippi and Alabama planters than "acclimated negroes" of any provenance.[31] When purchasing Chesapeake slaves, southwestern slaveholders customarily gave them time to "gain some knowledge of the cotton business" but also punished novices who failed or stubbornly refused to master the art of cotton picking.[32]

The tightening of plantation discipline and the unfamiliarity of many slaves with the cotton business, combined with various grievances stemming from the migration to the cotton frontier, infused a high level of tension into everyday workplace relations. Simmering conflicts often flared into open confrontation, especially during the picking season. The slaves supervised by Robert Beverly—most of them transplanted Virginians—engaged in a running battle with the overseer that intensified at harvest time. Beverly had arrived in Alabama determined to transform his force into cotton hands. Although he realized that the workers "cannot pick cotton, untill they have a good deal of practice," Beverly convinced himself that they could be "made to do it" by "floging and that quite often." But neither "practice" nor "floging" did the trick—and the latter doubtless contributed to the slaves' general disaffection. Beverly's cousin, who knew the slaves both before and after their move to the black belt, declared that they had nearly "baffled" the overseer: "They take the woods when pressed for work—it is shameful to reflect how completely they have been ruined here, from being the best hands in the county, they are now the meanest." The picking season brought out the worst in them.

The chief offender, a frequent truant who was aptly named Grief, exhibited "no idea of working except at his own gait, [and] will not pick cotton." His fellows evinced a "rebellious spirit" in the form of "a general disregard (with a few exceptions) of orders, running off when their services are most needed, and an unwillingness to be pressed hard at work."[33]

Just as the slaves under Beverly's charge asserted individually and collectively their determination not to be taxed beyond reasonable and customary bounds, so too did other slaves in the new black belt. Those brought to new plantations in the company of relatives and friends, as Beverly's slaves evidently were, drew immediately on shared knowledge and experiences in their response to unacceptable demands. But eventually even slaves who were initially strangers to one another developed a sense of the proper pace and intensity of field work under the gang system, which quickly assumed the trappings of custom. "All of them know what their duty is upon a plantation," declared a Mississippi planter in the 1840s, "and that they are generally willing to do, and nothing more." If pressed to surpass that standard, "they will not submit to it, but become turbulent and impatient of control, and all the whips in Christendom cannot drive them to perform more than they think they ought to do, or have been in the long habit of doing."[34] He spoke from an experience shared widely by his fellow planters, who had in earlier years been only partially successful at reshaping the slaves' notions of "duty" in accordance with the masters' ideal of labor on upland cotton plantations.

The gang system conditioned the slaves' conflict with their owners over matters of subsistence and independent production as well as field labor. During the evolution of slavery in the U.S. South, the entrenchment of the dawn-to-dusk workday under the gang system had been accompanied by stronger guarantees of subsistence to slaves. Rations increased in quantity and regularly included meat as well as corn meal. In the words of one observer, planters who worked their slaves under the gang system exacted "steady employment" while "giving the hands plenty to eat"—in contrast with the task regimen that prevailed on most low-country estates, which usually accorded slaves only minimal rations, often cornmeal alone, with the expectation that slaves would produce a substantial proportion of their own food after completing their task.[35] Although slaves on upland gang-labor estates seem to have had smaller amounts of land available for their own cultivation and less time to cultivate those plots, they also had less need to supplement their diets with food produced in their own time.

As a result, they could devote the products of garden plots and poultry yards, as well as fishing and hunting, to purposes other than immediate consumption, engaging in a broad range of transactions with other slaves, with their owners, and within local provision economies. On some upland cotton estates, too, slaves' crops extended to small patches of the staple crop, which they might sell to their owners or market themselves, according to local custom. When their owners permitted it, some slaves parlayed such petty production and exchange into personal property, including on occasion livestock.[36]

By wrenching slaves from the physical and social settings in which they had realized opportunities for independent production and petty trade, relocation to southwestern plantations reopened the question of their access to plantation resources and time in which to exploit them. Their forced migration tore slaves from familiar forests, fields, and garden patches and often required them to leave behind personal property that could not be easily moved.[37] Hoping at least to enjoy the same privileges in their new homes as they had in the old, slaves insisted that their owners not breach established traditions pertaining to subsistence and independent production.

Some migrant planters undoubtedly viewed the move to the cotton frontier as a chance to roll back slaves' self-directed productive activities in hopes of tightening their own hold over the slaves' labor. A sizable contingent of slaveholders in the older settled regions had long complained that allowing slaves to tend ground at night and on Sunday only fatigued them for the real work of the plantation, and that trading the produce of their gardens and "Negro crops" of cotton tempted them to theft or worse. "Allow it once to be understood by a negro that he is to provide for himself," warned one South Carolina planter, "and you that moment give him an undeniable claim on you for a portion of his time to make this provision; and should you from necessity, or any other cause, encroach upon his time, disappointment and discontent are seriously felt." Intent on instilling in his slaves "a habit of perfect dependence," he maintained "the doctrine that my negroes have no time whatever."[38] Acting upon similar convictions, the Alabama planter Charles Crommelin established a central garden on which slaves raised vegetables for his own table and theirs, rather than tending their own plots. He also stood squarely against slaves' ownership of poultry and livestock, insisting that he "must be the sole owner" of all property on the premises.[39]

But more often slaveholders acquiesced to the continuation of customary practices of garden plot cultivation, production of baskets and other handcrafted goods, fishing, and sometimes hunting. They did so both in the interest of social stability—to give slaves a tangible stake in remaining on the new plantation—and because they themselves derived immediate benefits from slaves' food production. Throughout the settlement period, and especially during the cotton boom of the 1830s, plantation proprietors were loath to devote scarce open land and valuable slave labor to food crops. They put the bulk of their fields into cotton and purchased most of their corn, meat, and other edibles from factors in New Orleans and Mobile, commission merchants in smaller towns, or local yeomen. As one planter in central Mississippi recalled, he and his neighbors "crowded every spot of their fields with cotton plants," whereas they imported "every grain of corn consumed upon their plantations." Immigration to newly settled regions quickly depleted local food surpluses and inflated prices, while shipments of provisions depended upon the vagaries of water transportation. Even when bulk goods did arrive, the monotonous diet of corn, salt pork, and game wore thin. In such circumstances, food produced in garden patches or procured in woods and waters not only helped feed people in the quarters but also those in the master's house and in other households in the neighborhood.[40]

On the cotton frontier as in the older settled regions, however, slaves were provided only conditional access to time and land, and rarely in ways that benefited them alone. Given the scarcity of cleared land in the newly opening black belt, slaves probably cultivated only the most marginal of land on their own or, alternatively, gained use of more productive tracts only by agreeing to clear them and have them subsumed into the plantation field the following year. Such an arrangement in effect amounted to a means of inducing slaves to perform extracurricular clearing.[41] Nor did slaves on the Alabama-Mississippi frontier receive any more time to work the plots than did slaves in the Chesapeake and in the piedmont cotton districts of the seaboard states. Few planters permitted slaves more "free" time than the customary Sunday, an occasional half-Saturday when the owner's crops were "forward," and a few days around Christmas and other holidays. Indeed, on a few plantations, owners actually saw fit to compel slaves to work their patches. When slaves were "too indolent to cultivate their own crops in their own time," declared a Mississippi planter, "a good overseer will always see that they do not neglect their own interest, any more than their master's."[42]

As the slaveholders' attempt to compel slaves to perform work on their "own" time suggests, whatever customary privileges slaves managed to retain or gain during the course of their relocation to the cotton frontier remained subject to revision or reinterpretation by their owners. For bondmen and women on cotton plantations in Alabama and Mississippi, the struggle to control their labor and its products would last far beyond the close of the 1830s.

7

SLAVE LIFE, SLAVE SOCIETY, AND TOBACCO PRODUCTION IN THE TIDEWATER CHESAPEAKE, 1620–1820

Lorena S. Walsh

TOBACCO SHAPED THE seventeenth- and early eighteenth-century Chesapeake. "Tobacco is our meat, drinke, cloathing and monies," Hugh Jones wrote in 1699. Thirty years later Benedict Leonard Calvert affirmed, "Tobacco, as our staple, is our all, and Indeed leaves no room for anything else."[1] The requirements of tobacco culture influenced everything from agricultural techniques and the yearly agricultural calendar, to types of housing, to settlement patterns and urban development (or the lack thereof), to the occupational structure and networks of trade and credit. Scholars have paid much attention to the links between the staple and white society, economy, and even mentality.[2] However, although tobacco and slaves have been judged sufficiently intertwined to serve as the title of a recent book on the Chesapeake between 1680 and 1800,[3] the intimate connections between the staple and slave society have been less intensively studied. The original sources, moreover, tell the story from the viewpoint of slaveowners—and mostly large ones at that. Shifting the perspective to that of the slaves is thus a challenging task.

Tobacco, more than anything else, brought black people to the Chesapeake. Planters by and large turned slaveholders when the supply of white indentured servants dwindled, providing too few new field hands for a revolving-door labor system that required a constant influx of workers. Once slavery was established, the price of tobacco determined the shape of the slave trade. Surges in slave imports tended—especially in the first half of the eighteenth century—to coincide with booms in the tobacco market, as had earlier peaks in migration of indentured servants.[4] When the tobacco market was good, planters wanted to expand production and had the cash or could get credit to purchase new workers. As Norfolk merchant Charles Stewart noted early in the 1750s, "Our planters have had great prices for their Tobacco these late years, and are full of Cash, which nothing but Negroes will draw forth, . . . the planters having left room in their Crops" for additional slaves.[5]

Since tobacco also influenced where slaves would live once they entered the region, it eventually determined the racial demography of the Chesapeake. There was less need for extra field hands in places like the lower Delmarva peninsula and the southside of the lower James River that had little good tobacco land. In addition, planters in these areas tended to be poorer, making them an unpromising market for human chattels. Slave ships therefore disgorged their merchandise in the places where rich planters who were expanding their labor forces were most numerous. As a result, slaves were concentrated in prime tidewater tobacco areas in the first quarter of the eighteenth century. By mid-century, most large tidewater planters no longer needed to buy additional workers; natural increase among their slaves supplied any extra hands they required. Then, as westward expansion into the piedmont accelerated, slaves migrated to or were sold at the outset in areas of expanding tobacco culture. After the Revolution, slavery expanded chiefly in the western piedmont of Virginia where—unlike in much of the tidewater, the Shenandoah valley, and western Maryland—tobacco remained the mainstay of the regional economy. A combination of slave migration westward and white out-migration resulted by 1810 in high concentrations of black people in those areas of the Chesapeake that remained most committed to tobacco.[6]

That many slaves lived alone or in small residential groups resulted from several circumstances, including the disease environment, sex ratios among imported slaves, and slaveowners' purchasing patterns and inheritance practices. In the seventeenth and early eighteenth centuries slaves encountered a harsh disease environment and suffered high rates of mortality. Among imported slaves men outnumbered women by roughly two to one, so that many men were unable to find wives and form families. African-born slave women were generally too sick or too alienated to begin bearing children until some time after they arrived in the Chesapeake. And, while a handful of grandees bought dozens of slaves at a time, most tobacco planters wealthy enough to buy slaves could afford to purchase only one or two per year. As the slave population in older areas changed from largely immigrant to native born and—in the second quarter of the eighteenth century—began to grow by natural increase, its demography became more normal. Still, residence groups remained small, in part because slaveholders tended to divide slaves among several heirs and in part because of the dispersed settlement pattern dictated by the requirements of tobacco culture.[7]

The persistence of small work and residence units into the nineteenth century resulted directly from the nature of the staple. Good tobacco soils occur in small plots scattered over the Chesapeake landscape. In order to make the most of the best soils and to maintain the long fallows necessary to restore soil fertility, small slaveholders tended to limit work forces in keeping with the long-term capacity of their farms. Large landowners, who were usually also some of the largest slaveowners, dispersed laborers among outlying quarters near the home farm or else on more distant holdings.

In addition to the limitations imposed by soil properties, there were few economies of scale in tobacco culture. Two or three workers could tend and harvest the crop more efficiently than one. Beyond this, however, successful tobacco culture required careful attention to a host of details throughout the growing season and during the subsequent harvesting and processing. Ordinarily overseers could supervise no more than ten working hands, and even the most skillful laboring slaveowners or estate agents no more than twenty. Consequently, while the size of slave work and residential units increased over time, with small quarters of one to five slaves becoming rarer, only at the great houses of the rich, where laborers pursued a variety of craft and diversified agricultural activities, could slaves expect to live together in large groups. Over time, too, as the numbers of slaves in older areas increased, the chances for socialization between and family formation among adjacent plantations multiplied. Nonetheless, tobacco culture continued to impose a high degree of residential isolation.[8]

Tobacco cultivation gave rise to a pattern of work both familiar and unfamiliar. Many features of early Chesapeake agriculture—especially hoe culture and long fallows—would have been familiar to farming peoples in any place where men and women were few and land plenty. The marked emphasis on production of a cash crop for distant, international markets, however, was probably less familiar. In most traditional societies, people use the labor time saved in raising sufficient food by extensive rather than intensive cultivation techniques for home manufactures and for various leisure activities— whereas Chesapeake planters devoted most of the extra labor time to producing tobacco.[9]

Seventeenth-century Chesapeake planters—both slaveless farm-ers and those with bound laborers, whether servants or slaves—exploited land, which was abundant and cheap, and sought to make the most of labor, which was scarce and dear. In the process of learn-ing how to survive in an often hostile environment and finding a staple that they could exchange for imports, colonists developed a new system of husbandry. Abandoning most European agricultural practices, planters adopted girdling or slash-and-burn clearing, long fallows, and hoe culture from local native Americans, as well as em-bracing maize and tobacco. The Europeans' main innovations were the introduction of domestic livestock and the use of metal tools. At first they concentrated on maximum production of tobacco from fresh lands. The annual work cycle was almost wholly shaped by the sea-sonal demands of tobacco, which required constant attention through-out most of the year. Production of food crops—primarily maize—was usually limited to the requirements of self-sufficiency, and almost all essential manufactured items imported. Until the last quarter of the seventeenth century, small farmers, who often owned a few inden-tured servants, were the major producers. Then, as the supply of European servants dwindled, richer planters turned to slaves as the primary source of bound labor. Large plantations (by Chesapeake standards) became more common, and wealth among whites more concentrated. Slaves produced an increasing proportion of the re-gion's cash crop.[10]

This initial system of Chesapeake agriculture, modified and diver-sified as settlements matured, would be repeated throughout the region as frontiers expanded. Although condemned as wasteful and inefficient, it saved labor, the scarcest resource, while exploiting the richness of virgin land in the short run. Planters rotated fields rather than crops, working only a small amount of land each year. Long fallows of about twenty years that followed six to eight years of cultiva-tion preserved much of the long-term fertility of the soil, while hill and hoe culture prevented serious erosion. As a result, there was little resource depletion before 1775, although abandoned old fields that reverted to natural vegetation made the landscape unsightly to Eu-ropean eyes. For Africans, native Americans, and creole planters, though, these cultivation practices simply reflected common sense.[11]

The system was successful, and everywhere tobacco output per laborer increased through 1690. The amount of tobacco one worker could produce in a single growing season rose from around three hundred pounds in the 1620s to over a thousand by the 1650s and 1660s, and in some places over two thousand pounds in the 1670s and

1680s. (Table 7.1, below, reports these changes in output over time and by subregion.)[12] Output rose because, over the first three quarters of the century, planters learned how to handle more tobacco plants per worker and developed improved plant strains. They also made improvements in curing and packing the crop. Through 1675 these increases in output were accompanied by decreasing costs for food, clothing, and tools, and for transportation and distribution of the crop. These savings allowed planters to continue to make a profit despite falling tobacco prices. But in order to profit handsomely, planters needed more workers. As the supply of European servants dwindled, they turned increasingly to slaves to remedy the labor shortage.[13]

The productivity of tobacco slaves was related to the ways workers resisted enslavement, their health, the weather, local natural resources, the managerial skills of owners and overseers, and differing techniques of crop management. In the late seventeenth and early eighteenth centuries output per laborer varied widely from farm to farm. A spate of bad growing seasons and, in some places, experiments with high-quality but lower-yielding strains caused drops of output per worker that had little to do with the composition of the labor force. But slave sickness, resistance, and alienation also lowered productivity on occasion. African slaves had little incentive to work diligently for their captors, and many planters and overseers did not know how to motivate them. From the outset Africans in the Chesapeake certainly resisted enslavement, but little evidence survives about the particular means they employed. Methods of resistance may have included refusing to work, running away, real or feigned misunderstanding of commands given in English, or simply denying the authority of their owners. Some slaves resisted the new regime strenuously; others could not or would not work hard. Some suffered harsh punishments as a result, while others—who appeared too sickly ever to become useful workers—were left to do whatever work they would, with minimal supervision and minimal care. Many black men and women perished in an unhealthy environment and climate colder than that to which they were accustomed, and many more were periodically or chronically ill. Some of the early tidewater plantations were located in particularly disease-prone places. The histories of individual farms show a link between low productivity per worker in both the cash crop (tobacco) and the subsistence crop (maize) on the one hand, and an unhealthy location, heightened slave resistance, and unsatisfactory performance and frequent turnover among overseers on the other.[14]

Nonetheless, the switch from predominantly servant to predomi-

TABLE 7.1. TOBACCO OUTPUT PER LABORER BY REGION

	Region One						Region Two						Region Three				Region Four							
	Lower James basin		Virginia Eastern Shore		Maryland lower Eastern Shore		Virginia Potomac basin		Maryland lower western shore		Maryland upper Eastern Shore		York basin		Lower Rappahannock basin		Va Piedmont-Rappahannock area		Va Piedmont James area		Virginia Southside		Shenandoah Valley	
Years	N	Mean	N	Mean	N	Mean	N	Mean	N	Mean	N	Mean	N	Mean	N	Mean	N	Mean	N	Mean	N	Mean	N	Mean
1623–1629	8	345																						
1630–1649	5	917	4	1,048					8	781	1	400	3	938										
1650–1669	7	897	12	1,138			7	802	20	1,539			13	1,087										
1670–1679	2	662	2	1,178	2	1,185	1	3,000	9	1,534	3	2,583	10	1,366	2	1,625								
1680–1699	6	973							7	2,167	1	2,584	12	1,453	5	1,355								
1700–1709							1	661	12	1,621	5	1,750	3	1,175	2	1,395								
1710–1719	1	918					6	938	5	1,120	16	1,831	12	806	3	1,408								
1720–1729					1	1,315	4	843	3	1,347	28	1,277	16	717	1	881			1	1,016				
1730–1739					1	2,083			4	1,009	27	1,352	36	635	5	611			1	686				
1740–1747					1	1,121	13	756	6	1,275	15	1,055	69	860	10	622								
1748–1753					1	853	6	862	4	1,078	9	1,026	36	980	28	773	1	922	1	789				
1754–1763	4	344					11	731	11	808	45	902	66	838	6	861	9	885	28	1,013				
1764–1769	7	193					20	660	17	748	17	665	56	777	29	717	1	988	26	977	1	1,011	6	1,032
1770–1774	3	400			2	639	10	908	15	839	26	732	40	898	9	590	18	837			9	1,036	2	1,463
1775–1781	6	788			2	342	11	424	19	747	41	631	12	422	13	773	7	484			8	479	9	1,104
1782–1789	1	28			1	227	13	448	11	749	24	1,048	46	572	30	580	2	883	5	639	1	464	3	629
1790–1799							7	797	33	715	32	647	19	581	14	878	1	495	15	1,150	7	1,139	3	1,007
1800–1807							3	727	29	655	13	862			21	636	2	699	18	750	5	1,545		
1808–1815									2	598	2	454			2	462	1	525	1	481	2	458		
1816–1820									7	415	4	466			12	121	1	300	4	1,258	1	1,579		

Sources: Plantation accounts, farm diaries, and probate inventories.
Notes: Tobacco output is measured in pounds. For methods of calculation, see note 12. N = number of crops for which size of labor force is known.

175

nantly slave labor did raise productivity on the majority of plantations, just as slave buyers had hoped. Output per worker peaked during the years in which the proportion of slaves in the bound labor force rose to half or more. More general estimates of output per worker that aggregate information from the entire region do not show this rise, but estimates broken down by subregions, or better yet, by country, confirm this pattern (see table 7.1).[15] Black slaves, not white servants, made most of the largest individual crops recorded, and most of these efficient workers were Africans, not creoles. African slaves arrived in the right places at the right time to exploit fresh lands for their owners. Planters could get new fields cleared more readily and thus expand their scale of operation. The initial preponderance of men among new slaves raised the proportion of prime laborers in the agricultural work force, and hence average crop sizes.

Planters also found new ways to exploit the strange new workers. So long as white servants made up most of the labor force, English work customs tended to prevail in the Chesapeake, customs that had evolved where there was a surplus of workers and a shortage of work. A climate in which summers were hotter and winters colder than in Britain also encouraged rest breaks in heat and slack times in cold. In the seventeenth-century Chesapeake, the workday ran from sunrise to sunset, but even during the growing season field laborers were permitted a rest in the heat of the day and given Saturday afternoon and various traditional holidays off. Little work was done in winter, aside from hunting, cutting firewood, preparing meals, and packing tobacco. So long as African slaves were few and intermingled with European servants, work rules designed for white laborers probably also applied to black ones.[16]

But once slaves came to dominate the bound labor force late in the seventeenth century, the experiences of slaves and servants diverged. Slaves had no claim to English workers' customary rights: food of reasonable quantity and quality, adequate clothing and shelter, and a certain amount of rest and leisure. Granted, slaveowners were unlikely to starve their expensive workers or to provide insufficient clothing or shelter, and planters frequently condemned those who failed to meet certain generally agreed upon standards, realizing that heightened slave resistance was a likely consequence. In 1732 William Byrd II encountered some badly provisioned slaves: "The poor Negroes upon [Colonel Jones's plantations] are a kind of Adamites, very scantily supplied with clothes and other necessaries. . . . However, they are even with their master and make him but indifferent crops, so that he gets nothing by his injustice but the scandal of it."[17] Nonetheless, in order to raise profits, slaveholders economized wherever possible with rations, clothing, bedding, and housing. They made little attempt to understand or to accommodate the blacks' preferences in diet or clothing, and they housed their slaves in small, insubstantial, and exceedingly cheap huts.[18]

More significantly, planters began imposing new, more stringent work routines. First, the number of workdays was increased. By about 1730 holidays were reduced to three a year—Christmas, the duration of this holiday being left to the master's discretion, and three days each at Easter and Whitsuntide. In addition, for almost all slaves Saturday became a full workday, and the same rule began to be applied to servants. Even Sundays were far from inviolate, although, with time, slaveowners found it prudent to compensate slaves for Sunday work with extra food or a little cash. (In the early eighteenth century slaveowners seem to have regarded a Sunday free of work as enjoined merely by their own religious sensibilities, but by mid-century the slaves had converted that practice into a right that could not be violated arbitrarily.) Slaves also had to respond to any situation the master declared to be an emergency. The slaves' workday, furthermore, was often extended into the night. Night work probably originated with the need to beat corn into meal with mortars and pestles daily. In the 1650s the Maryland provincial court ruled that a master could not keep his white servants in the fields so long that they must beat corn for their victuals at night. By the late 1670s, as slaves became more numerous, a traveler noted that "the servants and negroes after they have worn themselves down the whole day, and come home to rest, have yet to grind and pound the grain, which is generally maize, for their masters and all their families as well as themselves, and all the negroes, to eat."[19]

Slave women in the Chesapeake performed the same field labor as did slave men. In the seventeenth century, labor-short planters were also putting some white servant women to work at the hoe, albeit with a certain ambivalence about the types of work proper for servant women. Once slaves predominated in the labor force, however, white women servants all but disappeared from the fields. In contrast, every able-bodied slave woman and most slave girls aged twelve or more did regular field labor. Men and women toiled together at the same tasks in a single work group, and work requirements were the same for both sexes. When rating laborers as full or partial hands, planters made allowances for youth, disability, or advanced age but made no distinctions by sex. Most planters had too few slaves to divide their work force into men's and women's gangs, but even those who could divide their workers did not, at least until the middle of the eighteenth century. Before that time, any productivity increases that a division of the work force by sex might have created—an intensification of the pace of work in men's gangs, for example—were insufficient to offset the extra cost of supervising two gangs, or, more likely, to offset the drop in efficiency that would certainly occur when one overseer had to divide his attention between two groups.[20]

New customs evolved that governed work relations between masters and slaves, but these were specific to individual plantations. Slaves had no legal rights, as did servants, that courts might enforce. Plantation custom still defined the amount of work expected, the standard weekly food ration, and the kind and amount of new clothing to be provided each year. The work requirements might be harsh and the provisions scanty, but once minimums and maximums were set, slaves had some hedge against further exploitation. They could protest increased work demands, lack of sufficient food and clothing, or curtailment of privileges by appealing to their owners' or former owners' past practices or to current practices on neighboring plantations. If these arguments failed, they had to resort to work slowdowns, feigned illness, or running away. A few resisted violations of custom through direct, sometimes violent, confrontation with the offending owner or overseer, almost invariably suffering punishment as a result.

Whenever a new overseer attempted to change current privileges or work routines, the importance of customary practice became evident. Slaves resisted unfavorable changes, while the overseers' complaint was almost always that the slaves had become accustomed to doing too little work or were accustomed to working as they pleased. There was, then, a continuing contest about work requirements and about who would set the pace and determine the intensity of that work. Some slaveowners recognized that the more they allowed custom to define plantation work relations, the less their flexibility to make changes. Accordingly, they attempted to limit their slaves' ability to develop customary privileges and to control the work pace by changing overseers frequently—although incompetence on the part of the overseers or the irascibility of the slaveowners themselves sometimes produced the same result. Plantation records demonstrate that this was bad policy. Slaves usually expressed less open discontent and consistently made bigger crops on those quarters where overseers had long tenures. Indeed, by the early nineteenth century a candidate for a vacant overseer's post would solicit the job by promising not to interfere with whatever privileges the slaves had enjoyed under the previous overseer.[21]

Planters who owned bound laborers in the early eighteenth century sought to cut costs and to intensify labor requirements because they faced growing economic difficulties. They were caught between trade disruptions, rising costs of production, and diminishing tobacco yields. After the 1690s in all the older settled areas, tobacco output per laborer—and thus income from the major cash crop—began to fall, since tobacco prices remained low. The decline, which occurred well after slaves predominated in the unfree labor force, was a consequence of the interaction of changing populations with natural resources. Nonslaveowners, who generally had a growing number of dependent children in their households and who often farmed poorer quality land, experienced the same decline as did slaveowners. Some drop in tobacco output per full-time worker was an inevitable result of diminishing returns to available natural resources. Even prime fields, re-cultivated after a long fallow, failed to yield as well as virgin clearings, and over time, if they did not move somewhere else, planters began cropping more marginal, lower-yielding lands. As settlements matured, limits were soon reached on the amount of tobacco a worker—slave or free—could tend and consequently the size of crop he or she could produce. Only in the twentieth century, when chemical fertilizers became available, did tidewater tobacco growers achieve higher outputs per worker than they had between 1670 and 1700.[22] Moreover, once slaves began to form couples and have offspring, more black women and children joined the labor force. Women and teenagers, although counted as full field hands, could not produce as much tobacco as prime-aged men, which again lead to a drop in average crop size.

During the eighteenth century tobacco planters adopted several strategies to counter diminishing returns. When they could farm fresh land extensively, planters realized high outputs per person-hour. Once output per hour declined, ever more labor had to be expended in order to maintain returns. Farmers without slaves had either to work harder or accept a lower standard of living. Slaveowners sought to extract more work from their slaves. Since they could no longer expand tobacco output per worker, they added other kinds of activities that cut costs or generated additional revenues. These strategies included some on-farm production or local purchase of goods like coarse shoes, cloth, and basic tools to replace costly imports. In some parts of Virginia tobacco was further processed before export, adding to its value but increasing off-season work. Most slaveowners also added maize and wheat as major revenue crops.[23] By making these changes, planters realized relatively stable revenues per worker, in constant value, across the whole colonial period. Evidence from individual farms suggests that the annual gross revenue per hand from the major field crops was roughly £15 sterling constant value from the 1640s to the early 1680s, then probably fell to about £10 from about 1680 to 1740, but rose again to around £15 in the third quarter of the eighteenth century.[24] Slaves suffered disproportionately, since it was primarily their leisure that was sacrificed in the planters' drive to counter diminishing returns to the staple.

To a considerable degree, the course of later seventeenth-century and eighteenth-century Chesapeake agriculture can only be understood in terms of the differing patterns of development in several distinct subregions. Beginning in the 1680s three regions can be distinguished, although others emerge.[25]

The first of these subregions, the lower James basin and the lower Delmarva peninsula, had few soils suitable for tobacco. Planters in these areas dropped tobacco almost entirely when prices fell, turning to the production of naval stores, timber, cider, grain, corn and livestock, as well as to subsistence farming. They returned periodically to tobacco when prices were high, but these areas were never again important in the overall tobacco export trade. There were fewer slaves in the work force in this subregion, and they worked at more diverse activities.

The second subregion—Maryland's lower western and upper eastern shores, the Virginia side of the Potomac, and parts of the Rappahannock—was the major area of oronoco cultivation, the most common tobacco strain. Planters in these places continued to grow tobacco as a major cash crop until at least the 1770s. However, large crops of 2,500 to 3,000 pounds per hand had disappeared by the 1730s, and production per laborer slowly declined throughout the century. Planters compensated by adding wheat and maize to their market crop mixes, and from mid-century grains usually contributed about half of gross field crop revenues on big plantations. The adoption of tobacco inspection acts in the 1730s and 1740s may have reduced the size of marketable crops somewhat, but probably not by much. Before the Revolution, most planters did not switch from complete specialization in tobacco to complete specialization in wheat; they grew both, and corn as well. The development of new wheat and corn markets assured large planters that they could find buyers and continue to get a price for their produce that would more than cover costs even should they make steadily larger grain crops. And they learned how to grow more grain without reducing, or greatly reducing, tobacco crops.

In the third subregion, the York basin and parts of the Rappahannock—which produced the sweet-scented strain of tobacco most favored for the British domestic market—still another pattern prevailed. Planters enjoyed high prices during much of the depression of the late seventeenth and early eighteenth centuries, and production per laborer dropped markedly only in the 1720s and early 1730s, a period of low prices for the sweet-scented leaf, bad weather, and voluntary crop reductions in an attempt to limit quantity and raise the quality of the staple. York and Rappahannock planters found the standardization imposed by tobacco inspection acts, followed by a price rise beginning in the 1730s, sufficient encouragement to pitch larger crops per hand in the third quarter of the eighteenth century than they had in the second. These producers also began to plant more grain, especially maize since some of the area's soils were too acidic for wheat.[26]

Beginning in the 1730s a fourth subregion emerged—the expanding piedmont areas to the west—which contributed an ever-increasing share of tobacco exports. Planters and slaves working fresh lands at first produced bigger tobacco crops than did their contemporaries in the tidewater. While building farms, piedmont planters made only enough maize for plantation consumption. But once the farms were established, they began growing grain as well as tobacco on a commercial basis.

While tobacco remained the regional staple in all the parts of the Chesapeake except the lower James basin and lower Delmarva peninsula, grains became a more significant part of the agricultural mix. Beginning in some places in the 1720s and more generally by the 1730s, planters—especially large and middling slaveowners—responded to growing markets for grain in Europe and the West Indies by producing surpluses of corn and wheat. Throughout the Chesapeake grain production per worker rose from the 1730s onwards (see tables 7.2 and 7.3). Everywhere maize crops reached ten or more barrels per hand, a level of deliberate market production where about half of the crop was marketable surplus.[27] Wheat output per laborer varied greatly between regions, reflecting the low yields per acre most planters could effect with poor plows, weak draft animals, and on acid soils. The labor demands of corn and tobacco also limited the amount of land planters

TABLE 7.2. CORN OUTPUT PER LABORER BY REGION

| | Region One | | | | | | Region Two | | | | | | Region Three | | | | Region Four | | | | | | | |
| | Lower James basin | | Virginia Eastern Shore | | Maryland lower Eastern Shore | | Virginia Potomac basin | | Maryland lower western shore | | Maryland upper Eastern Shore | | York basin | | Lower Rappahannock basin | | Va Piedmont–Rappahannock area | | Va Piedmont James area | | Virginia Southside | | Shenandoah Valley | |
Years	N	Mean	N	Mean	N	Mean	N	Mean	N	Mean	N	Mean	N	Mean	N	Mean	N	Mean	N	Mean	N	Mean	N	Mean
1630–1649									3	7.8	1	4.0												
1650–1669	1	9.0	5	5.9					1	7.0			5	8.6										
1670–1679			1	7.0			1	18.0					1	4.5										
1680–1699	1	5.0							4	5.8			2	9.5	1	4.5								
1700–1709							1	4.0	4	8.3			5	8.9										
1710–1719	1	12.0					1	4.3	4	6.6			7	5.2	3	8.2								
1720–1729									3	8.6			7	7.9	4	10.9								
1730–1739					1	8.0			4	12.2	14	11.8	14	9.8	7	9.3	2	11.6	4	10.2				
1740–1747			(Md Head of Bay)				4	8.6	3	22.7	7	16.3	20	15.6	13	11.4	3	8.2	1	5.7				
1748–1753	1	10.0	4	15.1					3	9.0	8	17.1	34	18.6	1	2.5								
1754–1763	1	15.4	10	15.5			3	15.5	7	22.4	4	25.2	11	16.0	36	11.2	8	32.3	11	13.1			1	17.1
1764–1769	8	9.4	2	10.0			18	18.1	13	14.5	17	22.1	49	19.4	14	16.8	2	15.3	8	22.5			2	13.7
1770–1774	1	28.6			2	16.8	9	24.7	13	13.8	21	20.5	21	19.6	9	16.7	11	27.6	11	16.7	3	39.1	4	13.3
1775–1781	5	27.6	2	7.8	7	12.4	9	11.7	14	14.3	46	31.2	22	18.9	18	18.1	1	27.6	11	37.8	3	27.4	1	10.1
1782–1789	8	13.1			8	15.2	26	16.4	6	9.3	34	30.2	15	17.6	10	26.5	1	9.8	14	26.5	1	30.0	3	28.2
1790–1799	1	15.0	5	12.6	6	16.5	18	21.7	20	12.5	22	27.7	13	20.2	10	29.3	11	27.2	41	24.6				
1800–1807			2	13.2					10	14.3	26	22.8			32	30.9			6	17.2	7	30.9		
1808–1815	1	17.9	3	14.2					15	14.1	64	22.7			52	33.2	1	22.0	3	16.5	2	24.7		
1816–1820	1	28.6							6	13.6	21	26.7	6	16.0	21	37.6	1	11.8	7	29.3				

Sources: Plantation accounts, farm diaries, and probate inventories.

Notes: Corn output is measured in barrels. For methods of calculation, see note 12. Maryland Head of Bay, an area that dropped tobacco, is here added to Region One. N = number of crops for which size of labor force is known.

182

TABLE 7.3. WHEAT OUTPUT PER LABORER BY REGION

| | Region One | | | | | | Region Two | | | | | | Region Three | | | | Region Four | | | | | | | |
| | Lower James basin | | Maryland Head of Bay | | Maryland lower Eastern Shore | | Virginia Potomac basin | | Maryland lower western shore | | Maryland upper Eastern Shore | | York basin | | Lower Rappahannock basin | | Va Piedmont-Rappahannock area | | Va Piedmont James area | | Virginia Southside | | Shenandoah Valley | |
Years	N	Mean	N	Mean	N	Mean	N	Mean	N	Mean	N	Mean	N	Mean	N	Mean	N	Mean	N	Mean	N	Mean	N	Mean
1720–1739									2	6.6	6	11.1	4	7.4	1	3.5								
1740–1753			4	4.7					4	5.1	1	11.0	6	3.4										
1754–1763	1	4.8	5	7.6			1	8.7	6	8.8	22	35.1	8	9.0	7	7.6	3	12.0						
1764–1769	3	2.0	2	24.5			15	64.7	4	55.9	17	43.0	2	15.0	1	28.6	1	6.4	6	21.9				
1770–1774	2	31.7					8	61.2	11	18.0	23	34.6	15	14.2	8	23.3	1	1.8	2	9.9	1	5.3	3	27.5
1775–1781			1	30.4			5	28.5	9	8.3	47	36.0	5	7.2	2	15.1	1	12.5	1	10.0			1	25.0
1782–1789	5	15.4	3	67.5	5	7.2	3	13.5	6	15.7	37	73.1	8	11.3	2	6.8	5	45.3	19	33.7				
1790–1799	1	8.0	1	23.3	4	22.7	23	34.8	22	22.4	31	70.9	24	29.5	48	25.5					2	16.1	1	83.6
1800–1807			2	45.9			1	35.8	11	22.3	53	77.1	9	39.3	30	32.6					2	16.9		
1808–1815	1	18.9	1	31.5					13	19.1	79	82.1	4	24.3	58	50.1			5	63.2	2	30.1		
1816–1820	2	30.7							7	19.4	50	73.6	4	34.7	8	71.3	2	59.6	3	64.6				

Sources: Plantation accounts, farm diaries, and probate inventories.
Notes: Wheat output is measured in bushels. For methods of calculation, see note 12. N = number of crops for which size of labor force is known.

183

could cultivate in wheat. However, even small crops of wheat raised market income since, unlike maize (much of which was consumed on the plantation), about 90 percent of the wheat crop net of seed was sold.[28]

The addition of grains to the crop mix was, however, not easily accomplished. A major constraint on increased grain production throughout the period was inadequate livestock forage. If planters were to raise more grain per hand, they had to make greater use of plows, and they also needed more manure for fertilizer. And if they were going to pen stock and employ draft animals, they had either to grow or buy extra maize, fodder, hay, or cultivated grasses to feed the penned and especially the working animals. Many planters managed nothing beyond collecting and storing corn fodder more assiduously. Pasture improvement required a lot of extra work and hay a delicate meshing of seasonal schedules, since the wheat and hay harvests conflicted. Because of these constraints, many planters were slow to substitute plows for hoes. In a number of areas plows were far from universal farm equipment until the 1790s, and scarcity of forage remained a serious problem even in 1820. Plow culture supplanted the hoe more quickly in the piedmont than in the tidewater. There planters often succeeded in negotiating agreements with overseers, whereby the planters retained an extra share of corn and wheat crops in return for supplying plow teams.[29]

Scholars have generally failed to appreciate the forage constraint and have concluded in consequence that Chesapeake cultivation techniques were backward because slaves were poor workers who abused draft animals and who were unwilling or unable to use plows properly. Plantation records and planter correspondence do suggest that slaves were often careless with their owners' tools and that they appropriated part of the corn that was supposed to feed the stock. But planters and overseers generally agreed that draft animals performed poorly because they had insufficient food, and there is little to suggest that slaves consistently mistreated them. Neither did planters trust only native, more acculturated slaves with plows and carts. In two very old tidewater counties—York, Virginia, and St. Mary's, Maryland—only about half of all planters who left inventories owned plows in the 1770s. While slaves had arrived in number in both counties by the 1660s and had become self-reproducing around 1700, planters in both areas concentrated on hand-cultivated tobacco and made minimal use of plows, even when they grew extra corn or wheat. In contrast, in Kent and Talbot counties on Maryland's upper eastern shore, planters began to shift into wheat culture in the late 1720s. By the 1730s the majority of inventoried farmers and almost all the big slaveowners employed plows, although these counties developed later than either York or St. Mary's. Few planters acquired slaves until the 1690s, and large numbers of Africans were sold on the eastern shore in the 1710s and 1720s. Slaves, whatever their origins, began using plows consistently when and where planters began raising wheat as a major cash crop.[30]

In short, planters developed a second system of agriculture that depended on the plow to produce surplus corn and wheat. Albeit gradually in many places, these alterations to the Chesapeake system of husbandry had profound implications for slave work routines. Work patterns changed most on large plantations, for it was big slave-owners who took the lead in adopting the plow. So long as laborers employed hoes alone to prepare land for planting, the possibility of expanding grain production was limited: no more crops could be grown than hills to grow them on could be prepared. Plowing released labor time by speeding planting in spring and weeding during the growing season, thus enabling planters to double the production of corn. The extra corn could in turn be fed to the animals that pulled the plows and, when penned, produced manure for fertilizing, again increasing yields of corn and tobacco. Plowing was also essential for the expanded production of wheat, a crop that interfered less with the seasonal requirements of tobacco than did corn. The land could be prepared in off-seasons, and the grain seeded and plowed or harrowed in after the tobacco was harvested and before the corn needed gathering. Planters required extra labor only for the short harvest, and wheat growers had no difficulty hiring free whites or slaves belonging to planters who did not grow much grain.[31] Consequently, slaves on large plantations cultivated more acres per worker and spent more time plowing and raising grains than did slaves on small plantations where hoe-cultivated tobacco remained the major crop.

In addition to increased use of plows and manure, a second source of greater productivity came from greater exploitation of the work force. In the first three quarters of the seventeenth century, most bound laborers did not usually work after dark, and only sporadically in winter. As planters increased total crop output, they first eliminated a number of holidays and free Saturday afternoons. Gradually they increased requirements for night work, until by the middle of the eighteenth century slaves were often made to strip tobacco or husk corn by firelight, and planters sometimes whipped those who failed to complete their allotted task. Winter work intensified as well. As markets for timber and casks in the West Indies and the Wine Islands expanded and localized urban demand for firewood and lumber developed, more timber was cut and carted in winter. Small grains, threshed out immediately after harvest if possible, remained to be winnowed and the seed picked over in the off-season. Some began harvesting early spring runs of shad and herring with seines. Planters who wished to improve their lands found this an optimal period for grubbing swamps and cleaning pastures. The agricultural year was filled, with slaves fully employed the year round.[32]

When planters first ventured into diversification at the turn of the eighteenth century, the work patterns of laboring whites changed much more than did those of slaves. Initially, white men and women undertook most of the new or expanded skilled tasks, while slave men and women were kept at work in the fields. Free or indentured white men did almost all the artisanal work, such as shoemaking, coopering, smithing, and wagon making. The planter's wife, along with white women servants, did most of the domestic work and dairying. Around the middle of the century, however, the level of home industry increased markedly, and work patterns changed for everyone. With few European servant women entering the colonies, the planter's wife and his daughters—at least in slaveowning families—spent more time at the domestic production of fibers and at sewing, candle molding, butter making, and the like for their own families.

Slaves, especially those on large plantations, also began to experience a marked increase in the sexual division of labor. The new crops and routines required new tasks that were both varied and often involved some degree of skill—sowing and mowing grain, plowing, harrowing, carting, ditching, lumbering, fishing, and milling, for example. These new jobs fell primarily to slave men. By the end of the century men were thus performing a greater variety of tasks, and even on large plantations they sometimes worked on special projects by themselves or with only one or two mates, and not always under constant supervision. The great majority of slave women, however, did not share in the new opportunities, and probably lost considerably from agricultural change. A few became more involved in textile production and house service than in earlier years. However, poor free white women, especially spinsters and widows, did much of the spinning, weaving, and sewing that slaveowners needed done, while others worked as waged housekeepers. The great majority of black women continued to perform unskilled manual field labor, such as hand hoeing and weeding, and more often without the help of their menfolk. The new jobs assigned to slave women (or the old jobs formerly shared with men) included many of the least desirable chores: building fences, grubbing swamps, cleaning winnowed grain, breaking up new ground too rough or weedy to plow, cleaning stables, and loading and spreading manure. On large plantations, the work of slave women was less varied than that of the men, and they often labored together in gangs under the direct supervision of an overseer.[33]

Planters who adopted these practices considered themselves to be improving farmers. Some acknowledged that they had developed a new system of Chesapeake agriculture; others believed that they had adopted a course of "English husbandry," although this was far from the case. For a time, plow technology, the use of manure, and intensified grain culture—grafted onto traditional, long-fallow tobacco growing—raised total agricultural productivity. In part, farmers were responding to the harsh critiques of both European observers and native agrarian reformers of their supposedly primitive system of agriculture. In larger measure, they were also responding to changing market incentives. Between 1750 and 1775, while relative prices of wheat and tobacco oscillated, there was no clear trend in favor of one crop over the other, and most large planters raised both, but by 1775 planters had to make new choices, as the second system of Chesapeake agriculture was losing its viability. Population densities in the tidewater had reached a level at which there was not enough land available to rotate crops in long fallow, allowing for the forty to fifty acres required for each laborer.[34] Diminishing yields were inevitable without some change in either crop mix or cultivation techniques. Shifts in the relative prices of tobacco and grain after 1775—accompanied by European wars which closed major continental markets and made tobacco an exceedingly risky market crop—also encouraged a shift from tobacco to grain. Even if the American Revolution had not occurred, population growth would have forced basic alterations in agricultural practices. The nature of that war and the economic depression that followed pushed planters into particularly destructive kinds of change.

The Revolution brought both severe economic depression and social disruption to the Chesapeake. Nearly everyone suffered, and perhaps slaves suffered most. Many residents—ill-prepared to weather a trade cut-off—experienced shortages of salt, medicine, shoes, and cloth, and doubtless most slaveowners stinted their slaves before they stinted themselves. Some slaves who lacked shoes were excused from work in inclement weather, but others died from malnutrition or exposure to cold without adequate clothing. Conditions were worst in the lower tidewater and the piedmont, where trade was effectively blocked, and more favorable at the head of the Bay, on the eastern shore, and on the lower James, where some goods continued to trickle in and some produce get out. Residents were also exposed to greater risk of disease and death during the war from epidemics of smallpox, dysentery, and camp fever that erupted wherever troops were present in any numbers. Ill-clad and badly fed slaves were probably especially vulnerable. Some slaveowners arranged for mass smallpox inoculations for their slaves. This must have been a frightening experience for the slaves, although the risk of dying from the inoculation was much less than the risk of dying from smallpox itself. The routine inoculation of children that became more common on some plantations after the war may have improved chances of survival for some youngsters.[35]

Slaves' work routines changed during the Revolution. Planters who grew tobacco before the war cut back drastically during the fighting since they had few chances to sell export products, and they reassigned former field laborers to manufacturing and craft work. Many slave women learned how to spin and weave, and probably more slave men worked at crafts in order to replace white artisans who were serving in the army and militia. Ordinary field hands spent more time on self-sufficient activities such as gardening, hunting, and fishing, thus demonstrating that they could survive with little help from their owners. After the war this experience made it easier for some Afro-Americans to find full- or part-time employment, especially in towns.

The Revolution also altered relations between slaves and slaveowners in other fundamental ways. It was a profound educational experience for slaves. They learned much more about the geography and composition of the new nation. Some slaves traveled to distant places with owners who were serving in the Continental Army, the Continental Congress, or state governments. Some learned the lay of the land while transporting goods by horse and wagon, a task more slaves undertook during the war since waterways were no longer secure. Others saw new localities when they were sent to distant quarters to avoid British raids, while working in army or militia camps, or while serving as soldiers or sailors on state vessels or aboard privateers. Still others escaped to distant places, prompting friends and relatives to try to learn something of where they had gone. And those who tried to run away but failed had many a tale to share with those at home. All this new information caused slaves to rethink their world.[36]

The Revolution contributed to the political education of black Americans as it did to white ones. Free blacks embraced the goals proclaimed by the revolutionaries and hoped to improve their position in a more egalitarian political climate, as well as that of relatives still in bondage. Before the war slaveowners had no reason to discuss colonial politics or modes of government with their slaves, and slaves no reason to be interested: in most cases, the masters' laws were the only ones that counted. But when they started a revolution, masters could hardly avoid explaining to their slaves something about what they were doing—at the very least, that they were fighting a war—while simultaneously, and somewhat inconsistently, admonishing their slaves to remain faithful and continue to do their duty.[37]

Doubtless slaveowners sought to keep slaves ignorant of much that was happening, and some slaves may have been too apathetic to care. Nonetheless, given marked changes in their work routines, sharp reductions in customary issues of food and clothing, an obvious decline in their owners' standards of living, and the entry of some white and black men into military service, slaves doubtless pieced together something of what was taking place. With whites in the process of changing the rules of government for themselves, slaves had reason to learn about lawyers, courts, legislatures, and white opponents to slavery. These they too might utilize to change the rules in their own interest, and soon after the war some slaves began the attempt, often in sophisticated ways. The egalitarian political philosophy underlying the Declaration of Independence reverberated through the quarters and shortly found eloquent expression in slaves' petitions for freedom. They would now appeal to universal natural rights, not just to local custom.[38]

The experience of James Eagle, a Maryland overseer, who in 1803 quit a lucrative post in frustration, illustrated how intensified desire for freedom that arose among slaves during and after the Revolution affected labor relations. "I am now drawing towards 50 years of age I have spent 21 of that time on this place the first part of it much more agreeable than the latter," Eagle wrote his employer. The slaves he supervised had decided they, too, had an inalienable right to freedom. Eagle found "they Get much more Dissatisfied Every year & troublesome for they say that they all ought all to be at there liberty & they think that I am the Cause that they are not." He could not cope with their changed behavior: "By that means [they] Gaves me all the trouble that they can which keeps me one half of my time in hot blood & when that is the Case I Cannot Conduct my business as I ought to do."[39]

After the war economic recovery came slowly, with the result that the slaves' material condition was slow to improve. By 1781 planters found themselves in reduced if not desperate straits, as a result of owner absenteeism in government or military service, reduced income from market crops, destructive British raids, slave flight, depletion of livestock herds and timber reserves, loss of rent from tenants who could not or would not pay, high taxes, scarce specie, and deteriorating farm buildings and fences. Only those who had contrived successful speculations in alcohol or produce or those who had access to overland markets survived the war without major losses. Few planters were able to resume full crop production before 1785, and few were sanguine about future prospects until after the adoption of the Constitution and the reorganization of the national government. Market disruptions, falling land prices due to westward migration, scarce money and credit, unpaid prewar debts, and continued high taxes contributed to the economic malaise. Slaveowners who could not provide well for themselves were unlikely to provide well for their slaves. Slaves may have been forced to accept food and clothing of lesser quantity or quality than had been customary before the war.[40]

Once the tobacco market began to recover in the late 1780s planters resumed cropping with a vengeance, seeking to make up for lost time and lost revenues. Initially, the traditional staple seemed the best bet for turning quick profits. Work requirements for slaves were scaled up to prewar standards, and in prime tobacco areas yields per hand rebounded to prewar levels. By the end of the decade total regional tobacco production equaled that of the 1770s. Two sorts of evidence substantiate the intensification of work demands. First, annual outputs of tobacco per slave field hand rose, while outputs of corn and wheat either remained stable or inched upward. Second, while planters failed to mention increased slave resistance, some fired overseers who had become accustomed to lax routines during the war, and they increasingly complained of white wage laborers who refused to equal their expectations. In order to put more time into expanded tobacco production, most slave artisans—especially spinners and weavers—were returned to the fields, while their owners reverted to their prewar practice of buying imported manufactured goods or buying from white artisans. Slaves again wore clothes of imported rather than homespun cloth.[41]

But by the early 1790s, with the onset of European war, the tobacco market once more collapsed. A quick adjustment was in order. Planters in all parts of the Chesapeake—except the new western settlements and in pockets of older areas where there were still prime tobacco soils—diminished or abandoned altogether their commitment to the region's traditional staple, shifting instead to a mixture of maize, wheat, hay, cotton for slave clothing, dairy products, and livestock raising. When wheat prices soared in the 1810s some abandoned everything for wheat, trusting they could buy corn for slaves and stock from less specialized farmers. Alternatively, when trade embargoes or war closed grain markets, some former tobacco planters returned briefly to their former staple. Tobacco could be stored for a longer period than wheat, and high profits from temporary shortages were possible.[42]

Changes in markets offered some new opportunities. Towns and cities in the region—Baltimore, Norfolk, Richmond, Alexandria, Fredericksburg, Frederick, Lynchburg—became more important markets as urban populations grew and the demand for hay, dairy products, meat, and perishable produce rose. Regular water transportation increased possibilities for marketing perishables, and produce like potatoes, apples, and even turnip greens suddenly became valuable market crops. Planters deep in the hinterland as well as those near cities began rearing livestock for urban markets. Some slaves began to spend more time tending fruits and vegetables and making butter to feed townsfolk. Astute slave salesmen and women were assigned the job of peddling the produce in town, sometimes weekly, occasionally daily. Market days must have been a welcome time, affording some slaves a chance to escape the plantation and work without supervision, manage cash, and perhaps find ways to make a little money for themselves.

So far as can be determined from planters' records, slaves usually sold the produce they tended or gathered on their own time—chickens, eggs, oysters, fish, fruits, and vegetables—to their owners or to other nearby white families. Slaves who traded with neighboring families, who knew them personally and knew what sorts of dealings their owners sanctioned, were much less likely to be accused of stealing their wares, and they did not need a pass to go to nearby farms. Before the Revolution, slaves' opportunities for selling their wares were largely limited to local transactions. After the war, urban expansion offered slaves new outlets. Planters' records suggest that slaves who went to town markets sold only produce raised for the owner. If the slaves also peddled goods in town, either on their own account or for other slaves, it went unmentioned, and it seems likely that such traffic was of limited extent. But more perceptive planters also realized that slave or free black marketers sometimes made a few pennies by devious methods, for example, by underreporting sales, by watering the milk they were sent to sell, or by trading a bit of produce for whisky that they consumed on the trip home. Slaveowners who lived at a distance from the towns where their slaves traded tried to keep such expropriations to a minimum by requiring the slaves to account with a resident merchant and to turn over the proceeds to the representative. English immigrant Richard Parkinson, who raised produce and dairy products for the Baltimore market at the turn of the nineteenth century, found black hucksters superior to whites: "A Black man (in this case a free negro) is much better for this business than a white man; although they are in general ignorant, they are impudent." Selling produce was "an employment which they like, viz. riding to market in a cart, drinking whisky, and cheating you out of part of the money they get for the *truck*."[43] Slave marketers had to weigh the benefits of making something on the side with the risks of detection and possible revocation of trading privileges.

Although urban markets offered both planters and slaves new opportunities to profit from produce that a short time before had commanded little or no value, transportation remained a major obstacle to specialized agriculture. Only farmers living within two hours' travel time from market could risk relying much on highly perishable products such as fruit and milk. Most planters were reluctant to adopt radical changes in crop mix, opting instead to profit in town from the occasional windfall but trust in the main to traditional staples. The proceeds some planters realized from livestock, butter, hay, or potatoes were insufficient to warrant a shift to truck gardening, and the fact that a single planter could glut a town market like Baltimore with peaches, pumpkins, or rutabagas suggests their skepticism was not entirely misplaced. Otherwise, the effort was not commensurate to the returns; as Parkinson reported of his experiment in truck gardening and dairying on a farm three miles distant from Baltimore, "it was the general talk that we should kill ourselves; and I really think never three people [himself and two sons, not to mention his wife] worked so hard in the world for the length of time, and especially in such a climate," getting up daily between two and four in the morning in order to get their milk to market by sunup. Some kind of general agriculture remained the best strategy for most tidewater farmers.[44]

Between 1790 and 1820 most planters had to choose among three new courses of action, since neither traditional tobacco growing nor specializing in produce for urban markets was a viable option. Each of the three courses involved changes in crop mix, labor routines, and family security for slaves. Slaveowners who remained in the tidewater and who changed crop mix and farming techniques most drastically were increasingly likely to divide slave families in a quest for increased efficiency. Those who moved west, by the very fact of moving also divided slave families, without changing the crops they grew or the methods they expected their workers to use in growing them. Planters who neither moved nor changed, especially those who still owed heavy prewar debts, often fell victim to hard times. Either their owners' prosperity or their distress boded ill for the slaves.

A few planters became true improving farmers, investing more in land reclamation and improvement, fertilizers, artificial grasses, and new and better farm implements. On such plantations the slaves' work became ever more varied, and slave men at least usually acquired a greater degree of control over, and sometimes responsibility for, the nature and pace of their labor. The slaves of such improving farmers may also have enjoyed better living conditions but at an increasing risk to family security, unless their masters also developed moral qualms against dividing slave families. However, not many planters chose this course. Only as the second system of Chesapeake husbandry began everywhere to produce diminishing returns was there much impetus for change. By 1820, though, a number of large tidewater planters had adopted a new agricultural system that incorporated elements of advanced European practices. They rotated crops rather than fields, included clover and turnips in their crop mix, used manure extensively and lime a little, made adequate forage for draft animals and improved meat and dairy stock, constructed some permanent fences, and began to note yields per acre as well as per hand. Some progressive landlords also demanded that their tenants adopt improved practices.[45] Such advances did not necessarily make more capital available for further agricultural improvements, however, for prosperous planters began shifting some of their profits into non-agricultural investments—urban real estate, bank stock, and shares in internal improvement companies.[46]

Many planters found a second option more attractive: they chose to change where they lived rather than how they farmed. With the opening of new western settlements, they pulled up stakes and moved their slaves, wives, and children to fresh lands where they continued to farm in the old ways with better result. Slaves, who had no say in the matter, were forced to move far away from family and kin.

Even more farmers chose a third course, one that continued former methods of cultivation but with a greater emphasis on grain than on tobacco. Planters who neither migrated nor embraced improved agriculture found they could temporarily increase total farm production by using more labor to the acre and mining their lands with more intensive cultivation, often without either short fallowing or any use of animal or vegetable fertilizers. In addition, many landlords, anxious to increase rental income, began letting rental tracts only on short term leases with requirements that the tenants employ a *minimum* number of hands on the tract, rather than the land-conserving cap on the *maximum* number of workers usually found in prewar leases. Non-slaveholding tenant farmers were often squeezed off rented farms and the tracts leased to neighboring slaveowners, who worked the land with two or three times more hands. In some places the size of slave work units increased as well, as farmers eliminated small quarters in favor of fewer, consolidated farms.[47]

This third option had particularly unfortunate results. Wheat was far from an ideal alternative staple to tobacco, and its cultivation had an unforeseen adverse impact on the environment. Output per acre remained dismally low, since farmers could not hope to accumulate enough manure to fertilize wheat fields, which in any case were planted on old tobacco and corn land that had not been rested in long rotation. Grain growers, who were expanding production, expected their slaves to cultivate ever more acreage. The amount of land in agricultural production in southern Maryland, for example, may have increased from about 2 percent of the total in 1720 to nearly 40 percent in the early 1800s. Tobacco planters turned wheat-and-maize farmers proceeded to plow ever more extensively with no regard for land contours and to clear and cultivate marginal lands. Fallows were shortened or abandoned altogether. More complete plowing of fields and removal of tree stumps that had retarded runoff accelerated erosion, carrying off vital plant nutrients and before long a great deal of soil. Large expanses of cleared fields were also subject to wind erosion. Timber shortages—brought about by increased clearing, by the need to fence more fields, and by increasing sales of firewood to expanding town markets—became common. The result was widespread soil depletion and massive soil erosion that dates to precisely the period of expanded grain culture.[48] Erosion proceeded even more rapidly in the piedmont, where plowing was soon introduced and where steeper slopes became washed and gullied within twenty-five years of being cleared. Clearing and plowing in the piedmont increased rainwater runoff and the incidence of destructive freshes both locally and in the tidewater. By 1820 changing land use patterns were significantly altering the estuarine ecology and aquatic resources of the Bay.[49]

Many studies of Chesapeake agriculture have missed some of the links between the requirements and mode of cultivation of the region's staple crops and the effects on the environment. Of the three main market crops, tobacco has been most blamed for ecological degradation and economic decline. Indeed, its labor demands were so intense that wherever it remained a major crop, even as yields per laborer declined, its culture still shaped and limited all other agricultural efforts. Tobacco, however, was least responsible for long-term environmental destruction. As corn moved from being a subsistence crop requiring little labor to a market crop requiring relatively more, its reputation also declined, although poor cultivation techniques caused many of the problems encountered. Most post-Revolutionary advances in productivity occurred in wheat and other small grains, and these advances were substantial at least for a time.[50] But grain culture contributed most to the degradation of the environment, which proved exceedingly difficult to reverse. Planters traded one form of extractive agriculture for another and they, along with their overseers, in the words of John Taylor, "unite[d] in emptying the cup of fertility to the dregs."[51]

Planters who switched from tobacco to grains redirected most of the labor time that they saved into wheat. Few attempted to grow more maize than they had in the 1770s. By 1800 mean wheat crops per hand in most areas reached thirty bushels, a doubling of prewar levels. On Maryland's Eastern Shore mean crops exceeded seventy bushels per laborer, and a few slave gangs made over 150 bushels per hand. While tobacco cultivation allowed few economies of scale, there were considerable economies in wheat.[52] These included not only the obvious case of the harvest (for which most planters continued to hire extra labor) but also extended to ground preparation, seeding, threshing, cleaning, and transporting. Consequently, during the early nineteenth century, the revenues of large producers pulled far ahead of those of small ones. Big planters who shifted their crop mix to suit changing markets and who tailored their slave labor forces to the mix realized increasing returns from major field crops as well as growing revenues (not included in these estimates) from livestock sales. Gross crop revenues per hand among large slaveowners rose to about £25 sterling constant value between 1790 and 1807, and averaged over £35 between 1810 and 1818.[53]

However, the majority of planters did not do so well. Between 1790 and 1820 planters who owned no slaves or else owned fewer than two healthy adult workers realized gross revenues of only about £15 per worker, the prewar level. Small farms, where the slaves' work routines changed least, made few or no advances in productivity. Small planters often lacked both land and equipment for expanding their grain crops, and they may also have chosen neither to work harder nor to force their slaves to do so. Both hefty profits and, on the best-managed farms, ameliorative changes were primarily an option for the rich, who could forego some immediate income in order to divert labor to improvements. Even zealous advocates of improvement recognized the best that small farmers—who required "speedy supplies" of money to maintain their families—could do was to select the crops that sold for the most money. Their best hope was to draw the greatest possible product from the soil, "without entirely destroying future prospects of crops from their lands."[54]

Nor was soil mining necessarily an irrational response to economic change. Given the high returns per hand that large planters enjoyed between 1790 and 1818, it probably made a rational short-term choice. If land was certainly not as abundant as in the seventeenth century, it was still neither scarce nor dear. With increased westward migration after the Revolution, the white population ceased to grow in many older areas. Stagnant populations, combined with the availability of unlimited new land in the west, kept the price of land depressed in almost all of tidewater Virginia, as well as in some parts of Maryland, well beyond 1820.[55] At the same time, the expansion of the new south bid up the price of labor. Better then to continue skimming less valuable land while more efficiently exploiting still costly labor.

Everywhere planters tightened the screws on their slaves, coming to expect them to work "as much in the 24 hours as their strength without endangering the health, or constitution will allow of," and increasingly using watches to monitor the daily work pace in more precise units. Such farmers explicitly equated time with money.[56] Big planters' concentration on short-run profits tended also to direct their attention to short-run expenses—especially to the major expenses of slave maintenance and supervision. They measured cloth allotments by the inch rather than the yard, kept track of maize rations by the peck rather than the bushel, and intensified efforts to control the slaves' pilfering. Around the turn of the century many began to compensate overseers with an annual wage rather than with one or more shares of the crop—a shift usually interpreted as a move to diminish overseers' incentives to overdrive slaves and overwork land. Although this was sometimes the motive, many big planters probably adopted set wages as a way to limit the costs of supervision. By eliminating share payments, large planters retained a greater percentage of the proceeds of the larger grain crops their slaves were making.[57]

Readjustment of the labor force predominated over agricultural improvement, and by and large slavery proved adaptable to the new conditions. Planters who made marked changes in crop mix and cultivation techniques found land-labor ratios in older areas permanently altered. As they learned how to grow forage crops, they put more land into pasture and hay, changes that further reduced the acreage available for market crops and thus labor needs. And once they could count on animal power, planters needed fewer hoe hands. Wheat culture and general farming required smaller groups of strong, specialized, highly trained workers. Farmers pursuing this course began to reduce or at least to stabilize the size of their labor force by selling less productive workers, employing some slaves in nonagricultural pursuits, or hiring slaves out. Profits per hand could be increased by raising the proportion of adult men in the work force, just as had been the case in the seventeenth century.

In this new climate of cost consciousness, some slaveowners decided they could no longer afford—or no longer wished—to maintain hands who were not essential to their current operations, and especially to feed and clothe growing numbers of nonproductive children. Rather than retaining such slaves as an eventual inheritance for their children, more planters decided to let their offspring make their own arrangements, perhaps with a legacy of money rather than of laborers. Those who needed to raise capital found older, worn land difficult to unload, while slaves could be turned into ready cash with relative ease. Those whose sense of conscience had been heightened by either Revolutionary or evangelical Christian equalitarianism might opt instead to manumit some of their slaves. But most who did chose to free only women and children at the outset, while requiring men of prime age to serve five to ten years longer than women. Because able-bodied men were likely to remain slaves, their free wives and children were unable to function as independent households and had little choice but to serve as appendages to the planters' slave work force. Planters thus relieved themselves of maintenance costs of the least productive workers, retained the labor of the most productive, and had access to a pool of cheap seasonal labor as needed.[58] The most successful planters were the ones who retained their prime adult male slaves while disposing of "surplus" women and children through some combination of selective sales, forced westward migration, selective manumissions, apprenticeships, and increased slave hiring. Women and children were more often hired out or sold to whites seeking domestics or apprentices, or to small planters who wanted to expand their labor force. Others were sent west, where there was work enough for all sorts of hands. Planters opposed to dividing slave families often realized lesser revenues. Of course, slaves were the primary victims of this process of rationalizing farm work.[59]

Although slave families faced increasing risks of forced separation, some slaves found new ways to gain a measure of control over their working and living conditions. A few were allowed to find work off the plantation and to keep a portion of their wages, affording a chance for self-purchase. Planters allowed some of those slated to be hired out to select their new employers, rather than being placed with whoever bid the most for their services. Skilled field workers could protest worsened conditions effectively by refusing to work or by running away at critical times. Others might force owners to allow them a choice of occupation. For example, Ned, a Kent County, Maryland, field hand, informed his overseer in 1800 that he had "a great desire to be hired out to go by water (i.e., to work on boats) & says that he will not stay hear if [you] will [not] let him go for he says that he tires of working on the land." Both owner and overseer feared Ned would run away if his wishes were not accommodated.[60]

The Chesapeake economy had entered a long-term decline by 1820. Bad times arrived in 1818 with a cloud of hessian flies that greatly reduced wheat yields throughout the region. A commercial panic the next year put many of those who were overextended out of business. In 1820 overseas demand for grain dropped and wheat prices entered a long-term slump, even as the cheap, burgeoning produce of western farms began to flood the east. Tobacco prices also declined. Some improving farmers were eventually successful in adjusting to a system of mixed husbandry pursued with improved techniques.[61] Many others were unable to reverse the downward spiral in the face of falling prices and steadily deteriorating land. Their commitment to slavery made the necessary economic readjustment exceedingly painful. However, the collapse of wheat as viable staple, along with the environmental devastation to which its culture had contributed, was a problem shared by farmers along much of the eastern seaboard.[62]

Agricultural change, particularly the shift from the hoe to the plow, had profound effects on the living and working conditions of Chesapeake slaves that often differed for men, women, and children. Work routines shifted from seasons of intense effort that alternated with seasons of greater ease to full year-round employment. Tasks, especially for men, became more varied and specialized, whereas slave women gained little and perhaps lost more from the changing organization of labor. The context in which slaves struggled to establish some measure of control over the rhythm and pace of work was in constant flux. Economic diversification could mean greater independence from constant supervision but in other cases prompted planters to attempt to exert ever greater control. After the Revolution these struggles took place in a political climate that both fostered and frustrated slaves' efforts to gain greater control over their lives.

By the turn of the nineteenth century tobacco was no longer the "staple and all" in many parts of the Chesapeake. Slaves were concentrated in the remaining tobacco areas, where their labor was essential to the weed's demanding requirements. Eventually, many grain farmers also discovered that wheat and slaves were compatible. During that learning period, however, a number of slaves gained their freedom. Many of them left the rural Chesapeake. Among those who remained, ties to tobacco persisted. For freedmen able to rent a patch of land, tobacco—still the optimal poor man's crop—offered the best chance to make an independent living. In 1801, for example, Sawney, a free "man of color," pitched a crop of tobacco at Herring Bay in Anne Arundel County, Maryland. Short of labor, he took in Nace, a runaway slave from Baltimore County, members of whose family were suing for freedom in Maryland courts on the grounds that they had descended from a free white woman and were therefore entitled to freedom. Sawney and Nace agreed to work on shares, and together made two hogsheads of tobacco the first year—the very crop that had forced their ancestors into the region a century before.[63]

PART THREE

The Slaves' Economy

8

PROVISION GROUND AND PLANTATION LABOR IN FOUR WINDWARD ISLANDS: COMPETITION FOR RESOURCES DURING SLAVERY

Woodville K. Marshall

THE ROLE OF THE provision ground and internal marketing system in the context of plantation slavery has been a subject of increased interest over the last generation. Recent findings have greatly enriched comprehension of slave subsistence patterns, internal markets, the slaves' "protopeasant" activities, and even the quality of the slaves' diet.[1] However, no scholar has yet provided a full description of the provision-ground system, and only Sidney Mintz has attempted to link slaves' protopeasant activities with postslavery developments.[2] A description and analysis of the provision-ground system in the four Windward Islands of Grenada, St. Lucia, St. Vincent, and Tobago during the last fifty years of slavery can offer insight into these large subjects, leading to three tentative conclusions. First, and echoing Mintz, the provision-ground and internal-marketing system provided an extensive stage, as in Jamaica, for slaves' participation in independent activities. Second, the slaves' attempts to exploit the potential of these activities inevitably created intense competition between themselves and plantation owners and managers for labor services and land resources.[3] Third, slaves' success in creating and defending corners of independent existence fostered the growth of attitudes toward both plantation labor and independent activities that affected labor relations in the postslavery period.[4]

The four Windward Islands were, like Jamaica, "home fed" colonies.[5] Most of the slaves subsisted not on rations of imported or locally grown food but on produce cultivated on provision grounds, supplemented by weekly allowances of salt provisions—mackerel, cod, shad, or herring—provided by their owners. In emergencies caused by flood and drought or depletion of the soil of provision grounds, masters were usually expected (and often compelled by law) to supply weekly food rations of imported foodstuffs (grains, cornmeal or plantains) but in amounts that were not specified until the amelioration of slavery in the 1820s.[6] This pattern of slave feeding was firmly in place in Grenada, St. Vincent, and Tobaga by 1790; witnesses before one parliamentary committee said it was "universally the custom."[7]

However, the four Windwards adopted the provision-ground system at different times, depending on the rate of conversion to full slave-plantation economies. In general, it would appear that the first stage of plantation establishment, as well as the seasoning of all slaves, involved feeding slaves on rations of either imported food or a combination of imported food and ground provisions produced by gang labor. When land for the staples was cleared and planted, the provision-ground system took root but continued to coexist with other methods of slave feeding. In Grenada, where the plantation economy was well established by the 1750s, the provision-ground system was being subjected to legal regulation by 1766, suggesting that law was catching up with practice.[8] In St. Vincent, where the plantation was established after 1763, the governor, James Seton, indicated that by 1789 the provision-ground system was the dominant method of slave feeding.[9] In both Tobago and St. Lucia, where full plantation exploitation was constrained by frequent exchanges of ownership between England and France, the remnants of the original method of slave feeding could be found in slave laws as late as 1794 for Tobago and 1825 for St. Lucia. In both cases, the law directed planters to produce a quantity of provisions by gang labor in a fixed proportion to their slave population.[10]

Several factors influenced the adoption of the system. First, as Mintz points out, slaveowners had an obvious interest in maximizing "their returns from the slave labor" in a situation where the demand for slave labor was not constant all year round and where the cost of imported provisions meant a significant and regular outlay of capital.[11] Planter-witnesses before the parliamentary committees of 1789 to 1791 often linked the existence of provision grounds to reduced importation of foodstuffs, indicating that they were aware of the savings they had achieved.[12] Second, such savings became most important during the crises of slave subsistence that took place between 1776 and 1783, and again between 1794 and 1815. The effects of wars on established trading arrangements triggered a steep rise in the price of imported food, caused malnutrition and starvation, increased slave mortality, and forced planters to allocate more estate land to the production of food supplies.[13] Provision grounds therefore saved money and reduced the planters' risks.[14]

Third, the slaves' preference for provision grounds also merged with their masters' self-interest. For slaves, the advantages of a more secure and plentiful food supply, cash from the sale of surpluses, and periods of unsupervised activity were apparent. Indeed, slaves may have taken the initiative in modifying the patterns of feeding on some estates. In 1789 Ashton Warner Byam, a leading judicial official in Grenada and a proprietor in St. Vincent, told the parliamentary committee that when his slaves had made complete provision grounds for themselves, "they of their own accord offered to me that if I would give them the Saturday afternoon, out of crop time, they would require nothing but salt provisions from me."[15] Such an openly expressed preference quickly enabled masters to perceive the value of provision grounds as a mechanism for control. One year later, Alexander Campbell, one of the leading proprietors in Grenada, observed that it was "the custom" in Grenada to grant slaves as much land as they could work because it had been "universally considered the greatest benefit to a planter that his Negroes should have a sufficient quantity of provisions, and the more money the Negroes got for themselves, the more attached they were to the property."[16]

The topography of the Windwards was perhaps the most important factor in the planters' adoption and the slaves' consolidation of the provision-ground system. Grenada, St. Vincent, and St. Lucia were mountainous and Tobago at least hilly; all possessed wooded, mountainous interiors that restricted settlement to the coasts and coral lowlands, to the volcanic foothills, and to well-watered valleys leading to the sea.[17] The plantations, usually located in valleys facing the shore, often possessed land which ran into the foothills and "new ground" or "mountain runs" that were marginal or unsuited to sugar or other staple cultivation.[18] Lowland plantations, which were not so well endowed, often possessed "little vacant spots" on which, as David Collins—a St. Vincent physician—said, slaves were permitted to cultivate on their own account.[19] In those few cases where these vacant spots proved inadequate, planters purchased mountain land "for the purpose of negro ground."[20] Allocation of this type of land for provision cultivation was sometimes justified by the disingenuous argument that "these broken and steep places" did "answer very well for provisions."[21] But this inversion of the laws of husbandry could neither fully deflect criticism of the adequacy of slave-feeding methods nor obscure the fact that planters recognized how such an allocation advanced their vital interests in lowering production costs and increasing social control.

Provision grounds could consist of three different types of land allowance: yam grounds, gardens, and mountain land or mountain ground. Yam grounds, apparently distributed as customary allowances only in St. Vincent, may have been a remnant of earlier slave-feeding methods, which featured provision production by gang labor. These grounds were small portions, not exceeding forty square feet, of cane land being prepared for planting. Allotments were distributed to slaves on a declining scale according to age, and on these allotments slaves were expected to raise a yam crop before the new cane crop was planted. The allowance therefore served a dual purpose. It increased the slave's subsistence by assuring him of "a fair crop" out of the cultivation of good land, and it reduced the planter's labor costs by providing him with a "clean and ameliorated surface to plant first crop canes."[22]

Gardens, which can be confused with provision grounds because contemporaries sometimes used the terms interchangeably, were in the main not a land allowance at all.[23] In general, slaves created gardens from the land surrounding their houses, but sometimes garden allotments were provided by planters as partial substitutes for provision grounds. In Grenada a law passed in 1788 directed planters, who were prevented from providing provision grounds by the nature of soil or the "particular situation" of estates, to allot each adult slave at least one-fortieth of an acre "contiguous to the Negro Houses for the purpose of cultivating gardens for their sole use and benefit."[24]

Sketchy and contradictory contemporary comment makes difficult any assessment of the size, exploitation, and value of these gardens. Mrs. Carmichael, the wife of a West Indian planter, and John Bowen Colthurst, a special magistrate on St. Vincent, both of whom seemed intent of proving that slaves and apprentices were "plentifully maintained" by their own-account activities, described the St. Vincent gardens as of "a very comfortable size." For them, the gardens offered space for raising poultry and small stock and for cultivating tree crops, vines, and vegetables, which could meet the short-term food needs of the cultivators.[25] Another observer, John Anderson, noted that these gardens were generally neglected and unappreciated.[26] The point turns, no doubt, on the size and quality of this land. Since broken ground on the estate was likely to be the site planters preferred for slave villages, then, as abolitionist James Stephen argued, the garden's main utility would be to provide yards and passages between houses.[27] Gardens therefore had value to the extent that they contained conveniently located space for raising of small stock and poultry.

Mountain ground was the characteristic provision ground, and its location created problems for optimal cultivation. The distance between the grounds and slaves' residences was one difficulty. No direct information exists on how far slaves had to walk to their grounds, but various estate papers, slave codes, and local abolition acts suggest that it was often "considerable," probably as much as ten miles.[28] Such distances posed problems in terms of both efficiency and security. Time consumed in a long trek to and from provision grounds meant loss of labor and under-exploitation of the grounds; distant residence from growing crops also reduced the possibility of effective policing, increasing the risk of theft.

More important, problems with mountain grounds arose from the natural constraints on cultivation that such a location imposed. As the name suggests, such mountain land was difficult of access because of steep slopes, difficult to clear because of virgin forests, difficult to cultivate because of boulders and stones, and impossible to protect against threats of land slippage and erosion. No doubt, as John Bowen Colthurst suggested, some provision grounds were established in "deep rocky glens" containing some of the richest deposits of soil in St. Vincent, but the search for these locations could consume valuable time.[29] Moreover, success in the search might compound the problem of inconvenient distance from the slaves' residence.

Planters apparently cared little about the actual location of provision grounds. Only two contemporary commentators suggest that any criteria were applied in its selection. James Baillie, proprietor of estates in Grenada and St. Vincent, allotted fifty acres of "the most valuable and seasonable part" of his Grenada estate for provision grounds; Sir William Young "set apart" forty-six acres of "the richest ground" on his St. Vincent estate for "the negro gardens."[30] Those planters who possessed mountain runs, which automatically recommended themselves as provision grounds, seem to have left the exact locations to drivers and field slaves. The viability of the soil for provision grounds did not have to be pretested because of the presumed fitness of the land for the purpose. It was the slaves' responsibility to check its possibilities, identify its deficiencies, and indicate when new ground was required.[31] On lowland and smaller estates, however, inattention could not be the rule. Choices had to be made: how much land could be spared, whether gardens should substitute for provision grounds, and whether a specific quantity and quality of mountain land should be leased. Planters in general doubtless paid more attention to the distribution of individual lots, but that attention was probably misplaced because the location of the ground could determine the adequacy of the provisions to be derived from the individual lot.

The law did not define the size of the individual allotments until the last years of slavery. Late eighteenth-century legislation in Grenada directed that an adult slave (over fourteen years of age) should receive "his or her proper ground," but the assessment of its size and adequacy for maintenance was left to a loose inspection procedure controlled by planters themselves.[32] In the 1820s, under abolitionist pressure for greater precision, "*a sufficient portion of land* adapted to the growth of provisions" was stipulated, and the size of allotment was fixed at a quarter acre for adult slaves in Grenada and Tobago.[33] The greatest precision and most liberal provisions were achieved in St. Lucia: land "properly" adapted for provision cultivation and a half acre in size became the legal requirement.[34] This was a consequence of the island's constitutional position; direct British rule made possible by Crown Colony status prevented planters from obstructing the will of the British government to the extent possible in the other islands. The local abolition legislation generally echoed these provisions, though the Tobago legislature found it "desirable" to follow St. Lucia's example and increase the size of the allotment to a half acre for adult slaves.[35] Only in St. Vincent did vagueness about the allowance persist until the end of slavery. There, the local abolition act defined the size of the acreage and its quality in negative terms: the "sufficient portion" of provision ground would be "deemed adequate and proper for maintenance and support of every praedial apprentice *unless good and sufficient cause be shown to the contrary.*"[36]

Customary practices undoubtedly influenced the legal definition of the allowance. Some planters, eager to exonerate themselves from charges of underfeeding their slaves, suggested, somewhat vaguely, that the islands' topographical variety ensured that slaves had access to "great quantity" of ground and to "considerable tracts" which they cultivated "for their own benefit."[37] Planters probably recognized that a restrictive policy could be self-defeating; they could hardly spare the resources of personnel and time to enforce it. In any event, they could resume possession or restrict the size of the allotment whenever the imperatives of plantation expansion or slave discipline warranted. Moreover, the brute fact remained that the size of the allotment was effectively limited by its location, the quality of its soil, the available labor time, and the labor requirements of the particular cultigens.[38] Therefore, the amount of land that individual slaves actually managed to cultivate was probably no more than a quarter acre. In 1790 Alexander Campbell told a parliamentary committee that the provision-ground allowance in Grenada was never less than one acre for a family of six; two years later Sir William Young reported that each household on his St. Vincent estate had access to about half an acre; and John Bowen Colthurst suggested that a slave family in St. Vincent may have had access to a maximum of two acres during the 1830s.[39]

Throughout the slave period the time allowed for slaves to cultivate provision grounds was both minimal and seasonal. Before the 1820s it amounted to between fourteen and nineteen working days, which could be utilized only "out of crop" when the sugar canes had been reaped. After April or May the designated time, usually Saturday, was then doled out on the basis of a half day weekly or a full day fortnightly. Planters expected, as various witnesses explained to the parliamentary committees in 1790, that slaves would supplement the allowance by their "spare hours"—in the afternoon rest period, after sunset out of crop, on Sundays, and over the three-day holiday at Christmas.[40] This allocation schedule reflected planters' prejudices and priorities. According to Alexander Campbell, "very little labor" was required for planting and weeding the provision ground; thus, "the Negroes need not work half of the time allowed them in their gardens." Further, because provisions could not be planted before the rains in May and June, slaves had "no occasion to work in their gardens, but out of crop-time."[41] In brief, planters did not intend their production schedule to be damaged by any inconvenient dispersal of the labor force. Mrs. Carmichael declared that "no sugar could be made on Friday, Saturday or Monday," if labor time was granted during the grinding season: "the sugar made on Friday must be potted on the following morning, and canes cut on Friday would be sour by Monday morning."[42]

Abolitionist pressure forced an increase of roughly 50 percent in the allowance during the 1820s—from fourteen to nineteen days to between twenty-six and thirty-five days. But while "full working days" were substituted for the optional weekly half day, the seasonal stipulation was retained.[43] Little alteration occurred during the apprenticeship period, the final phase of slavery. The seasonal stipulation was dropped in Grenada, St. Vincent, and St. Lucia, but in Tobago the allowance was reduced from thirty-five to fourteen full working days and the seasonal restriction on the use of the allowance was extended to six months—July to December.[44]

Slaveowners did not supervise or assist slaves in the cultivation of provision grounds. Whether as individuals or as official "guardians," planters were responsible for providing land enough for the slaves' maintenance.[45] But that responsibility was discharged in perfunctory fashion. Planters did lay out grounds and distribute lots to individuals and families, but they paid little or no attention to the precise location of these lots and seldom bothered to demarcate their boundaries clearly.[46] Although some planters probably sent their gangs to assist in the heavy work of clearing forests for the establishment of provision grounds, the main business of clearing and preparing the ground was left to the slaves themselves.[47] Planters did need to be satisfied that provision grounds were productive—if only to ensure that their gangs would be fit for labor and that plantation stores and fields would not be raided for food. But their interest in the slaves' husbandry was usually excited only when slaves broke the prohibition against growing staple crops or created fire hazards for central plantation property by slash-and-burn methods of cultivation.[48] As a result, planters seldom inspected the grounds to check on the state of cultivation or the fertility of the soil, leaving slaves to indicate when the soil was depleted and new ground required.[49] Plantation supervisory staff probably mustered slaves for provision-ground duty on Saturday afternoons and on Sundays, but in all likelihood that action was more a police exercise against the threats of desertion and malingering than a deliberate effort to ensure the adequacy of slave maintenance. Dr. Collins's advice to the contrary, planters apparently offered little or no assistance to slaves with regard to supplies of plants and seeds, information about crop selection, rotation and preservation, or protection of crops against theft.[50] Therefore, slaves were generally forced to rely on their own scanty resources. How they coped with institutionalized neglect was illustrated by John Jeremie, president of the Royal Court in St. Lucia in 1825. Jeremie found that the slaves on St. Lucia were "extremely careful of their provision grounds," cultivating them "with assiduity" and guarding them "night and day," that they "never forgive a theft on them," and that "nothing is more likely to keep them at home than the cultivating of their gardens."[51]

Slaves' choice of crops reflected the pressure and circumstances that created and sustained the provision-ground system. The main staples of the slave diet were root crops and starches (yams, eddoes,

cassava, sweet potatoes), tree crops (plantain, banana, and bread-
fruit), and grains and legumes (Indian and Guinea corn, many varieties of peas and beans).[52] In addition, slaves produced some vegetables and fruit. Dietary preference was one element in the slaves'
choice, as the yam and plantain, traditional staples of the West African
diet, were "a favorite and good food," or "what the potato is to the
lower classes in Britain."[53] Quality of soil was another determinant.
Since cassava, arrowroot, peas, and vines could subsist in poor soil,
they occupied land perceived as unfit for staple crop cultivation. Restricted labor time both determined the amount of land that could be
cultivated and constrained the choice of crop. Slaves preferred crops
that did not require close and constant attention, high-yield crops like
plantains and bananas that quickly propagated themselves. Not surprisingly, the yam and sweet potato, whose growth inhibited weeds,
were featured in the slaves' crop regime. Moreover, most slaves raised
a variety of small stock in their gardens and backyards and exploited
the fishing resources of the islands' rivers.[54]

The produce of the provision ground and yard or garden formed
the basis for an expanding local market. In the Windward Islands,
eighteenth-century slave laws show that those markets, as in Jamaica,
made their appearance early in the life of the plantations. Legislation,
which had as its rationale the discouragement of theft, also sought to
outlaw door-to-door peddling by slaves, to reduce marketing by slaves
through enforcement of the pass laws, and to prohibit the trading of
cattle, plantation staples, precious metals and jewelry by slaves entirely. But these prohibitions themselves confirm the existence of unsupervised marketing by slaves. Moreover, the marketing of "logs of
wood, firewood, fresh fish and dunghill fowls, goats, hogs, and vegetables of any sort" by slaves was not interdicted.[55] This division in the
productive function provided unintended incentives for slaves to produce and trade surpluses. By 1790 planters pointed to the slaves'
virtual monopoly on the internal markets for locally produced food,
firewood and charcoal, and fodder. Urban dwellers purchased much
of their food from slaves, and the planters themselves depended on
slaves for the greater part of their supply of poultry and fresh meat.[56]
"A few poultry and hogs," Alexander Campbell observed, "are raised
by the proprietors, about their houses, but their chief consumption is
bought of the slaves."[57] By the end of slavery this "breach" in the slave
system was virtually complete: while the restriction on the trade in
plantation produce was retained, slave participation in the internal
markets was officially recognized by the formal concession of the

slaves' right to attend market on a designated day, and slaves were openly protesting the choice of market day and the organization of markets. Customary arrangements had overturned legal restrictions, and what had grown up outside the law had become recognized in law.[58]

Scattered evidence suggests that produce grown by plantation slaves animated elaborate urban markets in the Windward Islands.[59] Slave supply and urban demand stimulated commodity exchange and increased slaves' purchasing power. This in turn sustained an expanding distributive network linking slave producers to free and slave consumers, plantation to town, and slave to market. Plantation slaves, mainly women, marketed produce, either using hucksters as intermediaries or selling in the markets on their own account. Itinerant traders, usually colored slaves or freed persons, based in town or on the plantations, hawked dry goods around the countryside, tapping the savings of slaves or bartering their "finery" for the slaves' produce. Urban slave hucksters, operating either as slave hirelings or as agents for their owners, sometimes functioned as retailers for the plantation slaves' produce and were a steady source of the small items needed by plantation slaves. Merchants and shopkeepers furnished imported goods, which enhanced purchasing power brought within the reach of plantation slaves. Towns were central to this network—as sites of the main markets, as the main source of demand for slaves' produce, and as mercantile and financial centers. Slaves thus heightened the scale of urban activity in commodity exchange and increased employment and accumulation in internal markets.

Competition for market shares between small and large urban operators and between urban retailers and rural producers was a natural consequence of this expanding market. Barry Higman demonstrates that *free* merchants and shopkeepers sought to confine *slave* hucksters to the sale of locally produced goods. For example, in 1815 hucksters selling bread about the streets of St. George's, the capital of Grenada, had to be licensed.[60] For similar reasons, urban traders strongly supported the closure of Sunday markets, since they too perceived that their abolition would increase their own market share. Slave producers often did their retailing in the Sunday market, selling in the central market or in the street, effectively eliminating the urban middlemen. In 1823 the British government, in response to abolitionist pressure, ended or curtailed Sunday markets as a means of ameliorating the slaves' moral and material condition, a move that received strong support from urban traders. These traders reasoned that the abolition of Sunday markets would reduce competition offered by rural retailers on that day. Moreover, the substitution of a weekday as the new market day would strengthen their position in the exchange of slave produce, because the change of market day would disrupt the slaves' traditional commercial routine and deprive them of access to the large volume of business that was transacted on a weekend. Events on Grenada illustrate how this advantage was exploited. After 1828 hucksters in St. George's engrossed the produce brought into town by the rural slaves on Thursday, the new official market day, and then retailed it at inflated prices.[61]

The slaves' reaction to the formal abolition of Sunday markets reveals the extent to which they competed with free traders and perceived the effect on their own interests of a disturbance of traditional arrangements. By 1825 market day had been switched in Grenada and Tobago to Thursday and to Saturday in St. Lucia, while in St. Vincent the main market in the capital, Kingstown, was closed from ten on Sunday mornings. But four years later the governor of St. Vincent ruefully reported that he was issuing "the most peremptory orders" to the clerk of market and to the chief constable "to carry the law into complete effect."[62] In St. Lucia, in 1831, marketing on Sunday was still outlawed, but the governor was being directed by the Colonial Office to "appoint" a market day, even though the Legislative Council had recently switched the market from Saturday to Monday.[63] Slave resistance in the form of complaint and open defiance to such changes explains the gap between legislative enactment and implementation. In Grenada slaves greeted the change in the market day with "much dissatisfaction."[64] In St. Vincent the governor admitted that "nothing but absolute force" would shift slaves "from a long customary enjoyment (as it is estimated by them) of marketing on Sunday." Slaves had indicated that they thought "the abolition of this privilege" constituted "one of the greatest hardships imposed on them." The governor was fully alive to the economic implications of the switch in the market day, in that prices of provisions also were increased "to the great injury of domestics and other slaves in Kingstown, who rely upon the market for subsistence." He therefore concluded that the moral issue was likely to lose out to the economic: "until the Negroes shall have acquired a sufficient degree of religion to induce them to observe the Sabbath from a principle of morality, they will not give up their habits of trafficking on Sundays."[65]

The imprecision of available evidence makes it difficult to assess the slaves' material gains from provision grounds. Most contemporary observers, planter and official alike, suggested that the annual returns were substantial enough to provide "comparative wealth" or "an approach to real comfort," and that accumulation did take place.[66] Witnesses before the parliamentary committees of 1789 through 1791 estimated the slaves' annual earnings at £6 to £20, with "industrious" slaves on fertile soil earning as much as £30 to £40.[67] James Baillie, a Grenada planter, claimed that some slaves on his estate possessed property "worth forty, fifty, one hundred and even as far as two hundred pounds sterling" and that such property was "regularly conveyed from one generation to another, without any interference whatever."[68] Alexander Campbell was convinced that the slaves' earnings from the sale of surpluses of "provisions, poultry and hogs" amounted to "one half of the current specie" in the Ceded Islands (Dominica, Grenada, St. Vincent, and Tobago), and he illustrated that contention by pointing to their displays of "fine clothes" and to their lavish "feasts" for one to two hundred "other slaves."[69] Later commentators, like Mrs. Carmichael and John Bowen Colthurst, echoed these sentiments. For Mrs. Carmichael, any St. Vincent slave could earn £30 annually "and very many may save much more."[70] For Colthurst, the returns were less ample—£2.10 for any family and £7.10 for the "industrious" family.[71] For both of them, however, each element of the slaves' domestic economy brought material benefit and possibilities for accumulation. Provision-ground and garden produce fed slaves and stock; surplus produce was exchanged for dietary supplements, for "finery," and for the "little articles" like candles, soap and tobacco; small stock and poultry were marketed for cash, which was saved or used to purchase small luxuries. According to Mrs. Carmichael and Colthurst, some slaves saved "large sums," as much as £100 or £150.[72]

The accuracy of these estimates and the conclusions they underpin must be queried for at least three reasons. First, these observers were partisans of one stripe or another. Witnesses before these parliamentary committees were, like Sir William Young and Mrs. Carmichael, apologists for slavery. Colthurst, a self-proclaimed abolitionist, was perhaps eager to inflate the significance of evidence that slaves had adopted capitalistic values and had therefore vindicated all their supporters hoped of them.[73] Second, the claims took little account of the disparities in quality and size of provision grounds and of the capacity (or industry) of the slaves to exploit them. Most observers did qualify their more liberal estimates by linking them to the performance of "industrious" slaves. But, as Dr. Collins and James Stephen suggested, the terms "industrious slave" and "bad" and "lazy" slave carried special connotations.[74] The apparently ample returns of the industrious slave might relate as much to the quality of the land and to the availability of labor for its cultivation as to the drive and determination of the slave. Similarly, the poor returns achieved by lazy slaves who, by the estimate of the Chief Justice of St. Vincent, constituted the bulk of the slave population, might have been a consequence of depleted soils, debility induced by malnutrition, hunger and overwork, or a simple lack of interest. Third, the planter's evidence was internally inconsistent, if not contradictory. On the one hand, they pointed to an "abundance" of provisions, to well-stocked internal markets, "dimity jackets" and "muslins," furniture and substantial savings; on the other hand, they asserted that slaves "in general are subject to thieving" and accepted that there was a correlation between the incidence of theft and the adequacy of slaves' nutrition.[75] "All the estates," Alexander Campbell claimed, "are obliged to keep guards on the Negro provision gardens and to guard the cattle pens, storehouses, and rum cellars."[76] Finally, these sanguine conclusions overlooked the extreme vulnerability of the provision-ground sector of the economy. Provision grounds were defenseless against drought or flood: crops burned in drought, and floods washed away the mountain ground. In Grenada, after the 1831 hurricane, hunger drove slaves on the Lataste estate to eat unripe provisions, which made them ill, forcing them to rely on their masters for rations of expensive imported grain. Eventually, the slaves had to reestablish provision grounds on new land.[77] If provision grounds possibly provided slaves with a more secure source of nutrition, not all slaves were hardy enough to cope with the competing labor demands of plantations and provision ground. Only some could therefore create opportunities for the improvement of their standard of living.[78]

As Mintz has often pointed out, the participation of slaves in provision-ground cultivation and marketing exposed the contradictions and inconsistencies of the slave regime.[79] Slaves cultivated land and disposed of its produce without supervision from their owners. Slaves worked their provision grounds in family groups. Slaves selected crops and determined methods of cultivation, the extent of provision saving, and cash accumulation. They did so, moreover, with an energy and enthusiasm that sharply contrasted with their work habits and low productivity in regard to gang-labor plantation export staples.

Slave families in "the constant occupation" of provision ground forced their owners to recognize rights of occupancy to portions of plantation ground.[80] Slaves would not move from their ground without notice or without replacement grounds being provided, and they could bequeath rights of occupancy as well as property.[81] The increasing ability of slaves to produce marketable food surpluses and to consume imported goods created and sustained markets, and their involvement in those markets eventually secured them the legal right of participation.

These achievements were particularly remarkable because they were accomplished largely by the slaves themselves. Their owners contributed land and grudgingly donated small portions of the slaves' labor time, but they did not intend or expect more from the provision-ground system than a reduction in the cost of slave maintenance. In extending protopeasant activity, slaves often had to cope with planter hostility; the best that they could hope for was the unintended complicity of indifference. Therefore, while it may be possible to accept Bryan Edwards's "coalition of interests" in the elaboration of the plantation complex, it is difficult to see how it was a "happy" arrangement. Rather, its existence involved a barely disguised persistent and unequal competition for resources.

The competition was predicated upon, on the one hand, the slaves' perception that provision-ground cultivation and marketing offered a partial escape from the hard and long routine of supervised plantation labor, and, on the other, their recognition of the ever-present limitations on their ability to exploit this means of escape fully. The demand for *regular* plantation labor naturally deprived them of the time and energy to optimize the material and psychological returns from provision cultivation and marketing. The prime limiting factor was, of course, slavery itself. But if most slaves were seldom disposed toward suicidal confrontation with their owners and overseers, their resistance took the form of continuous efforts to explore and exploit what little the social system offered—to cope with slavery, not by direct confrontation, but by attempts to carve out lives of their own.[82] Resistance therefore may have been subsumed under a competition and scramble for land and labor resources.

Competition for land did not usually involve claims to larger portions of plantation ground. Competition instead revolved around the quality of land allotted to slaves, the distance of that land from slaves' residences, and the rights of occupancy to that land. A confrontation in 1831 between slaves and the manager-attorney on the Lataste estate in Grenada—which may be regarded as a form of industrial action— provides an excellent illustration. On that estate the slaves' provision ground was mountain land, but its occupancy had been rendered insecure by the dismissed attorney, William Houston, "who made no scruple at saying he would turn them away from those grounds at ten days' warning." In June 1831 the provision grounds were badly damaged by floods spawned by a hurricane. By September the slaves faced starvation, and they indicated that they were "quite dissatisfied" with the quality and location of their provision grounds and "anxious to get a new piece of land," and that they were cultivating the damaged grounds with "reluctance." In response, the manager-attorney admitted the validity of the complaints—"the land is poor and is now run out"—and, although he chided the slaves for murmuring at "the will of the Almighty," he quickly sought replacement ground. By late September he had succeeded in leasing "a piece of excellent new land for the Negroes," which was two miles nearer the estate than the old ground and with which the slaves seemed "well pleased."[83] Slaves had invoked their customary rights, and the manager-attorney had recognized the policy of satisfying them.

Essentially, slaves wanted what they did not control but what was within their masters' power to concede: adequate maintenance, to be provided by provision grounds with good soil in a convenient location and full rights to crops through secure occupancy of the grounds. Laws designed to guarantee them minimal levels of maintenance— the periodic inspection of provision grounds—were a dead letter. Slaves thus took it upon themselves to remind their masters that inadequate maintenance would be met with theft, desertion, and even insurrection. Their tactics included persistent complaint, "reluctance" (the go-slow), and desertion, perhaps in that order. The most commonly used tactic, however, was self-help. Some slaves took advantage of the negligible restrictions on the appropriation of land for provision grounds by scouring the mountains and high valleys for suitable soils. Therefore, what John Bowen Colthurst saw as the indulging of a "wandering propensity" was often the exercise of initiative, the far-ranging search for the adequate maintenance that masters failed to provide.[84]

Available evidence does not directly indicate how effective these various tactics were. However, inferences may be drawn from two developments. First, slaves consolidated the provision grounds and marketing complex, which implies a rising production and, perhaps, productivity of provision grounds. The slaves' success may therefore have forced planters to respond to their statements of grievance. Second, legislation near the end of the slavery period (usually local abolition acts) promised improvement in levels of maintenance. This was mainly the achievement of the abolitionists, and of James Stephen in particular. In 1824 his monumental work, *The Slavery of the British West India Colonies Delineated,* dissected as never before the practices of the slave system. But the story Stephen told was the story of the plight and struggle of West Indian slaves; so, to the extent that Stephen's work stimulated reform, the slaves' actions must be held partly responsible for the amelioration of their own condition.

Scramble for labor services was probably more intense than the competition for land, because labor was the slaves' scarcest resource. Supervised plantation labor normally occupied fifty-five hours in a six-day week, leaving little for slaves themselves. The portion of time they did control was small and intermittent, and might be reduced without notice by demands from their masters for extra duty or other chores on a Sunday.[85] Slaves were also faced with competing claims on their time—recuperation from the plantation routine, provision-ground cultivation, marketing, and leisure activities. If slaves gave too much priority to one claim, the effect on maintenance or health could be disastrous. Sickness or distance from provision grounds or markets could aggravate the situation. Therefore, the slaves' existence must have been hectic and full of frustrations, for it required some ingenuity to juggle competing claims and conserve energy for the tasks that awaited the small amount of time they controlled. Their problem, as rural producers, was how to maximize the use of available labor time in own-account activities and how, in the face of supervised plantation labor, to gain extra time for those activities.

Slaves tried to solve this double problem in at least three ways. The first tactic involved cooperation with masters and other slaves. Slaves in supervisory positions were permitted by masters either to hire or freely avail themselves of the labor services of other slaves.[86] Nonelite creole slaves sought their masters' patronage and may have competed with one another for the temporary labor services of newly arrived slaves during their seasoning period. Masters apprenticed new slaves to creole slaves, and, according to Sir William Young, the creoles' scramble for an allocation "was violent, and troublesome in the extreme."[87]

The second tactic stressed cooperation among slaves. Observers remarked on the higher average earnings which "Negroes and slaves having children" achieved compared to those of "single slaves."[88] Obviously, the pooling of land and labor resources in family groups created possibilities for a more efficient deployment of labor and for more intensive exploitation of provision ground and internal market. Children may have been mainly employed around the yards and gardens, tending the stock; women were the main market-people, preparing, transporting, and selling produce; and men presumably bore the major responsibility for clearing and preparing the grounds.

The third tactic turned on "theft" of masters' labor time. Slaves stole constantly because independent economic activities expanded but the allowance of labor time did not increase before the 1820s. This theft could seldom be obvious—absence from gang or late return from meal breaks—though such actions may have played a part. Supervision, however, and the certainty of punishment for malingering and temporary desertion most likely checked the incidence of overt malingering. Theft had to be subtle, theft through energy conservation and the deliberate reduction of performance levels. If one takes account of the length and intensity of the plantation work schedule, slaves' success in conserving their energy must chiefly explain the contrast between their "sodden, stupid and dull" demeanor in the plantation fields and their "lively, intelligent and even happy" behavior in their provision grounds and in the markets.[89] No doubt, as Mintz argues, unsupervised provision-ground cultivation did give slaves opportunities to express fully their humanity—but both that expression and provision-ground cultivation required reasonably high energy levels to sustain them.[90]

Protopeasant activity, the competition this generated, and the limited gains that slaves made in the competition nurtured and confirmed their attitudes about those activities and their relationship to plantation labor. These own-account activities and coerced labor, in an uneven mix, dominated the slaves' experience, with slaves employing protopeasant activity continuously during slavery to reduce the extent and impact of coerced labor. From the slaves' perspective, their own-account activities were probably as important as coerced labor in defining their status, their humanity, and their notions of freedom. Perhaps it is not too fanciful to suggest that they may have equated humanity and freedom with their independent activities. Further, slaves doubtless perceived that their forced involvement in plantation labor constrained their exploitation of the potential in protopeasant activity and was the critical limiting factor on their acquisition of freedom and full expression of humanity. Therefore, they may have concluded that, given a choice in the matter, they should rearrange the allocation of labor time to give priority to the transforming element of own-account activities.

Postslavery labor relations reveal the influence of such attitudes. Both apprentices and ex-slaves utilized the greater control of the labor time which slavery abolition conferred to deemphasize regular plantation labor and to emphasize own-account activities.[91] However, they tried to do all this *within the confines of the plantation,* which was still dependent on regular gang labor. Inevitably, then, the scope of that competition was to some extent culturally determined.

9

UNE PETITE GUINÉE:
PROVISION GROUND AND PLANTATION
IN MARTINIQUE, 1830–1848

Dale Tomich

URING THE NINETEENTH century the working activity of
slaves in the French West Indian colony of Martinique extended beyond the production of export commodities. The
planters of Martinique, under constant pressure to reduce costs,
obliged their slaves to produce for their own subsistence in their "free"
time, that is, outside of the time devoted to the plantation's commercial crop. Instead of receiving the legally required amounts of food and
clothing, slaves were commonly given plots of marginal land and a
free day on Saturday so that they could produce at least a portion of
their own consumption needs on their own account.[1] By encouraging
slaves to work for themselves the masters could avoid the effort and
expense of the large-scale cultivation of provisions. Instead, they had
only to furnish some clothing, a fixed weekly ration of salt meat or fish
and perhaps rum, and occasional medical care.[2]

This arrangement had obvious benefits for the master. The expense
of maintaining the slave population placed heavy economic burdens
on a planter. Imported goods were always expensive and their supply
often irregular, while the conditions of sugar production in Martinique
made available both land and time for provision-ground cultivation.
Planters perceived it as in their interest to spend as little money, time,
or energy as possible on slave maintenance—a perception that did not
change appreciably at least as long as the slave trade lasted, and for
many extended beyond the end of the slave trade and even of slavery
itself. Allowing slaves to produce for their own subsistence from
resources already at hand instead of purchasing the necessary items
on the market reduced the slaveholder's cash expenses. The burden of

reproduction costs was shifted directly to the slaves themselves, and they were kept usefully employed even during periods when there was no work to be done on the sugar crop. Although such practices meant that after long hours of toil in the cane fields the slaves had to work still more just to secure the basic necessities of life, many planters hoped that it would give the slaves a stake in the plantation and instill in them regular habits and the virtues of work and property.[3]

While provision-ground cultivation arose from the planter's attempts to reduce costs and create an interest for the slave in the well-being of the estate, it resulted in the formation of a sphere of slave-organized activity that ultimately became necessary for the operation of the plantation system. This sphere of activity neither was simply integrated into the organization of the sugar estate, nor, as some contend, did it form an independent "peasant breach" with a logic of its own.[4] Instead, provision-ground production and the commercial production of sugar were intimately bound to each other in ways simultaneously dependent and antagonistic. Although slave provision-ground cultivation was spatially and temporally separate from export commodity production, it developed within the constraints of estate agriculture. Not only did final authority over the use of the land and the disposition of labor reside with the master but the time and space for provision-ground cultivation also arose from the rhythm and organization of sugar production.

Nonetheless, such activity offered an opportunity for slave initiative and self-assertion that cannot simply be deduced from its economic form. The slave provision ground became, in the expression of Maléuvrier, the Intendant of Saint Domingue, *"une petite Guinée,"* where slaves could organize their own activities for their own purposes.[5] These practices both shaped and were shaped by Afro-Caribbean cultural forms, through which the definitions of social reality of slavery and the plantation were at once mediated and contested. Through this activity, slaves themselves created and controlled a secondary economic network which originated within the social and spatial boundaries of the plantation but which allowed for the construction of an alternative way of life that went beyond it.[6]

Provision-ground production and the activities associated with it developed within and through the antagonistic relation between master and slave. If for the master the provision ground was the means to guarantee cheap labor, for the slave it was the means to elaborate an autonomous style of life. From these conflicting perspectives evolved a continuing struggle—at times hidden, at times overt—over the division of the available labor time of the estate into export-crop production and provision-crop production. At issue was not only the amount and kind of work to be performed but also its social meaning and purpose. In this process, as much cultural as economic in both its causes and its consequences, the slaves contested the definition and meaning of time and space, labor and power.

The condition for the autonomous development of provision-ground cultivation and marketing was the slaves' appropriation of a portion of the labor time of the estate and its redefinition around their individual and collective interests, needs, and values within and against the predominant slave relation. The slaves' struggle for "free" time entailed and was conditioned by struggles to appropriate physical space, the right to property, and the disposition of their own activity. In turn, the consolidation of slave autonomy in provision-ground cultivation provided leverage to contest the conditions of staple crop production. These interrelated practices transformed and subverted the organization of labor within slavery even as they reinforced it. In this process, the bonds of dependence of slave upon master began slowly to dissolve, and the slaves' activities gradually transformed the foundations of slave society itself. The changing role and meaning of these independent activities were both cause of and response to the increased pressure for profitability on the plantation system during the first half of the nineteenth century. While these practices had existed virtually since the beginning of slavery in the colony, they assumed new importance with changing economic and political conditions and the imminent prospect of emancipation.[7]

Evolution

Masters had provided slaves with small gardens to supplement their rations since the beginning of slavery in the French colonies, but the practice of giving the slaves provision-grounds and a free day each week to grow their own food dated to the introduction of sugarcane into the French Antilles by Dutch refugees from Pernambuco during the first half of the seventeenth century. The origins of this latter practice can be traced back further still to São Tomé in the sixteenth century.[8] Thus, the diffusion of sugarcane entailed not merely the movement of a commodity but the spread of a whole way of life. With the appearance of sugar cultivation in the French Caribbean, subsistence crops for the slaves were neglected in favor of planting cane, and the

"Brazilian custom" was rapidly adopted by planters eager to reduce their expenses. Masters no longer distributed rations to their slaves. Instead, they expected slaves to provide their own food, shelter, clothing, and other material needs from the labor of their "free" day.

But this practice failed to ensure a regular and sufficient supply of food. Slaves were often poorly nourished. Indeed, frequent food shortages prevented masters from dispensing with the distribution of rations altogether. Provisions for these rations were produced as an estate crop by compulsory gang labor under the supervision of drivers and overseers. Further, critics of free Saturdays claimed that the custom gave the slaves too much freedom and encouraged theft and disorder. Too many slaves neglected their gardens, preferring to hire themselves out rather than grow food during their free time. They were said to squander their earnings and rob their masters and neighboring plantations for food. Nevertheless, despite these problems, the custom continued to spread slowly but steadily throughout the French colonies.[9]

Metropolitan authorities agreed with the critics and sought both to stop what they perceived to be the excesses resulting from the free Saturday and to ensure adequate nourishment for the slave population. The proclamation of the Royal Edict of 1685 or *Code Noir* by the metropolitan government was the first attempt to establish a uniform dietary standard for slaves in all the French colonies and to end the prevailing disorder. It sought to make masters totally responsible for the maintenance of their slaves and to prescribe standards for the food, shelter, and clothing to be provided to the slaves. Under the regulations the practice of relying on individual slave gardens and free Saturdays in lieu of rations was to be suppressed in favor of regular weekly food allowances of determined composition and quantity.[10]

This edict remained the fundamental legislation governing slavery in the French colonies throughout the ancien régime. The distribution of slave rations seems to have been more widely practiced in Martinique than elsewhere in the French Antilles, and slaves there had the reputation of being better fed than those elsewhere in the French colonies. Even so, throughout the eighteenth century administrators in Martinique complained continually that the slaveowners were concerned only with sugar, and, if they provided a part of the slaves' nourishment, the slaves were obliged to secure the rest on their own account. The persistent failure to regulate the slaves' diet and treatment and especially to prohibit the slave provision grounds is evident from the succession of declarations, edicts, ordinances, regulations, and decrees, too numerous to recount, promulgated by both metropolitan and colonial authorities during the seventeenth and eighteenth centuries. Colonial officials lacked the means to enforce the regulations in a society dominated by slaveholders who jealously guarded their "property rights," particularly when it cost them time or money. Planters expressed their preference for slave self-subsistence, and their reluctance to spend money on slave maintenance, especially food, persisted throughout the ancien régime and into the nineteenth century. Far from dying out, the practice of free Saturdays and slave provision grounds expanded and increasingly became an established part of colonial life.[11]

The revisions of the *Code Noir* enacted in 1784 and 1786 attempted to ameliorate the lot of slaves and reconcile the law with the growing importance of provision grounds in the colonies. The free Saturday was still forbidden, but instead of prohibiting slave provision grounds the new legislation recognized their existence and attempted to regulate them. It decreed that each adult slave was to receive a small plot of land to cultivate on his or her own account. The law still, however, required the distribution of rations. The produce of these plots was to supplement the *ordinaire*, not replace it. The prohibition against the substitution of the free Saturday for the legal ration was restated by the Royal Ordinance of October 29, 1828, which reformed the colonial penal code. But custom was stronger than law, and ministerial instructions advised colonial authorities to tolerate the replacement of the ration by the free Saturday when it was voluntary on the part of the slave.[12]

These modifications of the earlier legislation were a step toward recognizing the realities of colonial life, but the law still regarded provision-ground cultivation only as a supplemental activity and continued to insist on the distribution of the *ordinaire* as the primary means of providing for slave maintenance. However, depressed economic conditions after 1815 made complete dependence on the ration impractical, and scarcities caused planters to increase their reliance on provision-ground cultivation. In 1829 a parliamentary commission reported that before the sugar boom of 1823 most plantations in the French West Indies could only rarely provide their slaves with the *ordinaire*. Planters had to require slaves to provide for their own subsistence and were thus deprived of a portion of their labor. Yet the commission concluded that "almost all the Negroes now received the quantity of codfish and other food prescribed by the regulations, and their masters could employ them full-time in the cultivation of sugar cane." In his testimony before the commission, Jabrun, a planter from Guadeloupe, observed that slaves in that colony were better fed, better dressed, and better housed than they had been some years previously. Nevertheless, he also noted that, although produce from provision grounds normally supplemented the ration, poverty, shortage of credit, and the consequent difficulty in obtaining provisions still caused some planters to substitute the free Saturday for the ration. De Lavigne, a planter from Martinique, testified that in general the substitution of the free Saturday had ceased there. While this latter claim was certainly exaggerated, the evidence presented by both Jabrun and De Lavigne suggests a cyclical aspect to provision-ground cultivation. In contrast to periods of low sugar prices when land and labor could be given over to provision grounds, with the high prices of the sugar boom of the 1820s many planters may have devoted their attention entirely to sugar cultivation and purchased necessary provisions. Undoubtedly a variety of individual strategies were possible, and while continuous cultivation of provision grounds may be demonstrated for the colony as a whole, it may not necessarily be the case for individual estates.[13]

Despite the shortcomings and abuses of free Saturdays and slave provision grounds and the repeated attempts to suppress them, the scale of these activities grew steadily. By the nineteenth century they had become increasingly central to the functioning of the colonial economy. During the 1830s masters, with few exceptions, encouraged their slaves to grow their own foodstuffs, and the substitution of free Saturdays for the legally prescribed rations had become widespread. Slaves were given as much land as they could cultivate. They both produced and marketed crops without supervision and were so successful that the colony became dependent upon their produce for a substantial portion of its food. As one observer stated in the 1840s, "the plantations which produce foodstuffs [habitations vivrières] and the slaves who cultivate gardens more than guarantee that the colony is supplied with local produce." Measures prohibiting these activities were disregarded with the common consent of both masters and slaves. Enforcement would not only have inhibited the efforts of the slave cultivators but could also have reduced the island's food supply.[14]

By the 1840s authorities in both France and the colony no longer regarded these practices as threats to order, but rather felt that they contributed to social harmony. The reports of local officials stressed the social benefits of independent cultivation by slaves. One of them expressed the opinion that the free Saturday was an "effective means of giving [the slave] the taste for property and well-being, and consequently, to make them useful craftsmen and agriculturalists desirous of family ties." For another, writing in 1842, it meant nothing less than bringing slaves up to the standards of the civilized world: "But the slaves, for whom the custom of free Saturdays is established, prefer it to the ration because they work on their own account and find some profit from that state of affairs. It is clear evidence that man, even though a slave, has an interest in money and likes to enjoy the fruits of his labors while freely disposing of that which belongs to him. The black is forced to enter into types of social transactions that can only serve as a means of civilizing him." This "civilizing" aspect was seen to be especially important because of the imminent prospect of emancipation. The report continued: "In this regard, the custom of the free Saturday must be preferred to the legally sanctioned ration because, beyond everything else, it is a road toward free labor."[15]

The reforms of the July Monarchy were a decisive step in the recognition of existing practices in the colonies and prepared the way for emancipation. The law of July 18 and 19, 1845, known as the Mackau law, allowed the substitution of food grown on provision grounds for the *ordinaire*. While the land itself remained the property of the master, its produce belonged to the slave, and the state recognized the latter's legal personality and right to chattel property. The Mackau law confirmed and regularized what was already a customary practice, giving it legal sanction. In the words of its authors, "the law only recognizes a state that has long existed in practice and makes it a right to the great advantage of the black and without detriment to the master." These legally enforceable rights were less precarious and dependent upon the whim of the proprietor than the previous custom. Slaves could now assert their purposes with the support of the colonial state. The authorities saw in these practices not the source of disorder but the means to regulate slavery and provide a transition to free labor. The Mackau law sought to ease the transition to freedom by giving slaves skills, property, and therefore a stake in society. In the words of one local official, "on the eve of complete emancipation, it is the interest of the masters to see the taste for labor and the spirit of economy develop in the slaves. Now, without property there is no industrious activity. It is only for oneself that one has the heart to work. Without property there is no economy. One does not economize for another."[16]

Integration and Adaptation

According to French abolitionist Victor Schoelcher, the provision ground was the principal source of well-being for slaves in Martinique under the July Monarchy. Indeed, its importance grew as the crisis of the sugar industry and mounting indebtedness limited the planters' resources. Customarily, slaves who were given half a day free a week were allotted only half a ration, while those who received a full day were to provide food for themselves. In addition, Sundays, rest periods, and evenings during the week belonged to the slaves and could be devoted to subsistence activities. Schoelcher recorded that on a great number of plantations in Martinique such arrangements had become a sort of exchange between the master and his slaves. "This transaction," he wrote, "is very favorable for the master who no longer has capital to lay out to ensure the supply of provisions. And it is accepted with good will by the black who in working Saturday and Sunday in his garden derives great benefits."[17]

With few exceptions, masters encouraged their slaves to grow their own foodstuffs whenever possible. The practice of giving Saturdays to the slaves appears to have been far more common than the distribution of the *ordinaire* as the means of providing subsistence. Although some of the most prosperous planters preferred to give rations to their slaves, provision grounds were almost universal and appear to have existed even where the *ordinaire* was distributed. For example, according to one report, in Lamentin, one of the major sugar-growing regions of the colony, free Saturdays were denied on almost all the plantations and slaves received the legal allotments. Nevertheless, the slaves kept gardens and drew considerable revenues from sales to local markets. Not surprisingly, the distribution of clothing allowances was more widely practiced than that of food rations, although the *procureurs* (public prosecutors) reported that many planters expected their slaves to provide their own clothing as well as their food from the income of their gardens. This practice was especially widespread among the less prosperous planters, particularly in the poorer southern *arrondissement* of Fort Royal. Only wealthy planters could consistently afford to clothe their slaves. Others could do so only when the harvest was good, if at all. Several public prosecutors objected to planters making the slaves provide their own clothing and admonished the slaveholders to stop the practice. Thus, while diverse combinations and possibilities of conditions of subsistence existed, provision grounds and free Saturdays had become a common experience for the majority of slaves in Martinique during the nineteenth century. These slaves provided for their own maintenance, in whole or in part, through independent labor beyond their toil in the cane fields.[18]

The successful development of autonomous provision-ground cultivation and marketing in Martinique depended upon the initiative of the enslaved. It was the result of slaves adapting to New World conditions and acquiring the skills and habits necessary to produce and market these crops. At least one contemporary observer stressed the importance of cultural adaptation by the slaves in developing subsistence agriculture and also suggested that slave provision grounds became more prevalent after the slave trade ended in the early 1830s. "Thus, previously, the progress of the population did not take place in accordance with the laws of nature," he noted. "Each year, the irregular introduction of considerable numbers of blacks increased the possibility of a scarce food supply in the country. These new arrivals in the colonies, knowing neither the soil, the climate, nor the special agriculture of the Antilles, could not count on themselves for their support. It was necessary to provide sufficient and regular nourishment for them, but they had no skills to contribute. Thus, the proprietors were quite properly compelled to plant a certain amount of provisions since their slaves did not know how or were unable to plant enough." He continued, "The slaves of today have less need of constant tutelage than previously. They are able to supply themselves without depending upon the generosity of their masters. The latter hardly plant provisions at all any more because the slaves plant well beyond the amount that is necessary for consumption." Indeed, nineteenth-century accounts indicate that the slaves by and large preferred to have an extra day to themselves and raise their own provisions rather than receive an allowance of food from the master. "This practice," observed one government official, "is completely to the advantage of the slave who wants to work. A day spent by him cultivating his garden, or in some other manner, will bring him more than the value of the nourishment the law prescribes for him. I will add that there is no *atelier* which does not prefer this arrangement to the execution of the edict [*Code Noir*]. Once it has been set, it would be dangerous for the master to renounce it."[19]

The slaves who wanted to plant provisions were given as much land as they could work. These plots were usually located on the uncultivated lands on the margins of the estate, often scattered in the hills above the cane fields. However, both De Cassagnac, a local planter, and Schoelcher write that some planters in the 1840s allowed cane land to be used for provisions as a form of crop rotation. When the sugar cane had exhausted the soil in a field, the slaves were permitted to plant provisions there until the land was again fit for cane. The provision grounds were then shifted to other fields. (According to historian Gabriel Debien, larger grounds located away from the slave quarters only appeared after 1770, but these were still intended to supplement the rations provided by the master rather than furnish the main items of the slave diet. The staples of the slave diet—manioc, potatoes, and yams—were grown by the master in the fields belonging to the plantation.) The plots allotted to slaves were frequently quite extensive, as much as one or two acres according to Schoelcher. All available sources agree that the slave provision grounds were well kept. Produce was abundant, and the land was not allowed to stand idle. Manioc, the principal source of nourishment for the slave population, was harvested as often as four times a year. Besides manioc, the slaves raised bananas, potatoes, yams, and other vegetables on these plots.[20]

In addition to the provision grounds, there were also small gardens in the yards surrounding the slave cabins. They were intended to supplement the weekly ration, not replace it, and all the slaves, including those who received the *ordinaire*, had them. In these gardens slaves grew sorrel, squash, cucumbers from France and Guinea, green peppers, hot peppers, calabash vines, okra, and perhaps some tobacco. They also planted fruit trees and, if the master permitted, kept a few chickens there as well.[21]

Of course, not all slaves were willing or able to endure the burden of extra work in the provision grounds. Infants, the aged, the infirm, expectant mothers or those nursing children—all of whom could not provide for themselves—received a food allowance from the master, even on the plantations where the slaves grew their own foodstuffs. Also included among the nonparticipants were those slaves who refused to raise a garden. A public prosecutor in Fort Royal wrote that "only the lazy receive a ration and they are almost ashamed of it." Of these "lazy" slaves, Schoelcher commented: "We do not want to deny, however, that there are many Negroes who show a great indifference to the benefit of free Saturdays. It is necessary to force them to work for themselves on that day. It does not surprise us that beings, saturated with disgust and struck by malediction, are little concerned to improve their lot during the moments of respite that are given to them. Instead, they prefer to surrender to idleness to become intoxicated to the point of delirium from the melancholy agitation of their African dances." The free Saturday, while generally received enthusiastically by the slaves, was thus not universally accepted. For many slaves, it simply meant more work, and they refused. They withdrew their voluntary cooperation, throwing the burden of maintenance back on the master. De Cassagnac expressed surprise that on many planta-tions, if the slaves were given the free Saturday, they would not work. They had, in his view, to be treated like children and be forced to work for themselves. It was necessary to have a driver lead them to the gardens and watch them as carefully as when they were working for the estate.[22]

But compulsion was not usually necessary, and often individual planters went to great lengths to support the efforts of their slaves. Sieur Telliam-Maillet, who managed the Ceron plantation in Diamant, plowed his slaves' provision grounds. Even though he supplied the *ordinaire*, M. de Delite-Loture, who owned nearly three hundred slaves in the *quartier* of Sainte Anne, bought or rented land in the highlands of Rivière Pilote which he cleared so that his slaves could work it for themselves. Each week he had them taken nearly two leagues from the plantation to these gardens, and he paid for the transport of their produce as well. Schoelcher reports that in some *quartiers* the masters provided the slaves who worked such gardens with tools, carts, mules, and a *corvée* of workers, and the masters and the slave cultivators divided the harvest in half. Other masters, con-sidering such an arrangement beneath their dignity, simply aban-doned the land to the slaves.[23]

For even the most industrious slave, dependence on the planter was inescapable. As Schoelcher remarked, "the greater or lesser wealth of the slaves depends a great deal on the benevolence of the master." Whichever mode of providing for the slaves was adopted, one inspection report noted, "their nourishment is assured every-where, and the master is always ready . . . to come to the aid of the slave when the latter has need of him." Indeed, seasonal fluctuations could require the master to come to the assistance of his slaves. "In years of great drought," De Cassagnac wrote, "subsistence crops do not grow. Then planters who previously gave the free Saturday once again give the *ordinaire*. Those are disastrous years."[24]

Even at best, the slaves who produced their own provisions were exposed to risk and uncertainty. They were generally given land of inferior quality that was incapable of supporting sugar or coffee. At times the planters deprived them of their free day under various pretexts. If for some reason they fell ill and could not work, their food

supply was jeopardized. Drought or bad weather might make cultivation impossible. The prospect of theft and disorder was then increased, and, at the extreme, the physical well-being of the labor force
was threatened.[25]

Nevertheless, provision-ground cultivation could be advantageous
for the slave. Access to this property meant that the slaves' consumption was no longer entirely dependent on the economic condition of
the master. Rather, slaves could use their free time and the produce of
their gardens to improve their standard of living. Demonstrating exceptional initiative and skill, they used the opportunities presented to
them to secure at least relative control over their subsistence and a
degree of independence from the master. According to one contemporary estimate, the incentive provided by the gardens doubled slave
output. With the free day and the other free time that could be hus-
banded during rest periods and after tasks were finished, slaves could
produce beyond their immediate subsistence needs. The sale of this
produce in the towns and cities allowed slaves to improve both the
quantity and quality of goods available to them and to satisfy tastes
and desires that the master could not supply. Thus, improvement in
the slaves' well-being was due to their own effort, not to any amelioration of the regime.[26]

The slaves developed market networks that were an important
feature of the economic and social life in Martinique, and the colony
came to rely on the produce of the slave gardens for a substantial
portion of its food. Sunday was the major market day in the towns;
however, smaller markets were held on other days. Important market
towns, such as the ones at Lamentin, François, Trinité, and Robert,
attracted slaves from all parts of the island, bringing them into contact
with the world beyond the plantation. Soleau, a visitor to the island in
1835, described the Lamentin market: "This town is one of the most
frequently visited by the slaves of the colony. It has a fairly large
market where they come to sell their produce on Sunday. I have been
told that the number of slaves that gather there is often as high as five
or six thousand. I passed through there that day while going to the
quartier of Robert, and encountered many blacks on the road who were
going to the town. All were carrying something that they were doubt-
lessly going to sell—manioc flour, potatoes, yams, poultry, etc." An
astonishing variety of goods were exchanged at the town markets. In
addition to manioc, fruits, vegetables, yams, fresh or salted fish, animals, and slave handicrafts, these included manufactured goods such
as shoes, dry goods, porcelain, crystal, perfume, jewelry, and furniture. Barter undoubtedly played a large part in these exchanges, espe-

cially at local markets, but the money economy was significant, and prices were set in major towns for the main articles of trade. The scale of exchange at these town markets was so great that urban merchants began to complain. But their protests had little effect, for, as one planter noted, the town markets were a great resource for the interior of the island.[27]

The Sunday market was as much a social event as an occasion for exchanging goods. Slaves went to town to attend mass, to meet friends from other parts of the island, drink tafia, smoke, eat roast corn, exchange news and gossip, and perhaps dance, sing, or gamble. It was an opportunity for display, and the slaves wore their best. An observer painted a striking picture of the appearance of the slaves at the Lamentin market: "These slaves are almost always very well dressed and present the exterior signs of material well-being. The men have trousers, shirts, vests, and hats of oilskin or straw. The women have skirts of Indian cotton, white blouses, and scarves, some of which are luxurious, as well as earrings, pins and even some chains of gold." According to Soleau, the signs of prosperity presented by slaves of Martinique on market day were unusual in the Caribbean and even in rural France: "One thing struck me that I have never seen in Cayenne, Surinam, or Demerara. It is the cleanliness and the luxury of the clothing of the slaves that I encountered. The lazy, having nothing to sell, remained on the plantations. In France, generally, the peasants, except for their shoes, were not better dressed on Sunday and did not wear such fine material." The colorful and bustling markets punctuated the drudgery and isolation of plantation life. Slaves from town and country, young and old, male and female, along with freedmen, sailors, merchants, planters, and anyone who wanted to buy or sell, mingled in the crowds. These markets offered incentives to slaves, enabling them to improve the material conditions of life as well as to acquire skills, knowledge, and social contacts that allowed them to increase their independence, assert their individuality, and vary the texture of their lives. Their initiatives developed new economic and social patterns and mobilized productive forces that otherwise would have remained dormant.[28]

Appropriation

While provision grounds and free Saturdays never ceased to serve the interests of the slaveowner, they were not simply a functional adaptation to the requirements of the plantation economy. Rather, they form what Roger Bastide describes as a "niche" within slavery that allowed collective self-expression by the slaves—a niche where Afro-Caribbean culture could develop. The slaves had complete responsibility for the provision grounds and were thus able to organize their own activity there without supervision. The use of these parcels and their product was not simply a narrow economic activity but was integrated into broader cultural patterns. Preparing the soil, planting, cultivating, and harvesting, and the disposition of the product were organized through ritual, kinship, and mutual obligation. The provision grounds were important for aspects of slave life as diverse as kinship, religious belief, cuisine, and healing practices. There kin were buried, and singing, dancing, and storytelling took place. These activities provided an avenue for the slaves to exercise decision making and demonstrate self-worth that would otherwise have been closed off by slavery. But, except for Schoelcher's vague comment that the slaves cultivated their gardens "communally," there is little detailed information as to how they organized their activities. This lack of documentation is perhaps mute testimony to the genuine autonomy that the slaves enjoyed in the conduct of these activities.[29]

The provision grounds formed a nodal point within the social relations of slavery that allowed slave practices, values, and interests to emerge and develop and to assume autonomous forms of organization and expression. Long before the promulgation of the Mackau law, slaves established rights and prerogatives with regard to not only the produce of the land but also to the provision grounds and gardens themselves. Masters were compelled to recognize these claims. "The masters no longer acknowledge any rights over the gardens of the *atelier*. The slave is the sovereign master over the terrain that is conceded to him," admitted the Colonial Council of Martinique. "This practice has become a custom for the slaves who regard it as a right which cannot be taken from them without the possibility of disrupting the discipline and good order of the *ateliers*," confirmed one official. Slaves regarded the provision grounds as their own. When they died, the garden and its produce was passed on to their relatives. "They pass them on from father to son, from mother to daughter, and, if they do not have any children, they bequeath them to their nearest kin or even their friends," wrote Schoelcher. Often if no relatives remained on the estate, kinsmen came from other plantations to receive their inheritance with the consent of the master. Here, as elsewhere, the autonomous kinship organization of the slave community served as a counterpoint to the economic rationality of the plantation, and the master was obliged to respect its claims.[30]

Slaves defended their rights even at the masters' expense, and there was often a subtle game of give-and-take between the two. While traveling through the *quartier* of Robert, Schoelcher was surprised to find two small patches of manioc in the midst of a large, well-tended cane field. The proprietor explained that the slaves had planted the manioc when the field had been temporarily abandoned. When he wanted to cultivate the field, he offered to buy the crop, but they demanded an exorbitant price. The master then called upon the other slaves of the estate to set a fair price, but this too was rejected by the slaves who had planted the manioc. "I'll have to wait six or seven months until that damned manioc is ripe," the proprietor complained. Another planter, M. Latuillerie of Lamentin, upon returning from a long trip found that his slaves had abandoned the plots allotted to them in favor of his cane fields. He could not simply reclaim his land. Instead, he first had to agree to give the occupants another field. Schoelcher also observed large mango trees in the middle of cane fields which stunted the cane plants in their shadow. The masters would have cut them down, but they remained standing because they were bequeathed to some yet unborn slave. He noted that "there are some planters who do not have fruit trees on their plantations because tradition establishes that such and such a tree belongs to such and such a Negro, and they [the planters] have little hope of ever enjoying them because the slave bequeaths his tree just like the rest of his property."[31]

The elaboration of autonomous provision-ground cultivation remained intertwined with and dependent upon the larger organization of plantation labor not only spatially but temporally. The practice of the free Saturday transformed the character of the working day in the French Caribbean. An examination of this custom calls attention to the historical processes through which the cultural definitions of work and its relation to the larger matrix of plantation life were contested. As the slaves became socialized into the routine of plantation labor, they were able to lay claim to the free Saturday and use it for their own ends. They felt that they had a right to such "free" time and resisted any encroachment upon it. According to the report of one public prosecutor published in 1844: "It would be almost impossible for a planter to take even a little bit of time belonging to his slave, even if the authorities ignored the situation. There is a spirit of resistance among the slaves that prevents anyone from threatening what they consider to be their rights." Another official emphasized: "There would be discontent if the proprietors took away the free Saturday to give the provisions prescribed by the edict. . . . The Negroes prefer this method which assures them of an extra day each week. Everywhere that it has not been adopted the blacks desire it and beg for it. To try to abolish it where it was once been established would be to provoke disorder and revolt."[32]

The slaves thus effectively appropriated a part of the disposable labor time as their own. In practice, time on the plantation became divided between time belonging to the master and time belonging to the slaves. The time available for export commodity production was restricted, and the master had to bargain with the slaves. Time became a kind of currency, and a complex system of accounting emerged. If masters found that they needed slaves on a Saturday or at another time when the slaves had been exempted from labor, such work was voluntary and slaves were generally compensated for their services. Often, masters indemnified slaves with an equivalent amount of time rather than money. It was reported that the slaves on one plantation were made to work on Sunday during the harvest but were given the following Monday off. (This report added that the planter would be warned that this change was not in accord with religious rites and the regular habits of the slaves.) On the infrequent occasions when the master of another plantation needed the labor of his slaves on a free Saturday or a Sunday for some pressing work, they were given an equivalent amount of time on a weekday. A public prosecutor reported that this planter kept a precise account of the extra time that the slaves put in and indemnified them scrupulously.[33]

Thus, time belonging to the slaves was not only distinguished from that belonging to the masters but also opposed to it. At the extreme, the former encroached upon the latter. For slaves, the time separate from work was a sphere of autonomous activity; it was "free" time where they could dispose of their energies as they saw fit and within which they created a community organized around their beliefs, values, and collective action. Their use of this free time could subvert plantation discipline. According to Monk Lewis, a Jamaican planter, the slaves on his plantation referred to their free Saturday as "playday." The subversive element was especially apparent in the case of the slaves' nocturnal activities. Although prohibited by law from leaving the plantation after dark (in earlier times the *Code Noir* prescribed whipping and branding, and, for repeated offenses, even death), slaves enjoyed considerable freedom of movement at night. "During the week, when work is finished," noted one observer "the slaves leave the plantation and run to those where they have women. . . . The liberty of the night, that is, the right to use their nights as they wish, is a veritable plague. With this type of liberty, the Negroes have every means to indulge in their debauchery, to commit thefts, to smuggle, to repair to their secret meetings, and to prepare and take their revenge. And what good work can be expected during the day from people who stay out and revel the whole night? When the masters are asked why the slaves are allowed such a fatal liberty, they reply that they cannot take it away from them." De Cassagnac wrote that "for the blacks the night is a moment of supreme and incomparable sweetness that the whites will never understand." Night provided an opportunity for the exercise of individual freedom and collective self-expression away from the watchful eye of the authorities. It became the occasion for dancing, music, and religious rites—activities that expressed values antithetical to the subordination of life to work and the rejection of the role of sober, industrious, and self-regulated labor desired by the planters. If the slaves had learned to adapt to the exigencies of plantation labor, they nonetheless refused to reduce themselves to mere instruments of production.[34]

The free Saturday was important as the appropriation of a quantity of time and as the qualitative transformation of the meaning of that time. Through their activity, slaves were able, in some limited way, to define the nature of freedom for themselves. "Free" time became free for the slave and not merely a period when sugar was not being produced. The appropriation of this time provided a base for the assertion of the slaves' purposes, needs, and cultural forms in other aspects of plantation life, including the organization of work and the composition of the working day. Thus, the appropriated time became significant both because of its consequences for the material reproduction of the enslaved population and as an arena in which slaves were able to contest the conditions of domination and exploitation and the conceptions of social life imposed by the plantation regime. While slaves regarded "free" time as a resource to be protected and if possible expanded, masters had to contain the slaves' demands within the limits of economic efficiency and social order. In the development of this process, the historical trajectory and limits of slave production and the master-slave relation can be traced.

Instead of separating the direct producers from the means of subsistence, slavery provided them with the means of producing a livelihood. While slaves gained access to the use of property and had the opportunity to improve their material conditions of life, the price of subsistence was work beyond that required for sugar production. With these developments, the time devoted to the slaves' maintenance became separate from commodity production, and a de facto distinction between time belonging to the master and time belonging to the slave was created.

The planters responded to the slaves' appropriation of the free Saturday by attempting to transform their initiative into an instrument of labor discipline and social control. During the 1830s planters in Martinique implemented a system of task work to induce slaves to work and guarantee the performance of a given amount of labor during the day. Through experience, planters were able to calculate for each of the different types of work to be done on the plantation how much the average slave could do in a day without being overworked. Every morning each slave in the gang was assigned his or her daily task based on this customary amount of labor. On the one hand, slaves could do their daily quota of work as they liked and were free to dispose of the time remaining after its completion as they wished. Under the task system slaves might gain several hours each day which could be spent in the cultivation of their own gardens or in some other employment. The slaves thus had the opportunity to improve their condition, while slaveowners obtained the required amount of labor. On the other hand, slaves who did not use the time well had to spend the whole day working in the masters' fields in order to complete the required task. The punishment was proportional to the effort, or lack thereof, and if the slaves' failure to meet their assignment was too great, their free day could be jeopardized.[35]

Task work could only function when the slave population had sufficiently assimilated the routine of plantation labor to respond to its incentives. For self-regulation to replace external domination, slaves had to understand and accept the rhythm of work, organization of time, and system of rewards and punishments that characterized the plantation regime. Only then could the notion of free time appear as a reward to the slave. Only if the slaves formed a concept of their self-interest and appropriated time for themselves within this framework could the task system operate and the larger appropriation of the slaves' activity by the master take place. Such slave initiative and planter response contributed to the mutation of the relations of work. Once slaves had a recognized interest, their relation to the master could no longer rest upon absolute domination and authority. Instead, that relation had to admit bargaining and negotiation between interested parties—however unequal and antagonistic their relationship. Thus, implementation of task work marked a further transformation of the master-slave relation; it bears witness to the adaptation of the

African slave to the American environment that was both cause and effect of this change.[36]

Provision-ground cultivation and task work suggest the limits of pure coercion as a means of enforcing labor discipline. Their success was dependent upon the integration of the enslaved population into the productive and social processes of the slave plantation. For these measures to work, both master and slave had to recognize the existence of certain privileges and at least a limited degree of independence for the slave. Paradoxically, however, both master and slave became more closely tied to the maintenance of these privileges. The possible range of action for each was restricted, and the character if not the content of labor relations was altered decisively.

Task work was thus an expression of the social limit of the slave relation. While planters might influence individual behavior and set the parameters of the action of the group through the systematic manipulation of rewards and punishments, such measures merely adapted the slaves to the existing organization of production—with a greater or lesser degree of enthusiasm on the part of the slaves. The task system guaranteed the completion of a minimum amount of work and perhaps reduced the costs of supervision, but it did not alter the composition of the working day or increase surplus production. The self-interest created by this system was not a reward earned through commodity-producing activity, but was formed outside of this work and through a release from it. After slaves completed their predetermined task, they were free to look after their own affairs; literally, they were free to tend their own gardens. Such a system might provide slaves with an incentive to give a bit more of themselves, but it demonstrates the incapacity of slavery to create individual self-interest in production itself. Rather, individual self-interest and identification with the job and the plantation were created not in commodity production but in social reproduction. The economy of time and labor was dissolved into the maintenance of a given body of laborers on the one hand and the regular performance of a predetermined quantity of labor on the other: It thus resolved itself into a social-political question as the master-slave relation was challenged from within.

The slaves' appropriation of the free Saturday and their autonomous elaboration of the activities associated with it had far-reaching consequences for the development of slavery in the French West Indies and helped to shape the historical limits of the slave system in Martinique. It was an initiative by a population that, over the course of its historical experience, had learned to adapt to the labor routine, discipline, and organization of time of the slave plantation and confronted slavery from *within* its own relations and processes. The result was simultaneously to strengthen and weaken the slave system. On the one hand, the laboring population became more effectively integrated into the relations and processes of slave production and more responsive to its rewards and punishments. The operating expenses of the plantation were reduced, and a greater surplus was available to the planter. On the other hand, slaves were able to appropriate aspects of these processes and thereby to establish a degree of control over their own subsistence and reproduction. They claimed rights to property and disposition over time and labor that masters were forced to recognize, and they were able to resist infringements upon those rights. While provision-ground cultivation meant more work for the slaves, they were able substantially to improve their material well-being and increase their independence from the master. They restricted the master's capacity to exploit labor and presented a fixed obstacle to surplus production. The amount of labor time at the disposition of the planter was limited, and the slaves acquired a means of resisting the intensification of work at the very moment that the transformation of the world sugar market demanded higher levels of productivity and greater exploitation of labor from French West Indian plantations.

The very ability of masters to compel the participation of slaves in the new conditions of life and labor and the complexity and originality of the slaves' response altered the character of the master-slave relation. Within the context of continuing domination, exploitation, and material scarcity, new forms, meanings, and goals of social action emerged alongside older ones, becoming the focal points of a new constellation of conditions, needs, and capacities on both sides. The slaves' assertion of rights to provision grounds and free time and the autonomous use of these resources reduced their dependence on the master and undermined his authority. Custom, consent, and accommodation assumed greater weight in the conduct of daily life, where coercion had once prevailed. The acquisition of skills and property and the establishment of economic and social networks enabled the enslaved to realize important material and psychological gains. The slaves thus began to fashion an alternative way of life that played an important role both in eroding the slave regime and in creating the conditions for a transition to a new form of social and economic organization. Slaves' struggles for autonomy and planters' efforts to maintain their domination developed the slave relation to its fullest extent and created within slavery both the embryo of postemancipation class structure and the conditions for the transition to "free labor."[37]

Significantly, the autonomous provision-ground cultivation and marketing elaborated within slavery provided freed people with an alternative to plantation labor after emancipation. These activities played an important role in helping the former slaves to resist the new encroachments of plantation agriculture and shape a new relation between labor and capital. The very practices that planters had encouraged during slavery now incurred their wrath. Carlyle scorned Quashee and his pumpkin, but far from representing the "lazy Negro" Carlyle's ridicule was testimony to the capacity of the Afro-Caribbean population to learn, adapt, create, and articulate an alternative conception of their needs, despite the harshness of slavery. Probably few could escape the plantation entirely after emancipation, but provision-ground cultivation and marketing networks enabled the great majority of freed slaves to struggle effectively over the conditions of their labor. The skills, resources, and associations formed through these activities during slavery were decisive in enabling freed people to secure control over their own conditions of reproduction and to establish an independent bargaining position vis-à-vis the planters after slavery.[38]

The immediate consequences of emancipation in Martinique, as throughout the French and British Caribbean, were the withdrawal of labor—particularly the labor of women and children—from the plantation sector and struggles with the planters over time, wages, and conditions of work, struggles in which the laboring population asserted its independence and initiative. The success of these efforts forced a new relation of production on the plantation system itself as the planters attempted to recapture the labor of the emancipated population or find a substitute for it under conditions that guaranteed profitability. This resulted in the formation of new coercive forms of labor extraction in which the laboring population maintained control over subsistence activities and petty commodity production to one degree or another. Seen from this perspective, the reconstruction of the postemancipation plantation system and the transition from one form of coerced labor to another were not the inevitable results of unfolding capitalist rationality. Rather, both were processes whose outcome was problematic, requiring violence and compulsion on the part of planters and the colonial state to reassert control over labor in the face of material and social resources acquired by the laboring population while still enslaved. The transition is best understood as the product of the contradictory relation between production and social reproduction within slavery and of the struggle between masters and slaves over alternative purposes, conceptions of needs, and modes of organization of social and material life.

10

AS "A KIND OF FREEMAN"?: SLAVES' MARKET-RELATED ACTIVITIES IN THE SOUTH CAROLINA UP COUNTRY, 1800–1860

John Campbell

I N PRINCIPLE, SLAVEOWNERS enjoyed unfettered access to slave labor; in practice, they commonly allowed slaves to use a portion of their labor on their own account. As many scholars have long noted, slaves not only engaged in a variety of subsistence-related tasks, such as cooking and tending their garden plots, but they also performed remunerative work that thrust them into the market economy of their masters.[1] As market participants—who produced, sold, and purchased their own property—slaves temporarily experienced one of the central attributes of freedom: the purchase and sale of labor power and the enjoyment of its fruits. Presumably the slaves' presence on the terrain of freedom wrought important consequences for slaves and slaveowners alike. Yet it is only recently that scholars have come to grips with the nature and implications of slaves' independent production and related market activities. In his work on the Georgia–South Carolina low country, Philip Morgan shows how rice slaves used their opportunities for independent production to accumulate considerable wealth, expand their autonomy, and strengthen bonds of community among themselves. Participation in the market also facilitated slave theft of the master's property, argues Alex Lichtenstein, thus enabling slaves to better their economic position while damaging that of their masters. Indeed, the very process of exchange empowered slaves, suggests Lawrence McDonnell, simply because masters and slaves "confronted each other . . . as bearers of commodities, stripped of social dimensions." In short, the emerging portrait of slaves' independent production and related market activities highlights, on balance, the positive implications of these economic activities for slaves.[2]

The cumulative experience of slaves living in the cotton regions of the South Carolina up country supports this view—in part.[3] Participation in the market economy enabled up-country slaves to better themselves materially, assert greater control and independence in their lives, create and strengthen social relationships among themselves as well as with nonslaveholding white people, and challenge the interests and power of slaveholders. However, these benefits were not evenly distributed over time. Changes in the way that slaves earned and spent their incomes altered the impact and implications of slave market activities during the nineteenth century. In the century's first decades slaves worked as wage earners; in the late antebellum years they earned their income primarily as commodity—most notably, cotton—producers. This transformation heightened conflict between slaves and masters, culminating eventually in a number of "reforms" designed to reduce slave independence, and hence subversive activity, within the marketplace. As a result of these reforms, slaves enjoyed relatively less control over their economic affairs in the 1840s and 1850s than had their predecessors; at the same time, the last generation of cotton slaves derived greater material rewards from their market-related activities. An examination of these developments during the nineteenth century reveals the complex and contradictory nature of market participation for slaves living in the up country of South Carolina.

By the time Eli Whitney's cotton gin opened the South Carolina up country to large-scale, market-oriented cotton production in the 1790s, South Carolina slaves had already won the right to participate in the market. In 1740 South Carolina lawmakers set aside Sunday as a day when slaves did not have to work for their owners but instead could engage in their own pursuits.[4] During the course of the eighteenth century slaves living on the coastal rice plantations used the prevailing organization of work—the task system—to expand their independent economic activities. The organization of labor by tasks, in which each slave was assigned a measurable quantity of work, encouraged slaves to work quickly. Once they finished, the remainder of the day belonged to them, and they used it to produce and sell a range of goods, including rice, corn, tobacco, pumpkins, canoes, and baskets.[5] By the late eighteenth century rice planters had grudgingly conceded such arrangements; indeed, a 1796 South Carolina law implicitly ratified the custom of slaves selling and buying their own goods when it attempted to regulate—rather than prohibit—such market activities.[6]

On the emerging cotton plantations of the up country slaves also participated extensively in the market economy. However, the special conditions of up-country life structured the slaves' earning of income in distinct ways. The slaves' commodity production—whether of crops or manufactured items—was constrained by the amount of time and land available to slaves and, to a lesser extent, by their subsistence needs. Slaves laboring on both new and established cotton plantations did not have free time in the afternoon to work for themselves, for rather than working by the task up-country cotton slaves labored in gangs. Gang labor invariably meant that slaves remained in the fields until sundown. As a consequence, cotton slaves could pursue their own economic activities only at night, on Sundays, or on the occasional day when poor weather kept them from their owners' fields. A persistent feature of up-country cotton agriculture, the gang system permanently restricted the amount of time available for slaves to pursue their own economic interests.[7]

Yet the first generation of cotton slaves faced an additional constraint on their productive activities: a shortage, if not outright absence, of tillable farmland. During the first decades of settlement there was simply little land available for slaves to cultivate. It would take years of repeated tillage before there was a sizable quantity of cleared—if also worn-out—land that slaveowners could cede to slaves. With farmland scarce, at least from the perspective of slaves, it was difficult for individual slaves or slave families to gain access to the one- or two-acre plots that slaves regularly controlled in the 1840s and 1850s.[8] Instead, in the early years of the nineteenth century slaves made do with the small garden patches around their cabins or land "in some remote and unprofitable part of the estate, generally in the woods."[9]

Restricted access to time and land automatically limited the independent economic production of up-country slaves and their potential involvement in the marketplace as sellers of commodities, reducing the level of their activity below that of rice slaves. The size of the food allowance slaves customarily received from their masters also limited the scale of slave commodity production. According to Charles Ball, a slave who lived on an up-country plantation during the first decade of the nineteenth century, the quantity of corn and meat that slaveholders provided was insufficient to sustain him and his fellow slaves. As a result, they used their patches of land to grow food crops such as corn, potatoes, pumpkins, and melons.[10] Because slaves raised these crops as supplements to their subsistence allowance, they consumed—rather than sold—most of what they produced.

Nonetheless, even within these constraints, slaves still produced commodities for the market. When slaves grew food crops primarily for subsistence, they sometimes were able to sell a surplus. In 1803 slaves living on the plantation of Gabriel Guignard, located near present-day Columbia, sold eighteen bushels of corn for forty-two shillings, or roughly nine dollars. Some slaves also used their time and land to grow nonfood crops, like tobacco, which they sold at market. In addition to selling crops, slaves peddled a variety of useful articles, such as baskets, brooms, horse collars, and bowls, manufactured when inclement weather kept them out of the fields.[11]

Producing and selling commodities was not the only means by which the first generation of South Carolina cotton slaves earned income. They also worked for wages—and, in light of the history of cotton slaves' independent economic activities, wage work constituted a most distinctive development. The prominence of wage work during the early nineteenth century reflected shortages of labor and capital in the up country. Determined to maximize their profits, the first generation of cotton planters drove their slaves from sunup to sundown, six days a week. Despite this relentless pace, slaveowners still required additional labor. This need was especially pronounced among aspiring planters who, in the process of building their estates from scratch, had to lay out fields, clear trees, uproot rocks, and erect farm structures—all while getting a crop in the ground. But after 1800, when the price of cotton abruptly fell, even established planters needed additional labor if they hoped to offset the adverse economic consequences of lower cotton prices by increasing production.[12]

The process of harvesting cotton created an even more acute demand for—or, perhaps more accurately, persistent shortage of—plantation labor. The short-staple cotton grown in the pioneer up country was difficult to pick, "as the pods did not open widely." Problems in separating the cotton from the pods meant that slaves could harvest relatively little cotton in a day.[13] Between 1801 and 1804 slaves on the Guignard plantation picked an average of thirty pounds per day and only fifty pounds on the best days of the harvest. (In contrast, slaves commonly picked a hundred pounds a day during the late antebellum period.)[14] To increase productivity, especially after 1800, cotton planters sought, and would eventually find, a more pickable and productive variety of short-staple cotton. In the meantime, the only way that slaveowners could increase production was by acquiring additional workers, work time, or work effort during the harvest.

The slaveowners' labor needs spelled economic opportunity for slaves. To increase the amount of cotton slaves harvested, slaveowners frequently paid their slaves directly for each pound of cotton that they picked above a targeted amount, generally at the rate of a penny a pound. Rather than spend their free time tending their own crops, some slaves found it advantageous to work for wages. According to Charles Ball, it was "universal amongst the slaves on the cotton plantations" to work as wage earners on the Christian Sabbath. During the Guignard harvests, for example, slaves picked cotton for wages on Sunday. In other seasons of the year they earned cash clearing land, splitting rails, plowing, and hoeing cotton and potatoes.[15]

Slaves not only worked for their master but also traveled off the plantation on Sunday to work elsewhere. Charles Ball recalled how he and other slaves customarily left their home plantation to clear land and pick cotton for wages on neighboring estates. Individual slaveowners tried to stop this labor hemorrhage by offering their slaves more than the customary daily wage of fifty cents if only they would work on the home plantation. But even given the possibility of earning a higher wage slaves "often [left] the fields of their master . . . to go to the field of some neighboring planter. . . . [During the harvest] it is a matter of indifference to the slave, whether his master gets his cotton picked or not."[16]

As an income-earning activity, wage work carried contradictory consequences for slaves. In working for wages slaves unavoidably strengthened the very system that oppressed them. Whereas slave-produced commodities, such as cotton or tobacco, generated no direct economic benefit to slaveowners, slaves who provided additional labor as wage earners helped ensure the economic success of individual slaveowners, thus encouraging the slaveholders' continued commitment to slavery as a system of organizing and extracting labor. Yet participation in the Sunday labor market also gave slaves a temporary taste of freedom. In leaving the plantation slaves sold their labor power to whom they chose and became, if only briefly, someone else's employee, not their slave. Slaves themselves were impressed with the way that the Sunday labor system blurred the boundary between slavery and freedom. As Charles Ball put it, slaves who left the plantation to sell their labor power became "a kind of freeman on Sunday" as they "exercised [their] liberty on this day."[17] Thus, if wage work reinforced slavery, it also undermined it by allowing slaves to experience a kind of freedom and to see themselves as something other than slaves.

With their wages and other earnings some slaves did quite well as participants in the market economy. Charles Ball took special note of two diligent slaves, a man and a woman, who earned thirty-one and twenty-six dollars respectively as cotton pickers. Ball earned a comparable amount, both from wage work and from the wooden trays and vessels he made in his spare time and sold to local merchants and planters. The experience of other slaves, however, suggests that Ball's achievement was exceptional. Slaves on the Guignard plantation earned, on average, approximately three dollars annually during the period between 1802 and 1804. Overall, the typical field hand probably earned from three to eight dollars in a year.[18]

These earnings, whatever the size, nonetheless enabled slaves to improve their lives in two ways. Slaves could purchase "little articles of necessity or luxury," such as sugar, molasses, coffee, tobacco, and clothing, augmenting the all too bland and meager subsistence allowance they received from their masters.[19] Perhaps even more important, especially in light of future developments, slaves received their earnings in cash, rather than in credit or in kind. With cash in their pockets slaves could buy the goods they wanted when they wanted them. Slaves found crossroad shopkeepers more than willing "to rise at any time of the night to oblige [their slave] friends" by trading. Such service was much less likely, Charles Ball suggested, if slaves paid, as most white people did, by credit alone. Indeed, the possession of money itself encouraged slaves to leave the plantation surreptiously at night to spend their earnings as they desired—and thereby assert their independence. In this context, for many slaves money became synonymous with independence and control over their lives.[20]

If the nature of short-staple cotton—particularly the difficulty of separating cotton from pod—served as a surprising ally in slave efforts to carve out their own economic niche, it remained the bane of pioneer cotton planters. Keenly aware of how this variety of short-staple cotton shackled their economic aspirations, cotton planters attempted to develop more pickable varieties. During the second decade of the nineteenth century planters in the lower Mississippi valley crossbred common short-staple cotton with a Mexican variety. The resulting strain served the needs of planters marvelously: the bolls were noticeably larger than those of the common variety and, more to the point, were much easier to separate from the pod.[21]

Mexican short-staple cotton reached the Carolinas about 1816 or 1817 and, within a few years, many up-country planters had adopted it.[22] Given that Mexican cotton enabled slaves to pick far more cotton in a day, planters had fewer reasons to pay slaves for extra cotton picked during the regular workday or, more important, to hire slaves to pick on Sunday. Having established their plantations, planters also felt less pressure to expand the workweek by hiring slaves on Sunday. Thus, the arrival and adoption of Mexican cotton in the second decade of the nineteenth century signaled the demise of the Sunday wage system. Although masters would continue to pay slaves for performing a variety of plantation chores on Sunday, wage work would no longer constitute a central or predictable means by which slaves could earn an independent income.

Slaves themselves may have endorsed, if not initiated, the collapse of the Sunday wage system by choosing to spend their Sundays growing their own Mexican cotton. In earlier years the low productivity of the older varieties of cotton and the difficulty of picking it had discouraged slaves from planting cotton along with their food crops. Instead, slaves believed their time could be more fruitfully spent working for wages. With the arrival of Mexican cotton, however, they had at their disposal a variety whose weight and picking properties perhaps offered more financial rewards than wage work. In short, slaves may have withdrawn from the Sunday labor system on their own in order to plant, cultivate, and harvest their own cotton.

In any case, with the introduction of Mexican cotton into South Carolina after the War of 1812, cotton grown independently by slaves became an important feature of the up-country economy. In 1819 slaves living on five Darlington District plantations produced over 1,600 pounds of their own cotton. In the middle 1820s fifty-two slaves living on twenty-seven different Laurens District plantations produced well over 10,000 pounds of their own seed cotton. In the following decade, fifty-three slaves living on sixteen plantations produced and sold a comparable amount of cotton to the Society Hill merchant, Leach Carrigan.[23] During the 1840s and 1850s slaves on four plantations independently raised 7 percent of all cotton produced. When projected to the entire up country or the South as a whole, this level of production suggests that independent production by slaves played a direct role in making cotton king (see table 10.1).

Viewed in its entirety, the slaves' independent production and associated market activities during the forty years between 1820 and 1860 constitute a distinct period in the history of slaves' income-earning activities in the up country. The era did not reach its apogee, however, until late in the antebellum years. This delay reflected the fact that two important features of the wage-work era persisted into the cotton era: autonomy in work and relative access to and freedom within the marketplace.

TABLE 10.1. Slave cotton production
on four South Carolina upcountry
(Darlington District) plantations, 1841–1861

	Cotton production by slaves (lbs.)	Total cotton production (lbs.)	% of cotton production by slaves
Peter S. Wilds			
1841	5,141	98,014	5.2
1842	5,930	106,084	5.6
Total	11,071	204,098	5.4
Thomas C. Law			
1849	1,928	61,596	3.1
1858	7,679	124,035	6.2
1859	5,749	103,037	5.6
1860	4,750	103,687	4.6
Total	20,106	392,355	5.1
William Law			
1852	10,017	76,839	13.0
1854	9,112	84,181	10.8
1855	7,380	66,980	11.0
1856	7,902	56,750	13.9
1857	7,436	67,440	11.0
1858	5,940	61,634	9.6
1859	9,156	86,949	10.5
1860	6,066	58,560	10.4
1861	10,426	75,661	13.8
Total	73,435	634,994	11.6
Caleb Coker			
1858	9,640	125,640	7.7
1859	6,850	134,751	5.1
1860	4,238	131,075	3.2
1861	1,348	104,679	1.3
Total	22,076	496,145	4.4
All four			
Total	126,688	1,727,592	7.3

Sources: Wilds Family Papers, Darlington (South Carolina) Historic Commission; Thomas Cassels Law Papers, South Caroliniana Library; William Law Papers, Perkins Library, Duke University; Caleb Coker Plantation Book, South Caroliniana Library.
Note: All cotton measured in preginned pounds.

In the first years of the nineteenth century up-country slaves worked their crops after sundown or on Sunday, beyond the master's supervisory presence. Slaves who began growing their own cotton maintained a similar regimen. Before the onset of independent cotton cultivation, slaves traveled off their home plantations—unaccompanied by owners or overseers—to sell their labor power, crops, and manufactured goods, and to buy various consumer goods. In the very last years of the 1790s, for example, slaves from local farms and plantations in Laurens District traded at John Black's general store. Slaves who began to grow their own cotton maintained a similar degree of mobility. In 1819, for example, slaves from five Darlington District plantations carried their own seed cotton to the merchant firm of Law and DuBose, and, at the point of sale, decided whether to receive their payment in cash or goods. A few years later, in the mid-1820s, dozens of slave men and women regularly left Laurens District plantations to sell and buy with merchant Black.[24] These extra-plantation market activities were neither exceptional nor illegal; state law allowed slaves to leave the plantation and participate in the market as long as they had their master's permission.[25]

During the first third of the nineteenth century slaves used their access to the marketplace to pursue their own social and economic interests and, in the process, challenge those of their masters. Once away from the plantation slaves sought out men and women, most commonly nonslaveholding whites, who would sell them liquor "and other trashy goods" normally denied them by their masters. When accompanied by drink, gambling, and an overall spirit of conviviality, these transactions laid the basis for important—and, from the perspective of slaveowners, dangerous—relationships between slaves and their white trading partners.[26] For when "the poison of the one, invigorated by copious draughts of the inebriating beverage, [was] poured into the ready ear of the other . . . new and pernicious ideas" seeped into "the susceptible mind of the African." Under these poisonous influences, formerly contented slaves became despondent and, eventually, insubordinate and incapable of obeying "any domestic regulation" on the plantation.[27]

More subversive yet, these relationships of "perfect equality," as the planter Whitemarsh Seabrook called them, sometimes threatened slaveowner interests more directly. "Low [white] fellow[s]" would encourage a "negro to steal and bring to [them]—easing the poor fellow's conscience by making him believe what he takes is the fruit of his own labor and he is therefore entitled to it."[28] As John Brown, a slave, put it, "when these poor whites cannot obtain a living honestly, which they very seldom do, they get the slaves in their neighborhood to steal corn, poultry, and such like, from their masters, and bring these things to them."[29] While Brown may have overlooked the degree to which slaves acted on their own, without coaxing from white coconspirators, slaves employed these social relationships to better themselves materially—often at their masters' expense. It was precisely because slaves traveled, and with their masters' permission, that they could develop and sustain relationships with poor white people in the first place.

However much the wage-work and the cotton eras had in common in terms of labor patterns and market participation, the transition to independent cotton production changed the slaves' economy. Attached to the plantation as cotton producers, slaves no longer experienced the independence that derived from their ability to leave the plantation to work elsewhere on Sunday. Indeed, as long as slaveowners respected the slaves' right to move freely, even *threatening* to leave the plantation enabled slaves to strike better wage agreements with their master. With the eclipse of wage work this expression of the slaves' power disappeared.

The emergence of independent cotton production also reduced the liberating quality of slaves' market-oriented work. As cotton growers slaves no longer enjoyed the sense of freedom that Charles Ball associated with participation in the Sunday labor market, simply because their work occurred on their masters' plantation. While work itself, especially outside of the masters' immediate purview, still offered slaves a sense of independence, the context of work—the plantation—precluded a slave from acting like "a kind of freeman." For when the geographical domain of slaves' income-earning activities became coterminous with the boundary of the plantation, the liberating quality of slaves' work experience shrank sharply.

The geographic and economic shift in slave income-earning work also heightened tensions between masters and slaves. Within the realm of production, slaves pursued interests that invariably clashed with those of the master. Unwilling or unable to confine their work on their own crops—both cotton and provisions—to the early evening hours, slaves tended them late into the night; and, as slaveowners well knew, night work made slaves ill-fit for labor in the masters' field the following day. Moreover, slaveholders claimed that slaves, in tending crops outside of their presence, misused and damaged plantation equipment and work animals. After 1830, when masters attempted to shape the moral and religious beliefs of their slaves, the slaves' Sunday work was also seen as interfering with their proper religious development and moral deportment. All in all, the advent of cotton made production itself a terrain of escalating conflict between slaves and masters.[30]

Independent cotton production by slaves expanded old and created new opportunities for slaves to assert themselves, much to the dismay and detriment of their masters. With cotton seemingly everywhere slaves could steal with greater ease and thus with greater impunity than ever before. During the wage work era slaves sold stolen goods illicitly, at night, and under the cloud of possible detection and punishment. In September 1802, for example, two slaves in Edgefield District were caught selling pilfered cotton and tobacco at "about 12 or 1 o'clock in the night."[31] The dangers of selling stolen goods diminished considerably, however, once slaves earned their income primarily as producers and sellers of crops. For when slaves left the plantation to sell their own cotton and other crops, they could hide stolen property amid their marketable goods. In this way, slaves were able to fence stolen property conveniently, during the day, and as part of their "legitimate," master-sanctioned marketplace activity. Indeed, such a safe and direct way of disposing of stolen goods encouraged slaves to steal with greater frequency. As one South Carolina overseer put it, "by permitting [slaves] to leave the plantation with the view of selling and buying, more is lost by the owner than he is generally aware of." Much to the slaveowners' chagrin, such market-related theft became all the more pronounced *because* slaves had their own cotton to sell. Compared to corn, for example, cotton offered more temptations to theft because it was more easily carried, less easily detected, and of greater value. "A negro that would take one hundred pounds of cotton, in seed worth two dollars," observed an upcountry planter in 1832, "would hardly venture on the same weight of corn worth only seventy-five cents." For this planter, as for many others, slave theft could be reduced by restricting the slaves' independent production to corn and by preventing them from using their marketing activities as a cover for selling stolen crops. Instead, slave crops should be "disposed of" by the master.[32]

Slaveowners began searching for ways of reducing, if not eliminating, behavior they found disruptive, if not subversive. To this end, between 1830 and 1860 slaveowners adopted two strategies to reduce the problems foisted upon them by their slaves. Most drastically, some slaveowners simply prevented slaves from growing and selling their own cotton or other cash crops. James Henry Hammond, who entered the planter ranks in the 1830s, allowed his slaves to grow food crops solely for their own subsistence. In 1851 another planter reported how he "formerly gave [his slaves] crops," but had discontinued this practice "of late." Instead of crops, he paid his slaves a bonus at year's end, the size of which depended upon their behavior during the year. W. H. Evans of Darlington District argued that, as an alternative to producing their own cotton, slaves should be paid twenty-five cents for extra cotton picked on specially designated days during the harvest. Other slaveholders advocated less manipulative replacements for "negro crops" (as they were sometimes called), giving their slaves gifts of cash or material goods that would equal "what their crop (if they had one) would yield."[33]

A second group of slaveowners continued to allow their chattel to grow marketable crops such as cotton. But in order to reduce the subversive impact of slaves' market-related activities these planters exerted greater control over the entire range of slaves' independent production, selling, and buying activities. Within this new context slaves no longer experienced as much independence as they once had in the conduct of their economic activities. As a result, the social, psychological, and other noneconomic rewards of slaves' market-oriented activities narrowed considerably in the late antebellum period.

During the 1840s and 1850s the cotton era of slave market-related activities assumed its fullest form. Within the sphere of production slaveowners instituted two important changes in the slaves' economy. First, hoping to discourage their slaves from nighttime—or even Sunday—work, masters gave them additional time during daylight hours to work their crops. For some slaves, this extra time came regularly on Saturdays, a day that slaves had previously spent working on their owners' crop. According to Mary Johnson, a former slave of Newberry District, she and her fellow slaves "had Saturday afternoon off to do anything we wanted to do." Sylvia Cannon, a slave in Marion District, used this free time to work "dey extra crop." For slaves such as Johnson and Cannon, having Saturday to work their crops or engage in other activities became a customary feature of plantation life during the late antebellum years.[34]

While some planters systematically reduced the slaves' work week from six to five-and-a-half or even five days, others gave their slaves an occasional Saturday or even weekday off for tending their crops. On the estate of Thomas C. Law, a Darlington planter, slaves had a combination of Saturdays and weekdays for planting, hoeing, and plowing their own crops (see table 10.2). Similarly, on the Caleb Coker

TABLE 10.2. THE TIMING OF SLAVE WORK ON THEIR OWN CROPS, THOMAS C. LAW PLANTATION, DARLINGTON DISTRICT, SOUTH CAROLINA, 1841–1858

Year	Date	Activity
1841	4/17 Saturday	"plant my [Law's] cotton"
	4/19 Monday	"finished planting negro cotton—begin to shave cotton with scrapers"
	5/15 Saturday	"gave Negroes day to work their crop"
1843	7/8 Saturday	"gave Negroes day to work their crop"
1844	3/24 Sunday	"planted Negro cotton; finished 3/25"
	6/22 Saturday	"given to Negroes to plow and hoe their crops"
1846	5/16 Saturday	"ploughed negro crop"
1847	4/30 Friday	"finished planting my crop"
	5/1 Saturday	"planted negro crop"
1848	4/26 Wednesday	"planted negro crop"
	4/27 Thursday	"begin to plough cotton"
	6/17 Saturday	"ploughed negro crop"
1849	5/5 Saturday	"planted negro crop"
	6/21 Thursday	"ploughing negro crop and finished fresh land cotton"
1850	5/6 Monday	"finished planting cotton for myself"
	5/7 Tuesday	"planted negro cotton"
	5/25 Saturday	"finished ploughing cotton first time and ploughed negro crop"
	7/3 Wednesday	"ploughed negro crop 2nd time"
	7/6 Saturday	"begin to plough [my] cotton 3rd time"
1851	5/26 Monday	"finished ploughing corn 2nd time and ploughed negro crop"
	5/27 Tuesday	"begin to plow [my] cotton 2nd time"
	6/21 Saturday	"ploughed negro corn"
1852	4/17 Saturday	"stopped after dinner for hands to prepare their own lands"
	5/1 Saturday	"let negroes have 1½ days to plant their crop on the plantation"
	7/5 Monday	"ploughed negro cotton"
	7/10 Saturday	"gave all hands the day to work their own crop"
1853	6/18 Monday	"finished hoeing and putting to a stand cotton in 58 acres ploughing over negro crop"
	7/2 Saturday	"ploughed negro corn"
	7/9 Saturday	"ploughed negro cotton"
1854	4/1 Saturday	"Negroes mostly working for themselves to plant their corn"
	6/12 Monday	"ploughed negro cotton"
1855	5/19 Saturday	"planting negro corn"
	6/19 Tuesday	"ploughed negro corn"
1857	8/14 Friday	"finished ploughing [my] cotton"
	8/15 Saturday	"ploughed negro cotton"
1858	4/23 Friday	"finished planting cotton for self today"
	4/24 Saturday	"worked Negroes land"

Source: Thomas Cassels Law Papers, South Caroliniana Library.

255

plantation slaves received a few days late in the year to harvest their cotton. In 1859, for example, they picked their cotton on Friday, December 2, and on Saturday, December 3. The following year, on the Darlington plantation of H. G. Charles, slaves tended their owner's crop on Saturdays throughout the fall but still received two weekdays to pick their cotton in mid-December after the bulk of the owner's cotton had been harvested.[35]

Rather than allow slaves to manage these special workdays as they saw fit, however, masters supervised the slaves' supposedly independent activities. As long as masters permitted slaves to grow cash crops, they "should superintend the planting, working and gathering . . . and strictly forbid all working after dark," admonished one cotton planter. Likewise, Thomas Law argued in an address to the Darlington Agricultural Society in 1852 that slave crops should be "ploughed, under the owner's direction, as regularly as his own."[36]

This tactic was intended to keep slaves from mishandling work animals and equipment. Harvest-time supervision, whereby slaves picked their cotton under the watchful eye of their owner or overseer, might also discourage if not prevent slaves from stealing the owners' cotton. Not leaving anything to chance, slaveowners also weighed slave-grown cotton once it had been picked. By monitoring this procedure each master would be able to "detect theft if there should be any, as he is better able to judge of the quantity each would probably make from the ground cultivated, when it is submitted to his measurement."[37]

The masters' active, supervisory role unleashed a host of adverse consequences for up-country slaves. Slaves lost some of the independence that came when they worked their crops on Sunday or furtively at night. Diminished independence, especially at harvest, in turn made it harder for slaves to supplement their own crops with those of their masters. Moreover, the slaveowners' supervision of Sunday work impinged on long-established rights, jeopardizing customary practices. Work thus became less a means by which slaves could demonstrate their independence and assert control over their lives, and more a means of generating income.

Even so, slaves still controlled aspects of their market-related work. Despite owners' efforts to wean their slaves from evening work, slaves continued to labor "dat crop in de night, dat crop wha' dey buy dey Sunday clothes wid."[38] Slaves also helped determine when they received their special workdays. On the Thomas Law plantation, for example, the timing of such days depended in large part on the current status of Law's crop: that is, slaves received time to plant and plough only after they had finished planting or ploughing their owner's cotton. On Monday, April 19, 1841, slaves planted their cotton after having completed work on Law's crop the preceding Saturday. Similarly, on May 25, 1850, slaves ploughed their own crop after they had finished ploughing Law's earlier in the day. Conversely, the timing of when slaves worked their cotton determined, in effect, the subsequent work on their owners' crop, such as in May 1851, when Law's slaves began the second round of ploughing only after they had ploughed their crops once over.

The regularity described by Thomas Law in his 1852 speech was thus not a matter of frequency or priority but of predictability: that slaves would plant, hoe, and plow their crops only after they had finished performing the equivalent task on the masters' crop. Aware of the functional relationship between when they worked their crops and when they worked their masters' crop, slaves worked the latter more rapidly, thereby hastening the day when they could tend their own crops. Like rice slaves, cotton slaves also exercised some control over when they worked their crops in daylight hours. Their control, unlike that enjoyed by rice slaves, was asserted collectively, with the entire field force working together to complete the masters' work in a timely fashion.[39]

Slaves benefited from these special workdays in a number of ways. The time provided a brief respite from endless toil for their masters. As episodic as they were, these workdays gave slaves the choice of whether to use evening or Sunday hours for activities other than tending their crops. They also enabled slaves to tend their crops more efficiently than night work allowed. During the fall special workdays helped slaves harvest their cotton in a timely fashion, thereby preserving the quality and value of their cotton. For as all cotton growers— black and white, slave and free—well knew, prompt picking was essential if the ripe cotton bolls were to be spared damage by sudden frosts, rain, or even snow.[40]

Special workdays no doubt helped slaves increase their production and earnings. On four Darlington District plantations, individual slaves raised and sold roughly 200 to 350 pounds of seed cotton annually, while slaves living and working in family units produced considerably more.[41] The size of the cotton crop in any one year determined, in large part, the size of slave earnings. While slaves on these and other plantations produced and sold other commodities (corn, fodder, fowl, baskets, mats, tar, coal, and lumber) along with their cotton and performed miscellaneous labor for pay (such as digging ditches or wells), proceeds from the sale of cotton constituted the bulk of their income. Overall, the earnings of an individual slave ranged from four to nine dollars annually, although families might earn more.[42] It would appear that slaves earned more in the late antebellum era than they had earlier in the nineteenth century.[43]

Slaveowners were no less diligent in asserting their control over slaves' market activities as sellers of commodities. As a South Carolina overseer put it in 1836, "Negroes should in no instance be permitted to trade, except with their masters." In 1834 this position was echoed in the South Carolina legislature, which made it illegal for anyone to trade with slaves—day or night, Sunday or weekday, with or without permission from the slave's owner.[44] By outlawing interplantation trade between slaves and anyone else the 1834 law compelled slaveowners to oversee the disposal of their slaves' crops, whether as purchasers or factors. For without the owners' intercession slaves would have had no legal means of disposing of the crops which they had produced with their masters' approval in the first place.

Some slaveowners and merchants, for whatever reasons, failed to comply with the 1834 law. In publicly offering $500 for evidence that would convict anyone of buying "produce from my negroes without a special order from me in my own handwriting," one planter unabashedly admitted that he still allowed his slaves to trade on their own accord outside of the plantation.[45] Nonetheless, during the 1840s and 1850s slaveowners tended to supervise the disposal of the crops slaves produced on their own. On some plantations change came slowly, but it came nonetheless. Still purchasing large quantities of slave-grown cotton in the late 1830s, the Carrigan firm of Society Hill bought but one bale during the 1850s because its former slave trading partners now sold their cotton to their masters (or perhaps did not even grow cotton any more). Although Thomas Law allowed his slaves to sell their 1844 cotton crop off the plantation, by the late 1840s Law had changed his ways. Thereafter, Law purchased his slaves' cotton directly.[46]

Regardless of economic standing or locale, slaveholders, such as Thomas Law, evicted slaves from the marketplace as sellers, asserting direct control over the sale of slave-grown crops. Men such as Peter S. Bacot, who managed over one hundred slaves, bought their slaves' cotton, as did slaveholders of more modest means. Bacot's fellow Darlington planter, Peter S. Wilds, planted with thirty slaves and purchased his slaves' cotton in the early 1840s. Northwest of Darlington in York District, John Bratton bought his slaves' corn and cotton in the 1850s, as did Thomas C. Perrin, who lived even farther west along the Georgia border in Abbeville District. When slaveowners did not purchase slave cotton themselves, they still arranged to have it sold and shipped to someone else, as did the Darlington planter William Law.[47]

In short, during the last years of slavery slaveowners—partly in response to slaves' independent marketplace activity—overturned the long-standing custom of allowing slaves to leave the plantation and sell on their own account. By keeping slaves out of the marketplace slaveowners implicitly acknowledged the power that slaves had earlier wielded. By preventing such independence slaveowners eliminated one central means by which slaves could challenge their authority. With one swift stroke up-country masters shored up their hegemony on the plantation and throughout the surrounding countryside.

According to masters, slaves benefited from these new marketing arrangements. In purchasing slave-grown crops masters sometimes claimed that they did their slaves a favor by protecting them from "unprincipled men . . . who might cheat them out of their earnings." By buying the slaves' crops "more justice will be done them than if disposed of by themselves, which is always at a less price than can be obtained by the master." Thomas Law believed that the master should "always *purchase* what they have to *sell*" and always pay the "highest market price, whether he needs it or not, since it convinces [slaves] of your doing them justice and induces them to prefer you as the buyer."[48] This need to elicit the slaves' goodwill and the de facto acceptance of the master as purchaser worked to the economic advantage of Law's slaves. In November 1859 Thomas Law paid them eleven-and-a-half cents per pound of ginned cotton, an amount that exceeded the local market price of a little more than ten cents paid to the slaves of William Law, who had sold their cotton to a local merchant.[49] Indeed, the price received by Thomas Law's slaves reflected the higher prices of the Charleston cotton market (see table 10.3).

Yet the experience of Thomas Law's slaves was not typical. On balance, available evidence suggests that slaves failed to receive Charleston market prices and thus were underpaid for their cotton. Some planters, like Peter Bacot, deliberately shortchanged slaves when buying their cotton. Throughout the 1850s Bacot's slaves received a price consistently below the local market price as exemplified by the transactions of William Law's slaves during those same years. In 1854, for

TABLE 10.3. ACTUAL VERSUS POSSIBLE PRICE
FOR COTTON GROWN INDEPENDENTLY BY SLAVES,
ON FOUR DARLINGTON DISTRICT, SOUTH CAROLINA,
PLANTATIONS, 1841–1861

Owner/date[a]	Average price[b]	Owner's price[c]	Net price[d]	Slaves' price[e]	% difference in price[f]
Peter Wilds					
1841					
12/11/41	8.625	8.75	8.29	7.13	+16.4
1842					
10/29/42	7.875	7.0	6.40	4.87	+31.4
12/24/42	6.25	6.25	5.67	4.87	+16.4
03/14/43	5.875	5.0	4.66	4.87	−4.3
1843					
11/03/43	7.5	7.0	6.45	6.31	+2.2
01/09/44	9.25	9.0	8.42	6.31	+33.4
William Law					
1845					
04/26/45	6.19	6.125	5.617	4.0	+40.4
04/29/45	6.10	5.25	4.78	4.0	+19.6
1846					
12/06/47	7.5	6.75	5.62	8.625	−34.8
1852					
03/15/53	9.8	9.25	8.56	8.29	+3.2
06/07/53	11.0	10.75	10.10	8.29	+21.4
06/07/53	11.0	8.75	8.12	8.29	−2.0
1854					
12/30/54	8.125	7.25	7.189	8.0	−10.1
03/22/55	8.625	8.25	8.22	8.0	+2.8
05/18/55	9.9	10.125	10.06	8.0	+25.8
1855					
04/15/56	10.8	9.0	8.35	8.25	+1.2
04/15/56	10.8	10.5	9.89	8.25	+19.9
06/22/56	11.12	10.625	9.99	8.25	+21.1
1856					
12/08/56	12.0	11.5	10.74	12.25	−12.3
05/23/57	13.87	13.5	12.66	12.25	+3.3
1857					
10/08/57	12.375	13.375	12.64	8.0	+57.9
02/17/58	11.4	11.55	10.83	8.0	+35.4
04/21/58	12.125	13.0	12.24	8.0	+53.0
05/20/58	12.375	12.0	11.26	8.0	+40.8
06/12/58	12.06	10.625	9.57	8.0	+19.6
1858					
09/22/58	12.06	12.375	11.72	11.0	+6.5
10/26/58	12.06	11.0	10.39	11.0	−5.5

TABLE 10.3. *Continued*

Owner/date[a]	Average price[b]	Owner's price[c]	Net price[d]	Slaves' price[e]	% difference in price[f]
04/30/59	12.25	11.0	10.38	11.0	−5.6
04/13/59	12.25	12.165	11.47	11.0	+4.3
1859					
10/05/59	11.0	10.625	10.33	10.25	+.5
01/09/60	11.06	10.625	10.30	10.25	+.5
04/24/60	11.125	10.875	10.5	10.25	+2.4
1860					
10/26/60	10.9	10.875	10.252	9.0	+13.9
10/26/60	10.9	10.75	10.13	9.0	+12.6
10/26/60	10.9	10.375	9.76	9.0	+8.5
02/02/61	—	11.0	10.256	9.0	+14.0
Peter S. Bacot					
1852					
11/04/52	9.25	9.54	8.86	8.05	+10.1
12/03/52	8.8	8.75	8.176	8.05	+1.6
12/03/52	8.8	8.5	7.87	8.05	−2.2
02/17/53	9.5	8.0	7.33	8.05	−8.9
03/10/53	9.8	8.0	7.39	8.05	−8.2
03/10/53	9.8	8.165	7.57	8.05	−6.0
06/08/53	11.0	9.0	8.13	8.05	+1.0
06/08/53	11.0	11.0	10.09	8.05	+25.3
06/08/53	11.0	10.165	9.29	8.05	+15.4
1853					
11/23/53	9.68	10.25	9.626	6.63	+45.2
11/24/53	9.68	9.625	9.018	6.63	+36.0
11/16/54	9.68	10.125	9.481	6.63	+43.0
01/16/54	9.44	8.75	8.147	6.63	+22.9
02/23/54	9.19	9.25	8.645	6.63	+30.4
03/11/54	9.18	7.75	7.2	6.63	+8.6
03/11/54	9.18	9.125	8.55	6.63	+28.9
06/ /54	9.0	7.0	6.41	6.63	−3.4
06/ /54	9.0	6.5	5.885	6.63	−11.2
06/ /54	9.0	9.75	9.07	6.63	+36.8
1854					
12/26/54	8.125	6.75	6.22	6.58	−5.5
10/16/54	8.875	9.5	8.91	6.58	+33.5
11/29/54	8.93	8.125	7.545	6.58	+14.7
11/30/54	8.93	7.75	7.255	6.58	+10.3
02/19/55	8.18	7.25	6.70	6.58	+1.9
02/26/55	8.18	7.25	6.748	6.58	+2.6
03/13/55	8.625	8.125	7.557	6.58	+14.9

TABLE 10.3. CONTINUED

Owner/date[a]	Average price[b]	Owner's price[c]	Net price[d]	Slaves' price[e]	% difference in price[f]
1855					
11/26/55	8.93	9.125	8.261	6.58	+25.5
01/10/56	9.06	8.75	8.097	6.58	+22.8
03/05/56	10.06	10.0	9.432	6.58	+43.3
03/05/56	10.06	9.0	8.47	6.58	+28.7
05/24/56	10.875	10.0	9.369	6.58	+42.4
1856					
10/28/56	12.0	11.375	10.77	6.58	+63.7
01/04/56	11.68	12.0	11.42	6.58	+73.5
12/02/56	12.0	11.5	10.82	6.58	+64.5
12/12/56	12.0	11.25	10.55	6.58	+60.3
12/30/56	12.0	12.0	11.39	6.58	+73.1
02/ /57	13.125	11.75	11.1	6.58	+68.3
Thomas C. Law					
11/ /1859	10.94	10.69	10.05	11.5	−12.6

Sources: Data in Column B are calculated from Alfred Glaze Smith, Economic Readjustment of an Old Cotton State, South Carolina, 1820–1860 (Columbia, 1958), table 2, pp. 224–25. Smith provides the low and high cotton prices for each month; the average price for any given month is the average of Smith's low and high prices for that month.

Data on slaveowner and slave cotton are derived from the following collections: Peter S. Wilds Cotton Picking records, Wilds Family Papers, Darlington (South Carolina) Historic Commission; William Law Papers, Special Collections, Perkins Library, Duke University; Peter S. Bacot Papers, South Caroliniana Library, University of South Carolina; Peter S. Bacot Papers, Southern Historical Collection, University of North Carolina; Thomas Cassels Law Papers, South Caroliniana Library, University of South Carolina.

[a]Slaveowner, crop year, and date when owner's cotton was sold in Charleston, S.C.

[b]Average price per pound of cotton in the Charleston market during the month the owner's cotton was sold in this market.

[c]Price per pound of lint cotton (cents) received by the owner for his cotton.

[d]Price in Column C minus the percentage going to marketing expenses. Thus, the net possible price slaves would have received if they had sold in Charleston.

[e]The actual price received by slaves in selling to their owner or, in the case of William Law's slaves, to a local merchant.

[f]The net possible price (Column D) minus the actual slave price (Column E) divided by the actual slave price. That is, the percentage of increase or decrease of the possible price over the actual slave price.

example, Bacot paid his slaves less than seven cents per pound of ginned cotton, while Law's slaves received eight cents when selling to a local merchant; the difference became even more pronounced in 1856, when Law's slaves received nearly twice as much for their cotton as Bacot's.

Rather than set his price according to market fluctuations, Bacot simply paid his slaves a set price of roughly six and a half cents per pound. He did so despite the fact that his slaves produced a good quality cotton.[50] The prices realized by Bacot when he sold cotton were well within the range of market prices; thus, it can be reasonably inferred that the cotton he purchased from his slaves and then sold along with his own was of a good quality. At the least, it did not depress the prices he received from Charleston factors (see table 10.3). In short, Peter Bacot's slaves received a low price not because their cotton was of poor quality but because Bacot wanted to profit at his slaves' expense.[51]

Apart from deliberate gouging by their masters, slaves' earnings were reduced simply because their owners did not let them receive the benefit of market prices in Charleston. The prices received by masters when they sold their cotton in Charleston usually exceeded those paid to slaves when they sold to the master or to local merchants (see table 10.3).[52] In 1841, for instance, Peter Wilds paid his slaves slightly more than two cents per pound of seed cotton (or roughly seven cents per pound of ginned cotton); but when he sold this cotton—along with his original cotton—in Charleston, he received almost nine cents per pound of ginned cotton, roughly 22 percent more than what he paid his slaves. Similarly, the slaves of William Law received a fair local market price of eight cents in 1857 when they sold their cotton to a nearby merchant; yet this price was still 34 percent less than the average price of about twelve cents that Law himself earned when he sold his cotton in Charleston that year.[53]

There was, however, no guarantee that slaves would necessarily receive a better price if they sold their cotton in Charleston. If the slaves of William Law, for example, had sold their 1858 crop on April 30, 1859, when Law sold a portion of his cotton, they would have received the same price per pound (eleven cents) that they eventually got from a local merchant. Indeed, in this particular instance Law's slaves would have earned less from the Charleston than from the local sale. In selling locally slaves did not incur the various marketing expenses (freight, insurance, bagging and baling, weighing, storage, and factor's commission) that typically accompanied a sale in Charleston— and presumably Law would have made his slaves pay these charges if they had sent their cotton to be sold there.[54] When these expenses were taken into account, the resulting net price, as opposed to the gross price of eleven cents, slaves would have earned—namely, the price received by Law (eleven cents) less marketing expenses (5.6

percent)—would have been slightly more than ten cents per pound or 5.6 percent less than what they actually received.

Yet more often than not the various marketing expenses would not have made a Charleston sale less profitable than a local one. Of the seventy-four different occasions (price-date combinations) on which the cotton of Peter Bacot, William Law, and Peter Wilds was sold by their respective Charleston factors, there were fifty-nine occasions when slaves on these plantations would have received a better price— even after marketing costs were taken into account. Overall, selling in Charleston would have increased slave incomes by an average of roughly 18 percent. In actuality, of course, it was the master or local merchant who pocketed the extra earnings after they purchased and resold the slaves' cotton in Charleston.[55]

Thus, the new marketing arrangements instituted in the 1840s and 1850s brought considerable hardship on slaves. The one possible benefit slaves could have received—higher market prices—was lost as masters refused, by and large, to pay slaves the Charleston price or to market slave-grown cotton in Charleston. Instead of receiving the highest prices available, slaves bore the double burden of receiving local prices without at the same time being able to sell their cotton themselves. Confined to the plantation, slaves of the late antebellum era thus lost a valuable means for developing and sustaining relationships with merchants of their own choosing, even if they happened to be "unprincipled men." No longer being able to market their own goods independently meant in turn that they could no longer expropriate their owners' cotton and other property with the same impunity.

Indeed, aside from the fact that slaves had something to sell and were paid, there was precious little in "selling" to the master that bespoke a market experience, inasmuch as marketing refers to the processes of selecting a buyer and haggling over price. Even the market itself appeared in a distorted fashion: embodied in the master, who, as merchant, either purchased the goods or, as factor, arranged to have someone else purchase them. Rather than become leveling experiences whereby blacks were raised and "whites were lowered," these transactions—predicated as they were on the master's monopoly over the disposal of slave crops—reflected and reinforced the unequal distribution of power between masters and slaves.[56] In selling to or through the master, as opposed to traveling the countryside seeking their own customers, slaves found their dependence on their master increased rather than reduced. Instead of being an important moment of temporary independence for slaves, selling became a sharp reminder of their limited independence.

The long arm of the master also shaped the way slaves spent their earnings. Just as slaveowners of the late antebellum period reduced the slaves' participation in the marketplace as sellers of commodities, so they restricted slaves' activities as consumers. First, slaveowners gave their slaves fewer opportunities to leave the plantation as potential buyers by selling them consumer goods directly. William Law, for example, maintained a supply of molasses and tobacco, which his slaves purchased throughout the year. Other individuals went further, keeping, as one overseer advised in 1836, "a [plantation] store of such articles as slaves usually purchased elsewhere." When such a well-stocked store existed, as it did on the plantation of Thomas Law, slaves had little opportunity to shop elsewhere. By serving as retail merchants to their slaves masters limited the extent to which slaves participated in the marketplace as consumers and thus helped put slaves "out of the way of the temptation to roguery."[57]

Yet even when they doubled as merchants, some up-country planters allowed their slaves to travel off the plantation to spend some, if not most, of their earnings. Yet when these slaves left the plantation unaccompanied, their owners tried to retain control by giving their slaves credit, rather than cash, when they purchased their crops or when they compensated them for other economic endeavors. When buying goods from a local merchant, slaves thus bought against their credited earnings; eventually, the master received a bill for the amount of each slave's purchases and used the slaves' earnings to pay the merchant. In 1859, for example, William Law received a draft of credit for $305 for his slaves' cotton, which had been purchased by merchant R. A. Kendall of Cheraw. Law later used this money to pay the Darlington firm of Huggins and Brunson for goods that his slaves had purchased from that firm.[58] In effect, slaveowners such as Law served as factors to their slaves, first crediting slaves with the value of their independent economic endeavors and then deducting from each slave's account the cost of his or her purchases. Such transactions reduced the amount of money handled by slaves far below their earnings.

Both the paucity of money among slaves and the use of credit thus enabled masters to police and regulate slave purchases, even when they were made beyond the owners' immediate surveillance. Carrying so little money with them slaves had few means to buy liquor or other contraband from white traders, whom they might visit as they traveled to and from the marketplace. At the same time, the use of credit—

as either dispensed or withheld by the master—dictated where slaves could spend their earnings. Cash poor, credit rich, slaves could only purchase merchandise from merchants who would sell on credit—and merchants sold on credit to slaves only because slaveowners had arranged, ahead of time, to reimburse them for the amount of the slaves' purchases. For their part, slaveowners only made such arrangements with "reputable" men who would not sell contraband to slaves. In short, just as the use of a plantation store guaranteed that slaves would not acquire liquor or firearms, so the credit system enabled masters to prevent their slaves from purchasing such goods when they spent their earnings off of the plantation.

Indeed, slaveowners took additional steps to reduce slave independence and disruptiveness within the local marketplace. To doubly ensure that slaves did not acquire that most troublesome of contraband, liquor, the state legislature passed a law in 1834 making it illegal for merchants to sell "or otherwise deliver any spirituous liquors to any slave, except upon the written and express order" of the master. Similarly, the custom of slaves gambling, with dice or cards, while in the marketplace was also jeopardized by this law, which made it illegal for shopkeepers or any other white people to participate in "games of chance" with slaves. Even slaves' opportunity to make spontaneous, unplanned stops while away from the plantation would be curtailed sharply, as their written permits limited their travel to only those places approved by the master ahead of time and specified "the time during which" the slave "is permitted to be absent."[59]

Even within the constraints imposed upon them by the credit system, however, buying away from the plantation still proved beneficial and rewarding for slaves. Traveling off the plantation unchaperoned by a master or some other white person was no doubt a liberating experience, just as it had been earlier in the century. Not surprisingly, slaves exploited the owner's absence to pursue their own interests, spending more than what their master wanted or expected. In late 1853, for example, the slaves of William Law bought $200 worth of merchandise from the merchant F. W. Cooper. Apparently Law's slaves took advantage of their owner's absence, for Cooper later informed Law that the "amount of [the] Negroes indebtedness . . . is not as you desired," because of Cooper's "not having recd. your letter in time." But as Cooper pointed out, "most of them got what they wanted on Christmas Day or the accounts would not have been so large." Law's slaves were able to purchase as much as they wanted to because Cooper failed to receive Law's letter of instructions on time, as he claimed, or, as one might suspect, he ignored the instructions in order to sell more. Either way, purchasing outside of the masters' presence enabled Law's slaves to spend as they desired, contrary to the master's wishes.[60]

As the above episode suggests, slaves sometimes went into debt while participating in the market.[61] Although slaveowners such as William Law frowned upon slave indebtedness, they did little to discourage or prevent it. Rather than punish slaves for going into debt, Law and other slaveholders simply made their slaves pay their debts with future earnings. This mode of repayment, and hence indebtedness itself, benefited slaveowners because it ensured that at least some of slaves' future time would be spent in earning income—not in other, possibly disruptive activities on the plantation. Perhaps with this benefit in mind, slaveowners in the up country tolerated indebtedness as a normal feature of slave market participation.

This tolerance—combined with year-round spending, buying on credit, and the advantages of overspending for slaves—made it easy for slaves to fall into debt. Slaves who bought consumer goods months before they harvested and sold their crops ran the risk of spending more than they would eventually earn. Year-round spending helps explain, for example, why the slaves of Peter Bacot went into debt more frequently than did the slaves of Thomas and William Law, who spent most of their earnings only after they had harvested and sold their cotton.[62] Indebtedness also loomed large when slaves purchased consumer goods from local merchants on credit. Merchants such as F. W. Cooper had little reason to care about, much less encourage, careful spending by their slave customers. If anything, it was in their economic interest to encourage overspending, since they would sell more goods without running the risk of not being paid. For according to South Carolina law, slaveowners were the legal owners of slave property; thus, they were also responsible for any debts incurred by their slaves in purchasing this property. As long as masters were financially healthy, merchants were assured of repayment even when slaves spent more than they had earned.[63]

Slaves did not have to be seduced into spending beyond their means, however. Overspending was attractive to slaves because it allowed them to own and use more goods for a longer period of time than if they had avoided indebtedness. Conversely, remaining solvent meant that slaves had to defer the purchase and use of desired goods. Unwilling, perhaps, to make such short-term sacrifices, some slaves on the plantations of Thomas and William Law deliberately overspent, even though they knew how much they had earned and had available for spending (see table 10.4).[64]

On the other hand, overspending carried significant costs for slaves. By going into debt slaves consigned themselves to work in the future, whether they wanted to or not. Debts from one year also meant reduced purchasing power in the next, as slaves used a portion of their future earnings to balance their accounts. Moreover, indebtedness exposed some slaves to an additional possible loss of future income, namely, the possibility of having to pay interest. Such was the experience of slaves living on the Bacot plantation. From 1852 to 1860 some men and women incurred interest charges ranging from eight to eighty-eight cents. An average charge of thirty-three cents meant forsaking, for example, three yards of calico or three pounds of sugar—no small sacrifice for slaves whose annual income was five dollars and forty-two cents.[65]

Overall, these disadvantages—as well as the attractions of remaining solvent—actually encouraged most slaves to avoid indebtedness. Even with year-round spending Peter Bacot's slaves generally avoided indebtedness; indeed, more slaves on this plantation would have remained solvent if Bacot had paid them more fairly for their cotton. Buying primarily after the harvest of their crops helped seven out of ten slaves on the Thomas and William Law plantations to avoid debt. By staying out of debt slaves on these two plantations also saved roughly 15 percent of their earnings when buying on credit from either the master or local merchant.

By avoiding debt slaves acquired more control over their own affairs. Solvency allowed slaves to decide whether they needed to earn incomes in the future, while the possession of unspent earnings gave them the option of reducing their work effort without limiting their purchases. Given a surplus, slaves could also buy from or make loans to one another. The resulting web of economic and social interdependence could be dense indeed. During the 1850s the slaves of Peter Bacot, for example, initiated dozens of financial loans amongst themselves. While these loans did not necessarily involve cash transfers, since Bacot simply moved credit from one account to another, these transfers were significant as a means of strengthening the bonds of community among slaves.[66]

With a surplus, slaves also acquired one of the most illusive—and powerful—objects: money. Although slaves generally received their earnings as credit to be spent on merchandise, unspent portions were

TABLE 10.4. SLAVES' SPENDING AND SAVING PATTERNS
ON THREE DARLINGTON DISTRICT, SOUTH CAROLINA,
PLANTATIONS, 1852–1861

Year	No. of producing/ consuming units with accounts	Units with no debt[a]		Average spending rate for units with accounts[b]
William Law Plantation				
1854	18	9	(50.0%)	94.5
1856	14	14	(100.0%)	82.5
1857	16	14	(87.5%)	82.0
1858	16	9	(56.2%)	97.5
1859	19	18	(94.7%)	58.0
1860	18	13	(72.2%)	91.0
Total	101	77	(76.2%)	82.0
Bacot Plantation				
1852	61	33	(54.1%)	78.1
1853	71	35	(49.3%)	156.0
1854	49	34	(69.4%)	77.2
1855	39	12	(30.8%)	159.8
1856	44	34	(77.3%)	3.3
1857	32	17	(53.1%)	100.0
1858	38	19	(50.0%)	112.1
1859	21	6	(28.6%)	296.3
1860	23	8	(34.8%)	573.2
1861	33	18	(54.5%)	44.7
Total	411	216	(52.6%)	99.9
T. C. Law Plantation				
1859	24	16	(66.7%)	86.0
1860	22	15	(68.2%)	56.0
Total	46	31	(67.4%)	85.0

Sources: See source note for table 10.3.
[a]See note 64.
[b]The average spending rate is the percentage of a slave's total income spent on consumer goods in a given year, derived by dividing the value of total expenditure by the value of total income. The lower the percentage, the more the slaves saved; conversely, the higher the percentage, the more slaves spent. A percentage greater than 100 indicates indebtedness.

frequently given to them as cash. In contrast to receiving their surpluses as credit, which carried a heavy residue of dependence when dispensed by the master, the receipt of money increased slaves' independence. With money slaves could circumvent the master altogether when making loans to fellow slaves, thereby making these exchanges direct relationships between individual men and women—unlike the credit-based loans, which involved the bankerlike services of the master. With money slaves could purchase from each other, from itinerant peddlers, or even from illicit traders whom they might visit when they traveled off of the plantation to shop with "legitimate merchants." Finally, with money slaves could make loans or financial gifts directly to slaves living on other plantations, thereby creating or cementing relationships between different slave communities. In 1859, for example, Serena, a woman owned by Thomas Law, gave Excell, a slave man living on another estate, a three dollar coat. Later, when it became obvious that Serena had gone into debt, Excell reimbursed Serena.[67] In short, just as the possession of money empowered slaves in the early nineteenth century, so too did it give slaves such as Excell and Serena control over their economic affairs in the late antebellum years. That money and control accrued to slaves in those years only because they decided to avoid year-end indebtedness underscores the significance of such financial decisions.

Still, slaves enjoyed less independence as consumers in the late antebellum years than they had earlier. Not only did they possess far less money, but they had to avoid the snares of the credit system. In contrast, slaves in the early nineteenth century had received money—and the potential power that came with it—routinely, as payment for their wage work or other economic endeavors. Moreover, in the late antebellum years slaves enjoyed far less freedom of movement. Whereas their predecessors customarily left the plantation to buy where and even when they pleased, later generations of up-country slaves did not enjoy comparable mobility. Some spent most of their earnings on the plantation and rarely left it as consumers; others, who did leave, faced the restrictions imposed by the credit system, which—as manipulated by their masters—dictated where slaves spent their earnings and what they could or could not buy.

However, during the late antebellum years slaves enjoyed two distinct advantages over their predecessors. First, they had greater spending power per dollar. In the course of the nineteenth century, the price of consumer goods fell dramatically. While the index of consumer prices averaged 162 from 1800 to 1812, it hovered around 94 during the last twenty years of slavery.[68] This long-term decline in the price of consumer goods meant that each dollar earned by a slave in 1850 had roughly one-and-a-half times as much buying power as a dollar earned in 1810.[69] Such deflation enabled slaves of the late antebellum period to buy more consumer goods than their predecessors.

Slaves were able to put their greater spending power to good use. The passage of time also witnessed an explosion in the variety of goods produced in the burgeoning manufacturing centers of the United States and Europe. Slaves of the 1840s and 1850s were able to take advantage of these economic changes simply because they, like their forebears, did not have to use their earnings to pay for their basic subsistence. They did not face a slaveowner ultimatum—either pay for food and clothing or go without—and thus did not have to spend their earnings on subsistence.[70] Instead, within the limitations of their incomes they were relatively free to buy a wide variety of goods for themselves and their families.

Slaves with direct access to full-time retail merchants acquired a broad range of merchandise. In 1852 Toney, a slave of one Mrs. Brockington of Darlington District, used his income of thirty-eight dollars to purchase thirty-one different items from the merchant firm of Charles and Milling. The goods acquired by slaves when buying from the master were no less diverse. On an income of twenty-five dollars, Elleck, a slave owned by Thomas Law, purchased twenty-one items from Law's plantation store in 1859.[71] Overall, the slaves on Law's plantation purchased roughly sixty types of consumer goods in 1859, including tobacco, sugar, dishes, finished clothing such as shoes, dresses, and coats, and twenty-four varieties of fabric.

When slaves could not find what they wanted either in the plantation store or even at the shops of local merchants, they sometimes requested that their master buy the goods in distant cities. Throughout the 1850s, for example, the slaves of Peter Bacot acquired, through Bacot's intercession, coats, shawls, and dress patterns from Charleston shops. Even the retail establishments of South Carolina's leading city were within the reach of common field slaves living on up-country cotton plantations.[72]

In allowing slaves to produce marketable crops, earn their own incomes, acquire property, and participate in the market, slaveowners hoped permanently to transform slave values, attitudes, and behavior. "If slaves are industrious for themselves, they will be so for their masters," asserted one confident master defending slave market-related activities. The crops grown and goods purchased with their earnings would also "impress on [the slaves'] minds the advantages of holding property" and, presumably, respect for the owner's property as well.[73] Instead of making obedience or diligence a sine qua non of cash-crop production and related activities, masters believed that participation itself would eventually transform slaves into an obedient, property-respecting, and hard-working labor force. Where the system of Sunday wage work had, for masters, the clear short-term purpose of providing additional labor for necessary plantation work, producing and selling cash crops had the more fundamental, long-term purpose of socializing slaves in the masters' image.

From one perspective, participation in market-related economic activities did transform slaves, or at least promoted diligence, intentionality, and responsibility. In order to increase the size of their crops and earnings, slaves pooled the labor of family members when they worked their crops and purchased Peruvian guano, the fertilizer of choice among late antebellum cotton planters. Concerned with protecting their personal possessions, slaves sometimes purchased padlocks.[74] Generally unwilling to buy and accumulate with too cavalier an attitude, slaves spent their earnings carefully, thereby avoiding year-end indebtedness. All in all, slaves could not have disappointed their masters, as they were industrious in their work, respectful of property, and prudent in their financial affairs.

Yet when it came to the masters' crop, property, and interests, this seeming exercise in social engineering failed miserably. Despite their opportunities to buy and sell, produce and consume their own property, slaves remained a disobedient and troublesome labor force. Slaves who grew their own cotton for the market still disrupted the masters' work regime, as did three slave men, owned by H. G. Charles, Aron, Boston, and Andrew, who ran away at various times in 1860—though not in the fall when they harvested their own cotton. Even in the late antebellum years when masters had asserted greater control and supervision over slave economic affairs, slaves still stole—and proclaimed their right to do so. Mose, a slave living near Camden, who along with his fellow slaves produced and sold corn to their overseer, was suspected of stealing and "leaving bags full of something at certain houses in Camden." Fed, a slave living on the Bacot plantation, was a member in good standing of the Mechanicsville Baptist church until December 1847, when he was excluded for stealing and adultery.[75]

To add insult to injury, slaves not only mocked the putative power of their market-oriented activities but invoked the masters' own Christian ethics to justify continued depredations on the masters' property. As a slave of Thomas Law brazenly asserted to Law, he and other slaves could take what they worked for (even if it was nominally owned by the master) because "the Bible says a man has the right to the sweat of his eyebrows." The failure of independent economic activities to reform slaves was implicitly acknowledged by the slave-holding members of the Black Creek (Darlington District) Agricultural Society who, at their May 1860 meeting, debated—without resolution—the "general management of slaves and particularly their government so as to prevent their thieving from their masters."[76]

Despite this failure, slaveowners still reaped rewards from slaves' economic endeavors. By underpaying slaves for their crops slaveowners realized a profit on the resale of slave cotton. By situating slave workdays within the overall agricultural work regime cotton planters benefited from more diligent work from their slaves, who tended their master's crops more speedily in order to hasten the day when they could tend their own. More important, the very fact that slaves engaged in a plethora of production, selling, and buying activities meant that they had less time to engage in other, possibly subversive behavior on the plantation. These income-related activities filled time which, as one planter put it, "otherwise would be spent in the perpetration of some act that would subject [slaves] to severe punishment."[77] In effect, participation in the market economy channeled the slaves' time, energy, and attention into "safe" and nonthreatening activities, helping masters maintain order and stability on the plantation. These objectives were advanced all the more as slaveowners increased their control over the full range of slaves' market-related activities. Although this supervision was ultimately a rearguard action designed to overcome years of slave independence and disruptive activity as market participants, it nonetheless helped slaveowners maintain their power and authority in the up country.

Thus, for slaves of the late antebellum era participation in the market came at a high price: diminished control over their own affairs and additional exposure to slaveowner dictates. Slaves who did not participate enjoyed more day-to-day independence and escaped master interference in yet another aspect of their lives. Rather than making these slaves into "a kind of freeman," market participation in the 1840s and 1850s in many ways reinforced slaves' position of dependence and limited their control over their lives. As a result, up-country slaves derived relatively few noneconomic rewards from their involvement in the market. In contrast to their early nineteenth-century predecessors, the last generation of cotton slaves enjoyed fewer opportunities to forge social relationships beyond the plantation and to challenge the authority of their masters. Yet despite the restrictions on their market activities, these slaves still benefited from their economic pursuits. They enjoyed improved material conditions, especially in contrast to their predecessors. Market participation itself created new and important ways in which slaves asserted control over their affairs, enabling them to determine when they worked their crops, to choose whether to go into debt, and to decide how to use their unspent earnings. Indeed, participation in the market helped black people confront the opportunities and obstacles of the market once they were freed. It was as slaves, however, that many black people first experienced the contradictory nature of market participation.

11

INDEPENDENT ECONOMIC PRODUCTION
BY SLAVES ON ANTEBELLUM LOUISIANA
SUGAR PLANTATIONS

Roderick A. McDonald

URING THE LATE antebellum period slaves on Louisiana sugar plantations organized extensive and integrated economic systems, accumulating and disposing of capital and property within internal economies they themselves administered. Such economic systems probably functioned on every sugar estate in Louisiana, and their importance far outweighed the often limited pecuniary benefits slaves derived. The internal economy not only reflected the ways in which slaves organized their efforts to earn and spend money but also influenced the character and development of slave family and community life. The slaves' economy thus shaped patterns of slave life, providing the material basis for African American culture in the sugar-producing region.

Louisiana was the foremost sugar-producing state in the antebellum South. Between 1824 and 1861 cane sugar—which was climatically unsuited to cultivation in most of the North American continent— became the principal crop in southern Louisiana. Sugar production quintupled, reaching more than 500,000 hogsheads annually, and the number of sugar estates increased almost sevenfold, from 193 to 1,308. The slave population of the sugar region rose dramatically from just over 20,000 to around 125,000.[1]

Sugar production was confined to the southern part of Louisiana, the location of some of the largest and richest plantations in the South. Although only twenty-four of the state's sixty-four parishes grew sugar and less than 50 percent of their improved lands were ever in cane cultivation, the sugar region had a disproportionate number both of slaves and large estates. Louisiana's slave population, which numbered about 69,000 in 1820, rose to 109,600 in 1830, to 168,500 in 1840, and to 244,800 in 1850. On the eve of the Civil War it stood at 331,700. Slaves who worked on sugar estates numbered 21,000 in 1827 and by 1830 had reached 36,100, or about one-third of the state's total slave population. Thereafter, the number of sugar plantation slaves increased to approximately 50,700 in 1841, 65,300 in 1844, and by 1852 and 1853 stood at some 125,000—half of all the slaves in Louisiana.[2]

Land consolidation and the growth of large estates paralleled the sugar boom. Small holdings were common in the 1820s, even in prime sugar land that fronted the rivers and bayous. After 1830, however, small farms gave way to large estates. By 1860 the average sugar plantation contained 480 improved acres compared to 128 improved acres for noncane farms. Along with this consolidation, the number of slaves on each plantation increased steadily. By the Civil War plantations with slave populations numbering in the hundreds were commonplace. Sugar production soared, and the great estates, where most southern Louisiana slaves lived and worked, dominated the sugar economy.[3]

The cultivation of sugar was a race against time. Sugarcane cannot withstand the frosts that occur annually in Louisiana. Consequently, the sugarcane harvest came but nine or ten months after the date of planting, compared to the fourteen to eighteen months necessary for full maturation. Yet the longer the crop stayed in the ground, the higher its sugar content. Louisiana planters thus sought to plant the sugar crop as early as possible in the year and to harvest it at the last conceivable moment. Crucial to the determination of when to start the harvest were the planter's estimate both of the speed with which the crop could be cut and processed, and the date of the first killing frost.

The work routine of Louisiana sugar plantation slaves reflected the intensity of the sugar crop's cycle. Immediately following their annual Christmas and New Year holidays, slaves ploughed the fields in preparation for planting the canes, opening furrows some six to eight feet apart into which they placed seed cane set aside from the previous year's crop. Usually Louisiana planters allowed a given cane plot to ratoon for no more than two years before replanting.[4] Ratoons yielded less sugar than cane grown from seed, but ratooning also demanded less labor than planting, thus permitting cultivation of many more acres. After two years, low sugar yields required that the ratoons be dug up and the cane replanted from seed. Slaves thus planted about one-third of the estate's acreage of cane every year.

Slaves usually completed planting by the end of February. After the plant cane and ratoons sprouted, they tended the crop through the first months of its growth, hoeing and ploughing between the rows to keep the cane piece free of grass and weeds. By late June or early July the cane had grown tall enough to withstand weeds. Slaves then ploughed and hoed—"threw up"—the rows of cane in ridges to permit better drainage from the plants' roots. The cane was then "laid by" and left to grow untended until harvest time.

Tending the crop required less work than either planting or harvesting, which monopolized the time of the estate's labor force. During spring and early summer planters diverted some labor to such tasks as growing provisions and secondary cash crops, preparing for the sugar harvest, and maintaining and improving the estate. Through spring and summer slaveholders had the slaves plant one or two crops of corn, as well as perhaps potatoes, pumpkins, sweet potatoes, and other vegetables. Slaves harvested these crops and cut hay for fodder before the sugar harvest began. Slaves also mended roads and fences, built and repaired levees, made bricks for the construction and refurbishment of plantation buildings, dug and cleaned ditches, and gathered wood both for fuel and for use by the estate's coopers.

After the sugar crop was laid by slaves also began preparing for the sugar harvest. Before its commencement planters sought to have everything ready to see them through the harvest: sufficient wood to fuel the sugar mill, enough barrels and hogsheads to hold the crop, and adequate roads to transport the cane from field to works. Out of crop, during the nonharvest stage of production, slaves worked from sunup to sundown, with half an hour off for breakfast and a dinner break at noon, for five-and-a-half to six-and-a-half days per week, with time off on Saturdays and Sundays.

The sugar harvest usually began by mid-October. Once underway the work of cutting canes and processing the crop continued without stop until completion. Slaves first cut and matlayed—seed cane was literally laid out in mats and covered with a layer of earth to protect it from frost—the cane that was to be set aside for the next year's seed. Thereafter, the harvest began in earnest. Slaves worked sixteen or more hours a day, seven days a week, although factors such as bad weather, impassable roads, and breakdowns at the mill could disrupt this schedule. In addition to their tasks in the fields, slaves performed all the labor involved in processing the crop, from feeding and stoking the mill to loading hogsheads of sugar and barrels of molasses onto the river steamers at the plantation wharf.

Because of the threat of frost, harvest proceeded at a furious pace, slaves working in shifts through the night every day from late October through December. Freezing temperatures were most likely in the first couple of months of the new year, so planters tried to finish harvesting the crop by Christmas, at which time the slaves had their annual holidays. Often, however, the harvest continued until January. Thomas Hamilton, a British military officer who visited Louisiana in 1833, noted that "the crop in Louisiana is never considered safe till it is in the mill, and the consequence is that when cutting once begins, the slaves are taxed beyond their strength, and are goaded to labour until nature absolutely sinks under the effort."[5]

The gang system prevailed on Louisiana sugar plantations. Planters organized gangs according to the capacity of the slave labor force, incorporating their notions of the appropriate sexual division of labor. All adults worked in the fields, but the two most burdensome tasks on the estate, ditching and wood gathering, were men's work. Slave children also worked in gangs. Supervised by female slave drivers, they performed such light tasks as cleaning up around the sugar works and picking fodder. The work schedule of women with unweaned children accommodated their babies' feeding routine. Such women either had additional time off from labor in the gangs or worked in a "suckler's gang."

The combination of agriculture and industry required in sugar cultivation and processing placed tremendous demands on slave workers, with the result that Louisiana sugar plantations earned a dreadful reputation throughout the South. "The cultivation of sugar in Louisiana," commented Hamilton, "is carried on at an enormous expense of human life. Planters must buy to keep up their stock, and this supply principally comes from Maryland, Virginia, and North Carolina." Frances Trollope, a committed abolitionist, claimed that "to be sent south and sold [was] the dread of all the slaves north of Louisiana." E. S. Abdy, an Englishman who traveled through the South in the early 1830s, related how planters in the seaboard South disciplined slaves by threatening to sell them "down the river to Louisiana," while slaves incorporated the Louisiana sugar region's unenviable reputation in the chorus of a song:

> Old debble, Lousy Anna,
> Dat scarecrow for poor nigger,
> Where de sugar-cane grow to pine-tree,
> And de pine-tree turn to sugar.[6]

Sugar slaves suffered overwork, often compounded by undernourishment, harsh punishment, inadequate housing and clothing, high infant mortality, ill health, and a life span shortened by the grim plantation regime.

Slaves, however, struggled to transcend the brutality of plantation labor, the planters, and their agents. Slave community life throughout sugar's reign in Louisiana exhibited extraordinary creativity; the thousands of men and women who lived and died in bondage displayed resourcefulness, endeavor, dignity, courage—the full array of humanity's most prized attributes. The independence slaves displayed in their art and music, family and community development, and religion was also manifest in their economic activities. As their houses, gardens, and grounds provided the focus for slave family and community life, so too were they the base for their own economy.

While their independent economic activities had no sanction in law, slaves secured the tacit assent and approval of the planters. In much the same way as slaves used what control they had over the processes of production—by withholding their labor or laboring inefficiently— to get the planters to accede, for example, to better working conditions and standards of food, clothing, and shelter, planters also conceded to slaves the opportunity, during their time off from plantation labor, to work for themselves, to market the produce of their labor, and to keep the proceeds. Although subject to constant negotiation, the internal economy developed by sugar slaves expanded steadily until the Civil War.

Agricultural endeavors were a central component of the slaves' independent economic production. On most Louisiana sugar estates, slaves controlled some land, on which they raised livestock and grew crops for their personal consumption and sale. Slaves almost always had a small patch surrounding their house, where they tended gardens and kept some poultry and livestock. Travelers often commented on these gardens. "In the rear of each cottage, surrounded by a rude fence," observed journalist T. B. Thorpe in 1853, "you find a garden in more or less order, according to the industrious habits of the proprietor. In all you notice that the chicken-house seems to be in excellent condition." Describing the slave village on a Louisiana sugar estate, London *Times* correspondent William Howard Russell noted "the ground round the huts . . . amidst which pigs and poultry were recreating." A former slave, Elizabeth Ross Hite, confirmed Thorpe's and Russell's accounts, recalling that she and her fellow slaves "had a garden right in front of our quarter. We planted ev'rything in it. Had watermelon, mushmelon, and a flower garden." Similarly, ex-slave Catherine Cornelius remembered the "garden patch, wid mustard greens, cabbage, chickens too."[7]

Louisiana slaves put their kitchen gardens to diverse uses, raising fruits, vegetables, small livestock, and poultry. The close proximity of these gardens to the cane fields meant that slaves could work them at odd times through the week—during the midday break and in the evenings. Moreover, elderly slaves, who had few responsibilities for plantation work, could spend considerable time in the kitchen gardens. One former slave recalled that her grandmother did not go to work in the fields but "would tend to the lil patch of corn, raise chickens, and do all the work around the house."[8]

Besides their kitchen gardens, slaves had more extensive allotments of land, often known as "Negro grounds," elsewhere on the plantation. There they generally cultivated cash crops, most commonly corn, although they also raised some minor crops such as pumpkins, potatoes, and hay. While slaves consumed some of the kitchen-garden crops, they sold most of their provision-ground crops.

The "Negro grounds" were less accessible than the kitchen gardens, and slaves normally could not spend time in them during the regular workweek. Often they were located on the periphery of the plantation, beyond the land in sugar, sometimes a great distance from the sugar works, cane fields, and slave villages. Only on weekends—primarily on Sundays but also sometimes on part of Saturdays—could slaves tend them. Russell observed that slaves had "from noon on Saturday till dawn on Monday morning to do as they please." On some estates, however, slaves did regular plantation work for six days and light work for part of Sunday. Elizabeth Ross Hite recalled that "de Sunday wurk was light. Dey would only pull shucks of corn." Sunday work usually entailed the performance of a specific task, such as shelling corn, gathering fodder, branding livestock, or making hay, after which slaves had the rest of the day to themselves. Catherine Cornelius recalled that, on the West Baton Rouge Parish estate where she lived, the task-work system applied to Saturdays but slaves invariably had Sunday off except during the harvest. "Dat [Saturdays] was de day fo' ourselves," Cornelius explained. "We all had certain tasks to do. If we finished dem ahead of time, de rest of de day was ours."[9]

Slaves used their time off to cultivate their crops. Sometimes, generally just before the sugar harvest, slaves secured additional time off from the regular plantation schedule either to harvest or market their crop. For example, slaves on Duncan Kenner's Ashland Plantation "gathered their corn, made a large crop" one Sunday in early October

1852. Two days later "all but a few hands went to Donaldsonville," a nearby town, either to market their crop or spend their earnings. The next day, the sugar harvest began. From mid-October until at least the end of December, slaves harvested cane every day, including Sundays and Christmas.[10] The seven-day labor schedule, of course, precluded slaves from working in their grounds for the duration of the sugar harvest. Slaves did sometimes receive compensation, however, getting days off at the end of the harvest equal to the number of Sundays worked.[11]

Slaves valued time off prior to the sugar harvest, since it allowed them to secure their own crops before laboring full-time cutting and grinding cane. Slaves on Isaac Erwin's Shady Grove Plantation in Iberville Parish spent the two days' holiday before the 1849 sugar harvest "dig[g]ing their Potatoes & Pinders," while on Valcour Aime's St. James Parish plantation on the day preceding the commencement of the 1851 sugar harvest the slaves had a "free day to dig their potatoes." When such free time was not available, slaves did the best they could on their regularly scheduled days off. Slaves also worked for themselves during other annual holidays, which usually fell at Christmas and New Year, as well as at the end of the cane planting and when the sugar crop was laid by in midsummer.[12]

The plantation was not only the source of the slaves' independent production but also the principal market for the goods they produced. The growing and retailing of corn was the most lucrative dimension of the internal economy on Louisiana sugar plantations, and the one that involved the largest proportion of the slave population. Slaves marketed most of their produce on their home estate, since both they and the planters benefited from retailing the corn crop there. Planters wanted the crop because corn meal comprised a large proportion of the standard slave ration, and by purchasing it on the plantation, they were freed from the various fees attendant on buying through an agent, while slaves were saved the expense of shipping and marketing. Less frequently, slaves marketed their crop off the plantation. In 1849 Elu Landry recorded that he "gave [the slaves] permission & pass to sell their corn in the neighborhood—lent them teams for that purpose," while slaves on a Bayou Goula plantation sold their 1859 crop of 1,011 barrels of corn to the neighboring Nottoway Estate of J. H. Randolph for $758.[13] Although in these years the price slaves got for their corn—from thirty-seven-and-a-half to seventy-five cents a barrel—was somewhat below the commodity's market price in New Orleans, it was probably the equivalent of a local market price.[14]

Slave-grown corn was essential to the operation of many plantations. Because of its importance, slaves sometimes managed to obtain protection for their crops in case of loss or damage. In 1859 Lewis Stirling's Wakefield Estate accounts recorded that twelve slaves "lost all their corn" (a total of forty-seven barrels). They were, however, recompensed by the planter at the full price of fifty cents a barrel. In a similar instance two year previously, when plantation hogs had destroyed their corn crop, six slaves received payment of $22 from the planter as compensation. Such arrangements document the importance to the plantation of the slaves' private agricultural endeavors and the extent of planters' commitment to the slaves' continued involvement.[15]

Slaves grew and marketed a number of other cash crops. Some slave-controlled land was put into pumpkins. Although they sold for only pennies apiece, pumpkins could bring in a tidy sum. On Benjamin Tureaud's estate a slave named Big Mathilda received ten dollars for the seven hundred pumpkins she sold to the plantation in 1858, while the accounts of slaves for the Gay plantation in Iberville Parish reveal that in 1844 seven of the seventy-four slaves derived part of their earnings from the sale of pumpkins. In the previous year, the plantation's accounts record "Pumpkins 4000 bought of our Negroes . . . $80."[16] Slaves also raised potatoes, and their hay crops found a ready market on the plantation. In 1844 about the same proportion of the Gay plantation slaves as raised pumpkins sold hay to the estate at three dollars a load, while a year previous, the total crop was ten loads, or three thousand pounds.[17]

Poultry and hogs, the animals most commonly raised by slaves in Louisiana, also found their principal market on the plantation. Raising poultry was ideally suited to the economy of the slave community since it demanded little investment of time or effort, required minimal capital outlay, and provided a steady income through marketing both eggs and the birds themselves. Few travelers failed to comment on the slaves' proclivity to keep poultry, and their descriptions of slave villages on Louisiana sugar plantations invariably mention the chickens, ducks, turkeys, and geese ranging through the quarters. The prices paid by planters for fowl varied little during the antebellum years. Chickens sold at anywhere from ten to twenty-five cents each, and the price of eggs ranged from twelve-and-a-half to fifteen cents a dozen. On W. W. Pugh's Woodlawn Plantation in Assumption Parish, muscovy ducks fetched thirty-seven-and-a-half cents each in the early 1850s.[18]

Judging from the scene which William Howard Russell witnessed, slaves showed a trading acumen consistent with their position as independent retailers. "An avenue of trees runs down the negro street" on John Burnside's Houmas Plantation in Ascension Parish, Russell observed, "and behind each hut are rude poultry hutches, which, with the geese and turkeys and a few pigs, form the perquisites of the slaves, and the sole source from which they derive their acquaintance with currency." In the slaves' business transactions, "their terms are strictly cash." "An old negro brought up some ducks to Mr. Burnside," Russell related, "and offered the lot of six for three dollars. 'Very well, Louis; if you come tomorrow, I'll pay you'. 'No massa, me want de money now'. 'But won't you give me credit, Louis? Don't you think I'll pay the three dollars?' 'Oh, pay some day, massa, sure enough. Massa good to pay de tree dollar; but this nigger want money now to buy food and things for him leetle family. They will trust massa at Donaldsonville, but they won't trust this nigger.'" "I was told," Russell continued, "that a thrifty negro will sometimes make ten or twelve pounds a year from his corn and poultry."[19]

This exchange reveals the slave as a shrewd retailer with a knowledge both of the value of his commodity and the terms of the transaction. Indeed, Louis did not hesitate to contradict the planter in the course of the negotiations. The money Louis accrued from the sale was earmarked for purchases for himself and his family. Moreover, although he found a market for his goods on the plantation, Louis apparently planned to spend his cash off the estate in the nearby town of Donaldsonville, where, by virtue of his understanding of the terms demanded by the merchants there, he must have traded before.

The sale of crops, poultry, and livestock to the planter was not the only source of revenue for the slaves' independent economic activities on the plantation. Within the confines of the estate slaves had the opportunity to engage in various other money-making activities. Technological developments in the sugar industry that mechanized the grinding and milling of sugar gave slaves the opportunity to earn money, since the machines consumed huge quantities of fuel—almost without exception locally felled timber. The vast amounts of wood required by the Louisiana sugar mills can be estimated, since it took from two to four cords of wood to make one hogshead of sugar, and twice in the decade preceding the outbreak of the Civil War the sugar crop topped four hundred thousand hogsheads. The amount of wood that could be collected during regular plantation hours rarely met the estates' needs, and contracting for wood off the plantation was expensive. Buying wood that slaves chopped on their own thus proved the most efficient means for planters to supplement their fuel supply.

It also gave slaves the opportunity to earn substantial amounts of money. Payments to slaves for cutting wood on the Uncle Sam Plantation in St. James Parish, for example, totalled over $1,000 in 1859. In July 1860 fifty-three slaves received some $600 for woodcutting, and four months later $436 was paid to fifty-eight slaves. The following year sixty-one slaves cut nearly sixteen hundred cords, for which they were paid about $800 (the going rate in these years being fifty cents per cord). The most wood any one slave cut in 1861 was eighty cords and the least three cords, with the majority of slaves cutting between fifteen and forty cords.[20]

Slaves found advantages and disadvantages in lumbering. Although their compensation—from fifty to seventy-five cents per cord—was below the market price, slaves used the plantation's axes and saws and also had access to the estate's flatboats, work animals, and the tackle necessary to carry the wood out of the swamp and back to the mill. Moreover, they felled trees on land owned by the planters. Thus, since planters covered most of the slaves' capital costs, the price paid for wood may have been more equitable than it appears.[21] Woodcutting, however, was onerous, unpleasant work, since the wood had to be carried from swamps and bayous abutting the riverfront plantations. Slaves either worked from a flatboat or stood in the water, and they had to float or boat the wood out. Invariably, only men did this work.

Woodcutting was just one of many services for which planters would pay slaves. Planters also paid slaves to dig ditches, since sugar estates needed well-maintained irrigation systems and the amount of ditching done as part of the regular plantation labor schedule usually proved insufficient. Planters were thus obliged either to contract ditchers or pay slaves on the plantation for any ditching done on their time off.[22] On W. W. Pugh's estate slaves made shingles, staves, pickets, and boards, and Pugh bought slave-made shuck collars, barrels, and hogsheads. Slaves were also paid to haul wood, as well as to do regular work for the plantation on Sundays or holidays.[23] Slaves on the Gay family's sugar estate in Iberville Parish similarly were paid for work done on their time off from plantation labor. The proliferation of jobs included sugar potting, coopering, fixing and firing kettles, collecting fodder, forging iron hoops, mending shoes, counting hoop-poles, and serving as watchmen. Skilled slaves, moreover, made money during sugar harvest. In the mid-1840s the plantation sugar maker received thirty dollars for his services at harvest, while his deputy received fifteen dollars; the chief engineer and the kettle setter each got ten dollars. The firemen, kettle tenders, and the second engineer all received five dollars for their harvest season work.[24] On his estate Benjamin Tureaud paid slaves for making bricks, hogsheads, shuck collars, and baskets, while on the Wilton Plantation in St. James Parish estate accounts note cash payments to slaves for ditching, "levying," and making rails and handbarrows.[25]

Skilled slaves had an especially wide range of opportunities to work for themselves. Slave carpenters, coopers, and blacksmiths could use their training for their own profit, undertaking large-scale lucrative projects. For example, on the Gay family's plantation a slave named Thornton received twenty dollars for making a cart.[26] On some estates slave tradesmen did piecework, producing a specific quantity of items. On John Randolph's Nottoway Plantation, coopers received cash payments for producing more than a specified number of barrels. In December 1857 Cooper Henry received a payment of nineteen dollars and fifty cents for making twenty-six barrels and thirteen hogsheads above his quota, while his fellow tradesmen, Cooper William and Cooper Jack, earned sixteen dollars and eight dollars respectively for their extra production.[27]

Many paying jobs required physical stamina if not trained skills. Except for some tasks such as counting hoop-poles and collecting fodder, slaves lacking strength or skills had few opportunities other than making themselves available for day labor. Such work had to take into consideration the abilities of the individual slaves, since it was voluntary. Many slaves chose not to work for the plantation, however, preferring to tend to their farming, gardening, poultry and livestock raising, as well as their domestic crafts, while others combined working for themselves and for the plantation.

Cash could enter the internal economy from various other sources. Many sugar-plantation slaves found profit in nearby swamps and streams. Hunting and fishing supplemented the pork and corn ration supplied by planters and also offered slaves an opportunity to supplement their income, since they could sell or barter some of their catch to fellow slaves, traders, or planters.[28]

At Christmas some slaves received cash payments as a holiday bonus. Such was the case for the 150 slaves on the Nottoway Estate where, through the early 1850s, John Randolph made regular payments to the slaves. Indeed, extant plantation manuscripts contain numerous references to cash paid to slaves. An 1854 memorandum from the Stirling family's sugar plantation lists ninety-five slaves, fifty women and forty-five men, receiving cash payments totalling $314.

Most payments compensated slaves for goods and services; some of the larger amounts went to two partners for woodcutting. A similar list, probably dating from the following year, shows seventy-eight slaves receiving a total of $258. Similarly, in the early 1840s there were a number of cash payments to slaves on the Gay family plantation. For example, between December 1841 and January 1842 thirty-four men received a total of some $200, with individual payments ranging from one dollar to twenty dollars. The money probably paid either for slave crops or for harvest work but may have included holiday or Christmas bonuses and gifts.[29] Within the confines of the plantation slaves thus had a wide range of opportunities to earn money, which planter gifts supplemented.

Slaves also bypassed the plantation, selling their commodities elsewhere. Some were involved in marketing at major ports on the Mississippi River, as well as at local town markets and in the neighborhood of the plantation. They also transacted business with the traders who plied the waterways and highways of southern Louisiana.

Throughout the sugar region slaves worked for themselves collecting and drying Spanish moss, a plant that grew in profusion. Picking moss from the trees was relatively easy, since with the assistance of a long staff the plant could readily be detached from a tree's trunk and limbs. After it had been dried in the sun, slaves bound the moss into bales weighing 250 to 350 pounds ready for shipment. Hunton Love, who for the first twenty years of his life had been a slave on John Viguerie's sugar plantation on the Bayou Lafourche, testified to the importance of the collection and sale of moss. "Once I heard some men talkin'," he recalled in the 1930s, "an' one sed, 'You think money grows on trees,' an' the other one say, 'Hit do, git down that moss an' convert it into money,' an' I got to thinkin' an' sho' 'nuff, it do grow on trees."[30] The records of various plantations show slaves exploiting this market for moss. On Robert Ruffin Barrow's Bayou Lafourche estates slaves spent Sundays working their moss crop, while the accounts of Magnolia Plantation also recorded payments to slaves for moss.[31] Slaves consigned their dried moss to major entrepôts on the Mississippi, chiefly St. Louis, New Orleans, and Natchez, where they transacted business with the cities' retail agents.

The records of the Gay family's sugar estate contain rich documentation of moss gathering, including the collection and marketing patterns and payment schedules. In the mid-1840s Colonel Andrew Hynes and Joseph B. Craighead ran the plantation, while Edward Gay lived in St. Louis and acted as agent for the estate's produce. In 1844

Gay wrote to Hynes and Craighead, suggesting that the slaves pick moss and forward it to St. Louis where he guaranteed it would sell for a good price. Thereafter, moss became an integral part of the slaves' internal economy. Within a few months the first shipment of dried moss sold in St. Louis at two cents a pound with twenty-two slaves, two of whom were women, sending 9,705 pounds of moss in all and receiving a total of $162 ($196 less $34 freight and commission).[32] From 1844 to 1861 slaves on the Gay estate continued to send their moss to St. Louis for sale, where the price per pound ranged from two cents to one-and-a-quarter cents. Mississippi steamers took an average of four or five shipments per year. Slaves paid for the cartage aboard ship, and the agent's sales commission, which totaled from seventy-five cents to a dollar and a quarter per bale. When the receipts arrived at the plantation, slaves received the total net proceeds, usually around four to five dollars a bale.[33]

A record book documenting moss gathering and sale on the Gay plantation between the years of 1849 and 1861 shows the extent of the slave community's involvement. During that period 160 slaves—forty-one of whom were women—sold 1,101 bales of moss, with individual slaves selling between one and forty-eight bales. More than these 160 slaves were involved, however. Some of the shipments were sent jointly by husbands and wives, whose children and kin would also have assisted them in the project. Since the total slave population on the estate stood at 224 in 1850 and 240 in 1860, the great majority of adult slaves on the plantation were participating in this venture, from which, during the period, at least $4,000 entered the internal economy, an average of some $300 a year.[34]

Another commodity sold by slaves was molasses. On Duncan Kenner's Ashland Plantation the overseer recorded that in January 1852 he "sold the negroes molasses" and bought flour for them with the proceeds. Slaves on the Gay plantation also regularly shipped molasses for sale in St. Louis, where it fetched eight to twelve dollars a barrel. One such shipment consigned nineteen-and-a-half barrels, netting the fifteen slaves involved a total of $148.[35]

Slaves on Louisiana sugar estates had other options for marketing their crops and goods. Some transacted business in the general locale of their home plantation. Slaves on the Ventress estate, for example, contracted with a neighboring planter for the sale of their sizable corn crop of 1,011 barrels, while slaves on Elu Landry's plantation borrowed the estate's draft animals and wagons to peddle their crops throughout the neighborhood.[36] Others who lived near towns could trade at the village markets held on Sunday, the slaves' traditional day off. In 1860 the Reverend P. M. Goodwyn, a resident on Edward Gay's plantation, was amazed and horrified at the prevalence of Sunday trading. He saw slaves "going to and from the place of trade—wagons & carts, loaded and empty—servants walking and riding, carrying baskets—bundles—packages etc.," and asked, "why all this?—Can it be possible that there is a necessity for it?—If so, then it is excusable—and, vice versa,—Has the Master gone, or is he going to the house of God today?—How will he—how *ought* he to feel—as the thought comes up while he is attempting to worship—My Servant, or Servants, have a *permit* from me,—and *now*, while I am here, they are trading and trafficking in the stores of the town."[37]

Despite the misgivings of Goodwyn and other men of the cloth, Sunday remained the principal trading day for slaves able to journey to nearby towns. These markets were important to slaves as places both to sell their wares and to spend their earnings. The slave Louis, who had sold his ducks to John Burnside, was obviously well acquainted with the retail outlets in the nearby town of Donaldsonville. He insisted on a cash payment for the poultry, since he intended spending the money in the town's stores where "they will trust massa [with credit] . . . but they won't trust [him]."[38]

The market-day activities of Louisiana sugar slaves were not confined to retailing and purchasing goods. Some slaves used the day to shake the routine and restrictions of the plantation and, at market, spent some of their earnings on liquor, gaming, and other pleasures. The mayor of Plaquemine added his voice to that of other local officials when he complained that "Several Negroes were lately caught in this town drunk and gambling on Sunday in the day time in the house of a Free Negro woman." These illicit "shebeens" were, no doubt, a feature of market towns throughout the Louisiana sugar region.[39]

Even when their Sabbatarian scruples proscribed Sunday trading, slaves could still retail their goods in town. In 1853 planter William Weeks reported that a slave named "Amos has heard of the flat boats [trading vessels] being in New Town & has asked my permission to spend a portion of his crop on them—In consideration of his faithful services on all occasions, and his really conscientious scruples about trading on Sunday, I have concluded to let him go tomorrow." On Monday, a working day on the plantation, Amos went to town to trade on his own behalf.[40]

The vastness of Louisiana's sugar region and its paucity of towns meant, however, that most slaves did not have recourse to urban markets for buying and selling goods. Nevertheless, by transacting business with itinerant peddlers, slaves established trade networks over which planters had no control. Ex-slave Martha Stuart remembered the salesmen who "come thru the country," while Catherine Cornelius recalled how the slaves on the plantation where she lived would "git down to de ped'lers on de riber at nite tuh buy stuff." In fact, river traders had more extensive contact with plantation slaves than highway traders. Inadequate roads made travel by land difficult, while the large sugar plantations had direct access to navigable waterways. Moreover, river traders could move quietly and quickly and thus trade clandestinely in illicit goods. On the eve of the Civil War a Canadian traveler, William Kingsford, left an excellent description of river traders. From the deck of a Mississippi steamer he observed "the small vessels which, owned by pedlars, pass from plantation to plantation, trading with the negroes principally, taking in exchange the articles which they raise, or, when the latter are sold to the boats, offering to their owners the only temptations on which their money can be spent." Kingsford related how "now and then you come upon one of them, moving sluggishly down stream, or moored inshore, where the owner is dispensing his luxuries, in the shape of ribbons, tobacco, gaudy calicoes, and questionable whiskey."[41]

Slaves found the independence that the external trading network conferred extremely useful. It allowed slaves to divest themselves of the constraints of the plantation and engage in an independent economic system they themselves controlled. Planters had influence over neither the form of the trade nor the goods being traded. Indeed, often the river trade was carried on in violation of both plantation regulations and state law. Clandestine trading provided slaves the opportunity to sell goods planters would not buy and to buy goods planters would neither sell nor order. For example, while slaveholders rarely sold slaves liquor, river traders did, despite laws banning its sale. In turn, traders purchased a variety of commodities, including stolen goods, not traded between slaves and planters.[42]

Sugar planter Maunsell White revealed the disparity of interests between planters and river traders, on the one hand, and the identity of interests between slaves and river traders, on the other, when some of his slaves "were caught stealing molasses to sell to a Boat or 'Capota.'" White kept them under surveillance until "they were found on board the Boat, where they had hid themselves & were secreted by the owner; a man who called himself 'Block,' a German & another who called himself 'Bill.'" (Block's German nationality was not unusual, since many of these traders were immigrants.) When White and his companions searched "the Boat, an other negro was also found, who said he belonged to the Boat as did also the Men who owned it; but we soon found on arresting the whole of them, that the Boy confessed or said he belonged to [a fellow planter, George Lanaux]." When White interrogated Lanaux's slave the following morning, he found that the man had been a runaway "for 4 months; the whole of which time he said he spent in the City [New Orleans?] at work. Thirty five dollars and $^{50}/_{100}$ was found on his Person, & a Silver Watch . . . he afterwards said it was only 2 ½ months." River peddlers therefore not only gave slaves a means of enriching their lives in slavery but also provided them with an opportunity to escape slavery entirely.[43]

Theft played an integral role in the internal economy. Many slaves had no compunction about taking the planters' property, since they claimed that in appropriating plantation property they were taking what was rightly theirs. Transactions in stolen goods between slaves and peddlers were, according to Frederick Law Olmsted, common throughout the South. Olmsted noted, however, that there was a higher incidence of such trading in the Louisiana sugar region, because the sugar estates had navigable waterways and peddlers could more easily transport and conceal themselves. He observed that "the traders . . . moor at night on the shore, adjoining the negro-quarters and float away whenever they have obtained any booty, with very small chance of detection."[44] River peddlers had few inhibitions regarding what they were willing to purchase. The character of the trade militated against bulky consignments, the loading of which would require time and therefore increase the likelihood of detection. If they could avoid such logistical problems, however, peddlers were willing to purchase whatever slaves had to sell. Few of the planter's possessions were safe from the depredations of those involved in the trade. According to Olmsted, one planter had "a large brass cock and some pipe . . . stolen from his sugar-works." The planter "had ascertained that one of his negroes had taken it and sold it on board one of these boats for seventy-five cents, and had immediately spent the money, chiefly for whisky, on the same boat." It cost the planter $30 to replace the machinery. Another sugar planter informed Olmsted "that he had lately caught one of his own negroes going towards one of the 'chicken thieves,' (so the traders' boats are called) with a piece of machinery that he had unscrewed from his sugar works, which was worth eighty dollars, and which very likely might have been sold for a drink."[45]

Plantation records reveal the prevalence of slave theft and profile its most popular targets. Most thefts involved the plantations' produce and livestock. Slaves on Maunsell White's plantation stole molasses to sell to river traders, and William Weeks grumbled about "Simon that prince of runaways & troublesome negroes . . . [whose] last offence was to go into the sugar house & steal a portion of the little sugar I had kept for home use."[46] Livestock and poultry ranged free, providing particularly easy prey for slaves. Joseph Mather, superintendent of Judge Morgan's Aurora Plantation, recorded the "theft of chickens," and Ellen McCollam noted that she had "had 8 hens stowlen out of the yard." The threat of having his livestock stolen prompted Maunsell White to urge his overseer to make a picket pen "in order to save our hogs, pigs & sheep from all sorts of 'Varmints' two-legged as well as four." Similarly, planter J. E. Craighead complained that "the negroes steal our sheep as we have no safe place to keep them." One can judge the extent to which stealing poultry was viewed as characteristic of slaves by a claim incorporated in the lines of a Louisiana song:

> Negue pas capab marche san mais dans poche,
> Ce pou vole poule—
> Negro cannot walk without corn in his pocket,
> It is to steal chickens—[47]

Slaves stole the slaveholders' personal property as well. Planter Andrew McCollam and his wife Ellen, for example, lost items from their laundry. Once they had "8 shirts stolen out of the wash" and later "had a pair of sheets table cloth stolen out of the garden," whereas a visitor to Colonel Andrew Hynes's plantation had a trunk full of clothing stolen while his luggage was being loaded onto the steamer.[48]

Some stolen property supplemented the slaves' diet. Planter F. D. Richardson alluded to this in writing about slaves "committing depredations in the way of roberies," claiming that "the whole matter is no doubt attributable to the high price of pork—for many planters will not buy at the present rates & depend upon a little beef and other things as a substitute." The former slave Martha Stuart recalled that "ma Marster had a brother, they called him Charles Haynes and he was mean and he didn't feed his people . . . he didn't give 'em nuthin; 'twas the funniest thing tho; his niggers was all fat and fine cause dey'd go out and kill hogs—dey'd steal dem from de boss."[49] In addition to improving slaves' diet, clothing, and lodgings directly, goods stolen by slaves were traded for other commodities or for cash. Theft thus made an important contribution both to the slaves' economy and to their well-being.

Like the plantation economy, the slaves' independent economic production varied with the seasons. Fall and winter saw the injection of large sums of money into the internal economy, since slaves gained most of their income when they sold their cash crops and when they delivered wood prior to the beginning of the sugar harvest. Valcour Aime, a St. James Parish planter, paid $1,300 to slaves on his plantation for their 1848 corn crop, and in October 1859 slaves on the Uncle Sam Estate received over $1,000 for cutting wood and making barrels and bricks. The following year slaves on Uncle Sam earned about $500 for wood, bricks, and barrels, and the year after the total paid was $843. Similar payment schedules, involving sums from a few dollars to hundreds, occur regularly in plantation records.[50]

Stealing from the sugar house also was seasonal, since it had to be carried out between the time the crop was processed and was shipped off the estate. Furthermore, gifts from planters were usually distributed at the end of harvest or at Christmas. Christmas, according to T. B. Thorpe, was "the season when the planter makes presents of calico of flaming colors to the women and children, and a coat of extra fineness to patriarchal 'boys' of sixty-five and seventy. It is the time when negroes square their accounts with each other, and get 'master' and 'mistress' to pay up for innumerable eggs and chickens which they have frome time to time, since the last settling day, furnished the 'big house'. In short, it is a kind of jubilee, when the 'poor African' as he is termed in poetry, has a pocket full of silver, [and] a body covered with gay toggery."[51]

Not all of the entry of cash occurred in late fall and early winter. Poultry provided year-round earnings, as did theft, day labor, moss collecting, and other commercial ventures. The sugar harvest, however, was another matter, since the uninterrupted labor schedule left slaves little, if any, free time to devote to their own economic interests. At this time, slaves had to be preoccupied with the basic necessities of survival—food and rest. Apart from those paid for their services during harvest (such as kettlemen, firemen, sugar makers, and engineers) and those able to "appropriate" some of the sugar and molasses for themselves, slaves had little opportunity to advance their economic position. Additionally, they had little time to spend their money during harvest.

The internal economy therefore had a distinct seasonal profile. Earnings fluctuated considerably, since the labor demands of sugar slavery, especially during harvest, overlaid the seasonal nature of income derived from growing and marketing crops. Earnings potential also varied from year to year, since the slaves' cash crops were subject to the vagaries of the weather. Poor growing years diminished profitability for the slaves as well as the planters.

Not all slaves participated in the internal economy equally, and some may not have participated at all, although it was an integral part of community life on every sugar plantation in Louisiana. Considerable disparities existed in the earnings of slaves even within the same plantation. The money accumulated by individual slaves on Benjamin Tureaud's estate for 1858–59 ranged from $170 to $1 (during this period, 104 slaves on the estate earned a total of $3,423, with most adult slaves earning between $15 and $50). Some slaves, including twenty-two of the thirty women and two of the ninety-eight men, earned no money, although, since many received credit, there was the expectation of future earnings. Similarly, cash earned by slaves on the Gay family plantation in 1844 ranged from $82 to $1, with some slaves also getting credit: sixty-six slaves earned a total of $864 and ten slaves received $32 dollars in credit in that year. The twenty-three slaves paid for cutting wood on the Stirling estate in 1849 received sums of from $10 to $1 as their share of the total of $103 paid, while an 1854 list records payments of from $15 to ten cents in the total of $314 paid the fifty women and forty-five men.[52]

Plantation records, however, provide only a partial reckoning of the slaves' earnings, since they include payments only for certain commodities or work performed. They do not record income earned off the plantation. Other earnings would also have been unevenly distributed, although they did not necessarily benefit the same slaves. Those slaves who derived the greatest profit from dealings with river traders or through theft, for example, may not have been the same slaves who made the most money in transactions with the planter.

The internal economy permitted slaves to enjoy material benefits. Slaves used their earnings for self-improvement—to eat and dress better and to live in more comfortable homes, caring in these and other ways for themselves and for members of their families. Although earnings were often small and purchases modest—sugar plantation slaves could not, for example, expect to earn enough to purchase freedom for themselves or their families—they reflect the independent actions of slaves as consumers and offer insight into the way slaves dealt with their lives in bondage.

The purchases made by Louisiana slaves fell principally into six categories: food and drink, pipes and tobacco, clothing and other personal items, housewares, tools and implements, and livestock.

Within these six categories, however, slaves chose from a wide range of goods. They bought such foodstuffs as flour, molasses, meat, fish, coffee, beans, rice, potatoes, fruit, and bottles of cordial. They also purchased a variety of clothing and cloth from which they made their "best clothing." Among more elaborate purchases were "Elegant Bonnets," "fine Summer Coats," "Fine Russian Hats," "Chambray," white and colored shirts, jackets and waistcoats, silk dresses, gloves, oiled-cloth and "log cabin" pantaloons, and oiled-cloth winter coats. More usually, however, slaves purchased plainer goods: lengths of calico, checked, plain, and striped cotton, linen, cottonade, "domestic," blue drilling and thread, as well as simpler ready-made clothing like dresses, hose, shirts, pants, hats, shoes and boots, kerchiefs, suspenders, and shawls. Besides clothes, slaves bought such personal items as pocketknives, combs, fiddles, and umbrellas. Patrick, a slave "Engineer and Overseer" on the Gay family's plantation, even paid fifteen dollars for a watch. Slaves bought an equally diverse range of housewares. Their purchases included furniture, bedspreads, blankets, baskets, tin cups and buckets, copper kettles, chairs, bowls and pots, cutlery, locks, mosquito bars, soap and tallow, and spermaceti candles. Furthermore, Louisiana slaves made extensive use of chewing and pipe tobacco, which they bought along with pipes. Some of the other purchases slaves made represented an investment in their economic activities, including various implements and tools, such as shovels, saddles, bridles and bits, wire, twine, fishing hooks and line, "mud boots," and mitts. They also invested in pigs, shoats, and poultry.[53]

Obviously, not every slave bought such a wide range of goods. The foregoing derives from the records of purchases made by hundreds of slaves on some twenty Louisiana sugar plantations in the years between 1834 and the Civil War. This extensive listing, however, does indicate overall trends in slave purchases.

Slaves' buying practices underwent little change over time. Throughout the period they placed high priority on a limited number of commodities—specifically flour, cloth, and tobacco—with other goods given primacy including shoes and various items of ready-made clothing. This general pattern held not only over time but also from plantation to plantation. When slaves had only limited purchasing power, they tended to buy these few staple commodities, whereas slaves with larger earnings purchased other goods in addition to the staples.

Rations distributed by planters could, in specific cases, alter slaves' buying habits; slaves obviously did not have to buy goods if they were given them by the planter. On the Gay plantation, for example, slaves received a regular ration of tobacco, and hence an extensive itemization of purchases on that estate reveals them buying none.[54] The slaves' buying habits reveal that they wanted to enrich their diet, dress better, smoke tobacco, and drink liquor. Slaves considered the purchase of the more elaborate personal goods, housewares, and other items, of secondary import. They bought such goods only if they had money left over after buying the "staples."

Various plantation accounts provide evidence of this pattern. On one of Benjamin Tureaud's sugar plantations, for example, of the ninety-three men who bought goods through the plantation, seventy-six (82 percent) spent part of their earnings on tobacco, seventy-seven (83 percent) bought shoes, and seventy (75 percent) bought either meat or flour. In addition, the majority of the slaves (fifty-one out of the ninety-three—55 percent) bought some cloth or clothing other than shoes. Conversely, a minority of slaves bought such items as mosquito bars, locks, buckets, and sheet tin. The records of the Weeks family's Grande Cote Island sugar estate substantiate this pattern. The principal commodities slaves bought there were striped cotton, handkerchiefs, tobacco, flour, and coffee. Records of other Louisiana sugar plantations reveal similar purchasing patterns.[55]

Slaves managed their own earnings, purchasing needed goods and saving the rest. Planters cooperated with slaves in establishing plantation accounts, which credited slaves for work or goods and which slaves could use as depositories for earnings made off the plantation. Planters also acted as intermediaries in many of the expenditures made by slaves; that is, slaves made their purchases through the planter, the cost being debited from the slaves' personal accounts. Similarly, any money accrued from intracommunity transactions, such as T. B. Thorpe alluded to ("the time when negroes square their accounts with each other"), could be deposited with the planter. Given the extent to which slaves withdrew and deposited cash, the plantation slave communities were familiar with the medium of hard currency, albeit in small denominations, and were acquainted with both a barter system and a cash economy.[56]

Slaves were also conversant with the operation of a credit economy. On the Gay plantation, for example, nine slaves received a total of thirty-two dollars in credit in 1844. Six of the slaves used their credit to obtain flour and coffee, two withdrew theirs in cash, while one slave, Elias, spent part of his four dollars of credit on a "Fine Russian Hat bt.

in N. Orleans" that cost him three dollars. The other dollar went to pay a previous balance he owed on clothes. Similarly, on the Tureaud estate two slaves, Nash and David Big, received flour, meat, handkerchiefs, check cloth, shoes and tobacco on credit, while another slave, Charles Yellow, who had earned only two dollars cutting wood, bought tobacco, flour, shoes, hose, meat, handkerchiefs, cotton cloth, and a hat. The bill for these goods came to fifteen dollars and fifty cents, and the planter extended credit to Charles Yellow for the balance of thirteen dollars and fifty cents.[57]

Debiting systems and purchasing patterns indicate that the slave accounts were family accounts designated under the name of the head of household, almost always a man. Few slave women had accounts listed in their own names. On the Tureaud estate, for example, ninety-eight men all transacted business in their own names in 1858 and 1859, whereas, of the thirty women listed in the ledger, only eight accumulated any earnings; the other twenty-two had neither debits nor credits. Similarly, the Gay plantation records show only a handful of women with accounts in their own names, either in comparison to the number of men (six women and seventy men) or in comparison to the total number of seventy adult women living on the estate. That few women held accounts, of course, neither reflects their lack of involvement in the system nor suggests that they accrued fewer benefits from it.[58]

Wives had recourse to accounts listed under their husbands' names and made purchases through them. On John Randolph's Nottoway Plantation, for example, three slave women had their purchases of shoes deducted from the accounts of slave men. Two of these women, Mahala and Susan, each received a pair of shoes at the cost of one dollar, which was debited from the accounts of George and Gus, respectively, while in another case the journal records "Long William got 1 pr. Shoes (for Leana)—$1." An 1864 "List of Negroes" shows that George and Mahala were husband and wife, and one may assume that Gus and Susan, and Long William and Leana were also married or closely related, although it is also possible that they had some sort of nonkin working or contractual relationship. The accounts of slaves on the Gay plantation provide further evidence. In 1841 William Sanders had his account debited to pay for a "White Cambrice dress for wife." In 1839 Little Moses' account paid for shoes for his wife, Charity; five years later, Ned Davis was charged for "Coffee by your wife." A slave named Willis bought children's shoes from his account on the Tureaud estate, while Kenawa Moses, a slave on the Gay estate, paid for "meat for [his] children" from the money he earned. Other slaves on the Gay estate who were charged for goods for family members included Harry Cooper, who bought shoes for his wife and his daughter Tulip, and Alfred Cooper, who purchased calico for his daughter Louisiana and two "Elegant Bonnets" costing two dollars each, presumably for his wife Dedo and his daughter.[59]

The debiting systems and the purchasing patterns thus indicate that the slave accounts were family accounts, to which the family of the account-holder had access. Purchases went to improve the lives and comfort not only of the slaves who were debited for the goods but also of members of their families. Staple foodstuffs—meat and flour, for example—fed the entire family, while the lengths of cloth bought through the accounts would have been sewn by the women of the family to provide garments for all. Similarly, furniture, cutlery and other tableware, cooking utensils, blankets, locks, mosquito bars, soap, and candles would have been used by the household. Even where the records make no mention of kin relationship, as in the debit of twelve dollars and fifty cents from the account of Woodson, a slave on W. W. Pugh's estate, for a "Silk Dress for Rachel," and in the "cash [paid] to Aunt Julia" from Patrick's account on the Gay plantation, it seems likely that the men and women were kin.[60]

Records of the Gay estate reveal the familial basis of the slaves' accounts. A comparison of the 1844 slave accounts on the plantation with other slave lists compiled around the same time shows the family relationships of the account holders. Seventy-six people earned money and held accounts, seventy of whom were men. Of these seventy male account holders, thirty-seven were heads of households, six were sons in male-headed households, three were sons in female-headed households, and eighteen were single males without family affiliation. (The status of the remaining six men is unclear.) Of the six women holding accounts, two were heads of households, one was a daughter in a female-headed household, and one a single woman. The two other women held joint accounts; Clarissa with her husband Toney (Toney also held an account with another slave, Ned Teagle, who was a son in a female-headed household), and Anna with William, neither of whom can be traced elsewhere in the plantation records. Some of the slaves recorded as single and without family affiliation nevertheless had families who drew on their accounts. The slave named Kenawa Moses, for example, who was listed as single, paid from his account for "meat for [his] children." The accounts held by sons in either male- or female-headed households suggests a "coming of age" pattern. Young adults may have been listed individually, for example, when they assumed sole responsibility for a specific money-making endeavor.[61]

Slaves did not rely on the planters for all their purchases. Although they may or may not have kept accounts on the plantation, slaves frequently found reasons to buy elsewhere. Catherine Cornelius recalled that on the plantation where she lived the owner "wouldn't gib us combs en brushes, but we got some from pedlin."[62] Slaves also bought and traded for alcohol. Markets outside the plantation were usually the only source from which slaves could obtain liquor, since planters did not usually supply it (although they occasionally distributed it on holidays, like Christmas) and rarely allowed slaves to buy it through the plantation accounts.[63] Doubtless some of the cash slaves withdrew from their accounts went to purchase alcohol from river traders, illicit "shebeens" and grog shops, or "moonshiners," either on or off the plantation. Slaves also spent money gambling, as evidenced by reports of slaves "drunk and gambling" on Sundays in Plaquemine township. Cultural and religious items and locally crafted artifacts made by slave artisans were also purchased through agencies other than the planter.[64]

Participation in the internal economy offered slaves a number of less tangible benefits. Slaves who worked for themselves and accumulated money and goods not only supplemented their often meager rations and compensated for deficiencies in food and other necessities but also derived satisfaction from controlling a portion of their own lives. In assuming responsibility for structuring their independent economic activities, slaves chose the manner and extent of their involvement, decided which crops they would grow and how to distribute time between small-holding agricultural pursuits and work for which planters paid them, when to sell and what to buy—decisions not normally allowed them. Although the internal economy operated within the constraints imposed by chattel bondage, the opportunity for independent economic activity gave slaves a degree of control and autonomy at variance with the basic tenets of servitude. Slaves qua slaves operated within a structure of social and labor relations that deprived them of personal rights, autonomous actions, decision making, and self-motivated work regimes. As independent economic agents, however, they structured their own efforts, controlled "their" land and the manner of its cultivation, and decided how to market produce and dispose of the accumulated profits.

The independent activities of slaves on Mavis Grove Estate in Plaquemines Parish provide a telling example of the disparity between the slaves' lives as slaves and their lives as independent producers. On Sunday, September 13, 1857, the plantation journal recorded "Boys not cutting wood today, resting from the fatigues of last night's frolic." Although slaves on Mavis Grove normally spent Sunday chopping wood for sale to the planter, they themselves agreed to take that Sunday off. This balancing of work with social concerns demonstrates that slaves working within the confines of the internal economy determined how to order their time and labor and illustrates their priorities. Indeed, the structure of the slaves' internal economy, wherein they assumed the responsibility of deciding how to organize their work, resembled the economy of a landed peasantry.[65]

The processes by which slaves controlled their independent economies doubtless proved cathartic. Although involvement had potentially deleterious effects, such as overwork and physical stress, slaves found independent production rewarding. They derived great satisfaction from working for themselves, pacing their work, and organizing their own efforts, as well as from controlling the disposal of and profiting directly from the fruits of their labor. The independent economic activities, moreover, established the material foundations for slave family and community life. Patterns of production and marketing not only permitted economic independence and distance from the planters' control but also helped establish unique patterns of life within slave communities, providing an independent material basis for their society and culture. The diversity and ubiquity of the economic activities of slaves in Louisiana testifies to their creative initiative. Although planters no doubt found benefits in the slaves' internal economy, this system of independent production prompted enterprise, not subservience. Whereas the plantation economy followed the planters' will, the slaves' economy contradicted the very premises of chattel bondage, helping to shape patterns of African American life, culture, and economy that endured from slavery to freedom.

NOTES
CONTRIBUTORS
INDEX

NOTES

Introduction

1. This perspective is most evident in the studies of North American slavery. For example, see Eugene D. Genovese, *Roll, Jordan, Roll: The World the Slaves Made* (New York, 1974), although note Genovese's discussion of "Gardens," pp. 535–40; Herbert G. Gutman, *The Black Family in Slavery and Freedom, 1750–1925* (New York, 1976); John W. Blassingame, *The Slave Community: Plantation Life in the Antebellum South*, rev. ed. (New York, 1979); Lawrence W. Levine, *Black Culture and Black Consciousness: Afro-American Folk Thought from Slavery to Freedom* (New York, 1977); Albert J. Raboteau, *Slave Religion: The 'Invisible Institution' in the Antebellum South* (New York, 1978). For the Caribbean, see Mary Turner, *Slaves and Missionaries: The Disintegration of Jamaican Slave Society, 1787–1834* (Urbana, 1982); and Richard B. Sheridan, *Doctors and Slaves: A Medical and Demographic History of Slavery in the British West Indies, 1680–1834* (Cambridge, 1985).

2. Frederick Law Olmsted, quoted in Joseph P. Reidy, "Obligation and Right: Patterns of Labor, Subsistence, and Exchange in the Cotton Belt of Georgia, 1790–1860," Ch. 5 in this volume.

3. Although there has been little study of the ways in which slaves worked and the relationship between work process and slave culture, those connections have been much at issue in the study of wage workers. For the debate over the role of the work process in working-class activism, see David Montgomery, *Workers' Control in America: Studies in the History of Work, Technology, and Labor Struggles* (Cambridge, 1987), and *The Fall of the House of Labor: The Workplace, the State, and American Labor Activism, 1865–1925* (Cambridge, 1979); Patrick Joyce, *Work, Society and Politics: The Culture of the Factory in Later Victorian England* (New Brunswick, N.J., 1980); Bryan Palmer, *Skilled Workers and Industrial Capitalism in Hamilton, Ontario, 1860–1914* (Toronto, 1979); Andrew Zimbalist, *Case Studies in the Labor Process* (New York, 1979); and Richard Price, "The Labour Process and Labour History," *Social History* 8 (1983): 57–75, as well as the subsequent exchange between Price and Patrick Joyce. An important exception to the neglect of the work process in the study of slavery is Stuart B. Schwartz, *Sugar Plantations in the Formation of Brazilian Society* (Cambridge, 1986).

4. For pioneering and still invaluable work on the slaves' economy, see Sidney W. Mintz and Douglas Hall, *The Origins of the Jamaican Internal Marketing*

System, Yale University Publications in Anthropology no. 57 (New Haven, 1960), pp. 3–26; and Mintz, "The Jamaican Internal Marketing Pattern: Some Notes and Hypotheses," *Social and Economic Studies* 4 (1955): 95–103; "The Role of the Middleman in the Internal Distribution System of a Caribbean Peasant Economy," *Human Organization* 15 (1956): 18–23; "Internal Marketing Systems as a Mechanism of Social Articulation," *Proceedings of the American Ethnological Society* (1959): 20–30. The debate over the "peasant breach" in Brazil is summarized by Ciro Flamarion S. Cardoso, "The Peasant Breach in the Slave System: New Developments in Brazil," *Luso-Brazilian Review* 25 (1988): 49–57. Cardoso's own point of view is stated more fully in *Agricultura, escravidão e capitalismo* (Petrópolis, Brazil, 1979), ch. 4, and *Escravo ou Camponês: O proto-campesinato negro nas Américas* (São Paulo, 1987). Also see João José Reis and Eduardo Silva, *Negociação e conflito: A resistência negra no Brasil escravista* (São Paulo, 1988), and Stuart B. Schwartz, *Slaves, Peasants, and Rebels: Reconsidering Brazilian Slavery* (Urbana, Ill., 1992), especially ch. 2. For the British Caribbean, see B. W. Higman's encyclopedic *Slave Populations of the British Caribbean, 1807–1834* (Baltimore, 1984), especially pp. 53, 56, 60, and 204–18. Other important statements on the subject can be found in Robert Dirks, *The Black Saturnalia: Conflict and Its Ritual Expression on British West Indian Slave Plantations* (Gainesville, Fla., 1987); and Tadeusz Lepkowski, *Haiti,* 2 vols. (Havana, 1968–69), 1:59–60. Nothing of a similar nature exists for the mainland American South, but Philip D. Morgan, "Work and Culture: The Task System and the World of Lowcountry Blacks, 1700 to 1880," *William and Mary Quarterly,* 3d ser., 39 (1982): 563–99, and "The Ownership of Property by Slaves in the Mid-Nineteenth Century Low Country," *Journal of Southern History* 49 (1983): 399–420, as well as Leslie S. Rowland, "The Politics of Task Labor and Independent Production in Lowcountry South Carolina and Georgia" (unpublished essay, courtesy of the author), explore the subject for the South Carolina and the Georgia low country. Also useful is Lawrence T. McDonnell, "Money Knows No Master: Market Relations and the American Slave Community," in Winfred B. Moore, Jr., et al., eds., *Developing Dixie: Modernization in a Traditional Society* (New York, 1988), pp. 31–44.

5. See Higman, *Slave Populations of the British Caribbean,* pp. 181, 188; Robert William Fogel, *Without Consent or Contract: The Rise and Fall of American Slavery* (New York, 1989), p. 77; and J. R. Ward, *British West Indian Slavery, 1750–1834: The Process of Amelioration* (Oxford, 1988), pp. 14–18. Although work in the mines was onerous, it had its compensations: see Kathleen J. Higgins, "Masters and Slaves in a Mining Society: A Study of Eighteenth-Century Sabará, Minas Gerais," *Slavery and Abolition* 11 (1990): 58–73; and Donald Ramos, "Slavery in Brazil: A Case Study of Diamantina, Minas Gerais," *The Americas* 45 (1988): 47–59. Mortality and morbidity rates were of course influenced by climate, disease environment, and nutrition, as well as by labor demands. From this perspective, tropical climate and diseases compounded the difficulties faced by overworked and underfed slaves who cultivated sugar.

6. See Reidy, "Obligation and Right" and Steven F. Miller, "Plantation Labor Organization and Slave Life on the Cotton Frontier: The Alabama-Mississippi Black Belt, 1815–1840," both in this volume.

7. John J. McCusker and Russell R. Menard, *The Economy of British America, 1607–1789* (Chapel Hill, 1985), pp. 18–32; Richard Pares, *Merchants and Planters, Economic History Review,* Supplement, no. 4 (Cambridge, 1960), pp. 20–22, 40. For Minas Gerais, see Amilcar Martins Filho and Roberto B. Martins, "Slavery in a Nonexport Economy: Nineteenth-Century Minas Gerais Revisited," *Hispanic American Historical Review* 63 (1983): 537–68, along with the comments by Robert W. Slenes, Warren Dean, Stanley L. Engerman, and Eugene D. Genovese on pp. 569–90; Martins Filho and Roberto B. Martins, "Slavery in a Non-Export Economy: A Reply," *Hispanic American Historical Review* 64 (1984): 135–46; and Douglas Cole Libby, "Proto-Industrialization in a Slave Society: The Case of Minas Gerais," *Journal of Latin American Studies* 23 (1991), 1–35. Lorena S. Walsh demonstrates how Chesapeake planters responded to hard times in tobacco culture: "Slave Life, Slave Society, and Tobacco Production in the Tidewater Chesapeake, 1620–1820," Ch. 7 in this volume.

8. David Barry Gaspar, "Sugar Cultivation and Slave Life in Antigua before 1800," Ch. 3 in this volume.

9. For the classic statement of how the changing "rules of the game" shaped workplace struggles, see E. J. Hobsbawm, "Custom, Wages, and Work-Load in Nineteenth-Century Industry," in Asa Briggs and John Saville, eds., *Essays in Labour History* (London, 1960), 113–40. An attempt to join one strand of American labor history to the study of slavery can be found in Herbert Gutman's *Black Family.*

10. See Gaspar, "Sugar Cultivation and Slave Life in Antigua." The masters' acceptance of such unspoken agreement is affirmed by Lorena Walsh's observation that "a candidate for a vacant overseer's post would solicit the job by promising not to interfere with whatever privileges the slaves had enjoyed under the previous overseer." See "Slave Life, Slave Society, and Tobacco Production," p. 179 in this volume.

11. David P. Geggus, "Sugar and Coffee Cultivation in Saint Domingue and the Shaping of the Slave Labor Force," Ch. 2 in this volume; Fogel, *Without Consent or Contract,* p. 24. See also Philip D. Curtin, *The Rise and Fall of the Plantation Complex: Essays in Atlantic History* (Cambridge, 1990), pp. 3–28.

12. Geggus, "Sugar and Coffee Cultivation"; Michel-Rolph Trouillot, "Coffee Planters and Coffee Slaves in the Antilles: The Impact of a Secondary Crop"; and Walsh, "Slave Life, Slave Society, and Tobacco Production," all in this volume.

13. Trouillot, "Coffee Planters and Coffee Slaves," p. 133 in this volume; see also Higman, *Slave Populations of the British Caribbean,* pp. 113–14, 148, 150; and Fogel, *Without Consent or Contract,* pp. 169–70, 178–79, 182.

14. On interregional slave trades in sugar and cotton regions, see David

Eltis, "The Traffic in Slaves between the British West Indian Colonies, 1807–1833," *Economic History Review* 25 (1972): 55–64; and Robert William Fogel and Stanley L. Engerman, *Time on the Cross: The Economics of American Negro Slavery,* 2 vols. (Boston, 1974), 1:46. For the nineteenth-century United States, see Michael Tadman, *Speculators and Slaves: Masters, Traders, and Slaves in the Old South* (Madison, 1989).

15. Walsh, "Slave Life, Slave Society, and Tobacco Production," p. 173 in this volume; see also Richard S. Dunn, "Sugar Production and Slave Women in Jamaica"; Gaspar, "Sugar Cultivation and Slave Life in Antigua."

16. Trouillot, "Coffee Planters and Coffee Slaves"; and Geggus, "Sugar and Coffee Cultivation," both in this volume.

17. Dirks, *The Black Saturnalia;* Gaspar, "Sugar Cultivation and Slave Life in Antigua."

18. Geggus, "Sugar and Coffee Cultivation"; and Daniel C. Littlefield, *Rice and Slaves: Ethnicity and the Slave Trade in Colonial South Carolina* (Baton Rouge, 1981).

19. Dunn, "Sugar Production and Slave Women in Jamaica"; and Geggus, "Sugar and Coffee Cultivation."

20. Men were believed to be stronger than women and hence more useful for the heaviest field work, while slaveholders generally tried to avoid older slaves whose experience had made them "allways Obstinate, and Stubborn": Gaspar, "Sugar Cultivation and Slave Life in Antigua," p. 112 in this volume.

21. Miller, "Plantation Labor Organization," p. 159 in this volume; and Dunn, "Sugar Production and Slave Women in Jamaica." In addition, see Hilary Beckles, *Natural Rebels: A Social History of Enslaved Black Women in Barbados* (New Brunswick, N.J., 1989), especially pp. 7–54; and Barbara Bush, *Slave Women in Caribbean Society, 1650–1838* (Bloomington, Ind., 1990), pp. 36–37.

22. The essays by Trouillot and Geggus in this volume provide numerous examples. On the sexual composition of African cargoes, see, for example, David Geggus, "Sex Ratio, Age, and Ethnicity in the Atlantic Slave Trade: Data from French Shipping and Plantation Records," *Journal of African History* 30 (1989): 23–44; and David Eltis, "The Volume, Age/Sex Ratios, and African Impact of the Slave Trade: Some Refinements of Paul Lovejoy's Review of the Literature," *Journal of African History* 31 (1991): 485–92.

23. Higman, *Slave Populations of the British Caribbean,* pp. 179–80, 188, 200; Philip D. Morgan, "Task and Gang Systems: The Organization of Labor on New World Plantations," in Stephen Innes, ed., *Work and Labor in Early America* (Chapel Hill, 1988), pp. 189–220; Reidy, "Obligation and Right," Ch. 5 in this volume.

24. Reidy, "Obligation and Right"; and Drew Faust, *James Henry Hammond and the Old South: A Design for Mastery* (Baton Rouge, 1982).

25. Miller, "Plantation Labor Organization"; and Gaspar, "Sugar Cultivation and Slave Life in Antigua," pp. 166 and 111 in this volume.

26. Walsh, "Slave Life, Slave Society, and Tobacco Production," Ch. 7 in this volume. Also see William K. Scarborough, *The Overseer: Plantation Management in the Old South* (Baton Rouge, 1966).

27. Dunn, "Sugar Production and Slave Women in Jamaica"; and Gaspar, "Sugar Cultivation and Slave Life in Antigua," both in this volume.

28. Dunn, "Sugar Production and Slave Women in Jamaica."

29. Dunn, "Sugar Production and Slave Women in Jamaica"; Gaspar, "Sugar Cultivation and Slave Life in Antigua"; and Geggus, "Sugar and Coffee Cultivation," all in this volume; Higman, *Slave Populations of the British Caribbean*, p. 161.

30. Depending on the pattern of cultivation, processing, and marketing, other crops spawned yet other repertoires of skills. Rice lay somewhere between sugar and cotton, whereas cocoa, coffee, tobacco, and pimento were much like cotton, requiring few skilled specialists. For coffee, see Trouillot, "Coffee Planters and Coffee Slaves," and Geggus, "Sugar and Coffee Cultivation."

31. Gaspar, "Sugar Cultivation and Slave Life in Antigua," and Walsh, "Slave Life, Slave Society, and Tobacco Production." The changing place of free people of African descent in plantation societies can be glimpsed in David W. Cohen and Jack P. Greene, eds., *Neither Slave nor Free: The Freedman of African Descent in the Slave Societies of the New World* (Baltimore, 1972); and in Ira Berlin, *Slaves without Masters: The Free Negro in the Antebellum South* (New York, 1974).

32. Edmund S. Morgan, *Virginians at Home: Family Life in the Eighteenth Century* (Charlottesville, Va., 1963), p. 53.

33. Dunn, "Sugar Production and Slave Women in Jamaica," and Geggus, "Sugar and Coffee Cultivation."

34. Dunn, "Sugar Production and Slave Women in Jamaica." "Once slaves predominated in the labor force," Lorena Walsh observes, "white women servants all but disappeared from the fields. In contrast, every able-bodied slave woman and most slave girls aged twelve or more did regular field labor." Walsh, "Slave Life, Slave Society," p. 177 in this volume.

35. Gaspar, "Sugar Cultivation and Slave Life in Antigua," p. 110–11 in this volume. For other work on slave women in the Caribbean, see Beckles, *Natural Rebels;* Bush, *Slave Women;* and Marietta Morrissey, *Slave Women in the New World: Gender Stratification in the Caribbean* (Lawrence, Kans., 1989).

36. Miller, "Plantation Labor Organization," Ch. 6 in this volume.

37. Dunn, "Sugar Production and Slave Women in Jamaica," and Geggus, "Sugar and Coffee Cultivation," pp. 67 and 89 in this volume.

38. Walsh, "Slave Life, Slave Society, and Tobacco Production"; Miller, "Plantation Labor Organization"; Reidy, "Obligation and Right"; John Campbell, "As 'A Kind of Freeman': Slaves' Market-Related Activities in the South Carolina Up Country, 1800–1860"; and Dunn, "Sugar Production and Slave Women," all in this volume.

39. Dale Tomich, "*Une Petite Guinée:* Provision Ground and Plantation in Martinique, 1830–1848," p. 222 in this volume.

40. O. Nigel Bolland, "The Extraction of Timber in the Slave Society of Belize," in Ira Berlin and Philip Morgan, eds., *Slavery on the Periphery* (forthcoming); Walsh, "Slave Life, Slave Society, and Tobacco Production"; Campbell, "As 'A Kind of Freeman'"; Roderick A. McDonald, "Independent Economic Production by Slaves on Antebellum Louisiana Sugar Plantations," all in this volume; and John T. Schlotterbeck, "The Internal Economy of Slavery in Rural Piedmont Virginia," in Ira Berlin and Philip D. Morgan, eds., *The Slaves' Economy: Independent Production by Slaves in the Americas* (London, 1991), pp. 170–82.

41. See Tomich, "*Une Petite Guinée.*" See also Stuart B. Schwartz, "The Plantations of St. Benedict: The Benedictine Sugar Mills of Colonial Brazil," *The Americas* 39 (1982): 1–22.

42. William Frederick Sharp, *Slavery on the Spanish Frontier: The Colombian Choco, 1680–1810* (Norman, Okla., 1976), pp. 133–35; A. J. R. Russell-Wood, *The Black Man in Slavery and Freedom in Colonial Brazil* (New York, 1982), p. 118.

43. Woodville K. Marshall, "Provision Ground and Plantation Labor in Four Windward Islands: Competition for Resources during Slavery," Ch. 8 in this volume.

44. The Reverend Robert Robertson, quoted in Gaspar, "Sugar Cultivation and Slave Life in Antigua," p. 117 in this volume. See also Marshall, "Provision Ground and Plantation Labor in Four Windward Islands," Mary Turner, "Slave Workers, Subsistence, and Labour Bargaining: Amity Hall, Jamaica, 1805–1832," in Berlin and Morgan, eds., *The Slaves' Economy,* pp. 92–106.

45. Elsa V. Goveia, *Slave Society in the British Leeward Islands at the End of the Eighteenth Century* (New Haven, 1965), p. 137; Higman, *Slave Populations of the British Caribbean,* pp. 53, 56, 210–12; Trouillot, "Coffee Planters and Coffee Slaves."

46. Higman, *Slave Populations of the British Caribbean,* pp. 52–53; Orlando Patterson, *Sociology of Slavery: An Analysis of the Origins, Development, and Structure of Negro Slave Society in Jamaica* (London, 1967), pp. 66, 218; Turner, "Slave Workers, Subsistence, and Labour Bargaining," in Berlin and Morgan, eds., *The Slaves' Economy,* pp. 92–106.

47. Higman, *Slave Populations of the British Caribbean,* p. 208.

48. Although historians and economists admit regional differences, the debate over self-sufficiency in foodstuffs in the mainland American South has generally been decided in favor of self-sufficiency. See William K. Hutchinson and Samuel H. Williamson, "The Self-Sufficiency of the Antebellum South: Estimates of the Food Supply," *Journal of Economic History* 31 (1971): 591–612; Sam Bowers Hilliard, *Hog Meat and Hoecake: Food Supply in the Old South, 1840–1860* (Carbondale, Ill., 1972); Robert E. Gallman, "Self-Sufficiency in the Cotton Economy of the Antebellum South," and Diane L. Lindstrom, "Southern Dependence upon Interregional Grain Supplies: A Review of Trade Flows,

1840–1860" both in William N. Parker, ed., *The Structure of the Cotton Economy in the Antebellum South* (Washington, D.C., 1970); and Ralph V. Anderson and Robert E. Gallman, "Slaves as Fixed Capital: Slave Labor and Southern Economic Development," *Journal of American History*, 64 (1977): 24–46. To the best of our knowledge, no scholar has systematically explored the social as well as economic implications of the purchase of provisions by slaveowners from nonslaveowners.

49. Higman, *Slave Populations of the British Caribbean*, p. 205; Howard Johnson, "The Emergence of a Peasantry in the Bahamas during Slavery," *Slavery and Abolition* 10 (1989): 172–86; Anderson and Gallman, "Slaves as Fixed Capital"; Fogel, *Without Consent or Contract*, p. 192; Campbell, "As 'A Kind of Freeman' "; and McDonald, "Independent Economic Production by Slaves on Antebellum Louisiana Sugar Plantations."

50. J. Harry Bennett, Jr., *Bondsmen and Bishops: Slavery and Apprenticeship on the Codrington Plantations of Barbados, 1710–1838* (Berkeley, 1958), p. 37; Goveia, *Slave Society in the British Leeward Islands*, pp. 136–39; Patterson, *Sociology of Slavery*, p. 217; Ward, *British West Indian Slavery*, pp. 19, 65, 76; Peter H. Wood, *Black Majority: Negroes in Colonial South Carolina from 1670 through the Stono Rebellion* (New York, 1974), especially ch. 7; James T. McGowan, "Creation of a Slave Society: Louisiana Plantations in the Eighteenth Century" (Ph.D. diss., University of Rochester, 1976), pp. 139–45; Edmund Morgan, *American Slavery—American Freedom: The Ordeal of Colonial Virginia* (New York, 1975), pp. 154–57; Loren Schweninger, "The Underside of Slavery: The Internal Economy, Self-Hire, and Quasi-Freedom in Virginia, 1780–1865," *Slavery and Abolition* 12 (1991): 1–22.

51. Goveia, *Slave Society in the British Leeward Islands*, pp. 136–39; Ward, *British West Indian Slavery*, p. 18. For the French Caribbean, see Tomich's essay in this volume and Gabriel Debien, "La Nourriture des esclaves sur les plantations des Antilles françaises aux XVIIᵉ et XVIIIᵉ siècles," *Caribbean Studies* 4 (1964): 3–28.

52. Higman, *Slave Populations of the British Caribbean*, pp. 41, 210; Hilary McD. Beckles, "An Economic Life of Their Own: Slaves as Commodity Producers and Distributors in Barbados," in Berlin and Morgan, eds., *The Slaves' Economy*, pp. 31–47; Marshall, "Provision Ground and Plantation Labor in Four Windward Islands."

53. Richard B. Sheridan, "The Crisis of Slave Subsistence in the British West Indies during and after the American Revolution," *William and Mary Quarterly*, 3d ser., 33 (1976): 615–41, and *Doctors and Slaves*, pp. 154–62; Richard Pares, *A West-India Fortune* (London, 1950), pp. 106, 126–27; Bennett, *Bondsmen and Bishops*, pp. 101–2; Ward, *British West Indian Slavery*, pp. 41, 108–9, 113, 117; David Barry Gaspar, "Slavery, Amelioration, and Sunday Markets in Antigua, 1823–1831," *Slavery and Abolition* 9 (1988): 1–26; Gaspar, "Sugar Cultivation and Slave Life in Antigua."

54. J. Carlyle Sitterson, *Sugar Country: The Cane Sugar Industry in the South,*

1753–1950 (Lexington, Ky., 1953), ch. 1; Schwartz, *Sugar Plantations in the Formation of Brazilian Society,* pp. 343–44, 351, 423, 428, 449.

55. Frederic G. Cassidy, *Jamaica Talk: Three Hundred Years of the English Language in Jamaica* (London, 1961), pp. 43, 334–90; F. G. Cassidy and R. B. Le Page, eds., *Dictionary of Jamaican English,* 2d ed. (London, 1980); John H. Parry, "Plantation and Provision Ground: An Historical Sketch of the Introduction of Food Crops into Jamaica," *Revista de Historia de America* 39 (1955): 1–20 (the reference is to p. 1). For the variety of slave crops, see, for example, Dirks, *The Black Saturnalia,* p. 70; Higman, *Slave Populations of the British Caribbean,* p. 212; Jerome S. Handler, "The History of Arrowroot and the Origin of Peasantries in the British West Indies," *Journal of Caribbean History* 2 (1971): 46–93; Joseph William Jordan, *An Account of the Management of Certain Estates in the Island of Barbados* (London, 1826), p. 4; Henry Nelson Coleridge, *Six Months in the West Indies, in 1825* (London, 1832), pp. 125–26; Beckles, "An Economic Life of Their Own," and Richard Price, "Subsistence on the Plantation Periphery: Crops, Cooking, and Labour among Eighteenth-Century Suriname Maroons," both in Berlin and Morgan, eds., *The Slaves' Economy,* 31–47, 107–30; Marshall, "Provision Ground and Plantation Labor in Four Windward Islands"; and Tomich, "*Une Petite Guinée.*"

56. Genovese, *Roll, Jordan, Roll,* p. 535; Fogel, *Without Consent or Contract,* p. 192; Mintz and Hall, *Origins,* p. 17; Campbell, "As 'A Kind of Freeman.'"

57. Beckles, "An Economic Life of Their Own," in Berlin and Morgan, eds., *The Slaves' Economy,* p. 36. See also Alex Lichtenstein, "'That Disposition to Theft, With Which They have Been Branded': Moral Economy, Slave Management, and the Law," *Journal of Social History* 21 (1989): 413–40; Campbell, "As 'A Kind of Freeman'"; McDonald, "Independent Economic Production by Slaves on Antebellum Louisiana Sugar Plantations"; and Gaspar, "Sugar Cultivation and Slave Life in Antigua."

58. James Mercer to B. Muse, 8 April 1779, Battaille Muse Papers, Duke University, Durham; McDonald, "Independent Economic Production by Slaves on Antebellum Louisiana Sugar Plantations," p. 282 in this volume; Sir William Young, *Tour through the Several Islands of Barbadoes, Vincent, Antigua, Tobago, and Grenada, in the Years 1791 and 1792,* in Bryan Edwards, *History of the British Colonies . . . ,* 4 vols. (Philadelphia, 1806), 4:266 and 271. See also Dirks, *The Black Saturnalia,* pp. 70–72; Price, "Subsistence on the Plantation Periphery," and Schlotterbeck, "Internal Economy of Slavery," both in Berlin and Morgan, eds., *The Slaves' Economy,* pp. 107–30, 170–81.

59. Mintz and Hall, *Origins of the Jamaican Internal Marketing System,* pp. 15, 17; Ward, *British West Indian Slavery,* pp. 115, 199–200, 284–85; B. W. Higman, *Slave Population and Economy in Jamaica, 1807–1834* (Cambridge, 1976), p. 228; Patterson, *Sociology of Slavery,* p. 221; Goveia, *Slave Society in the British Leeward Islands,* p. 226; Pares, *West-India Fortune,* p. 122; Michael Craton, *Testing the Chains: Resistance to Slavery in the British West Indies* (Ithaca, N.Y., 1982), pp. 257–58; Morgan, "The Ownership of Property," pp. 399–420.

60. Evangeline Walker Andrews and Charles McLean Andrews, eds., *Journal of a Lady of Quality* (New Haven, 1923), pp. 176–77. See also Richard Price, "Subsistence on the Plantation Periphery," in Berlin and Morgan, eds., *The Slaves' Economy*, pp. 113–14, and "Caribbean Fishing and Fishermen: A Historical Sketch," *American Anthropologist*, 68 (1966): 1363–83; Sheridan, *Doctors and Slaves*, p. 95; Cassidy and Le Page, eds., *Dictionary of Jamaican English*, p. 483; Leland Ferguson, "Looking for the 'Afro' in Colono-Indian Pottery," in Robert L. Schuyler, ed., *Archaeological Perspectives on Ethnicity in America* (Farmingdale, N.Y., 1980), pp. 14–28, and *Uncommon Ground: Archaeology and Early African America, 1650–1800* (Washington, D.C., 1991). Archaeological investigations of slave sites reveal much evidence of slave hunting and fishing.

61. The literature is vast, but see, for example, Schlotterbeck, "Internal Economy of Slavery," in Berlin and Morgan, eds., *The Slaves' Economy*, pp. 170–81; Campbell, "As 'A Kind of Freeman'"; and McDonald, "Independent Economic Production by Slaves on Antebellum Louisiana Sugar Plantations."

62. Patterson, *Sociology of Slavery*, pp. 225–26; Sidney W. Mintz, "Was the Plantation Slave a Proletarian?" *Review* 2 (1978): 95; George Pinckard, *Notes on the West Indies*, 3 vols. (London, 1806), 1:369–70; John Luffman, *A Brief Account of the Island of Antigua* (London, 1788), pp. 94–95; Higman, *Slave Populations of the British Caribbean*, p. 208. See also Sidney W. Mintz, "Caribbean Marketplaces and Caribbean History," *Nova Americana* 1 (1980–81): 333–44; Daniel McKinnen, *A Tour through the British West Indies, in the Years 1802 and 1803: Giving a Particular Account of the Bahama Islands* (London, 1804), pp. 68–69; Neville Hall, "Slaves' Use of Their 'Free' Time in the Danish Virgin Islands in the Later Eighteenth and Early Nineteenth Century," *Journal of Caribbean History* 13 (1979): 28–29; Beckles, "An Economic Life of Their Own," in Berlin and Morgan, eds., *The Slaves' Economy*, pp. 31–47; Dale Tomich, "*Une Petite Guinée*," and Gaspar, "Slave Life and Sugar Production."

63. Walsh, "Slave Life, Slave Society, and Tobacco Production," p. 192 in this volume. See also Betty Wood, " 'White Society' and the Informal' Slave Economics of Lowcountry Georgia, 1763–1830," *Slavery and Abolition* 11 (1990): 313–31.

64. See Campbell, "As 'A Kind of Freeman'"; McDonald, "Independent Economic Production by Slaves on Antebellum Louisiana Sugar Plantations"; Trouillot, "Coffee Planters and Coffee Slaves," all in this volume; and Schlotterbeck, "Internal Economy of Slavery," in Berlin and Morgan, eds., *The Slaves' Economy*, pp. 170–81. For marketing in one mainland town, see Philip D. Morgan, "Black Life in Eighteenth-Century Charleston," *Perspectives in American History*, new ser., 1 (1984): 187–232, especially pp. 191, 194–97, 202–3.

65. Young, *A Tour through the Several Islands* in Edwards, *History of the British Colonies*, 4:271; Charles Leslie, *A New and Exact History of Jamaica* (Edinburgh, 1739), p. 306; McDonald, "Independent Economic Production by Slaves on Antebellum Louisiana Sugar Plantations"; and Reidy, "Obligation and Right in the Cotton South."

66. Goveia, *Slave Society in the British Leeward Islands,* p. 239.

67. Overwork was especially prevalent in various industrial work. See Robert S. Starobin, *Industrial Slavery in the Old South* (New York, 1970); Charles B. Dew, "Disciplining Slave Ironworkers in the Antebellum American South: Coercion, Conciliation, and Accommodation," *American Historical Review* 79 (1974): 393–418; Campbell, "As 'A Kind of Freeman' "; and McDonald, "Independent Economic Production by Slaves on Antebellum Louisiana Sugar Plantations."

68. Long, *History of Jamaica,* 2:410; Campbell, "As 'A Kind of Freeman' "; and Marshall, "Provision Ground and Plantation Labor in Four Windward Islands." See, however, Orlando Patterson's critique of Long, *Sociology of Slavery,* p. 229. For other examples of spectacular savings, see Sidney W. Mintz, "Currency Problems in Eighteenth-Century Jamaica and Gresham's Law" in Robert A. Manners, ed., *Process and Pattern in Culture* (Chicago, 1964), p. 253.

69. Long, *History of Jamaica,* 2:562; Campbell is quoted in Marshall, "Provision Ground and Plantation Labor in Four Windward Islands," p. 214 in this volume; see also Alice R. Huger Smith, *A Carolina Rice Plantation of the Fifties* (New York, 1936), p. 72.

70. William Beckford, *A Descriptive Account of the Island of Jamaica,* 2 vols. (London, 1790), 2:155; Morgan, "The Ownership of Property," p. 403. And see J. Stewart, *A View of the Past and Present State of the Island of Jamaica* (Edinburgh, 1823), p. 267; Jerome S. Handler and Frederick W. Lange, *Plantation Slavery in Barbados: An Archaeological and Historical Investigation* (Cambridge, Mass., 1978), pp. 173–74; Cassidy and LePage, eds., *Dictionary of Jamaican English,* p. 123; Long, *History of Jamaica,* 2:413; Marshall, "Provision Ground and Plantation Labor in Four Windward Islands"; McDonald, "Independent Economic Production by Slaves on Antebellum Louisiana Sugar Plantations"; Reidy, "Obligation and Right."

71. See, for example, "Petition of Colored Men of Mobile, Ala., to the Congress of the United States of America," January 1866, Unregistered Letters Received, ser. 9, Alabama Assistant Commissioner, RG 105, National Archives, Freedmen and Southern Society Project file number A-1735.

72. Tomich, *"Une Petite Guinée,"* p. 234 in this volume; Long, *History of Jamaica,* 2:410–11; Edwards, *History of the British Colonies,* 2:133; Bennett, *Bondsmen and Bishops,* p. 105; Morgan, "Work and Culture," p. 535.

73. B. W. Higman, *Jamaica Surveyed: Plantation Maps and Plans of the Eighteenth and Nineteenth Centuries* (Kingston, 1988), pp. 261–76, 291; Barham is quoted in Cassidy, *Jamaica Talk,* p. 345; Cassidy and LePage, eds., *Dictionary of Jamaican English,* pp. 139, 462; the Intendant of Saint Domingue is quoted in Tomich, *"Une Petite Guinée,"* p. 222 in this volume.

74. Ward, *British West Indian Slavery,* pp. 18, 110–11; and see Higman, *Slave Populations of the British Caribbean,* pp. 207 and 237–42, for relations between urban sellers and plantation slaves. For an excellent example of the individual differentiation in provision ground allotments, see Higman, *Jamaica Surveyed,*

pp. 269–73; and Marshall, "Provision Ground and Plantation Labor in Four Windward Islands."

75. Campbell, "As 'A Kind of Freeman' "; Tomich, "*Une Petite Guinée.*"

76. For the best data on the distances between estate and mountain grounds, see Higman, *Jamaica Surveyed*, p. 266. For other useful information on the drawbacks of the provision ground system, see Kenneth F. Kiple, *The Caribbean Slave: A Biological History* (New York, 1984), pp. 69–76; and Sheridan, *Doctors and Slaves*, pp. 164–69.

77. Higman, *Slave Population and Economy*, p. 129, and *Slave Populations of the British Caribbean*, p. 307; Ward, *British West Indian Slavery*, p. 254; Sheridan, *Doctors and Slaves*, pp. 174–77; the account of the differences between Virginia and South Carolina is drawn from Philip Morgan's research. For slave heights, see Fogel, *Without Consent or Contract*, pp. 138–41; Barry Higman, "Growth in Afro-Caribbean Slave Population," *American Journal of Physical Anthropology* 50 (1979): 373–85; and Gerald Friedman, "The Heights of Slaves in Trinidad," *Social Science History* 6 (1982): 482–515.

78. Higman, *Slave Populations of the British Caribbean*, p. 188.

79. Edwards, *History of the British Colonies*, 2:131; Pinckard, *Notes on the West Indies*, 1:368; the Grenadan is quoted in Marshall, "Provision Ground and Plantation Labor in Four Windward Islands," p. 205 in this volume; Rufus King, Jr. to William Washington, 13 September 1828, *American Farmer* 10 (1828): 346; William Read to Jacob Read, 22 March 1800, Read Family Papers, South Carolina Historical Society, Charleston. See also Manuela Carnerio da Cunha, " 'On the Amelioration of Slavery' by Henry Koster," *Slavery and Abolition* 11 (1990): 368–98, especially pp. 389–90.

80. Edwards, *History*, 2:161; Mintz, "Caribbean Marketplaces and Caribbean History," p. 336.

81. Campbell, "As 'A Kind of Freeman.' "

82. Dale Tomich, "*Une Petite Guinée*"; Turner, "Slave Workers, Subsistence, and Labour Bargaining," in Berlin and Morgan, eds., *The Slaves' Economy*, pp. 92–106.

83. Marshall, "Provision Ground and Plantation Labor in Four Windward Islands," p. 216 in this volume; and see Campbell, "As 'A Kind of Freeman.' "

84. Beckles, "An Economic Life of Their Own," in Berlin and Morgan, eds., *The Slaves' Economy*, pp. 31–47.

85. Stuart B. Schwartz, "Resistance and Accommodation in Eighteenth-Century Brazil: The Slaves' View of Slavery," *Hispanic American Historical Review* 57 (1977): 69–81; especially pp. 77–79.

Chapter 1

1. William Clark, *Ten Views in the Island of Antigua, in which are represented the process of sugar making, and the employment of the negroes.* . . . (London, 1823).

Eight of Clark's plates are reproduced as illustrations in Michael Craton, *Searching for the Invisible Man: Slaves and Plantation Life in Jamaica* (Cambridge, Mass., 1978), and four in Richard B. Sheridan, *Sugar and Slavery: An Economic History of the British West Indies, 1623–1775* (Baltimore, 1973).

2. B. W. Higman, *Slave Populations of the British Caribbean, 1807–1834* (Baltimore, 1984), pp. 69–71, 116–17, 418; Higman, *Slave Population and Economy in Jamaica, 1807–1834* (Cambridge, 1976), p. 72; and see the references in n. 15.

3. See also my "A Tale of Two Plantations: Slave Life at Mesopotamia in Jamaica and Mount Airy in Virginia, 1799 to 1828," *William and Mary Quarterly,* 3d ser., 34 (1977): 32–65; and especially " 'Dreadful Idlers' in the Cane Fields: The Slave Labor Pattern on a Jamaican Sugar Estate, 1762–1831," *Journal of Interdisciplinary History* 17 (1987): 795–822.

4. David W. Galenson, *Traders, Planters, and Slaves: Market Behavior in Early English America* (New York, 1986), p. 95. Of course, this sex ratio also reflected market conditions in West Africa, where women and children captured in tribal wars and raids were considered to be more suitable for local enslavement than adult male captives. But I question Herbert S. Klein's argument that European slavers were forced to settle for men because their African suppliers outbid them for women; see Klein, "African Women in the Atlantic Slave Trade," in Claire C. Robertson and Martin A. Klein, eds., *Women and Slavery in Africa* (Madison, Wisc., 1983), p. 36. The key point, I think, is that the European slavers wanted men more than women, and adults more than children.

5. Richard B. Sheridan, *Doctors and Slaves: A Medical and Demographic History of Slavery in the British West Indies, 1680–1834* (Cambridge, 1985), p. 107.

6. Herbert S. Klein, *The Middle Passage: Comparative Studies of the Atlantic Slave Trade* (Princeton, 1978), pp. 148–50.

7. David Geggus, analyzing a large sample of 177,000 slaves transported in French ships to the Caribbean between 1714 and 1792, finds an even higher sex ratio of 179; see his "Sex Ratio, Age, and Ethnicity in the Atlantic Slave Trade: Data from French Shipping and Plantation Records," *Journal of African History* 30 (1989): 25.

8. This admittedly small sample, consisting of 609 working men and boys and 579 working women and girls, is drawn from the personal property inventories, vols. 1–3 and 5, in the Jamaica Archives. For further evidence of a balanced sex ratio in the late seventeenth century, see Richard S. Dunn, *Sugar and Slaves: The Rise of the Planter Class in the English West Indies, 1624–1713* (Chapel Hill, 1972), pp. 315–17.

9. Richard B. Sheridan has sampled the eighteenth-century inventories in the Jamaica Archives but for the purpose of investigating planter wealth rather than slave life. See his "The Wealth of Jamaica in the Eighteenth Century," *Economic History Review,* 2d ser., 18 (1965): 292–311. The Jamaican censuses of 1661, 1673, 1680, 1730, and 1774 reveal very little about the composition of the slave population; see Robert V. Wells, *The Population of the British Colonies in America before 1776* (Princeton, 1975), pp. 194–202.

10. Additional MSS 12,435/33, British Library.

11. Higman, *Slave Population and Economy in Jamaica*, p. 72.

12. Ibid., pp. 16, 53, 61–62, 106–7, 116, 123, 256, 259. Both deathrates and birthrates were understated by an unknown but equal percentage in the Jamaican slave registration returns because the infants who died within a few days of birth were generally not reported at all.

13. Two nondemographic factors contributed to this decline: 5,373 slaves were manumitted in Jamaica between 1817 and 1832, and about 2,000 slaves escaped from their owners during this period. See Higman, *Slave Populations of the British Caribbean*, p. 690, and *Slave Population and Economy in Jamaica*, pp. 178–80.

14. Higman, *Slave Population and Economy in Jamaica*, pp. 14, 71–73.

15. Here I have compared the Westmoreland slave registration returns for 1817 (T 71/178, PRO) with the returns for 1834 (T 71/723).

16. The eighty-six Mesopotamia inventories are found in five boxes of the Barham Papers (hereafter identified as Barham): B34–38, Clarendon Manuscript Deposit, Bodleian Library, Oxford. They are dated 1736, 1743–44, 1751–52, and 1754–1831. Dual inventories were taken in 1756, 1762, and 1802. I wish to thank the Earl of Clarendon for permitting me to use these Mesopotamia records.

17. As with the islandwide Jamaican slave registration returns for 1817 to 1832 (see note 12), the birth and death figures at Mesopotamia are manifestly understated because the bookkeepers generally failed to report infants who died immediately after birth. In addition, no vital records at Mesopotamia have survived for 1737 to 1743 or 1745 to 1750.

18. See Gerald W. Mullin, *Flight and Rebellion: Slave Resistance in Eighteenth-Century Virginia* (New York, 1972), pp. 41–42. Unfortunately, African tribal scars were neither reported in the Mesopotamia inventories nor in the Jamaican slave registers. But they were carefully noted, along with the tribal identification of each African-born slave, in the Trinidad slave register for 1813. This Trinidad register indicates that practically every African-born female above the age of twelve—that is, every female who had passed through her tribal pubertal initiation rites before being shipped to America—bore country marks. See T 71/501, PRO.

19. The age statements for the older slaves were rounded and probably inflated, but not by much; forty of the fifty-seven slaves listed in their forties as of 1762 can be traced back nineteen years and were described as adults on the 1743 inventory, while twenty-two can be traced back twenty-six years and were described as adults on the 1736 inventory.

20. Daniel Barnyum to Joseph Foster Barham I, 22 April 1765, Barham C357.

21. This is not a randomly drawn sample. Most of these inventories I examined during the course of archival research in Britain and Jamaica, when I was looking for any evidence I could find about sex ratios. The portrayal here

would be greatly bolstered by inspection of the many hundred eighteenth-century inventories in the Jamaica Archives, which I have not examined, and the islandwide Jamaica slave registration returns for 1817 to 1834, which I have examined for Westmoreland parish only. Barry W. Higman has published two books analyzing these returns; see note 2.

22. Joseph Foster Barham II to Duncan Robertson and William Ridgard, 2 September 1829, Barham C428.

23. Between them, Beany and Dido had three living children as of December 1831. Beany bore two daughters in 1820 and 1823 (the second died in 1829), followed by three stillbirths between 1824 and 1826, and then a son in 1830. Dido bore a daughter in 1823, followed by stillborn twins in 1825 and another daughter in 1830, who died in infancy.

24. See Peter H. Wood, *Black Majority: Negroes in Colonial South Carolina* (New York, 1974), ch. 9; Allan Kulikoff, *Tobacco and Slaves: The Development of Southern Cultures in the Chesapeake, 1680–1800* (Chapel Hill, 1986), ch. 8.

25. This assumes that all of the thirty girls and one-third of the ninety-four women listed on the first inventory of 1736 were born on the estate; over the next ninety-five years the births of 261 girls were registered.

26. Katey was identified as Jamaica-born in the Westmoreland slave register of 1817; she died in 1821. Debby's maternal grandfather Handsome was a fifty-four-year-old invalid in 1792, and her grandmother Maria was a washerwoman of fifty-three.

27. The estimated ages of the older slaves transferred to Mesopotamia must be treated with suspicion, especially since many of them are clearly assigned approximate ages, grouped at five-year intervals (35, 40, 45, etc.). Nevertheless, any slave stated to be age forty—whether or not this figure is accurate—is a slave considered past her prime.

28. Sophia's two older sisters also bore mulatto children. Nancy had four children, two of whom were mulatto, and Bessy seven, the first of whom was mulatto.

29. Like many of the other Mesopotamia slaves, Sophia adopted a new baptismal name in the 1820s: Catherine Carr.

30. Altogether, perhaps 35 percent of the females who lived at Mesopotamia between 1736 and 1831 were born in Africa. This assumes that two-thirds of the ninety-four women listed in the first inventory of 1736 were Africans, and that half of the women purchased from other Jamaican estates during the eighteenth century were also Africans. Among the females purchased from other estates who were alive in 1817, the Jamaican slave register identifies forty-seven as born in Africa and seventy in Jamaica.

31. John Graham to Barham, 18 March 1792, Barham C357. Nine of these children were stated to be age eleven, nine were age thirteen, one was fourteen, one was fifteen. I suspect that these age estimates were based on the presence or absence of tribal scars or country marks. The children stated to be thirteen or older had probably passed through their adolescent initiation rites, whereas the eleven-year-olds had not.

32. Survey of the Mesopotamia work force, June 1802, Barham B36.

33. For descriptions of gang labor on a Jamaican sugar estate, see Orlando Patterson, *Sociology of Slavery: An Analysis of the Origins, Development, and Structure of Negro Slave Society in Jamaica* (Cranbury, N.J., 1969; orig. pub. London, 1967), ch. 2; Michael Craton and James Walvin, *A Jamaican Plantation* (Toronto, 1970), chs. 5 and 6; Craton, *Searching for the Invisible Man*, ch. 5; Higman, *Slave Population and Economy in Jamaica*, ch. 9.

34. Though the slaves aged 20 to 29 were in better health, those aged 25 to 34 fetched higher sales prices because of their combination of experience with relative youth. See Higman, *Slave Population and Economy in Jamaica*, pp. 190–95, 202–5.

35. For details, see Dunn, " 'Dreadful Idlers' in the Cane Fields," 795–822.

36. Ibid., pp. 809–10. These figures exclude the two mulatto women at Mesopotamia employed as domestics, because as a group the Mesopotamia mulattoes were strikingly unhealthy, died young, and had very short working careers. For example, one of the mulatto domestics, a girl named Mary, worked for only three years, was an invalid for two years, and died at age twenty-one.

37. The mothers of newborns were first systematically recorded on the 1774 inventory. All of the 136 women in this cohort have been traced annually from age twenty through age forty (if they lived so long), and most from age fifteen through age forty-five.

38. See Higman, *Slave Population and Economy in Jamaica*, pp. 116–17, 154, and *Slave Populations of the British Caribbean*, p. 358.

39. See in particular Herbert S. Klein and Stanley L. Engerman, "Fertility Differentials between Slaves in the United States and the West Indies," *William and Mary Quarterly*, 3d ser., 35 (1978): 357–73.

40. See Dunn, "A Tale of Two Plantations," pp. 60–61.

41. The Trinidad returns for 1813 (T 71/501–502, PRO) are particularly illuminating about African marriage patterns. See also B. W. Higman, "African and Creole Slave Family Patterns in Trinidad," *Journal of Family History* 3 (1978): 163–80.

42. Here I have examined the lists of slaves purchased for Mesopotamia from Three Mile River (1786), Southfield (1791), and Cairncurran (1814) estates, in Barham B33, 34, 36. See also B. W. Higman, "The Slave Family and Household in the British West Indies, 1800–1834," *Journal of Interdisciplinary History* 6 (1975): 261–87, and *Slave Population and Economy in Jamaica*, pp. 156–75; Michael Craton, "Changing Patterns of Slave Families in the British West Indies," *Journal of Interdisciplinary History* 10 (1979): 1–35.

43. Demographers tend to focus so heavily on infertility among the African women that they underestimate the general reproductive problem. See, for example, Jack Ericson Eblen, "On the Natural Increase of Slave Populations: The Example of the Cuban Black Population, 1775–1900," in Stanley L. Engerman and Eugene D. Genovese, eds., *Race and Slavery in the Western Hemisphere: Quantitative Studies* (Princeton, 1975), pp. 211–47.

44. See Kenneth F. Kiple, *The Caribbean Slave: A Biological History* (Cambridge, 1984), chs. 5–7.

45. See the data compiled by Higman in *Slave Populations of the British Caribbean*, pp. 281–82, 536–41; also Kiple, *The Caribbean Slave*, pp. 107–10.

46. Harriet died at thirty-eight, Jenny at twenty-nine, and Olive was thirty-six years old in December 1831.

47. Higman, *Slave Populations of the British Caribbean*, p. 188.

48. Matura was the first Mesopotamia field slave to be given this special treatment; in 1808 she was excused from the first gang upon the birth of her sixth child. In 1817 the threshold for retirement at Mesopotamia was reduced to five children, and in 1831 to four. Altogether, between 1808 and 1831 eleven women at Mesopotamia managed to escape from heavy physical labor on the grounds of motherhood.

49. Exact birth dates were reported at Mesopotamia between 1762 and 1831, death dates between 1751 and 1831. I have defined "infants" as children under the age of two. By way of comparison, see Higman's tabulation of the seasonality of slave births in Tobago, Berbice, and Dominica in *Slave Populations of the British Caribbean*, pp. 362–64, 686. He has no equivalent seasonal record of infant deaths.

50. Among adults at Mesopotamia, the peak death period was from August to October.

51. Journal of Thomas Thistlewood, 3 August 1765, Monson Manuscript Deposit, 31/16, Lincolnshire Archives, Lincoln. Thistlewood kept his diary in thirty-seven volumes, dating from 1750 to 1786.

52. Of Batty's six children, two were dead by 1830 and three had been freed from slavery. She left only one child on the estate, her sixteen-year-old daughter Hannah. This girl—being black rather than mulatto—was destined to be a field hand rather than a domestic. In 1831 she was promoted from the second gang to the first gang at the tender age of seventeen, even though she was afflicted with the yaws.

53. Robertson and Klein, eds., *Women and Slavery in Africa*, pp. 3–19, 49–65, 67–89, 95–109, 185–200.

54. I have reconstructed the careers of 450 female and 526 male slaves at Mount Airy plantation in Virginia between 1808 and 1865, in parallel fashion to my reconstruction of the Mesopotamia slave force. In this slave community I discovered only one woman who bore mulatto children; she had six children by two white, married overseers, which greatly distressed the plantation owner. William Henry Tayloe memorandum, 1868, Tayloe Papers D2123-35, Virginia Historical Society.

Chapter 2

1. The colonial censuses shed no light on this question. In addition to their questionable accuracy, they offer only summary statistics by parish, and most

of Saint Domingue's parishes included areas of plain and mountain. The main sources employed here are plantation inventories gleaned from more than twenty public and private archives. Supplemented by briefer descriptions of plantations found in contemporary and modern printed works, they provide basic information on more than four hundred plantations worked by about forty thousand slaves. The same types of information are not available for all cases, and not all records have been analyzed to the same degree. The sample spans the years from 1745 to 1797, but data are scant for the period before 1770. The slave lists of half of these plantations date from 1796 and 1797, the middle of the Haitian Revolution. Deriving from the British-occupied zone of Saint Domingue, where the slave regime was maintained with only partial success, they constitute something of a special case. They are used here only to provide corroborative evidence, as they have been analyzed in a previous article; see David Geggus, "The Slaves of British-Occupied Saint Domingue: An Analysis of the Workforces of 197 Absentee Plantations, 1796–97," *Caribbean Studies* 18 (1978): 5–41. Several corrections and additions have been made to material in this article, which derives from Domaines, Saint-Domingue, Administration Anglaise, 15 vols., Archives Nationales, Section d'Outre-Mer, Aix-en-Provence (hereafter ANOM), and T 64/228, Public Record Office, London.

2. Compare Ralph Korngold, *Citizen Toussaint* (New York, 1945), p. 51; Thomas Ott, *The Haitian Revolution* (Knoxville, 1973), p. 9; MS. 3453, 66, Bibliothèque Mazarine, Paris; MS. 1809, 44, 187, Bibliothèque Municipale, Nantes; "Liste des habitations incendiées," 107 AP 129, dossier 1, Archives Nationales, Paris (hereafter AN); Drouin de Bercy, *De Saint-Domingue* (Paris, 1814), 78; Torcuato S. di Tella, *La rebelión de esclavos de Haití* (Buenos Aires, 1984), 34; and 18 AP 3 (Bréda), AN; 107 AP 127-130 (Galliffet), AN; MS. 11/66 (Pébarte), South Carolina Historical Society, Charleston. The latter collection and the Chatard Papers (property of Dr. Ferdinand Chatard, Baltimore) reveal an interesting tendency among planters' descendants inadvertently to exaggerate their forbears' slaveholdings when annotating the family papers.

3. Jean Barré de Saint-Venant, *Des colonies modernes sous la zone torride et particulièrement de celle de St.-Domingue* (Paris, 1802), p. 447.

4. Saint Domingue did contain a number of estates, not used in this study, that reputedly housed four hundred or more slaves, such as Duplaa and D'Hericourt in the North Province, Damiens and Santo Domingo near Port au Prince, and the three Laborde estates near Les Cayes. Even so, one would have to add more than ten such giant estates to the list used here to raise the mean slaveholding to two hundred. The sample, in any case, probably over-represents the largest plantations, since their papers were more likely to survive in the collections of absentee owners in France. Sale advertisements in the colonial newspaper may overrepresent the very smallest plantations, those most likely to change hands. More research in notarial records seems the best way to further knowledge in this area.

5. $p = .0003$. All correlation coefficients cited are Spearman's.

6. Ratoons were second-growth canes allowed to germinate from the roots

of harvested canes. They obviated the backbreaking work of replanting but produced lower yields of sugar. Successful ratooning required fertile, well-watered, soil. Avalle, *Tableau comparatif des productions des colonies françaises aux Antilles* (Paris, 1799), pp. 1–5, similarly shows a 2:1 ratio on a model plantation of 100 carreaux (113 hectares), two-thirds planted in cane, with two hundred slaves. An identical model is presented in Drouin de Bercy, *Saint-Domingue*, appendix.

7. However, at the plantation level there was no observable relation between the slave to cane ratio and the extent of ratooning.

8. The figures presented in Robert Stein, *The French Sugar Business* (Baton Rouge, 1988), p. 67, show a much greater output per estate in the West than the North, but these contain an arithmetical error and make no allowance for converting muscovado to semirefined sugar. Cf. David Geggus, "The Major Port Towns of Saint Domingue in the Later Eighteenth Century," in Franklin Knight and Peggy Liss, eds., *Atlantic Port Cities: Economy, Society, and Culture* (Knoxville, 1991).

9. One slave over ten years of age per 1,000 trees was recommended in a "Mémoire sur la nature des terres" written in 1789: C9B/40, Colonies, AN.

10. Work-force size correlated highly with the slave to cane ratio ($p = .0002$; $r = .49$; $N = 53$) and less strongly but significantly with the ratio of slaves to coffee trees ($p = .0479$; $r = .25$; $N = 61$).

11. These figures derive from thirty-six sugar and fifty coffee plantations in the North Province.

12. However, at the plantation level, the mean sex ratios of the sugar and coffee samples were higher and more divergent—120 and 144. The contrast between the two plantation types may thus have been somewhat greater than appears in table 2.7. On the slave trade, see David Geggus, "The Demographic Composition of the French Caribbean Slave Trade," in Philip Boucher, ed., *Proceedings of the Thirteenth and Fourteenth Meetings of the French Colonial Historical Society* (Lanham, Md., 1990), tables 1 and 2.

13. G1/509, ANOM.

14. *Two Reports of the Committee of the Assembly of Jamaica on the Slave Trade* (London, 1789), p. 9, shows a sex ratio of 127 in 1789.

15. David Geggus, "Sex Ratio, Age, and Ethnicity in the Atlantic Slave Trade," *Journal of African History* 30 (1989): 24; Geggus, "Demographic Composition," table 1.

16. African males per 100 females numbered 133 (all provinces, 1721–97, $N = 13,334$); 139 (North sugar estates, 1780s, $N = 2,143$); 146 (North coffee plantations, 1780s, $N = 973$); 160 (West sugar estates, 1780s, $N = 1,042$). For the sex ratios of newly imported Africans, see Geggus, "Demographic Composition," table 1.

17. The loss of young males during the Revolution presumably accounts for the reduced presence of Congos in the 1796–97 columns in table 2.8.

18. Geggus, "Slaves of British-Occupied Saint-Domingue," 19–23; Geg-

gus, "Composition," table 2. Cf. David Geggus, "On the Eve of the Haitian Revolution: Slave Runaways in Saint Domingue in the Year 1790," in Gad Heuman, ed., *Out of the House of Bondage* (London, 1986), p. 19. It might be supposed that this sugar/coffee distinction should be attributed to the changing ethnic composition of slave imports through time, the coffee sector simply reflecting the most recent trends. However, although the trend was toward increasing purchases of Central Africans, these were most numerous in the North where work forces were oldest. Furthermore, ethnic groups such as the Hausa, Nupe, and Bariba that were sucked into the slave trade relatively late nonetheless show up primarily on sugar estates.

19. Gabriel Debien, *Plantations et esclaves à Saint-Domingue* (Dakar, 1964), 47.

20. For documentation regarding ethnic stereotypes, see Gabriel Debien, *Les esclaves aux Antilles françaises* (Basse Terre, 1974), 41–52; and Geggus, "Sex Ratio," nn. 56, 68.

21. Charles Malenfant, *Des colonies et particulièrement de celle de Saint-Domingue* (Paris, 1814), 210. However, the heights Malenfant gave (5'9" to 6'2") were much greater than table 2.9 shows for these groups.

22. Jan Vansina, *Ethnologie du Congo* (Kinshasa, n.d.), 14; Suzanne Miers and Igor Kopytoff, eds., *Slavery in Africa: Historical and Anthropological Perspectives* (Madison, Wisc., 1977), p. 238.

23. Médéric-Louis-Elie Moreau de Saint-Méry, *Description topographique, physique, civile, politique, et historique de la partie française de l'isle Saint-Domingue,* Etienne Taillemite and Blanche Maurel, eds., 3 vols. (Paris, 1958; orig. pub. 1797–98), 1: 51; Malenfant, *Des colonies,* p. 211.

24. Note that "Mundingoes" in Jamaica were several inches shorter than in Saint Domingue and Trinidad, though Igbos and Congos had approximately the same average height in all three places. See Orlando Patterson, *Sociology of Slavery* (2d ed., Rutherford, N.J., 1970; orig. pub. London, 1967), p. 138; Gerald C. Friedman, "Heights of Slaves in Trinidad," *Social Science History* 6 (1982): 487; and table 2.9, above. Jamaican planters disliked them but noted they consisted of "very distinct tribes," one of which was tall; see Bryan Edwards, *History, Civil and Commercial, of the British West Indies,* 2 vols. (London, 1793), 2:58–62. Cf. Geggus, "Slaves," 19, n. 35. In South Carolina Mundingoes were sought after and said to be tall; see Daniel C. Littlefield, *Rice and Slaves: Ethnicity and the Slave Trade in Colonial South Carolina* (Baton Rouge, 1981), pp. 10, 20.

25. The terms "Mesurade" and "Canga" were used in the North, and West and South Provinces, respectively, to designate an ethnic group from the region of modern Monrovia and its hinterland, possibly Bassa or Kpelle.

26. Cf. Moreau de Saint-Méry, *Description topographique,* 1:54; Jorge Dias, *Os Macondes de Moçambique,* 4 vols. (Lisbon, 1964), 1:44.

27. Numerous sources from different American societies attest to this carnivorous reputation. The Mondonga were a small tribe from the equatorial

forest, where cannibalism apparently was common. However, the name prob-
ably was applied to all Bantu with filed teeth and facial markings. Sold chiefly
in the port of Cabinda, they may have included many Teke (Bōōo), since the
latter were prominent in the regional slave trade but were never mentioned in
Saint Domingue, even though the two terms were distinguished in Louis
Degrandpré, *Voyage à la côte occidentale d'Afrique*, 2 vols. (Paris, 1801), 1:viii.
Moreau de Saint-Méry thought the Mondongues were neighbors of the
"Moussombe" (Nsundi) (*Description topographique*, 1:52–53). Others have
placed them south of Malebo Pool, as, for example, Gonzalo Aguirre Beltrán,
"Tribal Origins of African Slaves in Mexico," *Journal of Negro History* 31 (1946):
336. According to the missionary Oldendorp, "Mandongo" lived beyond the
Uoango (Kwango?) river, were widely disseminated, and consisted of three
tribes, the Bongolo (Imbangala?), Cando, and Colambo. See C. G. A. Oldendorp's *History of the Mission of the Evangelical Brethren on the Caribbean Islands of St.
Thomas, St. Croix, and St. John*, Johann Jakob Bossard, ed., Arnold Highfield
and Vladimir Barac, trans. (Ann Arbor, 1987), pp. 168, 177–78, 499.

28. MS 1809, 22–23, Bibliothèque Municipale, Nantes; Moreau de Saint-
Méry, *Description topographique*, 1:48; Gabriel Debien, "Les origines des esclaves aux Antilles," *Bulletin de l'Institut Français d'Afrique Noire*, ser. B (hereafter *BIFAN*) 23 (1961): 376; Malenfant, *Des colonies*, pp. 210–11.

29. To judge from the cases of forty-two Northern sugar estates, this was
true in both the 1770s and 1780s.

30. These figures come from fifty Northern coffee plantations, 1780–1791.

31. See Geggus, "Slaves of British-Occupied Saint Domingue," 31–34;
Michael Robinson, "Population Structure on Eight Saint Domingue Sugar
Plantations in the 1770s," unpublished paper, History Department, University
of Florida, 1988.

32. Or perhaps the Fulbe did not adapt well to field labor in a region of
heavy rainfall and so preferred to work indoors.

33. Geggus, "Slaves of British-Occupied Saint Domingue," 32. Were they
urban craftsmen, perhaps, accustomed to the heat of a furnace but not to
handling a hoe? The Yoruba were an unusually urbanized people, and data
from Brazil and Guadeloupe suggest that in the Americas they were differen-
tially selected for urban occupations. See the figures in Stuart B. Schwartz,
Sugar Plantations and the Formation of Brazilian Society (Cambridge, 1985), p. 475;
Nicole Vanony-Frisch, "Les esclaves à la Guadeloupe à la fin de l'Ancien
Régime," *Bulletin de la Société d'Histoire de la Guadeloupe* 63–64 (1985): 81.

34. MS 1809, 22–23, Bibliothèque Municipale, Nantes; Hilliard d'Auberteuil, *Considérations sur l'état présent de Saint Domingue*, 2 vols. (Paris, 1776–77),
2:60; Moreau de Saint-Méry, *Description topographique*, 1:48, 53; S. Ducoeurjoly,
Manuel des habitants de Saint Domingue, 2 vols. (Paris, 1802), 1:23–24.

35. However, indirect evidence from parish registers suggests that Sénégal females may have been disproportionately selected for urban employment. See Debien, "Origines des esclaves," *BIFAN* 29 (1967): 553.

36. To the three African fishermen found in the plantation lists, I added thirty-eight others, including one caulker, who belonged to an urban fishing enterprise described in Debien, "Origines," *BIFAN* 25 (1963): 240–41.

37. The percentage of men in the following groups on sugar estates who worked with livestock was as follows: all African men 7 percent, Fulbe 22 percent, Susu 19 percent, Nupe 15 percent, Sénégal 13 percent, Chamba 9 percent, Bambara 5 percent. The Bambara, although possessing horses in Africa, relied solely on Fulbe for herding and animal products (personal communication from Dr. K. Greene).

38. This is excluding slaves aged 60 and above described as *infirme*.

39. Inventories for twenty-one plantations show 11.3 percent of the slaves incapacitated, but inventories for twenty-three others show none at all. Such a stark contrast probably reflects differences in record keeping rather than in the work forces.

40. This is suggested by the cases of forty-four coffee and thirty-four sugar North Province plantations, 1778–91. However, the 1796–97 data produced a different result.

41. Weighting the data in table 2.9 according to the main groups' predominance in the African-born population reveals that the mean African height was about two centimeters below that of the mean creole height.

42. In most respects, these findings are supported by data from both the pre-Revolutionary and 1790s samples.

43. *Affiches Américaines,* Supplément, Feuille du Cap, 30 October and 3 November 1789.

44. Records for the five Galliffet plantations (sugar and coffee), which seem more reliable than most, suggest that 36 percent of newborns died before the age of two years. Average annual birthrates and deathrates were respectively 20 and 43 per thousand during the years between 1783 and 1791. The former was considered low, the latter high. See David Geggus, "Les esclaves de la plaine du Nord à la veille de la Révolution," part 3, *Revue de la Société Haïtienne d'Histoire,* 144 (1984): 32–38. Additional data are presented in Debien, *Les esclaves,* 339–68; and Geggus, "Les esclaves de la plaine du Nord à la veille de la Révolution," part 4, *Revue de la Société Haïtienne d'Histoire,* 149 (1985): 16–52.

45. Some caution is necessary here, as the strongest contrast results from the mid-1790s data, which may not have been typical. They derive from two quite limited areas where, although the plantations were kept in production, the slave regime may have been modified. Plantations that had suffered losses or damage were excluded from the sample. Research regarding other Caribbean colonies has produced mixed results on this question. See Barry Higman, *Slave Population and Economy in Jamaica, 1807–1834* (Cambridge, 1976), p. 123, and *Slave Populations of the British Caribbean, 1807–1834* (Baltimore, 1984), p. 361; Humphrey Lamur, "Fertility Differentials on Three Slave Plantations in Suriname," *Slavery and Abolition* 8 (1987): 313–35.

46. The best measure of work load on a sugar estate was assumed to be the ratio of the number of slaves to the area planted in canes. For the mountain plantations the ratio of slaves to coffee trees was chosen. Of course, neither is an ideal measure of the work performed by nubile females. Variations in soil fertility preclude the use of production statistics.

47. $p = .09$, $r = .29$, $N = 33$.

48. $p = .11$.

49. For the few plantations, most of them sugar estates, where the Africans' date of arrival was known, fertility indexes were adjusted upward accordingly.

50. Data were obtained by subtracting children's ages from those of their mothers who could be identified. To minimize the distortion associated with inaccurately reported ages only children under ten years were counted. Siblings of the same age were assumed to be twins and counted as one birth. Data were drawn from more than thirty sugar estates and seventeen coffee plantations. Further data can be found in Geggus, "Les esclaves de la plaine du Nord," part 3, p. 37.

51. Moreau de Saint-Méry, *Description topographique*, 1:60.

52. The mothers of slaves of mixed racial descent were almost always creoles. Moreau de Saint-Méry also noted that African women had a strong preference for black men, although under duress they did have relations with whites (*Description topographique*, 1:57–58).

53. Cf. David Geggus, "Slave and Free Colored Women in Saint Domingue," in Darlene C. Hine and D. Barry Gaspar, eds., *Black Women and Slavery* (Bloomington, Ind., forthcoming).

54. It was estimated in 1786 that the owners of 52 percent of the sugar estates and 9 percent of the coffee plantations lived in France: C9A/158, 177-8, AN. The mountain parishes generally had the highest ratios of whites to slaves and also the most prolific white families: censuses, G1/509, ANOM; and the tabular appendixes in François Barbé de Marbois, *Etat des finances de Saint-Domingue* (Paris, 1789); de Proisy, *Etat des Finances de Saint-Domingue* (Paris, 1790).

55. For some preliminary comments, see David Geggus, "Haitian Voodoo in the Eighteenth Century: Language, Culture, Resistance," *Jahrbuch für Geschichte von Staat, Wirtschaft und Gesellschaft Lateinamerikas* 28 (1991): 23, 36, 40, and "Le soulèvement de 1791 et ses liens avec le vaudou et le marronage," *Actes du Congrès International sur Haïti et la Révolution Française* (Port au Prince, forthcoming).

Chapter 3

1. Clement Tudway, "Instructions for Thomas Fenton," 21 December 1716, Tudway Papers, DD/TD, Box 16, Somerset Record Office, Taunton,

England. See also Michael P. Johnson, "Work, Culture, and the Slave Community: Slave Occupations in the Cotton Belt in 1860," *Labor History* 27 (1986): 325–55; Herbert G. Gutman, *Work Culture and Society in Industrializing America* (New York, 1977), pp. 3–78; and Sidney W. Mintz and Richard Price, *An Anthropological Approach to the Afro-American Past: A Caribbean Perspective* (Philadelphia, 1976).

2. John Yeamans to Board of Trade, 27 May 1734, *Colonial Office (CO) 152/V29*, Public Record Office, Kew, Surrey, England; Reverend Robert Robertson, *A Detection of the State and Situation of the Present Sugar Planters of Barbadoes and the Leward Islands* (London, 1732), p. 42. See also Richard B. Sheridan, *Sugar and Slavery: An Economic History of the British West Indies, 1623–1775* (Baltimore, 1973), pp. 184–207; Richard S. Dunn, *Sugar and Slaves: The Rise of the Planter Class in the English West Indies, 1624–1713* (Chapel Hill, 1972), pp. 117–48; and David Barry Gaspar, *Bondmen and Rebels: A Study of Master-Slave Relations in Antigua* (Baltimore, 1985), pp. 65–68, 93–99.

3. Gaspar, *Bondmen and Rebels*, ch. 4; Robert V. Wells, *The Population of the British Colonies in America before 1776: A Survey of Census Data* (Princeton, 1975), pp. 206–36.

4. William Mathew, "A State of H. M. Leeward Carribee Islands in America," 31 August 1734, in *Calendar of State Papers (CSP)*, Colonial Series, America and West Indies, 1734–1735, vol. 41 (London, 1953), no. 314ii, p. 207. See also Gaspar, *Bondmen and Rebels*, pp. 85–86.

5. Sidney W. Mintz, *Sweetness and Power: The Place of Sugar in Modern History* (New York, 1986), p. 48. See also Dunn, *Sugar and Slaves*, pp. 188–223; Richard B. Sheridan, *Doctors and Slaves: A Medical and Demographic History of Slavery in the British West Indies, 1680–1834* (Cambridge, 1985), pp. 127–84.

6. Sheridan, *Doctors and Slaves*, p. 141.

7. Inventory of the Slaves on the plantations of Main Swete, 26 November 1737, Swete Papers, 388M/E2 and E3, Devon Record Office, Exeter, England.

8. Gaspar, *Bondmen and Rebels*, pp. 95, 99–105; Richard B. Sheridan, "Samuel Martin, Innovating Sugar Planter of Antigua, 1750–1776," *Agricultural History* 34 (1960): 134–35; Robert Dirks, *The Black Saturnalia: Conflict and Its Ritual Expression on British West Indian Slave Plantations* (Gainesville, Fla., 1987), pp. 11–12, 22–27; Ward Barrett, "Caribbean Sugar Production Standards in the Seventeenth and Eighteenth Centuries," in John Parker, ed., *Merchants and Scholars: Essays in the History of Exploration and Trade* (Minneapolis, 1965), pp. 147–70; John Luffman, "A Brief Account of the Island of Antigua" (London, 1789), reprinted in Vere Langford Oliver, *The History of the Island of Antigua*, 3 vols. (London, 1894–99), 1:128–38, letters 21–23 (1 August–3 October 1787); Michael Craton, *Sinews of Empire: A Short History of British Slavery* (London, 1974), pp. 120–40; F. W. Pitman, "Slavery on the British West Indian Plantations in the Eighteenth Century," *Journal of Negro History* 11 (1926): 595–609.

9. Francis Farley to Charles Tudway, 23 July 1758, Tudway Papers, DD/TD, box 15; "Orders and Directions for Mr. [John] Jeffers at the Cottin Planta-

tion," 27 June 1715, Codrington Papers, D1610/C2, Gloucestershire County
Record Office, Gloucester, England. See also Sheridan, *Doctors and Slaves,*
pp. 131–34; D. W. Thoms, "Slavery in the Leeward Islands in the Mid Eighteenth Century: A Reappraisal," *Bulletin of the Institute of Historical Research* 42
(1969): 79; Ulrich B. Phillips, "A Jamaica Plantation," *Caribbean Quarterly* 1
(1949): 5–6; *House of Commons Sessional Papers of the Eighteenth Century* (hereafter *HCSP*), Sheila Lambert, ed. (Wilmington, 1975), 69:338, and 72:305–6.

10. "Stores wanted in the Estates for the Year 1771 not wrote for by Mr.
Walrond," 23 September 1770, Tudway Papers, DD/TD, box 11, bundle 4;
Luffman, "Brief Account of Antigua," 1 August 1787. See also Richard Pares,
Merchants and Planters (Cambridge, Eng., 1960), p. 23; Sheridan, "Samuel
Martin," p. 134; *HCSP* 72:309–10.

11. Elsa V. Goveia, *Slave Society in the British Leeward Islands at the End of the
Eighteenth Century* (New Haven, 1965), p. 119; *HCSP* 72:309–10, 350; 69:344.

12. Francis Farley to Charles Tudway, 23 July 1758, Tudway Papers, DD/
TD, box 15.

13. Main Swete Walrond to Clement Tudway, 23 April 1783, Tudway
Papers; Swete Plantation Accounts, 10 September 1738 to 13 August 1739,
Swete Papers, 388M/E4; Samuel Martin, "An Essay Upon Plantership," in
Annals of Agriculture and Other Useful Arts 18 (1792): 238; *HCSP* 69:330; James M.
Adair, *Unanswerable Arguments against the Abolition of the Slave Trade* (London,
[1790]), pp. 132–33. And see Sheridan, "Samuel Martin," p. 134.

14. Richard Pares, *A West-India Fortune* (repr., Hamden, Conn., 1968; orig.
pub. London, 1950), p. 16; "An Account of the Produce of Parham Plantation
Sugar and how Disposed of, for the Year 1737," Tudway Papers, DD/TD.

15. Martin, "An Essay Upon Plantership," p. 238. See also Luffman, "Brief
Account of Antigua," 3 October 1787; *British Parliamentary Papers,* Colonies,
West Indies, 1, session 3 February to 12 August 1842 (Shannon, Ireland, 1968),
p. 211, nos. 2773–74.

16. "An Act more effectually to provide for the Support, and to extend
certain Regulations for the Protection, of Slaves; to promote and encourage
their Increase; and generally to meliorate their Condition," 21 April 1798,
HCSP 122:103–4.

17. Philip D. Morgan, "Task and Gang Systems: The Organization of
Labor on New World Plantations," in Stephen Innes, ed., *Work and Labor in
Early America* (Chapel Hill, 1988), p. 189; Morgan, "Work and Culture: The
Task System and the World of Lowcountry Blacks, 1700 to 1880," *William and
Mary Quarterly,* 3d ser., 39 (1982): 565–69; Gaspar, *Bondmen and Rebels,* pp. 102–
3; Dirks, *Black Saturnalia,* pp. 49–50; James M. Clifton, "The Rice Driver: His
Role in Slave Management," *South Carolina Historical Magazine* 82 (1981): 331–
53; William L. Van Deburg, *The Slave Drivers: Black Agricultural Labor Supervisors
in the Antebellum South* (New York, 1979).

18. Parham Hill Plantation Inventory, February 1737, Tudway Papers,
DD/TD; Parham Plantation (Old Work) Inventory, 1750, Tudway Papers, DD/
TD, box 14.

19. Antigua, map no. 2, "The Island of Antigua by Herman Moll, Geographer," (1 inch to 1⅓ miles), *CO 700/2*. Tooley cites 1729 for the first edition; other editions appeared in 1732 and 1739: see R. V. Tooley, *The Printed Maps of Antigua, 1689–1899*, Map Collectors' Series, vol. 6, no. 55 (London, 1969), p. 5. See also P. A. Penfold, ed., *Maps and Plans in the Public Record Office*, 2 vols. (London, 1974), vol. 2; Antigua, map no. 3, "A New and Exact Map of the Island of Antigua in America, According to an Actual and Accurate Survey Made in the Years 1746, 1747, and 1748," by Robert Baker (2 inches to 1 mile) (London, 1748–49), *CO 700/3*; Antigua, map no. 4, "A New and Accurate Map of the Island of Antigua or Antegua taken from Surveys and Adjusted by Astronomical Observations," by Emanuel Bowen (1 inch to 2 miles) (London, 1752), *CO 700/4*. See also Gaspar, *Bondmen and Rebels*, pp. 98–99.

20. Instructions for John Jeffers, 27 June 1715; Instructions for John Griffith, 27 June 1715, Codrington Papers, D1610/C2; Account of Produce, Parham Hill Plantation, 1737; Walrond to Tudway, 21 March, 25 August 1774, Tudway Papers, DD/TD, box 11; *HCSP* 72:328–30; "Observations on the Inventory sent Sr. William Codrington 12 Aug. 1751," information relating to Betty's Hope Plantation, Codrington Papers, D1610/E5.

21. Richard B. Sheridan, *The Development of the Plantations to 1750: An Era of West Indian Prosperity, 1750–1775* (Barbados, 1970), p. 57; William Clark, *Ten Views of the Island of Antigua* (London, 1823), no. 4, "Cutting the Sugar-Cane."

22. *HCSP* 72:309, 329; Adair, *Unanswerable Arguments*, pp. 132–35.

23. Martin, "An Essay Upon Plantership," p. 243.

24. Clark, *Ten Views*, no. 4, "Cutting the Sugar-Cane."

25. Pares, *West-India Fortune*, pp. 116–19; Martin, "An Essay Upon Plantership," pp. 285–308; Barrett, "Caribbean Sugar Production Standards," pp. 159–63; *HCSP* 72:306.

26. Pitman, "Slavery on British West Indian Plantations," p. 598.

27. Tullideph to Ephraim Jordan, 25 October 1753, Tullideph Letter Book, MS., Scottish Record Office, Edinburgh, Scotland.

28. Walrond to Tudway, 21 March 1774; 23 April 1783; 31 October 1784. Tudway Papers, DD/TD, box 11.

29. Report on Betty's Hope Plantation [1740s], Codrington Papers, D1610/C5. See also Michael Craton, *Searching for the Invisible Man: Slaves and Plantation Life in Jamaica* (Cambridge, 1978), pp. 206–7.

30. Gaspar, *Bondmen and Rebels*, pp. 78–84, 99–107; Sheridan, *Doctors and Slaves*, pp. 141–47; B. W. Higman, *Slave Populations of the British Caribbean, 1807–1834* (Baltimore, 1984), pp. 158–225.

31. Walrond to Tudway, 23 April 1783, Tudway Papers, DD/TD, box 11.

32. Sheridan, *Doctors and Slaves*, pp. 72–97, 268–91; Swete Papers, 388M/E3.

33. Gaspar, *Bondmen and Rebels*, pp. 104–5; Orlando Patterson, *The Sociology of Slavery: An Analysis of the Origins, Development, and Structure of Negro Slave Society in Jamaica* (London, 1967), pp. 57–58; John W. Blassingame, "Status and Social Structure in the Slave Community: Evidence from New Sources," in

Harry P. Owens, ed., *Perspectives and Irony in American Slavery* (Jackson, Miss., 1976), pp. 139–40; Darlene Clark Hine and Kate Wittenstein, "Female Slave Resistance: The Economics of Sex," in Filomina Chioma Steady, ed., *The Black Woman Cross-Culturally* (Rochester, Vt., 1985), pp. 289–99; Barbara Bush, " 'The Family Tree Is Not Cut': Women and Cultural Resistance in Slave Family Life in the British Caribbean," in Gary Y. Okihiro, ed., *In Resistance: Studies in African, Caribbean, and Afro-American History* (Amherst, 1986), pp. 122–27; Hilary McD. Beckles, *Natural Rebels: A Social History of Enslaved Black Women in Barbados* (New Brunswick, N.J., 1989), pp. 55–71; Marietta Morrissey, *Slave Women in the New World: Gender Stratification in the Caribbean* (Lawrence, Kans., 1989), pp. 62–68.

34. Betty's Hope Plantation Inventory, 15 May 1740, Codrington Papers, D1610/E5; Parham Hill Plantation Inventory, 1 February 1737, Tudway Papers, DD/TD.

35. Joan W. Scott, "Gender: A Useful Category of Historical Analysis," *American Historical Review* 91 (December 1986): 1053–75; William Beckford, *Remarks Upon the Situation of Negroes in Jamaica* (London, 1788), pp. 13–14, quoted in Sheridan, *Doctors and Slaves*, p. 131; Lucille Mathurin, "Reluctant Matriarchs," *Savacou* 13 (1977): 3; Mathurin, *The Rebel Woman in the British West Indies during Slavery* (Kingston, Jamaica, 1975); Elizabeth Fox-Genovese, "Strategies and Forms of Resistance: Focus on Slave Women in the United States," in *In Resistance*, pp. 154–55; Fox-Genovese, *Within the Plantation Household: Black and White Women of the Old South* (Chapel Hill, 1988), pp. 172–91; Jacqueline Jones, *Labor of Love, Labor of Sorrow: Black Women, Work, and the Family from Slavery to the Present* (New York, 1985), p. 11–43; Deborah Gray White, *Ar'n't I a Woman? Female Slaves in the Plantation South* (New York, 1985), pp. 62–90.

36. Parham Hill Plantation Inventory, 1 February 1737, Tudway Papers, DD/TD.

37. British Parliamentary Papers [1842], pp. 211–12, 226; *HCSP* 72:304–5; Adair, *Unanswerable Arguments*, pp. 133–34.

38. Walrond to Tudway, 25 August 1774; 31 October 1784, Tudway Papers, DD/TD, box 11.

39. Report on Betty's Hope and the Garden Plantations [1740s], Codrington Papers, D1610/C5; Richard Clarke to Codrington, 8 June 1780, Codrington Papers, Nettie Lee Benson Latin American Collection, University of Texas at Austin, microfilm reels 2 and 3; Adair, *Unanswerable Arguments*, pp. 133–34.

40. Betty's Hope Plantation Inventory, 26 July 1751, Codrington Papers, D1610/E5.

41. James Ramsay, *An Essay on the Treatment and Conversion of African Slaves in the British Sugar Colonies* (London, 1784), p. 69, quoted in Sheridan, *Development of the Plantations*, p. 57. See also Sheridan, *Doctors and Slaves*, pp. 127–30; Sheridan, *Development of the Plantations*, pp. 56–58; Morgan, "Work and Culture," p. 569; Morgan, "Task and Gang Systems," pp. 189–220; and Martin, "An Essay Upon Plantership," p. 278.

42. Robertson, *A Letter to the Bishop of London* (London, 1730), pp. 12–13, 54. See also Gaspar, *Bondmen and Rebels*, pp. 207–9; and Sidney W. Mintz, *Caribbean Transformations* (Baltimore, 1974), pp. 75–81.

43. Dirks, *Black Saturnalia*, pp. 49–55; David Barry Gaspar, "Slavery, Amelioration, and Sunday Markets in Antigua, 1823–1831," *Slavery and Abolition* 9 (1988): 1–28; Neville Hall, "Slaves' Use of Their 'Free' Time in the Danish Virgin Islands in the Later Eighteenth and Early Nineteenth Century," *Journal of Caribbean History* 13 (1979): 21–43; Hall, "Slaves and the Law in the Towns of St. Croix, 1802–1807," *Slavery and Abolition* 8 (1987): 147–65.

44. "A Map of the Garden, Betty's Hope, The Cotton and the Cotton New-Work, Four Plantations in the Island of Antigua Belonging to Sir William Codrington Baronet" (1755), Samuel Clapham, Jr., surveyor, Codrington Papers, Nettie Lee Benson Latin American Collection, University of Texas at Austin, microfilm; Richard B. Sheridan, "Letters from a Sugar Plantation in Antigua, 1739–1758," *Agricultural History* 31 (1957): 3–23; Instructions for John Jeffers, 27 June 1715, Codrington Papers, D1610/C2; *HCSP* 72:306, 335. See also Dirks, *Black Saturnalia*, pp. 57–58, 65–66, 79–80; Gaspar, "Slavery, Amelioration, and Sunday Markets," pp. 4–6.

45. "Act for Planting Provision Proportionable to Negroes," 8 April 1682, (Nevis), *CO 154/2;* "An Act to restrain the Insolence of Slaves, and for preventing them from committing any Outrages, as also the better ordering such Slaves, &c," Act no. 36 of 1693, *Montserrat Code of Laws, From 1668 to 1788* (London, 1790), pp. 16–18. See also Bryan Edwards, *The History, Civil and Commercial, of the British Colonies in the West Indies*, 2 vols. (Dublin, 1793; repr. New York, 1972), 1:123–24; Martin, "An Essay Upon Plantership," pp. 238–40; [Dr. Collins], *Practical Rules for the Management and Medical Treatment of Negro Slaves, in the Sugar Colonies* (London, 1811; repr. New York, 1971), pp. 74–113; Sidney W. Mintz and Douglas Hall, *The Origins of the Jamaica Internal Marketing System*, Yale University Publications in Anthropology no. 57 (New Haven, 1960); Mintz; "The Jamaican Internal Marketing Pattern: Some Notes and Hypotheses," *Social and Economic Studies* 4 (1955): 95–103; Richard B. Sheridan, "The Domestic Economy," in Jack P. Greene and J. R. Pole, eds., *Colonial British America: Essays in the New History of the Early Modern Era* (Baltimore, 1984), pp. 43–53.

46. Tullideph to Lowes, 6 November 1756, Tullideph Letter Book; Richard B. Sheridan, "The Crisis of Slave Subsistence in the British West Indies during and after the American Revolution," *William and Mary Quarterly*, 3d ser., 33 (1976): 615–41; Robert Dirks, "Slaves' Holiday," *Natural History* 84 (1975): 86–87.

47. Robertson, *Detection*, pp. 48–49; "A Map of The Garden, Betty's Hope, The Cotton and the Cotton New-Work" (1755).

48. Robertson, *Letter*, pp. 12, 44; Gaspar, "Slavery, Amelioration, and Sunday Markets," pp. 3–9; Gaspar, *Bondmen and Rebels*, pp. 137–38, 145–48; Luffman, "Brief Account of Antigua," letters 30 (14 March 1788) and 31 (28 March 1788); *HCSP* 72:315, 318–19; Goveia, *Slave Society*, pp. 263–310.

49. Robertson, *Letter*, pp. 22, 46–48.

50. *HCSP* 69:326.

51. Gaspar, "Slavery, Amelioration, and Sunday Markets," pp. 9–21.

52. "An Act for the better Government of Slaves," December 16, 1697, *CO 8/3*, clauses 1, 5, 15; "An Act for the better Government of Slaves, and Free Negroes," Act no. 130, 28 June 1702, clause 22, in *The Laws of the Island of Antigua consisting of the Acts of the Leeward Islands, 1690–1798 and Acts of Antigua, 1668–1845* (hereafter *Laws of Antigua*), 4 vols. (London, 1805–46), vol. 1; Luffman, "Brief Account of Antigua," letter 31 (28 March 1788); Adair, *Unanswerable Arguments*, p. 221n.

53. Act no. 144, 2 September 1714, *Laws of Antigua*, vol. 1; Antigua Assembly Minutes, 9 August 1715, *CO 9/4*.

54. "An Act to repeal a certain Act of this Island concerning Negroes," Act no. 174, 1 February 1722, *Laws of Antigua*, vol. 1; Hart to Board of Trade, 9 April 1723, *CO 152/14, R 59*.

55. Gaspar, "Slavery, Amelioration, and Sunday Markets," pp. 5–9; Luffman, "Brief Account of Antigua," letters 30 (14 March 1788) and 31 (28 March 1788).

56. *HCSP* 72:335.

57. On this point the evidence for the 1800s is stronger. See T. Morgan to Methodist Missionary Society (MMS), 22 December 1826, Journal, Methodist Missionary Society Papers, box 123, no. 289, Library of the School of Oriental and African Studies, London; W. Dowson, et al. to MMS, 5 April 1831, box 130, no. 70; Clement Caines, *The History of the General Council and General Assembly of the Leeward Islands* (St. Christopher, 1804), 1:227–28.

58. Daniel McKinnen, *A Tour Through the British West Indies* (London, 1804), pp. 68–69; *HCSP* 72:315.

59. "An Act for attainting several slaves now run away from their Master's Service, and for the better Government of Slaves," Act no. 176, 9 December 1723, clauses 29, 30 (hereafter Act no. 176 of 1723), *Laws of Antigua*, vol. 1; Antigua Assembly Minutes, 25 June 1740, *CO 9/12*; Luffman, "Brief Account of Antigua," letters 30 (14 March 1788) and 31 (28 March 1788). See also Gaspar, *Bondmen and Rebels*, p. 138.

60. Robertson, *Letter*, pp. 45–46; Dirks, "Slaves' Holiday," p. 82; Dirks, "Resource Fluctuations and Competitive Transformations in West Indian Slave Societies," in Charles D. Laughlin, Jr. and Ivan A. Brady, eds., *Extinction and Survival in Human Populations* (New York, 1978), pp. 160–66; Dirks, "The Evolution of a Playful Ritual: The Garifuna's John Canoe in Comparative Perspective," in E. Norbeck and C. R. Farrer, eds., *Forms of Play of Native North Americans* (St. Paul, Minn., 1979), pp. 89–109; Dirks, *Black Saturnalia*, pp. 168–71; Richardson Wright, *Revels in Jamaica, 1682–1838* (New York, 1937), pp. 238–47; Luffman, "Brief Account of Antigua," letters 30 (14 March 1788) and 31 (28 March 1788); Janet Schaw, *Journal of a Lady of Quality*, Evangeline and Charles McLean Andrews, eds. (New Haven, 1921), pp. 88, 107–9; "An Act to

alter and amend the thirty-second and thirty-third Clauses of an Act of this Island, intitled, An Act for attainting several Slaves now run-away from their Masters' Service, and for the better Government of Slaves; and for regulating the Duty of the Militia during the Christmas Holidays," Act no. 390, 30 November 1778 (hereafter Act no. 390 of 1778), *Laws of Antigua*, vol. 1.

61. Dirks, "Slaves' Holiday," pp. 84–90; "Resource Fluctuations," pp. 160–66; and *Black Saturnalia*, pp. 167–90.

62. Board of Trade to Codrington, 24 March 1702, *CO 153/7*; Francis Le Jau, "Some Matters Relating to the Condition of the Clergy Employ'd in the Leeward Islands," Papers of the Society for the Propagation of the Gospel, 17, West Indian section, folios 291–92, Lambeth Palace Library, London; Act no. 176 of 1723, clause 32. This act said nothing about Easter, which fell during harvest. Perhaps both masters and slaves were more flexible about these holidays than those at Christmas, which normally preceded the start of harvest. See also, Gaspar, *Bondmen and Rebels*, pp. 140, 185–89.

63. Act no. 390 of 1778.

64. Gaspar, "Slavery, Amelioration, and Sunday Markets," p. 2; Goveia, *Slave Society*, pp. 55–58.

65. *HCSP* 122:103–4, 109, 113.

Chapter 4

My thanks to Ira Berlin, Sidney W. Mintz, and Philip Morgan for their comments on earlier versions of this paper.

1. Michel-Rolph Trouillot, "Motion in the System: Coffee, Color, and Slavery in Eighteenth-Century Saint-Domingue," *Review, A Journal of the Fernand Braudel Centre* 5 (1982): 331, 337; Barry Higman, *Slave Population and Economy in Jamaica, 1807–1834* (Cambridge, 1976), p. 213.

2. Francisco A. Scarano, *Sugar and Slavery in Puerto Rico: The Plantation Economy of Ponce, 1800–1850* (Madison, Wisc., 1984), p. 7; Raymond E. Crist, *Sugar Cane and Coffee in Puerto Rico* (Rio Piedras, 1948; reprinted from the *American Journal of Economics and Sociology* 7, nos. 2 and 3 [April and July 1948]), p. 6; Ramiro Guerra y Sanchez, *Sugar and Society in the Caribbean: An Economic History of Cuban Agriculture* (New Haven, 1964), p. 49; Felix Goizueta-Mimo, *Bitter Cuban Sugar: Monoculture and Economic Dependence from 1825–1899* (New York, 1987), pp. 8, 14.

3. Guerra y Sanchez, *Sugar and Society*, p. 49; Goizueta-Mimo, *Bitter Cuban Sugar*, pp. 8, 14; Dale W. Tomich, *Slavery in the Circuit of Sugar: Martinique and the World Economy, 1830–1848* (Baltimore, 1990), pp. 88–89; Nicole Vanony-Frisch, *Les esclaves de la Guadeloupe: A la fin de l'Ancien Régime d'après les sources notariales* (Aubenas d'Ardèche, 1985), p. 8; Higman, *Slave Populations of the British Caribbean, 1807–1834* (Baltimore, 1984), pp. 68–69.

4. This periodization was first sketched in Michel-Rolph Trouillot, "Con-

trapunto Caribeaño: El cafe en las Antillas (1734–1873)," *El Caribe* 6, nos. 16–17 (1990): 58–65.

5. Obviously, particular territories can be said to belong to one category at one time and to another in some other period. Only Dominica emerges clearly as a coffee-dominated colony for any extended period; see Michel-Rolph Trouillot, *Peasants and Capital: Dominica in the World Economy* (Baltimore, 1988). Since particular crops tended to flourish in specific ecological environments, their production always created some spatial patterns; the point at which these patterns can be said to create "enclaves" is, however, arbitrary. I have tended to list here the cases in which we can presume that definite spatial concentration overlapped the creation of "social niches."

6. Trouillot, "Motion in the System"; Thomas Atwood, *The History of the Island of Dominica, Containing a Description of Its Situation, Extent, Climate, Mountains, Rivers, Natural Productions, etc.* (London, 1971; orig. pub. 1791); Trouillot, *Peasants and Capital*, pp. 53–55; Inigo Abbad y Lasierra, *Historia geografica, civil, y natural de la isla San Juan Bautista de Puerto Rico* (San Juan, 1856; orig. pub., 1782); Fernando Pico, *Amargo Cafe: Los pequenos y medianos caficultores de Utado en al segundamitad siglo XIX* (Rio Piedras, 1981); Laird W. Bergad, *Coffee and the Growth of Agrarian Capitalism in Nineteenth-Century Puerto Rico* (Princeton, 1983); Goizueta-Mimo, *Bitter Cuban Sugar*.

7. Michel-Rolph Trouillot, "Peripheral Vibrations: The Case of Saint-Domingue's Coffee Revolution," in R. Rubinson, ed., *Dynamics of World Development, Political Economy of the World-System Annual*, (Beverly Hills, 1981); 4:27–41; Trouillot, "Motion in the System"; Médéric-Louis-Elie Moreau de Saint-Méry, *Description topographique, physique, civile, politique, et historique de la partie française de l'isle Saint-Domingue*, Etienne Taillemite and Blanche Maurel, eds., 3 vols. (Paris, 1958; orig. pub. 1797–98).

8. Edward L. Cox, *Free Coloreds in the Slave Societies of Grenada and St. Kitts, 1763–1833* (Knoxville, 1984), pp. 62–63; Atwood, *The History*; Trouillot, *Peasants and Capital*; Higman, *Slave Populations*, p. 110. For a comparison between free coloreds in Saint Domingue and Dominica, see Michel-Rolph Trouillot, "The Inconvenience of Freedom: Free People of Color and the Political Aftermath of Slavery in Dominica and Saint-Domingue/Haiti," in Frank McGlynn and Seymour Drescher, eds., *The Meaning of Freedom* (Pittsburgh, 1991), pp. 147–82.

9. Gabriel Debien, *Les esclaves aux Antilles françaises, XVIIe–XVIIIe siècles* (Basse-Terre, 1974–75); Debien, *Plantation à la Guadeloupe*; Higman, *Slave Population and Economy*; Trouillot, "Motion in the System," p. 348; Christian Schnakenbourg, *Histoire de l'industrie sucrière en Guadeloupe, XIXe–XXe siècles: La crise du système esclavagiste, 1835–1847* (Paris, 1980), p. 22.

10. Louis Abenon, *La Guadeloupe de 1671 à 1759: Etude politique, économique et sociale* (Paris, 1987), p. 93; Higman, *Slave Population and Economy*, p. 123.

11. Trouillot, *Peasants and Capital*, pp. 40–42, 185–91.

12. Trouillot, *Peasants and Capital*, pp. 39–42; 185–89.

13. Meredith A. John, *The Plantation Slaves of Trinidad, 1783–1816: A Mathematical and Demographic Enquiry* (Cambridge, 1988), pp. 117, 119.

14. Congos were reputedly more prone to disease. On coffee and slave populations in Saint Domingue, see Michel-René Hilliard d'Auberteuil, *Considérations sur la colonie française de Saint-Domingue*, 2 vols. (Geneva, 1779), 1:186–97; Debien, *Les Esclaves*, p. 145; Trouillot, "Motion in the System," pp. 378–79; David Geggus, "Sugar and Coffee Cultivation in Saint Domingue and the Shaping of the Slave Labor Force," ch. 2 in this volume. On the political contribution of "Congos" to the making of Haiti, see Michel-Rolph Trouillot, "The Three Faces of Sans Souci: Glory and Silences in the Haitian Revolution," in Gerald Sider and Gavin Smith, eds., *The Production of History: Silences and Commemorations* (forthcoming).

15. Higman, *Slave Population and Economy*, p. 73.

16. Bergad, *Coffee and the Growth of Agrarian Capitalism*, p. 58; Vanony-Frisch, *Les esclaves de la Guadeloupe*, p. 80. Admittedly, this sample has a high number of slaves of unknown origins (27 percent); see John, *Plantation Slaves of Trinidad*, p. 55.

17. Geggus, however, shows sex ratios on sugar and coffee plantations in Saint Domingue to be closer than first expected, in part because sugar planters placed a premium on males from the "favored" ethnic groups; see Geggus, "Sugar and Coffee Cultivation in Saint Domingue."

18. Gabriel Debien, "Le Plan et les débuts d'une caféière à Saint-Domingue: La plantation 'La Merveillère' aux Anses-à-Pitre (1789–1792)," *Revue de la Société d'histoire et de géographie d'Haïti* 14, no. 51 (1943): 12–32.

19. Higman, *Slave Population and Economy*, p. 224; Guerra y Sanchez, *Sugar and Society*, p. 52; Guy Lasserre, *La Guadeloupe: Etude géographique*, vol. 1, *Le milieu naturel: L'héritage du passé* (Bordeaux, 1961), pp. 368–69; Schnakenbourg, *Histoire de l'industrie sucrière en Guadeloupe*, p. 35; Tomich, *Slavery and the Circuit of Sugar*, pp. 86–88, 97.

20. In sharp contrast, a few years later Dominican sugarcane planters stubbornly refused to abandon production in spite of much worse conditions of production and sale; see Trouillot, *Peasants and Capital*, pp. 53–59.

21. Barry Higman warns against one case in which overemphasis on the history of settlement may lead to errors in analysis. He suggests that the higher mortality of males on *sugar* estates accounts better for the relatively high ratio of African males on coffee plantations in Jamaica than the historical expansion of settlement. The point is well taken, but it does not invalidate the suggestion that mortality rates may have reinforced patterns tied to the history of settlement. See Higman, *Slave Population and Economy*, pp. 73–74.

22. Although the production of coffee was sometimes combined with that of sugar, cocoa, provisions, pimento, indigo, cotton, or the hiring of labor in places such as Trinidad, Jamaica, Saint Domingue, and Dominica, most coffee plantations were monocultural, and the vast majority of slaves who worked on coffee as an export crop did so within these units. See John, *Plantation Slaves*

of Trinidad, p. 55; Higman, *Slave Population and Economy,* p. 13; Debien, *Les Esclaves,* p. 141.

23. Higman, *Slave Population and Economy,* p. 13. In 1822 the Maryland Plantation in Jamaica had 331 slaves and was managed by an attorney and an overseer, much like a sugar estate; see Higman, *Slave Population and Economy,* pp. 196–97. The average size of the labor force tended to increase with time, along with the cultivated acreage.

24. Trouillot, "Peripheral Vibrations," and "Motion in the System," pp. 346–48; Geggus, "Sugar and Coffee Cultivation in Saint Domingue."

25. Schnakenbourg, *Histoire de l'industrie sucrière en Guadeloupe,* p. 22; Higman, *Slave Populations,* p. 699; Tomich, *Slavery and the Circuit of Sugar,* p. 88.

26. Higman, *Slave Populations,* p. 434; and John, *Plantation Slaves of Trinidad,* p. 55. Using the same source, the Trinidad Slave Registers, Higman and John come up with slightly different totals for the number of slaves on coffee units of production.

27. Higman, *Slave Populations,* p. 434; Bergad, *Coffee and the Growth of Agrarian Capitalism,* p. 58.

28. P. J. Laborie, *The Coffee Planter of Saint Domingo* (London, 1798), pp. 163–69, 187–89. See also Trouillot, "Motion in the System"; Debien, *Plantation à la Guadeloupe;* "Archives de Planteurs"; and "Le Plan et les débuts."

29. Laborie, *The Coffee Planter,* pp. 178–79. Laborie was also suspicious of peddlers who were "never permitted to enter into, or to stay, in the negroe houses."

30. J. Girod de Chantrans, *Voyage d'un suisse dans différentes colonies d'Amérique* (Paris, 1980; orig. pub., 1785), pp. 219–20. Debien, *Les Esclaves,* pp. 141, 197–207; Laborie, *The Coffee Planter,* pp. 30–38, 193–95; Higman, *Slave Populations,* p. 586. On haciendas and plantations, see Sidney W. Mintz and Eric R. Wolf, "Haciendas and Plantations in Middle America and the Caribbean," *Social and Economic Studies* 6 (1957): 380–412.

31. Herbert Gutman, *The Black Family in Slavery and Freedom, 1750–1925* (New York, 1976); Sidney Mintz and Richard Price, *An Anthropological Approach to the Afro-American Past: A Caribbean Perspective* (Philadelphia, 1976); Michel-Rolph Trouillot, "Culture on the Edges: The Afro-American Plantation as Cultural Matrix," paper presented at the colloquium "The Plantation System in the Americas," Louisiana State University, Baton Rouge, April 1989.

32. Trouillot, "Motion in the system," p. 381.

33. If individual slaves could not find a priest, a midwife, or a musician of their preference within walking distance, they probably accommodated their tastes to the surroundings. But similarly, whoever emerged as a specialist had to accommodate to the tastes of the majority.

34. For instance, there were more slaves per hut in Saint Domingue's *caféières* than on sugar plantations. See Debien, *Les Esclaves,* pp. 219–32; and Laborie, *The Coffee Planter,* pp. 95–96.

35. Mintz and Price, *Anthropological Approach to the Afro-American Past,* 25.

36. Geggus, "Sugar and Coffee Cultivation in Saint Domingue."

37. See Trouillot, "Motion in the System," for the rivalry between sugar and coffee planters in eighteenth-century Saint Domingue. See also Hilliard d'Auberteuil, *Considérations sur la colonie française de Saint-Domingue*, 1:186–97; Jean Barré de Saint-Venant, *Des Colonies modernes sous la zone torride et particulièrement de celle de St.-Domingue* (Paris, 1802), p. 236; Higman, *Slave Population and Economy*, p. 121, and *Slave Populations*, p. 167; John, *Plantation Slaves in Trinidad*, p. 120.

38. Geggus notes comparable proportions of permanently sick slaves in sugar and coffee plantations but rightly argues that conditions at time of purchase influenced this result. Sugar planters tended to buy healthier slaves. See Geggus, "Sugar and Coffee Cultivation in Saint Domingue."

39. Debien, *Les Esclaves*, p. 142; Debien, "Le Plan et les débuts."

40. Laborie, *The Coffee Planter*, p. 18.

41. Most planters used nursery plants rather than seeds, in part because they flowered at least a year sooner. Distances between the trees varied greatly: a ten-acre field could have 12,000 to 20,000 trees, past and present methods of calculation notwithstanding. See Laborie, *The Coffee Planter*, pp. 113–15; Debien, "Le Plan et les débuts," and *Plantation à la Guadeloupe*; Lasserre, *La Guadeloupe*, pp. 366–67; Abenon, *La Guadeloupe de 1671 à 1759*, p. 91; Schnakenbourg, *Histoire de l'industrie sucrière en Guadeloupe*, p. 34.

42. Higman, *Slave Populations*, pp. 183–84; Laborie, *The Coffee Planter*, p. 34; Debien, *Les Esclaves*, p. 143; Girod de Chantrans, *Voyage d'un suisse*, p. 211.

43. Laborie, *The Coffee Planter*, p. 177.

44. Higman, *Slave Populations*, pp. 183–84, 188; Laborie, *The Coffee Planter*, 177; Debien, *Les Esclaves*, p. 143.

45. Vanony-Frisch, *Les esclaves de la Guadeloupe*, p. 78; Higman, *Slave Populations*, p. 586, and *Slave Population and Economy*, p. 23; Debien, *Les Esclaves*, p. 142; Geggus, "Sugar and Coffee Cultivation in Saint Domingue"; Girod de Chantrans, *Voyage d'un suisse*, p. 212.

46. Laborie, *The Coffee Planter*, p. 150.

47. Ibid., p. 150.

48. Philip D. Morgan, "Task and Gang Systems: The Organization of Labor on New World Plantations," in Stephen Innes, ed., *Work and Labor in Early America* (Chapel Hill, 1988), pp. 192–93. Laborie, *The Coffee Planter*, p. 150; Debien, *Les Esclaves*, p. 144.

49. Laborie, *The Coffee Planter*, p. 150; Morgan, "Task and Gang Systems," pp. 192–93.

50. Debien, *Les Esclaves*, p. 144.

51. Laborie, *The Coffee Planter*, p. 150.

52. The data for Saint Domingue and Jamaica suggest that in some cases the final analysis should be carried over to the level of internal regions or parishes.

Chapter 5

I am grateful to the Department of History of Howard University for a research grant that made possible the assistance of Emma S. Etuk.

1. James E. Callaway, *The Early Settlement of Georgia* (Athens, Ga., 1948), ch. 6. The discussion that follows derives from my larger study of nineteenth-century Georgia. Yet, in many structural respects, the expansion of short-staple cotton cultivation over the Georgia up country beginning in the 1790s differed little from its simultaneous spread into the South Carolina up country. For that reason, I have at times relied upon source material from South Carolina (for instance, the observations of Charles Ball, a Maryland slave sold first to South Carolina and then to Georgia), especially regarding the early period, for which details about field labor and subsistence practices in Georgia are scarce.

2. Historians of the U.S. South disagree in their assessment of the commercial commitment of pioneer agriculturalists. In contrast to the subsistence orientation argued here, see Joyce E. Chaplin, "Creating a Cotton South in Georgia and South Carolina, 1760–1815," *Journal of Southern History* 57 (1991): 171–200; and Lacy K. Ford, Jr., *Origins of Southern Radicalism: The South Carolina Upcountry, 1800–1860* (New York, 1988).

3. Callaway, *Early Settlement*, pp. 71–74; E. Merton Coulter, *Old Petersburg and the Broad River Valley of Georgia* (Athens, Ga., 1965). For parallel developments east of the Savannah River, see Thomas H. Pope, *The History of Newberry County, South Carolina, 1749–1860*, 2 vols. (Columbia, 1973), 1:111–12.

4. Quoted in Lewis Cecil Gray, *History of Agriculture in the Southern United States to 1860*, 2 vols. (Washington, D.C., 1933), 1:557.

5. See Joseph C. Robert, *The Story of Tobacco in America* (Chapel Hill, 1949); Paul G. E. Clemens, *The Atlantic Economy and Colonial Maryland's Eastern Shore: From Tobacco to Grain* (Ithaca, N.Y., 1980); John T. Schlotterbeck, "The 'Social Economy' of an Upper South Community: Orange and Greene Counties, Virginia, 1815–1860," in Orville Vernon Burton and Robert C. McMath, Jr., eds., *Class, Conflict, and Consensus: Antebellum Southern Community Studies* (Westport, Conn., 1982), pp. 3–28, especially pp. 11–12; Barbara Jeanne Fields, *Slavery and Freedom on the Middle Ground: Maryland during the Nineteenth Century* (New Haven, 1985); Allan Kulikoff, *Tobacco and Slaves: The Development of Southern Cultures in the Chesapeake, 1680–1800* (Chapel Hill, 1986); Lois Green Carr and Lorena S. Walsh, "Economic Diversification and Labor Organization in the Chesapeake, 1650–1820," in Stephen Innes, ed., *Work and Labor in Early America* (Chapel Hill, 1988), pp. 144–88; and Lorena S. Walsh, "Plantation Management in the Chesapeake, 1620–1820," *Journal of Economic History* 49 (1989): 393–406. The standard work on slavery in Jeffersonian Virginia indicates that slaves kept gardens and notes that masters who permitted cultivation of the patches on Saturday afternoon reduced rations proportionally. See Robert McColley, *Slavery and Jeffersonian Virginia*, 2d ed. (Urbana, Ill., 1973), p. 60; see also the essay by Lorena S. Walsh in this volume.

6. On the task system, see Ira Berlin, "Time, Space, and the Evolution of Afro-American Society on British Mainland North America," *American Historical Review* 85 (1980): 44–78, especially pp. 59–67; Philip D. Morgan, "Work and Culture: The Task System and the World of Lowcountry Blacks, 1700–1880," *William and Mary Quarterly*, 3d ser., 39 (1982): 563–99, and "Task and Gang Systems: The Organization of Labor on New World Plantations," in Innes, ed., *Work and Labor*, pp. 189–220; Ulrich Bonnell Phillips, *American Negro Slavery: A Survey of the Supply, Employment, and Control of Negro Labor as Determined by the Plantation Regime* (New York, 1918), pp. 247–60. On the preference for simple implements like the hoe, see Gray, *History of Agriculture*, 2:792–800, especially p. 794; and Eugene D. Genovese, *The Political Economy of Slavery: Studies in the Economy and Society of the Slave South* (New York, 1965), pp. 54–61, especially p. 55.

7. *Southern Agriculturist* 5 (1832): 181–84. For a closely reasoned defense of tasking as a key component in the proper "Management of Slaves," see *Southern Agriculturist* 6 (1833): 281–87.

8. For a commentary on such practices, see *Southern Agriculturist* 8 (1835): 343.

9. *Southern Agriculturist* 7 (1834): 404. For a discussion of an earlier generation of Virginia planters to impose similar discipline over their slave laborers, see Carr and Walsh, "Economic Diversification and Labor Organization," pp. 157–66.

10. In addition to the notorious interstate slave trade, which developed in response to the up-country settlers' demands for slaves, approximately sixty-three thousand slaves were imported from Africa to the up country during the final two decades when the international slave trade remained legal. See Allan Kulikoff, "Uprooted Peoples: Black Migrants in the Age of the American Revolution, 1790–1820," in Ira Berlin and Ronald Hoffman, eds., *Slavery and Freedom in the Age of the American Revolution* (Charlottesville, Va., 1983), table 1, p. 149.

11. Berlin, "Time, Space," p. 55; and Frederick Law Olmsted, *The Cotton Kingdom: A Traveler's Observations on Cotton and Slavery in the American Slave States*, ed. Arthur M. Schlesinger, Sr. (New York, 1984), pp. 391–92. For superb analyses of work routines on a small slaveholding, see J. William Harris, "The Organization of Work on a Yeoman Slaveholder's Farm," *Agricultural History* 64 (1990): 39–52, and "Portrait of a Small Slaveholder: The Journal of Benton Miller," *Georgia Historical Quarterly* 74 (1990): 1–19.

12. Charles Ball, *Fifty Years in Chains* (New York, 1970; orig. pub. 1837), pp. 38–39, 68–69, 131–32. John Blassingame has concluded that Ball's South Carolina residence was the plantation of General Wade Hampton; see *Slave Testimony: Two Centuries of Letters, Speeches, Interviews, and Autobiographies* (Baton Rouge, 1977), pp. xxv–xxvi.

13. Ball, *Fifty Years in Chains*, pp. 206, 215–18.

14. Ibid., pp. 56, 161, 206–7.

15. Ibid., pp. 276–83, 292–318.

16. Ibid., pp. 223, 230, 233, 262–63, 352–55. Ball enjoyed opossum on Sundays as a special treat. Laws to the contrary notwithstanding, scattered up-country slaves possessed firearms down to the Civil War. See, for instance, Charles and Tess Hoffmann, "The Limits of Paternalism: Driver-Master Relations on a Bryan County Plantation," *Georgia Historical Quarterly* 68 (1983): 329. Along the coast rice planters customarily equipped slaves with guns during the rice-bird season, and some even permitted slaves to purchase arms and ammunition of their own. See Olmsted, *The Cotton Kingdom*, p. 200.

17. See Ball, *Fifty Years in Chains*, pp. 107, 166–67, 189, 203; Blassingame, *Slave Testimony*, p. 132.

18. Ball, *Fifty Years in Chains*, pp. 351–52, 273, 186. By the late antebellum period, the Georgia code mandated a fine of $100 for masters who employed slaves on Sunday—"a day of rest of Divine appointment"—except in "work of absolute necessity and the necessary occasions of the family": R. H. Clark, T. R. R. Cobb, and D. Irwin, comps., *The Code of the State of Georgia, 1861* (Atlanta, 1861), p. 368.

19. Ball, *Fifty Years in Chains*, pp. 273, 187; Olmsted, *The Cotton Kingdom*, p. 83. For fuller treatment of the phenomenon of Sunday labor, see the essay by John Campbell in this volume.

20. Ball, *Fifty Years in Chains*, pp. 108, 188, 190, 194–95, 355; *Southern Agriculturist* 9 (1836): 582. Olmsted, *The Cotton Kingdom*, p. 81, noted that slaves in Virginia sometimes traded their rations.

21. The Georgia Code expressly prohibited "any boat hand or negro" from engaging in such petty trade. See *Georgia Code, 1861*, p. 310. At various times, the legislature added specific prohibitions against trade between fishing vessels and slaves, especially during the 1850s, when legislators especially feared abolitionism (see n. 32, below). A Mississippi law restricting trade with slaves drew special attention to "slave, negro or mulatto" teamsters. *Mississippi Laws, 1850* (Jackson, 1850), pp. 100–102. It is likely that slave teamsters throughout the South engaged in petty trade.

22. *Southern Agriculturist* 11 (1838): 512–13. In addition to the *Southern Agriculturist*, prominent agricultural journals such as the *Farmer's Register* and the *Southern Cultivator* also abounded with articles on plantation management. Northern journals did likewise but within a different context of agricultural production.

23. *Southern Agriculturist* 11 (1838): 512–13.

24. Drew Gilpin Faust, *James Henry Hammond and the Old South: A Design for Mastery* (Baton Rouge, 1982), pp. 74–75 and chs. 5 and 6. On another plantation not far from Hammond's the prominent Georgia planter Alexander Telfair permitted tasking in work that was conducive to that kind of organization; the size of the task depended on the "state of the ground and the strength of the negro." See Ulrich B. Phillips, *Plantation and Frontier, 1649–1863*, 2 vols. (Cleveland, 1910), 1:126. See also *Southern Agriculturist* 1 (1828): 529. For a fuller comparison of task and gang labor, see Morgan, "Task and Gang Systems."

25. *Southern Agriculturist* 7 (1834): 406–7.

26. *Southern Agriculturist* 5 (1832): 118.

27. *Southern Agriculturist* 7 (1834): 408.

28. This is not to be confused with the common practice of establishing a "task" for cotton picking, which included no provision for those who had finished to leave the field early but rather stipulated a minimum number of pounds to be picked per day. Any slave who failed to meet the quota was subject to the lash. Again, see Morgan, "Task and Gang Systems."

29. *Southern Agriculturist* 10 (1837): 240. I would like to thank Leslie Rowland and Steven Miller for this reference. See also Phillips, *American Negro Slavery*, pp. 259–60.

30. *Georgia Acts*, 1831 (Milledgeville, Ga., 1832), pp. 214–15 (brackets in original). See also *Georgia Acts*, 1829 (Milledgeville, Ga., 1830), pp. 152–53; *Georgia Acts*, 1857 (Columbus, Ga., 1858), pp. 288–90.

31. *Georgia Acts*, 1857, pp. 249–50; *Georgia Acts*, 1831, pp. 214–15.

32. Georgia legislators aimed to restrict the interaction between slaves and persons aboard rivercraft. Early in the period concern centered around illicit trade in plantation staples and liquor, but by the late antebellum period fears of commercial fishermen and "incendiary publications" also operated. The preamble to an 1857 law aimed at "preventing obstructions" on several major waterways specifically noted the operations of "companies from the Northern states and others." See *Georgia Acts*, 1849–50 (Milledgeville, Ga., 1850), pp. 357–59; *Georgia Acts*, 1857, pp. 289–90.

33. See, for instance, *Georgia Acts*, 1855–56 (Milledgeville, Ga., 1856), pp. 411–12; *Georgia Acts*, 1857, pp. 249, 252–54; *Georgia Acts*, 1858 (Columbus, Ga., 1859), p. 163. Such laws aimed especially at nonresidents of designated counties or of the state.

34. *Southern Agriculturist* 4 (1831): 198, and 6 (1833): 425; *Southern Cultivator*, new ser. 3 (1845): 58. Northern farmers no less than southern farmers suffered the depredations of "sheep-killing cur[s]." See *Solon Robinson: Pioneer and Agriculturist*, Herbert Anthony Keller, ed., 2 vols. (Indianapolis, 1936), 2:438.

35. Testimony of Caroline Ates, Rias Body, Mary Childs, Fannie Fulcher, Hannah Murphy, and Olin Williams in George P. Rawick, Jan Hillegas, and Ken Lawrence, eds., *The American Slave: A Composite Autobiography*, Supplement, series 1, 12 vols. (Westport, Conn., 1977), 3:22, 72, 201–2, 252; 4:467, 644.

36. Ulrich Bonnell Phillips, *Life and Labor in the Old South* (Boston, 1929), p. 272; George P. Rawick, *From Sundown to Sunup: The Making of the Black Community* (Westport, Conn., 1972), p. 70.

37. Ball, *Fifty Years in Chains*, p. 190. For a planter's insightful description of how labor patterns changed according to the season and the weather, see *Southern Cultivator* 8 (1850): 162–64. The planter noted his objections to granting garden privileges and his requirement that slaves work after dark on fall

and winter nights—the women at spinning or making bed quilts. He also observed that at times he required women to patch clothing "of wet days when they are compelled to be in the house."

38. Phillips, *American Negro Slavery*, pp. 268, 277. See also Olmsted, *The Cotton Kingdom*, p. 482.

39. Phillips, *American Negro Slavery*, pp. 238, 305. Testimony of Elsie Moreland appears in Rawick, Hillegas, and Lawrence, eds., *The American Slave*, 4:456. Some masters gave their slaves a share of cotton profits; see Phillips, *American Negro Slavery*, p. 279; and Weymouth T. Jordan, *Hugh Davis and His Alabama Plantation* (University, Ala., 1948), pp. 104–5. Still others let slaves cultivate a cotton field, the proceeds of which purchased Christmas presents. For a fuller examination of this practice see the essay by John Campbell in this volume.

40. *Georgia Code*, 1861, pp. 271–72, specifies the requirements of legal fences and the respective rights and liabilities of landowners and animal owners. As Steven Hahn has demonstrated, such common rights provoked intense struggle between landowners and animal owners after the Civil War. See his "Hunting, Fishing, and Foraging: Common Rights and Class Relations in the Postbellum South," *Radical History Review* 26 (1982): 37–64, as well as *The Roots of Southern Populism: Yeoman Farmers and the Transformation of the Georgia Upcountry, 1850–1890* (New York, 1983). But before the war, the supremacy of private rights over common rights was not clearly established. In Georgia as elsewhere the citizenry at large retained assorted rights to privately owned but unimproved land. Besides the subsistence rights of gathering firewood and foraging animals, these also included commercial rights. As late as 1857, for instance, persons in certain counties could cut timber for sale on land they did not own, unless the landowner or his agent posted written notice on the courthouse door specifically "forbidding any person from trespassing on said land or lands" (*Georgia Acts*, 1857, p. 250). The 1850s clearly mark a transitional period in the narrowing of common rights in the interest of private rights. Proprietors of riparian lands steadily advanced their rights over riverbanks and to some extent over the watercourses themselves (*Georgia Acts*, 1855–56, pp. 12–13). And whereas the legislature circumscribed landowners' rights against commercial exploitation in some counties, it extended them in others, for instance by flatly prohibiting any person from cutting trees for sale "knowing the same to be the property of another" (*Georgia Acts*, 1857, p. 253, and 1858, p. 162). It is noteworthy that none of the relevant legislation banned taking wood for home use. For a recent interpretation that depicts antebellum Southern property rights as unqualifiedly absolute, see James Oakes, *Slavery and Freedom: An Interpretation of the Old South* (New York, 1990), ch. 2.

41. See Phillips, ed., *Plantation and Frontier*, 1:169.

42. Ball, *Fifty Years in Chains*, pp. 167, 262–63; Olmsted, *The Cotton Kingdom*, p. 372; Phillips, ed., *Plantation and Frontier*, 1:171. For anthropological perspectives on the sexual division of labor in agricultural settings, see George P. Murdock and Caterina Provost, "Factors in the Division of Labor by

Sex: A Cross-Cultural Analysis," *Ethnology* 12 (1973): 203–25; and Michael L. Burton and Douglas R. White, "Sexual Division of Labor in Agriculture," *American Anthropologist* 86 (1984): 568–83.

43. *Southern Agriculturist* 10 (1837): 239. See also Phillips, *American Negro Slavery,* ch. 12; Gray, *History of Southern Agriculture;* Arthur F. Raper, *Tenants of the Almighty* (New York, 1943), pp. 44–45; Chester McArthur Destler, "David Dickson's 'System of Farming' and the Agricultural Revolution in the Deep South, 1850–1885," *Agricultural History* 31 (1957): 30–39; John Hebron Moore, *Agriculture in Ante-Bellum Mississippi* (New York, 1958); James C. Bonner, *A History of Georgia Agriculture, 1732–1860* (Athens, 1964); and Pope, *History of Newberry County,* 1:118–21. On fences, see *Southern Agriculturist* 1 (1828): 306–8; *Southern Cultivator* 2 (1844): 19, 173.

44. *Southern Agriculturist* 6 (1833): 67–69, and 3 (1830): 123.

45. For the quoted planter, see *Southern Cultivator* 4 (1846): 127; for illustrations, see also *Southern Cultivator* 5 (1847): 60–61, 161.

46. See Olmsted's description of "Plow-Girls" in *A Journey in the Back Country* (New York, 1970), pp. 81–82.

47. Sam Bowers Hilliard, *Atlas of Antebellum Southern Agriculture* (Baton Rouge, 1984), maps 64–75. For Ball's observation, see *Fifty Years in Chains,* p. 318. Frederick Douglass provided vivid testimony of a slave's first attempt at handling ornery work animals; see his *Narrative of the Life of Frederick Douglass an American Slave Written by Himself,* Benjamin Quarles, ed. (Cambridge, Mass., 1988), pp. 89–91.

48. Although George Fitzhugh gave classic expression to this point in *Cannibals All! Or, Slaves without Masters* (Cambridge, Mass., 1960), countless other ideologues have echoed the same refrain. See, for example, *Southern Cultivator* 3 (1845): 148.

49. Genovese, *Roll, Jordan, Roll: The World the Slaves Made* (New York, 1974), p. 538; Bonner, *History of Georgia Agriculture,* p. 198.

50. *Georgia Code,* 1861, pp. 368–69.

51. Olmsted, *The Cotton Kingdom,* pp. 257–58.

52. For opposition to trafficking, see *Southern Agriculturist* 5 (1832): 183, and 6 (1833): 285–86. For opposition to gardening and other productive activity, see *Southern Agriculturist* 9 (1836): 230, 518–20; also *Southern Cultivator* 8 (1850): 163. More generally, see Lawrence T. McDonnell, "Money Knows No Master: Market Relations and the American Slave Community," in Winfred B. Moore, Jr., Joseph F. Tripp, and Lyon G. Tyler, Jr., eds., *Developing Dixie: Modernization in a Traditional Society* (Westport, Conn., 1988), pp. 31–44.

53. Bonner, *History of Georgia Agriculture,* pp. 118–19.

Chapter 6

1. For general accounts of the movement of slavery into the upland cotton South, see Allan Kulikoff, "Uprooted Peoples: Black Migrants in the Age of the

American Revolution, 1790–1820," in Ira Berlin and Ronald Hoffman, eds., *Slavery and Freedom in the Age of the American Revolution* (Charlottesville, Va., 1983), pp. 143–71; Ulrich Bonnell Phillips, "The Origin and Growth of the Southern Black Belts," in Phillips, *The Slave Economy of the Old South: Selected Essays in Economic and Social History,* ed. with an introduction by Eugene D. Genovese (Baton Rouge, 1968), pp. 95–116 (orig. pub. 1906); Thomas Perkins Abernethy, *The South in the New Nation, 1789–1819* (Baton Rouge, 1961), ch. 16; Everett Dick, *The Dixie Frontier: A Social History of the Southern Frontier from the First Transmontane Beginnings to the Civil War* (New York, 1948), chs. 5–7. Useful surveys of Chesapeake and low-country slave societies in the late eighteenth and early nineteenth centuries include Allan Kulikoff, *Tobacco and Slaves: The Development of Southern Cultures in the Chesapeake, 1680–1800* (Chapel Hill, 1986); Richard S. Dunn, "Black Society in the Chesapeake, 1776–1810," and Philip D. Morgan, "Black Society in the Lowcountry, 1760–1810," both in Berlin and Hoffman, eds., *Slavery and Freedom in the Age of the American Revolution,* pp. 49–141.

2. Lewis Cecil Gray, *History of Agriculture in the Southern United States to 1860,* 2 vols. (Washington, D.C., 1933), 2:683–89, 888–905. Population figures calculated from U.S. Census Office, *Population of the United States in 1860* (Washington, D.C., 1864); the "Southern states" include all those that would later join the Confederacy, plus Maryland, Kentucky, and Missouri.

3. Gray, *History of Agriculture,* 2:691–700, 898–90; Gavin Wright, "Slavery and the Cotton Boom," *Explorations in Economic History* 12 (1975): 439–51.

4. On the economics and politics of settlement, see Mary E. Young, *Red- skins, Ruffleshirts, and Rednecks: Indian Allotments in Alabama and Mississippi, 1830–1860* (Norman, Okla., 1961).

5. The 1830 and 1840 figures are calculated from the manuscript census schedules, slave population, Lowndes County, Mississippi, microfilm, National Archives, Washington. Figures on slaves brought into the county by their owners are calculated from "Lowndes County slave list," microfilm, Special Collections, Mitchell Memorial Library, Mississippi State University, Starkville. The list (presumably kept in accordance with a Mississippi law that, between 1836 and 1847, prohibited the importation of slaves into the state by anyone other than their owner or authorized agent and required the registration of those brought in legally) provides the following information for 469 slaveholdings brought into Lowndes County: name of owner, number of slaves, and date of registration. In the majority of cases, it describes the holdings as containing specified numbers of men, women, "boys," "girls," and children, allowing for rough disaggregation by age and sex.

6. Henry A. Tayloe to Benj. Ogle Tayloe, 29 July 1839, Tayloe Family Papers, Virginia Historical Society, Richmond (hereafter VHS); Jno. Knight to William M. Beall, 27 January 1844, John Knight Papers, Perkins Library, Duke University, Durham, N.C. (hereafter Duke). The predominance of young slaves in the interstate slave trade is amply documented in Michael Tadman,

Speculators and Slaves: Masters, Traders, and Slaves in the Old South (Madison, Wisc., 1990). A number of large slaveholders, particularly in the Chesapeake, seem to have purchased cotton plantations in Alabama or Mississippi, intending more or less systematically to relocate young slaves whom they could work more profitably there than back east. The papers of John Hartwell Cocke in the Cocke Deposit, Alderman Library, University of Virginia, Charlottesville (hereafter UV) provide a wealth of information on this pattern, as do those of the Tayloe Family at the Virginia Historical Society. On the Tayloes, see also Richard S. Dunn, "A Tale of Two Plantations: Slave Life at Mesopotamia in Jamaica and Mount Airy in Virginia, 1799 to 1828," *William and Mary Quarterly*, 3d ser., 36 (1977): 32–65.

7. Calculated from U.S. Census Office, *Sixth Census, Or Enumeration of the Inhabitants of the United States, as Corrected at the Department of State, in 1840* (Washington, D.C., 1841).

8. For assessments of the significance of this forced migration, see especially Kulikoff, "Uprooted Peoples," and Herbert G. Gutman and Richard Sutch, "The Slave Family: Protected Agent of Capitalist Masters or Victim of the Slave Trade?" in *Reckoning with Slavery: A Critical Study in the Quantitative History of American Negro Slavery* (New York, 1976), ch. 3. Much of the discussion in the historical literature continues to center on the probably unanswerable question of how many slaves were moved via slave traders versus how many moved with their owners. See, most notably, Frederic Bancroft, *Slave Trading in the Old South* (Baltimore, 1931); William Calderhead, "How Extensive Was the Border State Slave Trade? Another Look," *Civil War History* 43 (1972): 42–55; Robert W. Fogel and Stanley L. Engerman, *Time on the Cross: The Economics of American Negro Slavery*, 2 vols. (Boston, 1974), 1:44–57; Tadman, *Speculators and Slaves*, and "Slave Trading in the Ante-Bellum South: An Estimate of the Extent of the Inter-Regional Slave Trade," *Journal of American Studies* 13 (1979): 192–220.

9. The discussion of the character of slave migrations derives from Bancroft, *Slave Trading*, pp. 280–89; E. A. Andrews, *Slavery and the Domestic Slave Trade in the United States* (Boston, 1836), p. 149; James Benson Sellers, *Slavery in Alabama* (University, Ala., 1950), p. 153; as well as manuscripts scattered about the collections cited in these notes.

10. Nathl. A. Hooe to William A. Harrison, 18 November 1832, Hooe-Harrison Papers, UV.

11. William B. Beverly to Robert Beverly, 3 December 1830, 21 January 1831, 9 June 1831, 1 August 1831, Beverly Family Papers, VHS.

12. On the paucity of open land in one region, see Merle Wentworth Meyers, "Geography of the Mississippi Black Prairie" (Ph.D. diss., Clark University, 1948), p. 256.

13. On land-clearing practices in the early and mid-nineteenth-century South, see *Southern Cultivator* 1 (1843): 173; 4 (1846): 58; 5 (1847): 25; 11 (1853): 209; 16 (1858): 213–14; *The Cultivator*, new ser., 2 (1835): 302; William B. Dana,

Cotton from Seed to Loom: A Handbook of Facts for the Daily Use of Producer, Merchant and Consumer (New York, 1878), pp. 84–85.

14. Obviously, the amount of land a slave could clear depended on the nature of the land as well as the vigor and skill of the slave. One-eighth of an acre was the standard daily task for clearing work in the low country. See Philip D. Morgan, "Work and Culture: The Task System and the World of Lowcountry Blacks, 1700 to 1880," *William and Mary Quarterly,* 3d ser., 39 (1982): 575. In newly opening areas, the average was probably a good deal less. It took two months for a group of eight men and three women to clear forty acres of virgin land in frontier Georgia, for example; assuming that nine of the eleven slaves worked at clearing for twenty-five days per month, each hand averaged less than one-tenth of an acre per day. See Charles Ball, *Slavery in the United States: A Narrative of the Life and Adventures of Charles Ball . . .* (Lewistown, Pa., 1836), pp. 260–63. For roughly comparable estimates, see Lois Green Carr and Lorena S. Walsh, "Economic Diversification and Labor Organization in the Chesapeake, 1650–1820," in Stephen D. Innes, ed., *Work and Labor in Early America* (Chapel Hill, 1988), p. 151.

15. Ray Mathis, *John Horry Dent, South Carolina Aristocrat on the Alabama Frontier* (University, Ala., 1979), p. 34. Preparing to open a southwest Georgia plantation "all in the woods," a planter warned a would-be partner that, because of the difficulty in clearing, "we could make nothing on the place for nearly three years." See John B. Lamar to Howell Cobb, 29 December 1846, in Ulrich B. Phillips, ed., *Plantation and Frontier,* 2 vols. (Cleveland, 1909), 1:178–81.

16. William B. Beverly to Robert Beverly, 9 June 1831, 13 September 1834; Robert Beverly to Robert Beverly, 28 August 1832, 20 August 1833, Beverly Family Papers, VHS. From similar reasoning, Thomas Harrison of up-country South Carolina, who was preparing to send a portion of his slaves to his son in Mississippi, took it for granted that in the early going "it would be out of the question to buy provisions for the women and children, and no one would hire them without a sufficient proportion of working hands." See Thomas Harrison to James T. Harrison, 4 January 1836, Harrison Family Papers, Southern Historical Collection, University of North Carolina, Chapel Hill (hereafter SHC).

17. On the sexual division of field labor on cotton plantations, see Elizabeth Fox-Genovese, *Within the Plantation Household: Black and White Women of the Old South* (Chapel Hill, 1988), pp. 172–77; Ball, *Slavery in the United States,* p. 162; Morgan, "Black Society in the Lowcountry, 1760–1810," p. 107; John Witherspoon DuBose, "The Canebrake Negro, 1850–1865," typescript, John Witherspoon DuBose Papers, Alabama Department of Archives and History, Montgomery (hereafter ADAH).

18. On the relative scarcity of skilled slaves on New World cotton plantations vis-à-vis those of staples such as sugar, see B. W. Higman, *Slave Populations of the British Caribbean, 1807–1834* (Baltimore, 1984), pp. 167–72. On the

relatively high proportion of skilled slaves in the low country, see Morgan, "Black Society in the Lowcountry," pp. 97–104.

19. Overall, working-aged men outnumbered women in the same group only slightly (between 105 and 120 men per 100 women) in the slave population of black-belt counties during the settlement period.

20. See, among a plethora of examples, Martha B. Wilson to Charles Tait, 13 January 1835, Tait Papers, ADAH; Nathl. A. Hooe to William A. Harrison, 23 March 1832; Hooe-Harrison Papers, UV; Fletcher M. Green, ed., *The Lides Go South . . . and West: The Record of a Planter Migration in 1835* (Columbia, S.C., 1952), pp. v, 9; Dick, *Dixie Frontier*, pp. 55–56; Henry A. Tayloe to Benjamin Ogle Tayloe, 27 December 1833, 1 September 1835, 20 July 1839, 15 October 1839, Tayloe Family Papers, VHS; James Graham to William Graham, 7 February 1833, in J. G. DeRoulhac Hamilton, ed., *The Papers of William Graham*, 7 vols. (Raleigh, N.C., 1957), 1:250–52.

21. This paragraph and the one that follows are based upon James A. Tait to Charles Tait, 21 January 1818, 7 February 1818, 19 January 1819; Charles Tait to James A. Tait, 14 October 1818, 10 November 1818, all in Tait Papers, ADAH.

22. On slave-hire arrangements among frontier cotton planters, see Alfred Graham to William Graham, 20 February 1832, Joseph Graham to William Graham, 22 December 1833, James A. King to William Graham, 13 October 1838, in Hamilton, ed., *Papers of William Graham*, 1:232–34, 2:14–15; P. R. Beverly to Robert Beverly, 10 September 1829, and Robert Beverly to Robert Beverly, 28 August 1837, Beverly Family Papers, VHS; Nathl. A. Hooe to William A. Harrison, 16 February 1832 and 23 March 1832, Hooe-Harrison Papers, UV; Mathis, *John Horry Dent*, pp. 97–98; Thomas Harrison to James T. Harrison, 4 January 1836, Harrison Family Papers, SHC; Sarah L. Fountain to Hannah L. Coker, 10 February 1836, in Green, ed., *Lides Go South*, p. 11; Solomon Northrup, *Twelve Years a Slave* (Buffalo, 1853), pp. 152–53; John R. Long to William Long, 15 June 1838, William Long Papers, North Carolina State Department of Archives and History, Raleigh (hereafter NCDAH). Especially revealing are the accounts and memoranda in Henry Toole Clark Papers, Duke.

23. Accounts and memoranda in Henry Toole Clark Papers, Duke.

24. Louis Hughes, *Thirty Years a Slave: From Bondage to Freedom* (1897; reprint, New York, 1969), pp. 36–37. See also J. R. Long to William Long, 18 January 1838, William Long Papers, NCDAH; Franklin L. Riley, ed., "Diary of a Mississippi Planter, January 1, 1840, to April 1863," *Publications of the Mississippi Historical Society* 10 (1909): 305–481, passim, but especially the entries for early 1840 beginning on p. 312; William Ethelbert Ervin Plantation Book, SHC, vol. 1, especially the entries for 1839. On the increasing participation of Chesapeake slave women in clearing-related tasks during the late eighteenth and early nineteenth centuries, see Carr and Walsh, "Economic Diversification and Labor Organization," especially pp. 175–88. For an ac-

count of slave women who took their turns with the axe as well as with the grubbing hoe, see Northrup, *Twelve Years a Slave*, pp. 152–53.

25. Hughes, *Thirty Years a Slave*, pp. 36–37; Riley, ed., "Diary of a Mississippi Planter," passim; Sellers, *Slavery in Alabama*, p. 73; "Report of the Committee of the Barnwell Agricultural Society on the Culture of Cotton," *Southern Cultivator* 3 (1845): 114–15; *Southern Cultivator* 4 (1846): 11; J. W. Monett, essay on the culture of cotton, printed as an appendix in [Joseph Holt Ingraham], *The South-West, By a Yankee*, 2 vols. (New York, 1835), 1:281.

26. Dick, *Dixie Frontier*, p. 81; Gideon Lincecum, "The Autobiography of Gideon Lincecum," *Publications of the Mississippi Historical Society* 8 (1913): 471–72; Hughes, *Thirty Years a Slave*, pp. 36–37; William J. Barbee, *The Cotton Question: The Production, Export, Manufacture, and Consumption of Cotton* (New York, 1866), p. 84; Dana, *Cotton from Seed to Loom*, p. 85.

27. On the significance of new upland cotton strains, see John Hebron Moore, *Agriculture in Ante-Bellum Mississippi* (New York, 1958), pp. 28–36, 46. On implements, see John Hebron Moore, *The Emergence of the Cotton Kingdom in the Old Southwest: Mississippi, 1770–1860* (Baton Rouge, 1988), ch. 3; *Southern Agriculturist* 7 (1834): 22; *Southern Cultivator* 3 (1845): 100.

28. On the gang system generally, see Gray, *History of Agriculture*, 1:550–56; Philip D. Morgan, "Task and Gang Systems: The Organization of Labor on New World Plantations," in Innes, ed., *Work and Labor in Early America*. On its prevalence in the southwest, see Charles Sackett Sydnor, *Slavery in Mississippi* (New York, 1933), p. 9. For an example of a Mississippi planter who routinely divided his force into squads, see the William Ethelbert Ervin Plantation Book, SHC, vol. 1, passim. For explications of the rationale behind the shift from task to gang organization, see, for example, *Farmers' Register* 5 (1838): 269–71; Drew Gilpin Faust, *James Henry Hammond and the Old South: A Design for Mastery* (Baton Rouge, 1982), ch. 5, especially pp. 74–75, 92.

29. On Tait and task work, see Sellers, *Slavery in Alabama*, 66–74. For an example of a low-country planter's conversion from task to gang labor on setting up in Alabama, see "The Canebrake Negro, 1850–1865," typescript, John Witherspoon DuBose Papers, ADAH. For another instance of what appears to have been task organization on an Alabama plantation, see George P. Rawick, Jan Hillegas, and Ken Lawrence, eds., *The American Slave: A Composite Autobiography*, supp. ser. 1, *Alabama Narratives*, 1:48. Encountering evidence that, on some upland cotton estates some operations (usually plowing or hoeing) were organized by the task, historians have occasionally concluded that the "task system" was widely implemented. See, for example, Sellers, *Slavery in Alabama*, pp. 66–70; Moore, *Emergence of the Cotton Kingdom*, pp. 95–96, which goes so far as to suggest that "a revised version of the task system . . . gradually replaced the gang system" on Mississippi plantations after 1840; and Morgan, "Task and Gang Systems," especially pp. 199, 206–7. The evidence is too thin to support such a conclusion. Especially erroneous is any equation between task organization and the use of quotas during the cotton-picking season, despite their superficial similarities. Almost universally the quota consti-

tuted the minimum acceptable product of a full day's labor; few slaveholders permitted slaves to quit work upon attaining it. Hands who exceeded the minimum sometimes received rewards for doing so, while those who fell short faced punishment. Moreover, evidence strongly suggests that masters and overseers based quotas upon the maximum output of each individual slave or each "class" of hands, as a means of forcing slaves to work harder to finish picking before exposure to winter weather damaged the standing crop. See, for example, Monett, essay on the culture of cotton, in [Ingraham], *Southwest, by a Yankee,* 2:285–86; Sydnor, *Slavery in Mississippi,* pp. 15–21; Northrup, *Twelve Years a Slave,* pp. 165–71; Hughes, *Thirty Years a Slave,* pp. 31–32.

30. Ball, *Slavery in the United States,* pp. 39–40, 57–58, 165–68. See also Joseph B. Lyman, *Cotton Culture* (New York, 1868), pp. 15–16.

31. Jackson *Mississippian,* 6 January 1837; Huntsville *Democrat,* 14 March 1840; Tadman, *Speculators and Slaves,* p. 128. Even after emancipation, one authority on cotton planting emphasized that it was "very desirable to hire laborers that are accustomed to cotton." See Lyman, *Cotton Culture,* p. 16.

32. Jno. Knight to William M. Beall, 27 January 1844, John Knight Papers, Duke. See also Robert Beverly to Robert Beverly, 3 September 1833, Beverly Family Papers, VHS; Susan Dabney Smedes, *Memorials of a Southern Planter* (Baltimore, 1887), p. 69; Northrup, *Twelve Years a Slave,* pp. 178–79.

33. William B. Beverly to Robert Beverly, 4 June 1835; Robert Beverly to Robert Beverly, 15 October 1835 and 1 January 1841, Beverly Family Papers, VHS.

34. Quoted in Herbert Anthony Kellar, ed., *Solon Robinson: Pioneer and Agriculturist,* 2 vols. (Indianapolis, 1936), 2:296.

35. *American Agriculturist,* as quoted in J. A. Turner, *The Cotton Planters Manual: Being a Compilation of Facts from the Best Authorities on the Culture of Cotton* (New York, 1857), pp. 133–34; see also the essay by Joseph P. Reidy in this volume. Leslie S. Rowland has written on the implications of low-country provisioning practices: "The Politics of Task Labor and Independent Production in Lowcountry South Carolina and Georgia" (unpublished essay courtesy of the author).

36. Useful sources pertaining to garden plots on upland cotton plantations include Mathis, *John Horry Dent,* p. 93; Sellers, *Slavery in Alabama,* pp. 73–74; Charles S. Davis, *The Cotton Kingdom in Alabama* (Montgomery, Ala., 1939), pp. 60–61; Weymouth T. Jordan, *Hugh Davis and His Alabama Plantation* (University, Ala., 1948), pp. 104–6; Frederick Law Olmsted, *A Journey in the Back Country* (1860; reprint, New York, 1970), pp. 74–75; Rawick, Hillegas, and Lawrence, eds., *American Slave,* supp. ser. 1, *Alabama Narratives* 1:40, 159, 161–62; supp. ser. 1, *Mississippi Narratives* 8:823; and supp. ser. 1, *Mississippi Narratives* 10:2021; Ball, *Slavery in the United States,* especially pp. 128, 145–46. Ball's narrative provides an essential starting point for understanding the political economy of slave gardens in the early nineteenth-century upland South. On the broader context of slave gardens and provision grounds in the Americas, see Ira Berlin and Philip D. Morgan, "Introduction," in "The Slaves'

Economy: Independent Production by Slaves in the Americas," special issue of *Slavery and Abolition* 12 (May 1991); Eugene D. Genovese, *Roll, Jordan, Roll: The World the Slaves Made* (New York, 1974), pp. 535–40.

37. Before the slaves of Thomas Dabney embarked with their owner from Virginia to central Mississippi in the early 1830s, one of them recalled half a century later, they had to "sell all our things." See Smedes, *Memorials of a Southern Planter*, p. 54.

38. *Southern Agriculturist*, as reprinted in *Southern Cultivator* 4 (1846): 43–45. On the debate among planters over "Negro crops," see the essay by John Campbell in this volume; James Breeden, *Advice among Masters: The Ideal in Slave Management in the Old South* (Westport, Conn., 1980); Lawrence T. McDonnell, "Money Knows No Master: Market Relations and the American Slave Community," in *Developing Dixie: Modernization in a Traditional Society*, Winfred B. Moore, Jr., Joseph F. Tripp, and Lyon G. Tyler, Jr., eds. (New York, 1988), pp. 31–44.

39. Sellers, *Slavery in Alabama*, pp. 55–56.

40. *Raymond Times*, 7 May 1841, as quoted in Moore, *Emergence of the Cotton Kingdom*, p. 15. A Mississippi planter, who in early 1837 urged his fellows that it was in "the interest of the planter" to raise more food on the plantation, nevertheless acknowledged that earlier in the decade it may have been "in the interests of planters to purchase [provisions], especially as they had not land open sufficient to make a good crop of cotton and corn": Jackson *Mississippian*, 24 February 1837. On local food shortages and the high price of provisions, see, for example, Sophia Witherspoon to William Graham, 14 April 1828, in Hamilton, ed., *Papers of William Graham*, 1:177–79; Eli H. Lide to Caleb Coker, 25 October 1836, in Green, ed., *Lides Go South*, p. 23; Gaius Whitfield to William Whitfield, 15 April 1833, James B. Whitfield Papers, ADAH; Robert Beverly to Robert Beverly, 3 September 1833, Beverly Family Papers, VHS; Vernon[?] Terrell to John D. Terrell, 21 January 1835, John D. Terrell Papers, ADAH.

41. John W. Blassingame, *Slave Testimony: Two Centuries of Letters, Speeches, Interviews, and Autobiographies* (Baton Rouge, 1971), p. 132. After emancipation, an elderly North Carolina freedman informed a Northern minister that "he had built eight houses for himself on his master's plantation. His heartless lord would give him a building spot, and suffer him to live there until he had cleared the land around his dwelling, and then would drive him out, to repeat the process in a new location": Horace James, *Annual Report of the Superintendent of Negro Affairs in North Carolina, 1864* (Boston, 1865), p. 27.

42. Kellar, ed., *Solon Robinson*, 2:295–96.

Chapter 7

1. Michael Kammen, ed., "Maryland in 1699: A Letter from the Rev. Hugh Jones," *Journal of Southern History* 29 (1963): 369–70; William Hand Browne, et al., eds., *Archives of Maryland*, 72 vols. (Baltimore, 1883–1972), 25:602.

2. This paper is based on preliminary results of a manuscript in progress on plantation agriculture in the Chesapeake region, tentatively entitled " 'To Labour for Profit': Plantation Management in the Chesapeake, 1620–1820." The primary sources are planter correspondence, plantation account books, and selected probate inventories throughout all parts of the region where tobacco was at one time an important crop. The bulk of the evidence comes from a few middling and many large servant and slaveowners, although small planters are taken into account. The project draws especially on the work of Lois Carr, Paul Clemens, Carville Earle, Lewis Gray, Allan Kulikoff, John McCusker, Russell Menard, Edward Papenfuse, David Percy, and Joseph Robert, as well as upon numerous county studies, studies of individual planters, and works on Chesapeake merchants and the Chesapeake economy. I am indebted to all, though there are a number of areas where my interpretations differ from theirs. Some preliminary results of the project are summarized in Lorena S. Walsh, "Plantation Management in the Chesapeake, 1620–1820," *Journal of Economic History* 49 (1989): 393–406. For a bibliography of recent literature see John J. McCusker and Russell R. Menard, *The Economy of British America, 1607–1789* (Chapel Hill, 1985), ch. 6.

3. Allan Kulikoff, *Tobacco and Slaves: The Development of Southern Cultures in the Chesapeake, 1680–1800* (Chapel Hill, 1986). Also see T. H. Breen, *Tobacco Culture: The Mentality of the Great Tidewater Planters on the Eve of the Revolution* (Princeton, 1985).

4. Kulikoff, *Tobacco and Slaves*, chs. 2 and 8.

5. Letters of 3 July and 5 July 1751 and 27 February 1752, Charles Stewart Letterbook, 1751–53, MS., Historical Society of Pennsylvania, Philadelphia; a microfilm copy is available at the Colonial Williamsburg Foundation Research Library, Williamsburg, Virginia.

6. Kulikoff, *Tobacco and Slaves*, part 3; Richard S. Dunn, "Black Society in the Chesapeake, 1776–1810," in *Slavery and Freedom in the Age of the American Revolution*, Ira Berlin and Ronald Hoffman, eds. (Charlottesville, Va., 1983), 49–82; Philip D. Morgan and Michael L. Nicholls, "Slaves in Piedmont Virginia, 1720–1790," *William and Mary Quarterly*, 3d ser., 46 (1989): 211–51.

7. Sources dealing with size of work units include Kulikoff, *Tobacco and Slaves*; Russell R. Menard, "The Maryland Slave Population, 1658 to 1730: A Demographic Profile of Blacks in Four Counties," *William and Mary Quarterly*, 3d ser., 32 (1975): 29–54; Gloria L. Main, *Tobacco Colony: Life in Early Maryland, 1650–1720* (Princeton, 1982), ch. 3; Jean Butenhoff Lee, "The Problem of Slave Community in the Eighteenth-Century Chesapeake," *William and Mary Quarterly*, 3d ser., 43 (1986): 333–61; and Lois Green Carr and Lorena S. Walsh, "Economic Diversification and Labor Organization in the Chesapeake, 1650–1820," in Stephen Innes, ed., *Work and Labor in Early America* (Chapel Hill, 1988), pp. 144–88.

8. Kulikoff, *Tobacco and Slaves*, ch. 9; Lorena S. Walsh, " 'To Labour for Profit': Plantation Management in the Chesapeake, 1620–1820," manuscript in progress.

9. For characteristics of such agricultural systems, see Ester Boserup, *Population and Technological Change: A Study of Long-Term Trends* (Chicago, 1981).

10. This agricultural system is described and analyzed in Lois Green Carr, Russell R. Menard, and Lorena S. Walsh, *Robert Cole's World: Agriculture and Society in Early Maryland* (Chapel Hill, 1991).

11. Ibid., and Lorena S. Walsh, "Enlightened Practice or Egregious Blunder? Agricultural Change and the Chesapeake Ecology, 1650–1820," paper presented at the annual meeting of the Social Science History Association, November 1988.

12. The crop outputs per laborer, termed "shares per hand" in most contemporary records, include both exact observations of crop divisions and some estimates. The exact observations, most of which come from planter account books, report the size of the total crop on a given plantation, the number of field laborers, their ranking as full or half sharers, and the number of shares awarded the overseer. In order to make output figures comparable, I recalculated some shares reported in the account books. Overseers, where present, were always counted as one laborer in the crop; yields were recalculated when overseers received more than a single share. Shares retained by planters for draft animals, where present, were reallocated among the labor force. I have also used some estimates derived from probate inventories and plantation accounts that report the size of the total crop and the approximate number of field hands. I used only those results that appeared "reasonable"; to be included, an estimated output had to fall within the range of the exact observations. My definition of a hand is that universally employed by planters themselves: any able-bodied adult man or woman. Planters rated only older or partially disabled slaves or youngsters between twelve and fifteen as half shares; when making estimates, I have followed this rating used in the account books. The crop output data is thus standardized but not sex specific. There is no evidence in contemporary plantation records that Chesapeake planters rated female field hands any differently from males. Only William Tatham asserted that women were counted as three-quarter hands: William Tatham, *An Historical and Practical Essay on the Culture and Commerce of Tobacco* (1800; reprinted in Melvin G. Herndon, ed., *William Tatham and the Culture of Tobacco* [Coral Gables, Fla., 1969], pp. 101–2). Still, interpretation must take into account shifts in the sex and age composition of the labor force as well as increases in the hours of work per day and the number of days worked. Median outputs, not here reported, were with a few exceptions quite similar to the mean.

13. Russell R. Menard, "The Tobacco Industry in the Chesapeake Colonies, 1617–1730: An Interpretation," *Research in Economic History* 5 (1980): 109–77; Russell R. Menard, "From Servants to Slaves: The Transformation of the Chesapeake Labor System," *Southern Studies* 16 (1977): 355–90.

14. This link emerges in the analysis of many individual plantations; it will be further explored in Walsh, " 'To Labour for Profit.' "

15. I have made such comparisons for York County, Virginia, and St. Mary's, Charles, Talbot, and Queen Anne counties, Maryland, for which there was sufficient data to plot annual series. In each case tobacco crop shares peak during the period when probate inventories indicate that the labor force was shifting primarily to slaves. However, I have yet to detect any correlation between further changes in the composition of the labor force and the timing of upward shifts in corn and wheat. These shifts appear more related to market access.

16. Carr and Walsh, "Economic Diversification and Labor Organization."

17. William Byrd II, *Prose Works*, Louis B. Wright, ed. (Cambridge, Mass., 1966), pp. 349–50. Materials in the Jones Family Papers, MS., Library of Congress, corroborate Byrd's observation.

18. Carr and Walsh, "Economic Diversification and Labor Organization." This is not to imply that many white servants and poor free whites did not live in similar small, flimsy houses. However, as the eighteenth century progressed, successful planters provided themselves, their overseers, and their white servants with better shelters. Slaves, however, continued to be housed in the cheapest quarters that could possibly be constructed until at least the end of the century and, even then, improved quarters were constructed only on home plantations, not on outlying quarters. For a review of slave housing, see Mechal Sobel, *The World They Made Together: Black and White Values in Eighteenth-Century Virginia* (Princeton, 1987), ch. 9.

19. Carr and Walsh, "Economic Diversification and Labor Organization," quoting the *Journal of Jasper Danckaerts, 1679–1680*, Bartlett Burleigh James and J. Franklin Jameson, eds. (New York, 1913), p. 133.

20. Carr and Walsh, "Economic Diversification and Labor Organization."

21. Walsh, " 'To Labour for Profit' "; Galloway-Maxcy-Markoe Papers, MS., Library of Congress, no. 13416. On frequent changes of overseers as a management strategy designed to prevent slaves from becoming "too set in their way" (or exerting too much control), see William Kauffman Scarborough, *The Overseer: Plantation Management in the Old South* (Athens, Ga., 1984), pp. 38–40, 125–27. Some Chesapeake planters also thought that "overseers tire as cornfields do." See, for example, *The Diary of Col. Landon Carter of Sabine Hall, 1752–1778*, Jack P. Greene, ed. (Charlottesville, Va., 1965), pp. 301–2; also William Bolling, quoted in Ulrich B. Phillips, *Life and Labor in the Old South* (Boston, 1963), pp. 237–38.

22. Walsh, "Enlightened Practice"; U.S. Department of Agriculture Soil Conservation Service, *Soil Survey of Charles County, Maryland* (Washington, D.C., 1974), pp. 91–92; Lewis Cecil Gray, *History of Agriculture in the Southern United States to 1860* (1932; reprint, Gloucester, Mass., 1985), ch. 32.

23. Carr and Walsh, "Economic Diversification and Labor Organization."

24. Values for annual gross revenues per laborer from major field crops were converted from Maryland or Virginia currency into sterling using John J. McCusker, *Money and Exchange in Europe and America, 1600–1775: A Handbook*

(Chapel Hill, 1978). They were then deflated by a sterling commodity price index developed for the St. Mary's City Commission by P. M. G. Harris, base years 1700–1709. Averages were compiled from observations of the revenues on individual plantations where information was available on the size and selling price of the major field crops being grown. The bulk of this evidence comes from records of crop divisions between planters or stewards and overseers. While such records survive only for larger planters, I have no reason to suppose they are biased towards more successful planters. Everyone who employed an overseer had to come to some kind of accounting.

25. Regional variations over time will be documented in Walsh, " 'To Labour for Profit.' "

26. My research on prices of sweet-scented tobacco, combined with data compiled by Peter Bergstrom and Harold Gill of Colonial Williamsburg, has permitted construction of a price series from price observations in planter and merchant account books, probate inventories and accounts, and county court records for the period between 1650 and 1810. This price series diverges most markedly from that of oronoco between 1700 and 1725. I will discuss other regional differences between oronoco and sweet-scented regions in " 'To Labour for Profit,' " ch. 3. It should be noted that crop shares of sweet-scented tobacco are often not equivalent to shares of oronoco. Sweet-scented was often stemmed before packing, which resulted in a loss in weight of 25 to 30 percent over leaf. Not all sweet-scented was stemmed, however, the choice varying from year to year and plantation to plantation, depending on the quality of the crop, the forwardness or backwardness of the seasons, the availability of labor, changing legislation, and shifts in buyer tastes. Oronoco was almost never stemmed.

27. The figure of ten barrels is derived from plantation records that detail the allocation of whole crops among slave and livestock food, overseers' shares, seed, and marketed surplus. Maize yields over two-and-a-half but less than ten barrels per hand might produce surpluses as well, depending on the relative number of black and white laborers and dependents on the plantation.

28. Plantation accounts indicate that slave rations almost never included any wheat and that white families, except for those who kept great establishments, consumed no more than two to five bushels of wheat per year. The proportion of the remainder required for seed varied from as little as 11 percent to as much as 100 percent.

29. St. Mary's City Commission inventory files, available at the Maryland State Archives, indicate the presence or absence of plows in eighteen Maryland and Virginia counties for selected time periods between 1650 and 1775. For the 1790s, see Lorena S. Walsh, "Selected Agricultural and Food-Related Items in York County, Virginia, and St. Mary's Country, Maryland, Inventories, 1783–1820," Colonial Williamsburg Research, 1991. On the scarcity of forage, see the correspondence in *The American Farmer*, an agricultural newspaper, from 1819 to 1821, and Julius Rubin, "The Limits of Agricultural Progress in the Nineteenth-Century South," *Agricultural History* 49 (1975): 362–75.

30. This point will be elaborated in " 'To Labour for Profit.' " For opposing views, see Kulikoff, *Tobacco and Slaves*, ch. 10, and Eugene D. Genovese, *The Political Economy of Slavery: Studies in the Economy and Society of the Slave South* (New York, 1966), ch. 5.

31. Lois Green Carr and Russell R. Menard, "Land, Labor, and Economies of Scale in Early Maryland: Some Limits to Growth in the Chesapeake System of Husbandry," *Journal of Economic History* 49 (1989): 407–18. Manure was applied to the hilled crops, corn and tobacco. Seventeenth-century planters had not used manure because of the difficulty of feeding penned animals and because manure was said to affect the taste of the product. This caveat did not apply to the tobacco used for snuff, which was introduced early in the eighteenth century.

32. Carr and Walsh, "Economic Diversification and Labor Organization." For another perspective on diversification and year-round utilization of the labor force, see Ralph V. Anderson, "Labor Utilization and Productivity, Diversification, and Self-Sufficiency, Southern Plantations, 1800–1840" (Ph.D. diss., University of North Carolina, 1974).

33. Carr and Walsh, "Economic Diversification and Labor Organization."

34. Edward C. Papenfuse, Jr., "Planter Behavior and Economic Opportunity in a Staple Economy," *Agricultural History* 46 (1972): 297–311.

35. These assertions are discussed and documented in Lorena S. Walsh, "Rural African Americans in the Constitutional Era in Maryland, 1776–1810," *Maryland Historical Magazine* 84 (1989): 327–41. Some slaves, however, probably found smallpox inoculation familiar, since inoculation was practiced among some contemporary tribes in Africa. Some of the slaves transported to the colonies had undergone the treatment, although whether native-born slaves had or continued to have knowledge of the procedure is unknown. See Eugenia W. Herbert, "Smallpox Inoculation in Africa," *Journal of African History* 16 (1975): 539–59.

36. Walsh, "Rural African Americans."

37. For an example of a slaveowner's presentation to his slaves, see Louis Morton, *Robert Carter of Nomini Hall: A Virginia Tobacco Planter of the Eighteenth Century* (Williamsburg, Va., 1941), pp. 55–56.

38. Walsh, "Rural African Americans." For the Afro-Americans response to the Revolution, see Benjamin Quarles, *The Negro in the American Revolution* (Chapel Hill, 1961); Benjamin Quarles, "The Revolutionary War as a Black Declaration of Independence," in Berlin and Hoffman, eds., *Slavery and Freedom in the Age of the American Revolution*, pp. 283–301; and Ira Berlin, "The Revolution in Black Life," in Alfred F. Young, ed., *The American Revolution* (Dekalb, Ill., 1976), pp. 348–82.

39. Galloway-Maxcy-Markoe Papers, no. 13412, Library of Congress. Similarly, George Washington reported in 1798 that "negros are growing more and more insolant and difficult to govern." See *The Writings of George Washington, 1745–1799*, John C. Fitzpatrick, ed., 39 vols. (Washington, D.C., 1931–44), 36:443–47.

40. Walsh, " 'To Labour for Profit,' " chs. 5 and 6.

41. Ibid.

42. Ibid., ch. 8.

43. Richard Parkinson, *A Tour in America in 1798, 1799, and 1800* (London, 1805), pp. 175–76, 218–19, 303–10, 433–34, 446. For other references to slaves selling produce in towns, see Henry Bradshaw Fearon, *Sketchés of America* (New York, 1818; reprint, 1969), p. 287; Morris Birbeck, *Notes on a Journey in America from the Coast of Virginia to the Territory of Illinois*, 4th ed. (London, 1818), p. 11; and Robert Sutcliff, *Travels in Some Parts of North America, In the Years 1804, 1805, and 1806* (New York, 1811), pp. 96, 195–96. For references to a slave marketer accounting to an urban representative, see the letters of George Gardiner to Francis Jerdone of 23 January and 1 December 1797, 20 February 1798, and 7 February 1799, Francis Jerdone Papers, MS. 39.1 J47, Swem Library, College of William and Mary, box 2. For a record of slaves marketing their owner's produce in Baltimore, see the Thomas Jones Record Books, 1779–1812, MS. 517, Maryland Historical Society, Baltimore. The account books and diaries of almost all later eighteenth-century Virginia and Maryland planters that include a record of cash expenditures mention purchases of produce from local slaves; especially revealing is the Francis Taylor Diary, 1786–1799, MS., Virginia State Library, Richmond.

44. Parkinson, *Tour in America*, p. 174. Crop mixes will be discussed in Walsh, " 'To Labour for Profit,' " ch. 8.

45. There is a greater likelihood that surviving post-Revolutionary and especially early nineteenth-century plantation records are biased toward more efficient plantations. In the first place, papers of the post-Revolutionary generation have not been as carefully preserved as those of the Founding Fathers. In addition, many planters switched from paying overseers a proportion of the crop to paying them a set wage. Hence, records of crops per hand become scarcer, and I suspect that, with the rationale of settling with overseers no longer present, "improving" planters were more likely to keep records than were indifferent managers. To counter some of this bias, I am currently studying inventories of lesser planters in selected counties.

46. Winifred B. Rothenberg, "The Emergence of a Capital Market in Rural Massachusetts, 1730–1838," in Ronald Hoffman, John J. McCusker, and Russell R. Menard, eds., *The Economy of Early America: The Revolutionary Period, 1763–1790* (Charlottesville, Va., 1986), pp. 126–65. Rothenberg notes a similar appearance of internal improvement and bank securities in the holdings of wealthy rural Massachusetts farmers.

47. Lorena S. Walsh, "Land, Landlord, and Leaseholder: Estate Management and Tenant Fortunes in Southern Maryland, 1642–1820," *Agricultural History* 59 (1985): 373–96; Willard F. Bliss, "The Rise of Tenancy in Virginia," *Virginia Magazine of History and Biography* 58 (1950): 427–41; Dunn, "Black Society in the Chesapeake," p. 79; Kulikoff, *Tobacco and Slaves*, pp. 397–98.

48. Henry M. Miller, "Transforming a 'Splendid and Delightsome Land':

Colonists and Ecological Change in the Chesapeake, 1607–1820," *Journal of the Washington Academy of Sciences* 76 (1986): 173–87; N. L. Froomer, "Geomorphic Change in Some Western Shore Estuaries during Historic Times" (Ph.D. diss., Johns Hopkins University, 1978); Joseph Scott, *A Geographical Description of the States of Maryland and Delaware* (Philadelphia, 1807); Papenfuse, "Planter Behavior and Economic Opportunity."

49. By 1820 sediments in Chesapeake estuaries were accumulating two to twenty times faster than they had during the period of hoe culture. Many streams, navigable by ships in the 1770s, had become silted up by the early nineteenth century. Enough silt and chemical nutrients were washing into the rivers to change the predominant species of fish in some Chesapeake waters. Some bottom-oriented species, highly regarded as foodfish in the seventeenth and eighteenth centuries, were gone by the mid-nineteenth century. See Grace S. Brush, "Geology and Paleoecology of Chesapeake Bay: A Long-term Monitoring Tool for Management," *Journal of the Washington Academy of Science* 76 (1986): 146–60; Miller, "Transforming a 'Splendid and Delightsome Land.' "

50. Not all planters raised other small grains, but where they did, there were similar increases in output per hand in oats, rye, and spelts, as well as in crops such as pumpkins, Irish potatoes, turnips, carrots, and jerusalem artichokes.

51. [John Taylor], *Arator: Being a Series of Agricultural Essays, Practical and Political: In Sixty-four Numbers*, M. E. Bradford, ed. (1818; reprint, Indianapolis, 1977), p. 128.

52. James R. Irwin, "Exploring the Affinity of Wheat and Slavery in the Virginia Piedmont," *Explorations in Economic History* 25 (1988): 295–322, finds that in 1850 and 1860 there were probably scale effects in wheat production. With the exception of harvest, however, he did not explore other possible scale effects.

53. Lorena S. Walsh, "Plantation Management in the Chesapeake, 1620–1820," *Journal of Economic History* 49 (1989): 393–406.

54. Address of Athanasius Fenwick to the Agricultural Society of St. Mary's County, *The American Farmer*, no. 24 (1819).

55. William Strickland, *Observations on the Agriculture of the United States of America* (London, 1801), p. 25; Gray, *History of Agriculture*, 1:640–46.

56. *The Writings of George Washington*, 30:175–76 (quote) and 36:110–14; Thomas Jones Record Books, MS. 517, and James Wilson Farm Account Book, MS. 915, Maryland Historical Society, Baltimore.

57. That the switch to salaries was intended to cap overseers' wages at a time of rising slave productivity seems corroborated by several things. First, when initially set, salary levels were close to average returns from crop shares; thereafter, salaries tended not to rise, regardless of changes in productivity (Scarborough, *The Overseer*, ch. 2). Second, planters who continued to remunerate overseers with portions of the crop more frequently paid them a set proportion, say a tenth or a twelfth, regardless of the number of workers

supervised. Planters could then add workers without increasing an overseer's compensation. Third, at about the same time, some landlords shifted from letting prime lands—and sometimes slaves, stock, and equipment as well—for a fixed rent to renting them for some proportion of the crops raised.

58. Berlin, "Revolution in Black Life"; and Thomas E. Davidson, "The Demography of Freedom: Manumission Practices and the Shaping of the Eastern Shore's Free African American Population, 1776–1810," paper presented at the conference "Freedom Fettered: Blacks and the Constitutional Era in Maryland: 1776–1810," Morgan State University, October 1987. See also Barbara Jeanne Fields, *Slavery and Freedom on the Middle Ground: Maryland during the Nineteenth Century* (New Haven, 1985), ch. 2.

59. These ideas are developed in Lorena S. Walsh, "The Rationalization of the Chesapeake Tidewater Labor Force, 1720–1820," paper presented to the annual meeting of the Association of Caribbean Historians, April 1986, and in Walsh, "Rural African Americans."

60. Thomas Jones Record Books; Galloway-Maxcy-Markoe Papers, vols. 28 and 29; the examples are in nos. 13286 and 13328.

61. Kathleen Bruce, "Virginian Agricultural Decline to 1860: A Fallacy," *Agricultural History* 6 (1932): 3–13; N. F. Cabell, "Some Fragments of An Intended Report on the Post Revolutionary History of Agriculture in Virginia," *William and Mary Quarterly*, 1st ser., 26 (1917): 145–58; David F. Allmendinger, Jr., "The Early Career of Edmund Ruffin, 1810–1840," *Virginia Magazine of History and Biography* 93 (1985): 127–54; James Blaine Gouger III, "Agricultural Change in the Northern Neck of Virginia, 1700–1860: An Historical Geography" (Ph.D. diss., University of Florida, 1976); Peter Joseph Albert, "The Protean Institution: The Geography, Economy, and Ideology of Slavery in Post-Revolutionary Virginia" (Ph.D. diss., University of Maryland, 1976); Joseph Clarke Robert, *The Tobacco Kingdom: Plantation, Market, and Factory in Virginia and North Carolina, 1800–1860* (1938; reprint, Gloucester, Mass., 1965); Paul W. Gates, *The Farmer's Age: Agriculture 1815–1860* (New York, 1960); Gray, *History of Agriculture*, vol. 2; and Robert McColley, *Slavery and Jeffersonian Virginia*, 2d ed. (Urbana, Ill., 1973). The above sources make varying assessments of the health or morbidity of Chesapeake agriculture between 1820 and 1860.

62. Percy Wells Bidwell and John I. Falconer, *History of Agriculture in the Northern United States, 1620–1860* (1925; reprint, New York, 1941); Cornelius Oliver Cathey, *Agricultural Developments in North Carolina, 1783–1860* (Chapel Hill, 1956); John McCallum, *Unequal Beginnings: Agriculture and Economic Development in Quebec and Ontario until 1870* (Toronto, 1980); Gates, *The Farmer's Age*.

63. Galloway-Maxcy-Markoe Papers, no. 13346.

Chapter 8

1. See Sidney W. Mintz and Douglas G. Hall, *The Origins of the Jamaican Internal Marketing System* (New Haven, 1960), pp. 3–26; Mintz, *Caribbean Trans-*

formations (Chicago, 1974); "Caribbean Marketplaces and Caribbean History," *Nova Americana* 1 (1978): 333–44; and "Was the Plantation Slave a Proletarian?" *Review* 2 (1978): 81–98; Robert Dirks, *The Black Saturnalia: Conflict and Its Ritual Expression on British West Indian Slave Plantations* (Gainesville, Fla., 1987); "Regional Fluctuations and Competitive Transformations in West Indian Societies," in C. D. Laughlin and I. A. Brady, eds., *Extinction and Survival in Human Populations* (New York, 1978); B. W. Higman, *Slave Populations of the British Caribbean, 1807–1834* (Baltimore, 1984); Kenneth F. Kiple, *The Caribbean Slave: A Biological History* (New York, 1984); Richard B. Sheridan, *Doctors and Slaves: A Medical and Demographic History of Slavery in the British West Indies, 1680–1834* (Cambridge, 1985).

2. See, in particular, Sidney W. Mintz, "Slavery and the Rise of Peasantries," *Historical Reflections* 6 (1979): 213–42.

3. What I mean here by "competition" is not much different from what Dirks outlines in *Black Saturnalia*, pp. 98–102. But I am not sure how the ecological formulation clarifies the political issues that were present.

4. The primary sources for a description and analysis of the provision-ground system in the Windward Islands are limited. The earliest description can be found in absentee proprietor Sir William Young's "A Tour through the several Islands of Barbados, St. Vincent, Antigua, Tobago and Grenada in the years 1791 and 1792," in Bryan Edwards, *History, Civil and Commercial, of the British Colonies in the West Indies*, 33 vols. (London, 1801), 3:249–84. A second was produced by David Collins, a successful doctor-planter resident in St. Vincent for over twenty years, who published *Practical Rules for the Management and Medical Treatment of Negro Slaves in the Sugar Colonies* (1803; reprint, Freeport, N.Y., 1971). The fullest account is provided by Mrs. A. C. Carmichael in her *Domestic Manners and Social Condition of the White, Colored, and Negro Population of the West Indies*, 2 vols. (London, 1833). She lived in St. Vincent between 1820 and 1823 and was a keen observer and assiduous collector of information, although she favored the planters on the abolition question. One final description can be found in the journal of Special Magistrate John Bowen Colthurst, who served in St. Vincent during the last seven months of the Apprenticeship; see W. K. Marshall, ed., *The Colthurst Journal* (Millwood, N.Y., 1977).

Two supplementary sources amplify this information: the slave laws, particularly those enacted under abolitionist pressure for slavery amelioration, and the testimony provided by witnesses before the parliamentary committees of 1789 to 1791 on the slave trade and slavery. See the *House of Commons Sessional Papers of the Eighteenth Century*, Sheila Lambert, ed. (Wilmington, 1975), vols. 69, 70, 71, 77, 82 (hereafter *HCSP*). Nine witnesses gave evidence on conditions in Grenada, St. Vincent, and Tobago, including leading proprietors and officials, nearly all of whom qualified for expert status because of their professional experience and long residence in the islands.

5. James Stephen, *The Slavery of the British West India Colonies Delineated*, 2 vols. (London, 1824), 2:261.

6. Higman, *Slave Populations*, p. 204.

7. See *HCSP* 71:141, 145, for the evidence of Alexander Campbell. See also evidence given by Gilbert Francklyn of Tobago, *HCSP* 71:83, and by James Seton, Governor of St. Vincent, *HCSP* 69:427.

8. See Grenada Act no. 2 of 1766, quoted in B. A. Marshall, "Society and Economy in the British Windward Islands, 1763–1823" (Ph.D. diss., University of the West Indies, 1972), p. 302.

9. *HCSP* 69:427, evidence given by Governor Seton.

10. *British Parliamentary Papers* (Dublin, 1969, 1971), 71:155; 77:435 (hereafter *BPP*); B. Marshall, "Society and Economy," p. 303. In Tobago the stipulation was one acre "well planted with provisions" for every five slaves. In St. Lucia it was five hundred plants of manioc or other vegetable for each slave.

11. Mintz, "Caribbean Marketplaces," p. 335.

12. See the evidence of Gilbert Francklyn and Ashton Warner Byam, *HCSP* 71:83, 103.

13. Richard B. Sheridan, "The Crisis of Slave Subsistence in the British West Indies during and after the American Revolution," *William and Mary Quarterly*, 3d series, 33 (1976): 615–41.

14. Mintz and Hall, *Origins*, p. 3.

15. *HCSP* 71:103.

16. *HCSP* 71:141. This point was elaborated by Edward Kamau Brathwaite in "Controlling Slaves in Jamaica," paper presented at the Conference of Caribbean Historians, Georgetown 1971.

17. J. D. Momsen, "The Geography of Land Use and Population in the Caribbean with Special Reference to Barbados and the Windward Islands" (Ph.D. diss., University of London, 1969), pp. 132–33; D. L. Niddrie, *Land Use and Population in Tobago* (Bude, England, 1961), pp. 17, 43; W. M. Davis, *The Lesser Antilles* (New York, 1926), p. 8.

18. See the evidence of Alexander Campbell and James Baillie, *HCSP* 71:141, 184, 187, 195.

19. Collins, *Practical Rules*, 76.

20. *Parliamentary Papers*, 1842, vol. 13 (hereafter *PP*); evidence of Henry Barkly before the Select Committee on West India Colonies (Question 2661).

21. *HCSP* 69:428, evidence of Governor Seton. See *PP*, vol. 13, evidence of H. M. Grant before the Select Committee on West India Colonies (Questions 31–72).

22. *Colthurst Journal*, p. 171. See also John Anderson, "Journal and Recollections," p. 26, Aberdeen University Library, Scotland.

23. For example, Sir William Young in Edwards, *History*, 3:248; John Jeremie, First President of the Royal Court in St. Lucia, in *BPP* 71:223; and W. C. Mitchell, Attorney of Lataste estate in Grenada in Mitchell to Baumer, 3 September 1831, Lataste Estate Papers, Moccas Court Collection, National Library of Wales, Aberystwyth.

24. *HCSP* 70:132, Grenada Act of 3 November 1788; B. Marshall, "Society and Economy," p. 319.

25. *Colthurst Journal,* p. 170; Carmichael, *Domestic Manners,* 1:135–37.

26. Anderson, "Journal," p. 26.

27. Stephen, *Slavery,* 2:262.

28. The Grenada Abolition Act referred to provision grounds located "a considerable distance from their place of abode." See also Higman, *Slave Populations,* p. 204.

29. *Colthurst Journal,* p. 171.

30. *HCSP* 71:195; Edwards, *History,* 3:271.

31. *HCSP* 71:130, evidence of Gilbert Francklyn; Lataste Estate Papers, Mitchell to Baumer, 3 and 25 September 1831.

32. *HCSP* 70:131, Grenada Acts of 10 December 1766 and 3 November 1788. Inspectors, later called Guardians, were given the responsibility of inspecting provision grounds, of determining their adequacy for maintenance, and of fining planters for infractions of the law.

33. *BPP* 71:57–58, Grenada Consolidated Slave Law, 1825; *BPP* 77:140–41, Tobago Slave Act, 1829.

34. *BPP* 77:369, St. Lucia Second Supplementary Ordinance, 1830; *BPP* 79:126, Order in Council, 1831. The local ordinance in 1830 had stipulated "at least one *carré* [3⅓ acres] for every two full grown slaves," but the Order in Council of 1831 reduced the size to half an acre for each slave fifteen years and over.

35. Section 10 of Tobago Slavery Abolition Act, 1834.

36. Section 10 of St. Vincent Slavery Abolition Act, 1834. Emphasis added.

37. *HCSP* 71:83, 195, evidence of Gilbert Francklyn and James Baillie; Edwards, *History,* 3:274.

38. Dirks, *Black Saturnalia,* p. 75.

39. *HCSP* 71:69; Edwards, *History,* 3:271; *Colthurst Journal,* p. 170.

40. *HCSP* 71:105, 142, 195–96, evidence of Ashton Warner Byam, Alexander Campbell, and James Baillie; *HCSP* 69:428, evidence of Governor Seton; *HCSP* 82:163, evidence of Drewery Ottley.

41. *HCSP* 71:143, evidence of Alexander Campbell; also evidence of Ashton Warner Byam, *HCSP* 71:105; Carmichael, *Domestic Manners,* 1:174–75.

42. Carmichael, *Domestic Manners,* 1:174.

43. *BPP* 71:57, 95, Grenada Consolidated Slave Law, 1825, and St. Vincent Consolidated Slave Act, 1825; *BPP* 77:140, 369, Tobago Slave Act, 1829, and St. Lucia 2nd Supplementary Ordinance, 1830.

44. Section 11 of Tobago Abolition Act.

45. B. Marshall, "Society and Economy," pp. 301–3, 318–22.

46. *HCSP* 71:141–42, 195–96, evidence of Alexander Campbell and James Baillie; Collins, *Practical Rules,* pp. 87–89.

47. *HCSP* 71:130, 195–96, evidence of Gilbert Francklyn and James Baillie.

48. *BPP* 71:106, 228, St. Vincent Consolidated Slave Act, 1825, and St. Lucia Ordinance, 1825.

49. *HCSP* 71:130, evidence of Gilbert Francklyn; Lataste Estate Papers, Mitchell to Baumer, 3 and 25 September 1831.

50. *HCSP* 71:142, 195–96, evidence of Alexander Campbell and James Baillie; Collins, *Practical Rules*, pp. 91–99.

51. *BPP* 71:223, enclosed in Acting Governor to Bathurst, 30 August 1825.

52. *HCSP* 71:143, evidence of Alexander Campbell; Carmichael, *Domestic Manners*, 1:162–78.

53. *HCSP* 71:143, evidence of Alexander Campbell; Carmichael, *Domestic Manners*, 1:162.

54. Carmichael, *Domestic Manners*, 1:51–53, 179.

55. *HCSP* 70:149, St. Vincent Act for the Better Government of Slaves, 11 July 1767, Section X; B. Marshall, "Society and Economy," pp. 292–96.

56. *HCSP* 71:84, 105–6, 187, evidence of Gilbert Francklyn, Ashton Warner Byam, and James Baillie.

57. *HCSP* 71:170, evidence of Alexander Campbell.

58. Mintz, "Caribbean Marketplaces," p. 336; Mintz and Hall, *Origins*, pp. 12–13.

59. The argument in this paragraph is based mainly on the analysis of Higman in *Slave Populations*, pp. 237–42.

60. *St. George's Chronicle*, 13 May 1815, quoted in Higman, *Slave Populations*, p. 238.

61. *Grenada Free Press*, 19 August 1829, quoted in Higman, *Slave Populations*, p. 241.

62. *BPP* 77:136, Brisbane to Murray, 22 May 1829. Emphasis added.

63. *BPP* 77:366, First Subsidiary Ordinance, 1830, to H. M.'s Order in Council; *BPP* 79:101–3, Order in Council, 1831.

64. *BPP* 71:78, Patterson to Bathurst, 23 November 1825.

65. *BPP* 77:136, Brisbane to Murray, 22 May 1829. For the comparable response in Antigua, see David Barry Gaspar, "Slavery, Amelioration, and Sunday Markets in Antigua, 1823–1831," *Slavery and Abolition* 9 (1988): 11–21.

66. Edwards, *History*, 3:271; Carmichael, *Domestic Manners*, 1:5.

67. *HCSP* 71:105–6, 145, evidence of Ashton Warner Byam and Alexander Campbell; *HCSP* 82:162–63, evidence of Drewery Ottley.

68. *HCSP* 71:187.

69. *HCSP* 71:145–46. See also evidence of Gilbert Francklyn, *HCSP* 71:93–94.

70. Carmichael, *Domestic Manners*, 1:176–79.

71. *Colthurst Journal*, pp. 163, 171.

72. Ibid., p. 171; Carmichael, *Domestic Manners*, 1:194–97.

73. For example, Drewery Ottley (*HCSP* 82:163) suggested that, on an estate of two hundred slaves, only about twelve to eighteen would earn annually the £6 to £8 which was within the reach of "an industrious but ordinary Field Slave."

74. Collins, *Practical Rules*, pp. 77–79; Stephen, *Slavery*, 2:264–71.

75. *HCSP* 71:141–46, evidence of Alexander Campbell. See also the evidence of John Giles, *HCSP* 82:75.

76. *HCSP* 71:148. See also the evidence of Gilbert Francklyn, *HCSP* 71:85, and of John Giles and Drewery Ottley, *HCSP* 82:75, 175.

77. Lataste Estate Papers, Mitchell to Baumer, 3 and 25 September 1831.

78. Stephen, *Slavery*, 2:270–71; Higman, *Slave Populations*, pp. 212–18.

79. See Mintz, "Was the Plantation Slave a Proletarian?" and "Caribbean Marketplaces and Caribbean History."

80. *Colthurst Journal*, p. 10.

81. Lataste Estate Papers, Mitchell to Baumer, 3 and 25 September 1831; Carmichael, *Domestic Manners*, 1:197; *HCSP* 71:95, 191, evidence of James Baillie and Gilbert Francklyn.

82. Mintz, *Caribbean Transformations*, p. 212.

83. Lataste Estate papers, Mitchell to Baumer, 3 and 25 September 1831.

84. *Colthurst Journal*, p. 171.

85. *HCSP*, 82:75, 109, evidence of John Giles and John Terry. Both observed that the plantation chore of "picking of grass" on Sundays and in the afternoon break was "a great hardship on slaves." Giles also complained that slaves received no compensation in time for the loss of their Sundays to guard duty.

86. *HCSP* 71:105, evidence of Ashton Warner Byam; Higman, *Slave Populations*, p. 212.

87. Edwards, *History*, 3:272; *HCSP* 71:144–45, evidence of Alexander Campbell.

88. *HCSP* 71:145, evidence of Alexander Campbell. See also Gilbert Francklyn's evidence, *HCSP* 71:84, 92–94, and *Colthurst Journal*, p. 171.

89. Mintz, "Was the Plantation Slave a Proletarian?" p. 94.

90. Mintz, "Caribbean Marketplaces," p. 340; *Caribbean Transformations*, pp. 151–52.

92. See W. K. Marshall, "Commentary One" on "Slavery and the Rise of Peasantries" in *Historical Reflections* 6 (1979): 243–48, and "Apprenticeship and Labor Relations in Four Windward Islands," in David Richardson, ed., *Abolition and its Aftermath* (London, 1985), pp. 202–24.

Chapter 9

Material for this article is drawn from my book *Slavery in the Circuit of Sugar: Martinique in the World Economy, 1830–1848* (Baltimore, 1990) and appears with the permission of The Johns Hopkins University Press.

1. Some planters gave only half a day on Saturday and continued to supply a part of the slaves' rations themselves. In addition, slaves in Martinique commonly had Sundays free.

2. A. Soleau, *Notes sur les Guyanes française, hollandaise, anglaise, et sur les Antilles françaises (Cayenne, Surinam, Demerary, la Martinique, la Guadeloupe)* (Paris, 1835), pp. 9–10; France, Ministère de la Marine et des Colonies, *Commis-*

sion instituée par décision royale du 26 mai 1840, pour l'examen des questions relatives à l'esclavage et à la constitution politique des colonies (Paris, 1840–43), p. 205.

3. Félix Renouard, Marquis de Sainte Croix, *Statistique de la Martinique*, 2 vols. (Paris, 1822), 2:105.

4. Ciro Flammarion S. Cardoso, *Agricultura, Escravidão e Capitalismo* (Petropolis, 1979); Tadeusz Lepkowski, *Haiti*, 2 vols. (Havana, 1968).

5. Cardoso, *Agricultura, Escravidão e Capitalismo*, p. 145.

6. These simultaneously complementary and antagonistic processes crystallized in the practices and embryonic property relations that Sidney Mintz has described as the formation of a "proto-peasantry." He uses this term to characterize those activities by people still enslaved that would allow their subsequent adaptation to a peasant way of life. As Mintz emphasizes, the formation of this protopeasantry is both a mode of response and a mode of resistance on the part of the enslaved to the conditions imposed upon them by the plantation system. Thus, a protopeasantry is not a traditional peasantry attacked from outside by commodity production, the market economy, and the colonial state. Rather, it is formed from within the processes of historical development of slavery and the plantation system. See Sidney W. Mintz, *Caribbean Transformations* (Chicago, 1974); "Slavery and the Rise of Peasantries," *Historical Reflections* 6 (1979): 213–42; "Currency Problems in Eighteenth Century Jamaica and Gresham's Law," in Robert A. Manners, ed., *Process and Pattern in Culture* (Chicago, 1964), pp. 248–65; Sidney W. Mintz and Douglas Hall, *The Origins of the Jamaican Internal Market:ng System*, Yale University Publications in Anthropology, no. 57 (New Haven, 1960), pp. 3–26.

7. Walter Rodney, "Plantation Society in Guyana," *Review* 4 (1981): 643–66; Sidney W. Mintz, "Decrying the Peasantry," *Review* 6 (1982): 209–25.

8. Gabriel Debien, *Les esclaves aux Antilles françaises (XVIIᵉ–XVIIIᵉ siècles)* (Basse-Terre, Fort-de-France, 1974), pp. 178–79; Marian Malowist, "Les débuts du système de plantations dans la période des grandes découvertes," *Africana Bulletin* 10 (1969): 9–30.

9. Debien, *Les esclaves aux Antilles françaises*, pp. 178–86; Lucien Peytraud, *L'Esclavage aux Antilles françaises avant 1789 d'après des documents inédits des Archives Coloniales* (Pointe-à-Pitre, Guadeloupe, 1973), p. 217.

10. The *Code Noir* legally prescribed the weekly food ration for an adult at two-and-a-half pots of manioc flour (1 pot = 2.75 livres) or seven-and-a-half livres of cassava and three livres of fish or two livres of salt beef. This allotment was known as the *ordinaire*. The master was also obligated to provide the slave with two changes of clothes per year, one change to be distributed every six months. The men were to receive a shirt, trousers, and a hat, while the women were given a shirt, skirt, scarf, and hat. Children received only a shirt. In addition, each individual was given one cloth jacket each year. France, Ministère de la Marine et des Colonies, *Exposé général des résultats du patronage des esclaves dans les colonies françaises* (Paris, 1844), pp. 177, 219–25; Debien, *Les esclaves aux Antilles françaises*, pp. 176–77, 181, 183–85; Antoine Gisler, *L'Es-*

clavage aux Antilles françaises (XVIIᵉ–XIXᵉ siècles): Contribution au problème de l'esclavage (Fribourg, 1965), pp. 23–25, 35–38; Peytraud, *L'Esclavage aux Antilles françaises*, pp. 216–24.

11. Debien, *Les esclaves aux Antilles françaises*, pp. 176–77, 181, 183–86, 215; Gisler, *L'Esclavage aux Antilles françaises*, pp. 23–25, 35–38; Peytraud, *L'Esclavage aux Antilles françaises*, pp. 216–24; Ministère de la Marine, *Commission du 26 mai 1840*, p. 205.

12. Victor Schoelcher, *Des Colonies françaises: Abolition immédiate de l'esclavage* (Paris, 1842), pp. 8–9; Ministère de la Marine, *Exposé général des résultats du patronage*, pp. 177, 267; Louis-Philippe May, *Le Mercier de la Rivière (1719–1801)*, 2 vols. (Aix-Marseille, 1975), 1:119–21.

13. France, Ministère du Commerce et des Manufactures, *Commission formée avec l'approbation du Roi . . . pour l'examen de certaines questions de législation commerciale: Enquête sur les sucres* (Paris, 1829), pp. 23, 52, 67, 156, 248.

14. Sainte Croix, *Statistique*, 2:105; P. Lavollée, *Notes sur les cultures et la production de la Martinique et de la Guadeloupe* (Paris, 1841), p. 10; Ministère de la Marine, *Exposé général des résultats du patronage*, pp. 182–87; *Commission du 26 mai 1840*, p. 205.

15. Ministère de la Marine, *Exposé général des résultats du patronage*, pp. 183–84, 290.

16. Ibid., pp. 177–88, 288–91, 332–33; Ministère de la Marine, *Commission du 26 mai 1840*, pp. 205–6, 208–9.

17. Schoelcher, *Abolition immédiate*, p. 11; Lavollée, *Notes sur les cultures*, p. 123.

18. Ministère de la Marine, *Exposé général des résultats du patronage*, pp. 89–90, 182–85, 177, 219–25, 288–91, 332–33; France, Archives Nationales-Section Outre Mer (hereafter ANSOM), *Généralités*, carton 9, dossier 99, De Moges, "Mémoire."

19. Ministère de la Marine, *Exposé général des résultats du patronage*, pp. 104–5, 180–88, 290; ANSOM, *Généralités*, carton 144, dossier 1221, "Exécution de l'ordonnance royale," 2:40, 51.

20. Debien, *Les esclaves aux Antilles françaises*, pp. 178–91, 205–7; Ministère de la Marine, *Exposé général des résultats du patronage*, pp. 182–87, 290; *Commission du 26 mai 1840*, 206; Adolphe Granier de Cassagnac, *Voyage aux Antilles* (Paris, 1842), pp. 174–75; Schoelcher, *Abolition immédiate*, pp. 9–12; Lavollée, *Notes sur les cultures*, p. 10; Sainte Croix, *Statistique*, 2:105.

21. Ministère de la Marine, *Exposé général des résultats du patronage*, pp. 180–88, 290; Schoelcher, *Abolition immédiate*, pp. 9–13; ANSOM, *Généralités*, carton 144, dossier 1221, "Exécution de l'ordonnance royale," 2:40, 51; Debien, *Les esclaves aux Antilles françaises*, pp. 178–91; Mintz, *Caribbean Transformations*, pp. 225–50.

22. De Cassagnac, *Voyage aux Antilles*, p. 176; Schoelcher, *Abolition immédiate*, p. 12; [Collins], *Practical Rules for the Management and Medical Treatment of Negro Slaves in the Sugar Colonies* (London, 1811), pp. 87–94.

23. De Cassagnac, *Voyage aux Antilles*, pp. 174–75; Schoelcher, *Abolition immédiate*, 12; Ministère de la Marine, *Exposé général des résultats du patronage*, pp. 182–85, 288–91, 332–33; ANSOM, *Généralités*, carton 9, dossier 99, De Moges, "Memoire."

24. Ministère de la Marine, *Exposé général des résultats du patronage*, pp. 180–88, 290; Schoelcher, *Abolition immédiate*, pp. 12–13; De Cassagnac, *Voyage aux Antilles*, pp. 174–75; ANSOM, *Martinique*, carton 7, dossier 83, Dupotêt à Ministre de la Marine et des Colonies, Fort Royal, 5 April 1832.

25. Soleau, *Notes sur les Guyanes*, pp. 9–10; Lavollée, *Notes sur les cultures*, p. 123; Debien, *Les esclaves aux Antilles françaises*, pp. 178–80; Peytraud, *L'Esclavage aux Antilles françaises*, p. 217; Gisler, *L'Esclavage aux Antilles françaises*, p. 48.

26. Mintz, *Caribbean Transformations*; Ministère de la Marine, *Exposé général des résultats du patronage*, pp. 110, 188, 303–35; B. W. Higman, *Slave Population and Economy in Jamaica, 1807–1834* (Cambridge, 1976), p. 129; Soleau, *Notes sur les Guyanes*, pp. 9–10; ANSOM, *Martinique*, carton 7, dossier 83, Dupotêt à Ministre de la Marine et des Colonies, Fort Royal, 5 April 1832.

27. Soleau, *Notes sur les Guyanes*, p. 59; ANSOM, *Généralités*, carton 144, dossier 1221, "Exécution de l'ordonnance royale," p. 51; *Martinique*, carton 7, dossier 83, Mathieu à Ministre de la Marine et des Colonies, 10 March 1847, no. 1508; Sainte Croix, *Statistique*, 2:13–15; M. Le Compte E. de la Cornillère, *La Martinique en 1842: Intérêts coloniaux, souvenirs du voyage* (Paris, 1843), pp. 123–24.

28. De la Cornillère, *La Martinique en 1842*, pp. 123–24; Soleau, *Notes sur les Guyanes*, p. 59; Ministère de la Marine, *Exposé général des résultats du patronage*, p. 102.

29. Jean Besson has demonstrated the importance of family land for distinctively Afro-Caribbean conceptions of kinship and property in the free villages of postemancipation Jamaica; see "Family Land and Caribbean Society: Toward an Ethnography of Afro-Caribbean Peasantries," in Elizabeth M. Thomas-Hope, ed., *Perspectives on Caribbean Regional Identity*, Center for Latin American Studies, University of Liverpool, Monograph Series no. 11 (Liverpool, 1984), pp. 57–83, and "Land Tenure in the Free Villages of Trelawny, Jamaica: A Case Study in the Caribbean Peasant Response to Emancipation," *Slavery and Abolition* 5 (1984): 3–23. See also Melville J. Herskovits, *Life in a Haitian Valley* (New York, 1937), pp. 67–68, 76–81; Schoelcher, *Abolition immédiate*, p. 9; M. G. Lewis, *Journal of a West India Proprietor, 1815–1817* (Boston, 1929), p. 88; Roger Bastide, *The African Religions of Brazil: Toward a Sociology of the Interpenetration of Civilizations*, trans. Helen Sebba (Baltimore, 1978), p. 58.

30. Schoelcher, *Abolition immédiate*, pp. 9–13; Ministère de la Marine, *Exposé général des résultats du patronage*, pp. 180–88, 290; Ministère de la Marine, *Commission du 26 mai 1840*, pp. 208–9; ANSOM, *Généralités*, carton 144, dossier 1221, "Exécution de l'ordonnance royale," 2:40, 51.

31. Ministère de la Marine, *Exposé général des résultats du patronage*, pp. 180–

88, 290; Schoelcher, *Abolition immédiate,* pp. 9–13; ANSOM, *Généralités,* carton 144, dossier 1221, "Exécution de l'ordonnance royale," 2:40, 51.

32. Mintz, *Caribbean Transformations;* Ministère de la Marine, *Exposé général des résultats du patronage,* pp. 180–88, 290, 303–5.

33. Ibid., pp. 303–5.

34. Debien, *Les esclaves aux Antilles françaises,* p. 209; Lavollée, *Notes sur les cultures,* pp. 123–24; Lewis, *Journal of a West India Proprietor,* p. 81; Peytraud, *L'Esclavage aux Antilles françaises,* p. 156; De Cassagnac, *Voyage aux Antilles,* p. 168, 211. Cf. Schoelcher, *Abolition immédiate,* p. 53n.; Yvan Debbasch, "Le marronage: Essai sur la désertion de l'esclave antillais," *Année Sociologique,* 3d ser. (1962), pp. 131–38.

35. Soleau, *Notes sur les Guyanes,* pp. 8–10.

36. Ibid., pp. 8–9; Edward Brathwaite, *The Development of Creole Society in Jamaica, 1770–1820* (Oxford, 1971), pp. 298–99.

37. Mintz, *Caribbean Transformations.*

38. Ibid.; Douglas Hall, "The Flight from the Plantations Reconsidered: The British West Indies, 1838–1842," *Journal of Caribbean History* 10–11 (1978): 7–23.

Chapter 10

I would like to thank Karen Anderson, Ira Berlin, Stanley Engerman, Sara Evans, Stephen Gudeman, Colette Hyman, Barbara Laslett, Russell Menard, Philip Morgan, and Stuart Schwartz for reading and commenting on earlier versions of this essay.

1. Orville V. Burton, *In My Father's House Are Many Mansions: Family and Community in Edgefield, South Carolina* (Chapel Hill, 1985), pp. 161–62; Eugene D. Genovese, *Roll, Jordan, Roll: The World the Slaves Made* (New York, 1974), p. 535; Jacqueline Jones, *Labor of Love, Labor of Sorrow: Black Women, Work, and the Family, From Slavery to the Present* (New York, 1985), p. 36; Allan Kulikoff, *Tobacco and Slaves: The Development of Southern Colonies in the Chesapeake, 1680–1800* (Chapel Hill, 1986), pp. 392; Leslie Howard Owens, *This Species of Property: Slave Life and Culture in the Old South* (New York, 1976), pp. 53–54; Kenneth M. Stampp, *The Peculiar Institution: Slavery in the Antebellum South* (New York, 1956), p. 164; Deborah Gray White, *Ar'n't I a Woman? Female Slaves in the Plantation South* (New York, 1985), pp. 155–56.

2. Philip D. Morgan, "Work and Culture: The Task System and the World of Lowcountry Blacks, 1700 to 1880," *William and Mary Quarterly,* 3d ser., 39 (1982): 563–99; "The Ownership of Property by Slaves in the Mid-Nineteenth Century Low Country," *Journal of Southern History* 49 (1983): 399–420. Alex Lichtenstein, "'That Disposition to Theft, with Which They Have Been Branded': Moral Economy, Slave Management, and the Law," *Journal of Social History* 21 (1988): 413–40; Lawrence T. McDonnell, "Money Knows No Master:

Market Relations and the American Slave Community" in Winifred B. Moore, Jr., Joseph F. Tripp, and Lyon G. Tyler, eds., *Developing Dixie: Modernization in a Traditional Society* (Westport, Conn., 1988), pp. 31–44.

3. In this essay the term "up country" refers both to the bulk of South Carolina located inland from the low country of the coast and, more important, to that vast area where short-staple cotton—as opposed to rice and long-staple cotton—was cultivated. My use of "up country" thus joins together the middle country—the area south of the fall line and inland from the coastal rice districts—and the "real" up country—that area north of the fall line.

4. John Belton O'Neall, ed., *The Negro Law of South Carolina* (Columbia, 1848), p. 21.

5. Morgan, "Work and Culture," pp. 566, 573–74.

6. The 1796 act attempted to regulate slaves' marketing activities by increasing to $200 the maximum penalty for trading with a slave who did not carry a permit to trade from the master. The stiffened penalty was intended to discourage individuals from trading illicitly with slaves. See Howell M. Henry, *The Police Control of the Slave in South Carolina* (Emory, Va., 1914), pp. 81–82; Lichtenstein, " 'That Disposition to Theft,' " pp. 429–30.

7. Robert W. Fogel and Stanley L. Engerman, *Time on the Cross: The Economics of American Negro Slavery,* 2 vols. (Boston, 1974), 1:203–6; Lewis C. Gray, *History of Agriculture in the Southern United States to 1860,* 2 vols. (Washington, D.C., 1933), 1:550–56; Philip D. Morgan, "Task and Gang Systems: The Organization of Labor on New World Plantations" in Stephen Innes, ed., *Work and Labor in Early America* (Chapel Hill, 1988), pp. 189–220; U. B. Phillips, *American Negro Slavery* (1918; reprint, Gloucester, Mass., 1959), p. 247.

8. George Rawick, ed., *The American Slave: A Composite Autobiography* (Westport, Conn., 1977), 2, pt. 1: 191 (Sylvia Cannon); 3, pt. 4: 221 (Genia Woodberry).

9. Charles Ball, *Slavery in the United States: A Narrative of the Life and Adventures of Charles Ball, A Black Man* (1837; reprint, New York, 1969), p. 166.

10. Ibid.

11. Plantation Volume, 1801–12, p. 53, Guignard Family Papers, South Caroliniana Library, University of South Carolina, Columbia (hereafter SCL); Guignard began planting in 1801 with sixteen slaves. See also McDonnell, "Money Knows No Master," p. 36; Ball, *Slavery in the United States,* pp. 190, 195.

12. The price of ginned cotton averaged roughly thirty-five cents per pound from 1790 to 1800. From 1800 to 1801, the price dropped from forty-four to nineteen cents. For the next twenty years the price would remain below twenty cents, with occasional exceptions. Gray, *History of Agriculture,* 2:681, 682, 1027 (table 41).

13. Ibid., 2:689–90. Long-staple (sometimes known as sea island) cotton was even more difficult to pick. See Phillips, *American Negro Slavery,* p. 224.

14. John Campbell, "The Gender Division of Labor, Slave Reproduction,

and the Slave Family Economy on Southern Cotton Plantations, 1800–1865,"
Ph.D. diss., University of Minnesota, 1988, ch. 2.

15. Ball, *Slavery in the United States*, pp. 187, 189, 217, 271–73; Plantation
Volume, 1801–12, pp. 48, 53, 54, 63, 64, 69, 71, 76, 136, Guignard Family
Papers, SCL.

16. Ball, *Slavery in the United States*, pp. 273, 187. Ball himself worked for
twenty different employers.

17. Ibid., p. 273.

18. This range reflects the differing experience of slaves living on the
Guignard plantation and those with whom Charles Ball was acquainted.
Although Ball did not indicate how much the typical slave earned, it may be
conjectured that, at fifty cents per day, they might have earned $8 in the fall
(fifty cents times the sixteen Sundays between September and December). Of
course, this amount was probably less for some slaves who, as Ball says,
"would not work constantly on Sunday" (*Slavery in the United States*, p. 272).
Future research may well revise these estimates, however.

19. Ibid., pp. 108, 167, 188, 190, 202, 270. The Guignard slaves typically
received, as part of their allowance, shoes, blankets, hats, and cloth and thus
presumably used their earnings to supplement these subsistence goods. See
Plantation Volume, 1801–12, pp. 36, 67, 75, 88, 118, 136, 137, 146, 148, 160,
Guignard Family Papers, SCL.

20. Ball, *Slavery in the United States*, p. 191.

21. John Hebron Moore, *Agriculture in Ante-Bellum Mississippi* (New York,
1971), chs. 1 and 2.

22. Gray, *History of Agriculture*, 2:689; James L. Watkins, *King Cotton: A
Historical and Statistical Review, 1790–1908* (1908; reprint, New York, 1969),
p. 75.

23. Law-DuBose Cash and Barter Book, 1818–20, William Law Papers,
Special Collections, Perkins Library, Duke University (hereafter Duke); Slave
Account Book, 1824–27, John Black Papers, SCL; Cotton Record Book, 1836–
38, Leach Carrigan Records, SCL; McDonnell, "Money Knows No Master,"
p. 33.

24. Ball, *Slavery in the United States*, pp. 190, 191, 195; Ledger, 1796–99,
John Black Papers, SCL; Law and DuBose Cash and Barter Book, 1818–20,
William Law Papers, Duke; "Slave Account Book, 1824–27," John Black Pa-
pers, SCL.

25. The law allowed slaves to trade away from the plantation provided
they had a written permit from the master. An updated law, passed by the
General Assembly in 1817, continued to allow slaves to trade on their own but
increased the penalties for individuals convicted of trading with slaves who
did not have their owner's permission. The new maximum fine was $1,000 and
no less than one month—but no more than a year—in jail. See O'Neall, *The
Negro Law*, p. 46.

26. Ball, *Slavery in the United States*, pp. 167, 191, 192, 291, 307–8; A Practi-

cal Farmer, "Observations on the Management of Negroes," *Southern Agricul-turalist* 5 (1832): 181–84; "On the Management of Slaves," *Southern Agricultur-alist* 6 (1833): 281–87; Tattler, "Management of Negroes," *Southern Cultivator* 8 (1850): 162–64.

27. Whitemarsh B. Seabrook, *An Essay on the Management of Slaves* (Charleston, S.C., 1834), p. 8.

28. Ibid., p. 8; undated speech, p. 4, Thomas Cassels Law Papers, SCL. This speech may have been an early version of an address given by Thomas C. Law on 10 August 1852 to the Darlington Agricultural Society, entitled "The Report on the Management of Slaves—Duty of Overseers and Employers." The final version omits the quoted phrase on slave theft.

29. F. N. Boney, ed., *Slave Life in Georgia: A Narrative of the Life, Sufferings, and Escape of John Brown, A Fugitive Slave* (1855; reprint, Savannah, Ga., 1972), pp. 47–48. Among these poor whites were the apparently underpaid civil servants of antebellum America, such as Robert McQueen, postmaster at Cheraw, South Carolina, who supplemented his salary by purchasing stolen cotton from slaves and who was eventually convicted of this crime in 1832; Laurence Prince to Stephen Miller, 12 April 1832, box 3, folder 3, Chestnut Family Papers, State Historical Society of Wisconsin (hereafter SHSW).

30. A Practical Farmer, "Observations on the Management of Negroes," pp. 181–84; Tattler, "Management of Negroes," pp. 162–64; Thomas C. Law, "On the Management of Slaves," 10 August 1852, Thomas Cassels Law Papers, SCL. These tensions within production, as well as in other aspects of slaves' market-related activities, existed throughout the South. See, for example, A Mississippi Planter, "Management of Negroes upon Southern Estates," *De Bow's Review* 10 (1851): 621–27.

31. Folder 184–93, Thomas Waties Papers, SCL; for another example of slaves selling stolen goods at night, see also folder 283-92.

32. An Overseer, "On the Conduct and Management of Overseers, Driver, and Slave," *Southern Agriculturalist* 9 (1836): 225–31; A Practical Farmer, "Observations on the Management of Negroes," pp. 181–84.

33. Drew Gilpin Faust, *James Henry Hammond and the Old South: A Design for Mastery* (Baton Rouge, 1985), p. 74; James M. Townes, "Management of Negroes," *Southern Cultivator* 9 (1851): 87–88; W. H. Evans, "Report of the Committee on Cotton: Read before the Darlington (South Carolina) Agricultural Society, at its Last Meeting," *The Rural Register* 2 (1860): 180; Tattler, "Management of Negroes," 162–64; A Mississippi Planter, "Management of Negroes upon Southern Estates," pp. 621–27. Like South Carolina and Mississippi cotton planters, those in Georgia also became disillusioned with slave crops and market-related activities over time. According to one Georgia planter, "It was at one period much the custom of planters to give each hand a small piece of land to cultivate on their own account, if they chose to do so; but this system has not been found to result well. . . . It is much better to give each hand, whose conduct has been such as to merit it, an equivalent in money at the end

of the year": Robert Collins, "Essay on the Treatment and Management of Slaves," *Southern Cultivator* 12 (1854): 205–6.

34. Rawick, ed., *The American Slave*, vol. 3, pt. 3: 56 (Mary Johnson); vol. 2, pt. 1: 185 (Sylvia Cannon).

35. Farming Books, 1841–42, 1843–44 [but actually up to 1852], 1853–54, 1854–55, 1856–57, 1856–59, 1860–63, Thomas Cassels Law Papers, SCL. Data missing for some years in table 10.2 probably reflects Law's failure to describe plantation work, whether performed on his own crops or his slaves' crops, in the same detail from year to year. From 1859 through 1861 slaves on the Caleb Coker Plantation received four Saturdays and five weekdays to harvest their own cotton: 2 and 3 December 1859; 12, 15, and 29 September 1860; 9 and 10 November 1860, 16 September and 29 October 1861, Caleb Coker Plantation Book, 1856–61, SCL. The slaves of H. G. Charles and Company received two days—13 and 14 December—to pick their cotton: H. G. Charles Plantation Volume, 1860, Charles and Company, Darlington Merchant Records, SCL. In addition, slaves on the William Law plantation commenced planting their cotton on Friday, 23 April 1858, the day after they finished planting Law's cotton. See "A Minute of Farming Operations-Year 1858," folder 1857-59, William Law Papers, Duke.

36. Hurricane, "The Negro and His Management," *Southern Cultivator* 18 (1860): 276–77; Thomas C. Law, "On the Management of Slaves."

37. Thomas C. Law, "On the Management of Slaves." See also A Practical Farmer, "Observations on the Management of Negroes," pp. 181–84.

38. Rawick, ed., *The American Slave*, vol. 3, pt. 4: 221; see also vol. 2, pt. 2: 143–44.

39. The same work pattern existed on the Chester District plantation of John Strong. In his plantation record book Strong recorded on Wednesday, 12 May 1852, that they "finished ploughing middles today . . . the Negroes ploughed their crop this evening." A month later, on Tuesday, 15 June, Strong wrote: "ploughed the hillsides over at James got done about half past ten o'clock . . . ploughed part of the Darkies' corn": folder 4, unbound plantation volume (15 April 1852 to 17 August 1852), Strong Family Papers, SCL.

40. Cotton damage due to snow was a very real possibility. On the H. G. Charles plantation, slaves finished harvesting their 1860 cotton crop on 14 December, a scant one day before snow fell: H. G. Charles Plantation Book, Charles and Company Records, SCL.

41. The owners of these plantations were Peter S. Bacot, Thomas Law, William Law, and Peter S. Wilds; see Campbell, "Gender Division of Labor," ch. 6.

42. Income inequality within and among plantations—as well as between different regions, such as the rice low country and cotton up country—indicates another way in which slaves' income-earning activities played an ambiguous role in slave life. Inequality created, at a minimum, a source of economic difference among slaves and, more significantly, possible discord within plan-

tation slave communities. Although I consider the possible implications of income inequality in my dissertation, "Gender Division of Labor," a more systematic discussion is beyond the scope of the present essay.

43. Fogel and Engerman, *Time on the Cross*, 1:148, report that some slaves in Texas earned as much $100 annually from their cotton crops.

44. An Overseer, "On the Conduct and Management," pp. 225–31. Under this new law the penalties for trading illegally with a slave remained as they were under the 1817 law (see note 25, above). See also O'Neall, *The Negro Law*, p. 46; and Henry, *Police Control*, p. 82.

45. Quoted in Henry, *Police Control*, p. 83.

46. McDonnell, "Money Knows No Master," p. 33; for Law, see the sources cited in note 35 and Negro [Accounts] Book, 1859–60, Thomas Cassels Law Papers, SCL.

47. Slave account books, Peter S. Bacot Papers, SCL; Peter S. Wilds cotton picking records, Wilds Family Papers, Darlington (South Carolina) Historic Commission (hereafter DHC); Ledger 1847–62, Bratton and Rainey Ledgers, SCL; folder 2: 1840–49, folder 3: 1850–56, folder 4: 1857–59, folder 5: 1860–80, folder 6: Undated, Thomas C. Perrin Papers, Southern Historical Collection, University of North Carolina, Chapel Hill (hereafter SHC); folders 1837–39, 1843–45, 1848–49, 1850–53, 1854–56, 1857–59, 1860–62, 1863–66, Undated, William Law Papers, Duke. For other planters who purchased slave crops, see also Caleb Coker Plantation Book, SCL; McRae to Mr. Christmas, 5 March 1858, vol. 7, John McRae Letterbooks, SHSW; Cotton Book, 1858, Mary Hart Means Papers, SCL; Witherspoon Plantation Record Book, 1839–59, Witherspoon Family Papers, SCL.

48. A Practical Farmer, "Observations on the Management of Negroes," pp. 181–84; Law, "The Report on the Management of Slaves," Thomas Cassels Law Papers, SCL.

49. In his analysis of the Carrigan cotton records, McDonnell found that slaves earned the same prices received by white people who sold their cotton to the Carrigan firm. Thus, for the present purpose I am assuming that when the slaves of William Law sold their cotton locally under Law's auspices they received a fair local price.

50. Although Bacot did not describe the quality of his slaves' cotton, his peers were quick to note any deficiencies and paid accordingly. In 1841, for example, Peter Wilds paid his slaves two cents per pound of yellow (that is, inferior) cotton as opposed to two-and-two-tenths for their better cotton. Such careful pricing was understandable given that Charleston factors judged the cotton very strictly when *they* determined its price and reminded planters that mixing low and high quality cotton in the same bale reduced the value of the entire bale. In 1824, for example, the Charleston factorage firm of Parker and Brailsford wrote Stephen Miller of Stateburg, advising him to "direct your overseer not to mix the prime cotton in the same bale with the inferior . . . as it not only injures, but renders it difficult to accomplish a sale to advantage":

folder 7: 1824, Chesnut Family Papers, SHSW. In light of these meticulous grading standards, it is reasonable to assume that, because the prices received by Bacot were generally in line with Charleston prices, the cotton produced by his slaves was not yellow or otherwise inferior.

51. When selling consumer goods to his slaves, Bacot did not exploit his slaves by charging excessive prices: a comparison of the prices he charged and the prices he paid when buying the same consumer goods revealed no differences. Overall, the Bacot slaves spent 30 percent of their earnings on the plantation.

52. This analysis is possible because factor invoices for the sale of the owner's cotton exist for all four plantations studied in this section. These invoices provide information on the number and weight of the owner's bales of cotton, the price received by the owner, and the various marketing costs, such as freight, insurance, weighing, storage, and factor's commission, incurred in sending cotton to Charleston.

53. The prices in the distant Charleston market were higher than those in the local area—all other things being equal—for two reasons. First, producers who delayed the sale of their cotton by sending it to a distant market received a risk payment as part of the price that they eventually received. For in refusing to accept a price they were certain of in the local market, these producers took the risk that prices at the distant market would fall between the time they could have sold their cotton locally and the time of its sale in Charleston. Second, by delaying the sale of their crop—for up to six months after the harvest, in some instances—planters also received an interest payment as part of the price, since in not selling their cotton immediately they deprived themselves of the possible interest on the income earned when their cotton was sold soon after harvest. In short, the price structures of distant, centralized marketplaces were automatically higher than those of the local marketplace.

54. On one occasion, in 1857, Law's slaves did have to pay shipping expenses of one dollar and sixty-and-one-half cents per bale (one dollar for freight, forty-eight cents for bagging and rope, and twelve-and-one-half cents for weighing) when selling their cotton to an up-country merchant who lived a slight distance away from them, in Cheraw. Revealingly, these costs were standard, regardless of how far one shipped one's cotton; throughout the 1840s and 1850s, Law paid the same amounts when he sent his bales to Charleston. In effect, then, in 1857 Law's slaves paid some of the cost of shipping their cotton to Charleston—but without sending it there and thus possibly receiving a higher price.

55. Overall, a Charleston sale would have increased slave incomes by roughly 16 percent, 12 percent, and 25 percent for slaves living on the Wilds, William Law, and Bacot plantations, respectively.

56. McDonnell, "Money Knows No Master," p. 35.

57. William Law Papers, Duke, folders 1857–59, 1860–62. The William Law slaves generally spent most of their incomes off the plantation, as did the

slaves of Peter S. Bacot. Negro Book, 1859–60, Thomas Cassels Law Papers, SCL; An Overseer, "On the Conduct," p. 230.

58. Folders 1857–59, 1860–62, William Law Papers, Duke.

59. Thomas Cooper and David J. McCord, eds., *The Statutes at Large of South Carolina*, 7 (Columbia, S.C., 1840), pp. 468–70: "An Act to Amend the Laws in Relation to Slaves and Free Persons of Color"; ibid., 12 (Columbia, S.C., 1874), p. 734: "An Act to Prescribe the Form of Permits for Slaves to Be Absent from the Owner's Premises." Typically, in the early years of the nineteenth century, slaves' permits to travel to the marketplace had not specified slaves' eventual destination, thereby giving slaves considerable latitude about the places they might visit.

60. Folder 1850–53, William Law Papers, Duke.

61. Unfortunately, there are no records which indicate how much Law's slaves earned from their crops in 1853. Thus, there is no way of determining how many slaves went into debt and by what amount.

62. The findings presented in table 10.4 are based on my reconstruction of each slave's economic and financial affairs in a given year. To determine a slave's year-end financial status, I subtracted his or her total expenditures in a year—goods purchased, money loaned out, interest payments made, etc.—from the slave's total income—crop and other earnings, money received from other slaves, credit for consumer goods returned. The table presents the aggregate experience of all the slaves on the plantation for each year. Technically, the unit of analysis is not individual slaves per se but discrete slave producing-selling-buying-consumer units. For slaves who operated as individuals, outside of a family context, the selling-buying unit was the individual slave, but for slaves who lived in identifiable family units on the plantation, the unit of analysis is the family. Each family's overall financial status includes the buying and selling activities of all of its members. Typically, more than one family member appeared in the records as buying and selling—most commonly, both the husband and wife each had their own separate accounts of their economic activity. I am assuming that even though spouses, for example, may have had separate accounts, they nonetheless earned their incomes, spent their earnings, used consumer goods, and made economic decisions within the context of the family—not as solitary individuals who just happened to live together. For an initial analysis of the extent and implications of slave participation in market-related activities by gender, see Campbell, "Gender Division of Labor," ch. 6.

63. "A slave may, by the consent of his master, acquire and hold *personal* property. All, thus acquired, is regarded in law as that of the master. . . . A slave cannot contract, and be contracted with": O'Neall, *The Negro Law*, pp. 21–22.

64. Table 10.4 presents slaves' year-end financial status in terms of the year slaves produced their crops, which was not necessarily the same year in which slaves made their purchases. The slaves of William Law, for example,

appear to have spent their 1857 earnings in January or February of the following year; rather than treat these purchases as part of their 1858 financial affairs, I include them as part of their 1857 economic activities—just as Law himself did when balancing slaves' accounts in February of 1858. William Law and his brother, Thomas Law, generally noted when slaves made their purchases, which makes it relatively easy to determine which purchases should be included in which year when calculating slaves year-end financial status. The same cannot be said, however, for Peter Bacot, who did not always indicate when slaves made their purchases or whether their purchases were bought with unspent earnings from the previous year or bought against future earnings for crops not yet harvested and sold. As a result of these ambiguities, I may have assigned purchases to the wrong years, thereby misrepresenting the year-end financial picture for individual slaves and, hence, for the entire Bacot slave community. With this in mind, it is best to view the Bacot findings as approximations of slaves' year-to-year financial status on this plantation.

65. Calculations made from data collated from the Slave Account Books, Peter S. Bacot Papers, SCL.

66. Ibid. Of course, loans between slaves may also mask tensions stemming from income inequality within the slave population.

67. Negro [Accounts] Book, 1859–60, Thomas Cassels Law Papers, SCL. It is unlikely that the slaves studied here saved a portion of their earnings each year in order to buy their freedom at a later date. The amount of money earned, much less saved, by these slaves was simply far too small to finance their self-purchase, even after years of savings.

68. Glenn Porter, ed., *Encyclopedia of American Economic History* (New York, 1980), p. 234, table 1. The base period is 1910–14, with 100 as the base. Index values less than 100 signify lower consumer prices (deflation) than in the 1910–14 period; values greater than 100 indicate higher prices for consumer goods.

69. For example, a yard of flannel cost seventy-five cents in 1819 but less than thirty cents in the 1850s; Folder 1811–19, Thomas Waties Papers, SCL; and Campbell, "The Gender Division of Labor," pp. 279–80.

70. Examples of late antebellum planters who gave slaves subsistence goods, thereby enabling slaves to spend their incomes on an array of "luxury," nonsubsistence goods, abound. See Peter S. Bacot Papers, SCL; William Law Papers, Duke; Witherspoon Family Papers, SCL; Thomas C. Perrin Papers, SHC; Mary Hart Means Papers, SCL.

71. Charles and Company, Merchant Records, SCL; Negro [Accounts] Book, 1859–60, Thomas Cassels Law Papers, SCL. Actually, Elleck purchased twenty-seven dollars worth of goods and thus went into debt by two dollars. But given the size of his income, he would have still purchased, in all likelihood, a large number of different goods even if he had not overspent.

72. Campbell, "The Gender Division of Labor," pp. 278–79; Slave Planta-

tion Books, Peter S. Bacot Papers, SCL. For the extent and implications of slave participation in market-related activities by gender, see Campbell, "Gender Division of Labor," ch. 6.

73. R. King, Jr., "On the Management of the Butler Estate and the Cultivation of Sugar Cane," *Southern Agriculturalist* 1 (1828): 523–29.

74. On guano and padlock purchases see the Negro [Accounts] Book, 1859–60, Thomas Cassels Law Papers, SCL; for padlocks, also see the Slave Plantation Books, Peter S. Bacot Papers, SCL.

75. H. G. Charles Plantation Volume, 1860, Charles and Company Merchant Records, SCL; McRae to Christmas, vol. 7, p. 479, John McRae Letterbooks, SHSW; Mechanicsville (Darlington District) Baptist Church Records, p. 83, SCL.

76. "On the Management of Slaves," Thomas Cassels Law Papers, SCL; Black Creek Agricultural Society Minute Book, p. 5, SCL. Although the various measures adopted by late antebellum slaveowners to reduce slave theft—from greater supervision during production to control over the marketing of slave crops—no doubt made it harder for slaves to steal, slaves still stole. Indeed, slave theft seems to have reached epidemic proportions by the late antebellum period. Although South Carolina slaveowners and their allies continued to press the legislature to pass even sterner laws against individuals who traded illicitly with slaves, theft and illicit trade continued unabated. Eventually, slaveowners throughout South Carolina took the law into their own hands, leading, in extreme cases, to bloodshed. In March 1858, for example, sixty or so members of the Darlington Vigilante Committee assaulted and killed two white men who were known traders with slaves (Campbell, "The Gender Division of Labor," ch. 5). For further discussions of slave theft and slaveowner response during the late antebellum period, see J. William Harris, *Plain Folk and Gentry in a Slave Society: White Liberty and Black Slavery in Augusta's Hinterlands* (Middletown, Conn., 1985), pp. 52–61; Henry, *Police Control*, ch. 8; Michael Stephen Hindus, *Prison and Punishment: Crime, Justice, and Authority in Massachusetts and South Carolina, 1767–1878* (Chapel Hill, 1980), ch. 6; Lichtenstein, "'That Disposition to Theft,'" pp. 426–33; McDonnell, "Money Knows No Master," pp. 35–37.

77. James O. Breeden, ed., *Advice among Masters: The Ideal in Slave Management in the Old South* (Westport, Conn., 1980), p. 267.

Chapter 11

1. J. Carlyle Sitterson, *Sugar Country: The Cane Sugar Industry in the South* (Lexington, Ky., 1953), pp. 28–30, 60.

2. Ibid., 48; *Hunt's Merchant's Magazine and Commercial Review* 7 (1842): 133–47, 242; 30 (1854): 499; 31 (1854): 675–91; 35 (1856): 248–49; *De Bow's Review* 1 (1846): 54–55; Joseph C. C. Kennedy, *Population of the United States in 1860;*

compiled from the Original Returns of the Eighth Census (Washington, D.C., 1864), pp. 188–93. Here and throughout, numbers have been rounded off.

3. Sitterson, *Sugar Country*, pp. 30, 48–50; *De Bow's Review* 1 (1846): 54–55; 19 (1855): 354; *Hunt's Merchant's Magazine* 30 (1854): 499; 35 (1856): 248–49; 42 (1860): 163.

4. Sugarcane did not have to be replanted following each harvest since the stubble left after cutting sprouted new shoots, or ratoons.

5. Captain Thomas Hamilton, *Men and Manners in America*, 2 vols. (Edinburgh and London, 1833), 2:229–30.

6. Ibid., 2:229; Frances Milton Trollope, *Domestic Manners of the Americans*, Donald Smalley, ed. (New York, 1949), p. 246; E. S. Abdy, *Journal of a Residence and Tour in the United States of North America, from April 1833 to October 1834*, 3 vols. (London, 1835), 3:103–4.

7. T. B. Thorpe, "Sugar and the Sugar Region of Louisiana," *Harper's New Monthly Magazine* 7 (1853): 753; William Howard Russell, *My Diary North and South* (London, 1863), p. 371; Interview conducted under the auspices of the Slave Narrative Collection Project, Federal Writers' Project, Works Progress Administration. Interviewee: Elizabeth Ross Hite; Interviewer: Robert McKinney; Date: c. 1940, Louisiana Writers' Project File, Louisiana State Library, Baton Rouge, Louisiana (hereafter LWPF, LSL). Interview conducted under the auspices of a Slave Narrative Collection Project organized by Dillard University (hereafter DUSNCP) using only black interviewers, a project which developed alongside the Federal Writers' Project program. Interviewee: Catherine Cornelius; Interviewer: Octave Lilly, Jr.; Date: c. 1939, Archives and Manuscripts Department, Earl K. Long Library, University of New Orleans, New Orleans, Louisiana.

8. Interviewee: Melinda [last name unknown]; Interviewer: Arguedas; Date: c. 1940: F. W P. Interviews, Federal Writers' Project Files, Melrose Collection, Archives Division, Northwestern State University of Louisiana, Natchitoches, Louisiana (hereafter LWPF, NSU).

9. Russell, *My Diary*, p. 399; Interview with Elizabeth Ross Hite, LWPF, LSL; Plantation Diary, vol. 1, 1838–40, Samuel McCutcheon Papers, Department of Archives and Manuscripts, Louisiana State University, Baton Rouge; Interview with Catherine Cornelius, DUSNCP.

10. Ashland Plantation Record Book, Archives, LSU.

11. Isaac Erwin Diary, Archives, LSU; Plantation Diary of Valcour Aime, Louisiana Historical Center, Louisiana State Museum, New Orleans.

12. Plantation Diary and Ledger, Elu Landry Estate, Archives, LSU.

13. Plantation Diary and Ledger, Landry Papers; Journal 6, Plantation Book, 1853–63, John H. Randolph Papers, Archives, LSU.

14. *De Bow's Review* 4 (1847): 393; 6 (1848): 436; 7 (1849): 420; 9 (1850): 456; 11 (1851): 496; 13 (1852): 512; 15 (1853): 528; 17 (1854): 530; 19 (1855): 458; 21 (1856): 368; 23 (1857): 365; 25 (1858): 469; 27 (1859): 477; 29 (1860): 521; Sam Bowers Hilliard, *Hog Meat and Hoecake* (Carbondale, Ill., 1972), p. 155.

15. "Negroes Corn for 1857," box 9, folder 54; "Negroes Corn 1859," box 9, folder 57, Lewis Stirling and Family Papers, Archives, LSU.

16. Ledger, 1858–72, Benjamin Tureaud Papers, Archives, LSU; Daybook, 1843–47, vol. 5, Edward J. Gay and Family Papers, Archives, LSU.

17. Plantation Diary of Valcour Aime; Daybook, 1843–47, vol. 5, Gay Papers.

18. Thorpe, "Sugar and the Sugar Region," p. 753; Russell, *My Diary*, p. 373; Thomas Haley to Mrs. Mary Weeks, 11 April 1841, box 9, folder 29, David Weeks and Family Papers, Archives, LSU; Notebook, 1853–57, vol. 9, Weeks Hall Memorial Collection, David Weeks and Family Collection, Archives, LSU; Daybook, 1843–47, vol. 5, Gay Papers; Ledger, 1851–56, vol. 18, George Lanaux and Family Papers, Archives, LSU; Cashbook for Negroes, 1848–55, vol. 6, W. W. Pugh Papers, Archives, LSU.

19. Russell, *My Diary*, p. 396.

20. "Statements of the Sugar and Rice Crops Made in Louisiana," by L. Bouchereau (New Orleans, 1871), box 1, folder 1, UU-211, #555, Pharr Family Papers, Archives, LSU; box 7, folder 39, Stirling Papers; boxes 1 and 2, Uncle Sam Plantation Papers, Archives, LSU; Joseph K. Menn, *The Large Slaveholders of Louisiana—1860* (New Orleans, 1964), pp. 353–54; Plantation Record Book, 1849–60, vol. 36, Gay Papers; Journal, 1851–60, vol. 14, Lanaux Papers.

21. Plantation Diary, 1842–59, 1867, William T. Palfrey and George D. Palfrey Account Books, Archives, LSU.

22. Diary, 1847, vol. 1, Kenner Family Papers, Archives, LSU; Plantation Record Book, 1849–60, vol. 36, Gay Papers; Cashbook for Negroes, 1848–55, vol. 6, W. W. Pugh Papers.

23. Cashbook for Negroes, 1848–55, vol. 6, W. W. Pugh Papers; Plantation Record Book, 1849–60, vol. 36, Gay Papers.

24. Daybook, 1843–47, vol. 5; Plantation Record Book, 1849–60, vol. 36; "Memorandum relative to payments to negroes, Dec. 1844," box 11, folder 81, Gay Papers.

25. Ledger, 1858–72, Tureaud Papers; S-124 (9) #2668, Bruce, Seddon and Wilkins Plantation Records, Archives, LSU.

26. Plantation Record Book, 1849–60, vol. 36, Gay Papers.

27. Journal 6, Plantation Book, 1853–63, Randolph Papers.

28. Interviewee: Martha Stuart; Interviewer: Octave Lilly, Jr.; Date: c. 1938, DUSNCP; Interview with Elizabeth Ross Hite, LWPF, LSU.

29. Journal/Plantation Book, 1847–52, vol. 5; Journal 6, Plantation Book, 1853–63, Randolph Papers; box 8, folders 49 and 51, Stirling Papers; Estate Record Book, 1832–45, vol. 8; Cashbook/Daybook, 1837–43, vol. 18, Gay Papers.

30. Interviewee: Hunton Love; Interviewer: unknown; Date: c. 1940, LWPF, LSL.

31. J. L. Rogers to Robert Ruffin Barrow, 29 October 1853, box 2, folder 1850s-20; Residence Journal of R. R. Barrow, 1 January 1857 to 13 June 1858

(copied from an original manuscript in Southern Historical Collection, University of North Carolina, Chapel Hill, North Carolina), Department of Archives, Tulane University, New Orleans; Book of Accounts of the Magnolia Plantation, 1829–53, Louisiana State Museum.

32. Edward Gay to Hynes and Craighead, 6 April 1844; "Account 1844, Memorandum, Sale of moss for the negroes," box 11, folder 81, Gay Papers.

33. Moss Record Book, 1849–61, vol. 35; boxes 11–13, folders 81–96, Gay Papers; Residence Journal of R. R. Barrow, 1857–58, Barrow Papers.

34. Moss Record Book, 1849–61, vol. 35; Estate Record Book, 1848–55, vol. 34, Gay Papers; Menn, *Large Slaveholders,* pp. 244–45.

35. Ashland Plantation Record Book; Daybook 1843–47, vol. 5; box 12, folder 86; "Sales of Moss & Molasses belonging to the Negroes," box 13, folder 100; box 12, folder 93; box 13, folder 96, Gay Papers.

36. Journal 6, Plantation Book, 1853–63, Randolph Papers; Plantation Diary and Ledger, Landry Papers.

37. P. M. Goodwyn to Edward Gay, 27 August 1860, box 29, folder 255, Gay Papers.

38. Russell, *My Diary,* p. 396.

39. Ibid., p. 373; P. E. Jennings to Edward Gay, 25 August 1858, box 25, folder 221, Gay Papers.

40. W. F. Weeks to Mary C. Moore, 31 January 1853, box 31, folder 82, Weeks Papers.

41. Interviewee: Frances Doby; Interviewers: Arguedas-McKinney; Date: 1938, LWPF, NSU; Interview with Catherine Cornelius, DUSNCP; [William Kingsford], *Impressions of the West and South during a Six Weeks' Holiday* (Toronto, 1858), pp. 47–48.

42. U. B. Phillips, comp., *The Revised Statutes of Louisiana* (New Orleans, 1856), pp. 48–65.

43. Maunsell White to G. Lanneau, 15 April 1859, box 3, folder 1, Lanaux Papers.

44. Frederick Law Olmsted, *A Journey in the Seaboard Slave States* (New York, 1856), p. 674.

45. Ibid., p. 675.

46. William F. Weeks to Mary C. Moore, 20 June 1860, box 36, folder 180, Weeks Papers.

47. Joseph Mather Diary, 1852–59, Archives, LSU; Diary and Plantation Record of Ellen E. McCollam, Andrew and Ellen E. McCollam Papers, Archives, LSU; Maunsell White to James P. Bracewell, 10 August 1859, Maunsell White Letterbook, Archives, LSU; J. E. Craighead to John B. Craighead, 11 September 1847, box 14, folder 102, Gay Papers; Lyle Saxon, comp., *Gumbo Ya-Ya* (Boston, 1945), p. 430.

48. Diary and Plantation Record of Ellen McCollam, McCollam Papers; Plantation Diary and Ledger, Landry Papers; Nicholas Phipps to Colonel Andrew Hynes, February 1847, box 13, folder 97, Gay Papers.

49. F. D. Richardson to Moses Liddell, 18 July 1852, safe 12, folder 3, Moses and St. John R. Liddell and Family Papers, Archives, LSU; Interview with Martha Stuart, DUSNCP.

50. Plantation Diary of Valcour Aime, 1847–52; Boxes 1 and 2, Uncle Sam Papers.

51. T. B. Thorpe, "Christmas in the South," *Frank Leslie's Illustrated Newspaper* 5 (26 December 1857): 62.

52. Ledger, 1858–72, Tureaud Papers; Daybook, 1843–47, vol. 5; Moss Record Book, 1849–61, vol. 35, Gay Papers; "List of Wood Cut by Slaves and Payment Made," box 7, folder 39; box 8, folder 39, Stirling Papers.

53. Ledger, 1858–72, Tureaud Papers; Daybook, 1843–47, Gay Papers; Journal/Plantation Book, 1848–52, Randolph Papers; Plantation Record Book, 1849–60, Gay Papers; Wilton Plantation Daily Journal, 1853, Bruce, Seddon and Wilkins Records; Journal, 1851–60, Journal, 1851–56, Lanaux Papers; Cashbook for Negroes, 1848–55, W. W. Pugh Papers.

54. P. O. Daigre to Edward J. Gay, 15 August 1858, box 25, folder 221, Gay Papers.

55. Ledger, 1858–72, Tureaud Papers; Notebook, 1853–57, vol. 9, Weeks Collection.

56. Ledger, 1858–72, Tureaud Papers; Daybook, 1843–47, Gay Papers; T. B. Thorpe, "Christmas," 62.

57. Ledger, 1858–72, Tureaud Papers; Daybook, 1843–47, Gay Papers.

58. Ledger, 1858–72, Tureaud Papers; Daybook, 1843–47, Gay Papers.

59. Ledger, 1862–65, vol. 8, Randolph Papers; Memorandum Book, 1840–41, vol. 28; Estate Record Book, 1831–45, vol. 8, Gay Papers.

60. Cashbook for Negroes, 1848–55, W. W. Pugh Papers; Daybook, 1843–47, Gay Papers.

61. Estate Record Book, 1831–45, vol. 8; Cashbook/Daybook, 1837–43, vol. 18, Gay Papers.

62. Interview with Catherine Cornelius, DUSNCP.

63. Kingsford, *Impressions,* pp. 47–48; V. Alton Moody, *Slavery on Louisiana Sugar Plantations* (New Orleans, 1924), p. 68. Slaves on the Gay family's estate, for example, were occasionally given whiskey. On 28 December 1846 "whiskey for Negroes dinner" cost $1.50 and on 25 December 1850 "Whiskey for Negroes" cost $2.50. The planter paid for these items. Estate Record Book, 1842–44, vol. 12; Estate Record Book, 1848–55, vol. 34, Gay Papers.

64. P. E. Jennings to Edward J. Gay, 25 August 1858, box 25, folder 221, Gay Papers.

65. Journal of Mavis Grove Plantation, 1856, Louisiana State Museum.

CONTRIBUTORS

IRA BERLIN is Professor of History at the University of Maryland. He is the founder and former director of the Freedmen and Southern Society Project, a coeditor of *Freedom: A Documentary History of Emancipation* (1983–), and the author of *Slaves without Masters: The Free Negro in the Antebellum South* (1974), as well as numerous other studies of the American South.

JOHN CAMPBELL teaches in the Department of History at the University of Arizona. He is completing a study of the slave family economy, entitled *The Peculium and the Peculiar Institution: Slave Market Activity in the South Carolina Cotton Country, 1790–1860.*

RICHARD S. DUNN is the Roy F. and Jeannette P. Nichols Professor of American History at the University of Pennsylvania. The author of *Sugar and Slaves: The Rise of the Planter Class in the English West Indies, 1624–1713* (1972) and a number of essays on slave labor in English America, he is currently writing a comparative study of slave life and work on two plantations, Mesopotamia in Jamaica and Mount Airy in Virginia.

DAVID BARRY GASPAR is Professor of History at Duke University. He is the author of *Bondmen and Rebels: A Study of Master-Slave Relations in Antigua* and the coeditor, with Darlene Clark Hine, of *Black Women and Slavery in the Americas* and, with David Geggus, of *The French Revolution and the Greater Caribbean,* both forthcoming.

DAVID GEGGUS teaches in the History Department at the University of Florida, Gainesville. He is the author of *Slavery, War and Revolution: The British Occupation of Saint Domingue* (1982) and of numerous other studies. The recipient of many awards, including Guggenheim and National Humanities Center Fellowships, he works primarily on the Haitian Revolution and the eighteenth-century Caribbean.

WOODVILLE K. MARSHALL is Professor of History at the University of the West Indies, Cave Hill Campus, Barbados. His research interests center on postslavery adjustments in the British Caribbean, and he has published a number of articles on labor systems, peasantries, and villages in the British Windward Islands.

379

RODERICK A. MCDONALD is Associate Professor of History at Rider College. The author of _The Economy and Material Culture of Slaves: Goods and Chattels on the Sugar Plantations of Jamaica and Louisiana_ (1993), he is presently at work on _The Journal of John Anderson, St. Vincent Special Magistrate, 1836–1839._

STEVEN F. MILLER is a member of the Freedmen and Southern Society Project at the University of Maryland. He is coeditor, with other members of the project, of _Freedom: A Documentary History of Emancipation_ (1983), and coauthor of _Slaves No More: Three Essays on Emancipation and the Civil War_ (1992) and of _Free at Last: A Documentary History of Slavery, Freedom, and the Civil War_ (1992).

PHILIP D. MORGAN is Professor of History at Florida State University. An editor, with Lois Green Carr and Jean B. Russo, of _Colonial Chesapeake Society_ (1988) and, with Bernard Bailyn, of _Strangers within the Realm_ and the author of a study of slavery in colonial mainland North America, _Slave Counterpoint: Black Culture in the Eighteenth Century_ (1993).

JOSEPH P. REIDY is Associate Professor of History at Howard University. He is the author of _From Slavery to Agrarian Capitalism in the Cotton Plantation South: Central Georgia, 1800–1880_ (1992), a study of the transformation of antebellum society. As a former member of the Freedmen and Southern Society Project, he is coeditor of _Freedom: A Documentary History of Emancipation._

DALE TOMICH is Associate Professor of Sociology at the State University of New York at Binghamton. The author of _Slavery in the Circuit of Sugar: Martinique in the World Economy, 1830–1848_, he is currently engaged in a study of slavery in Cuba, Brazil, and the U.S. South and its role in the nineteenth-century world economy.

MICHEL-ROLPH TROUILLOT is Professor of Anthropology at the Johns Hopkins University. He has published articles on Caribbean societies and cultures, on historical discourse, and on anthropological theory. His books include _Peasants and Capital: Dominica in the World Economy_ (1988) and _Haiti, State against Nation: The Origins and Legacy of Duvalierism_ (1990).

LORENA S. WALSH is a historian in the Research Department of the Colonial Williamsburg Foundation and adjunct lecturer in American Studies at the College of William and Mary. She is coauthor, with Lois Carr and Russell Menard, of _Robert Cole's World: Agriculture and Society in Early Maryland_ (1991) and has written widely on Chesapeake agriculture, labor systems, consumption patterns, and family history.

INDEX